Web Design
with Macromedia
Studio MX 2004

Web Design with Macromedia® Studio MX 2004

Eric Hunley

CHARLES RIVER MEDIA, INC.
Hingham, Massachusetts

Acquisitions Editor: James Walsh
Production: Publishers' Design and Production Services, Inc.
Cover Image: Eric Hunley
Cover Design: The Printed Image

Photographs used with permission , © 2004 John Dukes Photography Web site, *www.jdukesphoto.com*. All rights reserved.

Macromedia and Macromedia Studio are trademarks or registered trademarks of Macromedia, Inc. in the United States and/or other countries. Copyright © 2003. Macromedia, Inc., 600 Townsend Street, San Francisco, CA 94103 USA. All rights reserved.

CHARLES RIVER MEDIA, INC.
10 Downer Avenue
Hingham, Massachusetts 02043
781-740-0400
781-740-8816 (FAX)
info@charlesriver.com
www.charlesriver.com

This book is printed on acid-free paper.

Eric Hunley. *Web Design with Macromedia® Studio MX 2004*.
ISBN: 1-58450-283-5

All brand names and product names mentioned in this book are trademarks or service marks of their respective companies. Any omission or misuse (of any kind) of service marks or trademarks should not be regarded as intent to infringe on the property of others. The publisher recognizes and respects all marks used by companies, manufacturers, and developers as a means to distinguish their products.

Library of Congress Cataloging-in-Publication Data
Hunley, Eric.
    Web design with Macromedia Studio MX 2004 / Eric Hunley.
        p.   cm.
    ISBN 1-58450-283-5 (pbk. with CD-ROM : alk. paper)
    1. Web sites—Design.   2. Web site development.   3. Macromedia Studio MX. I. Title.
    TK5105.888.H89 2004
    005.7'2—dc22
                            2004001697

Printed in the United States of America
04 7 6 5 4 3 2 First Edition

CHARLES RIVER MEDIA titles are available for site license or bulk purchase by institutions, user groups, corporations, etc. For additional information, please contact the Special Sales Department at 781-740-0400.

Requests for replacement of a defective CD-ROM must be accompanied by the original disc, your mailing address, telephone number, date of purchase and purchase price. Please state the nature of the problem, and send the information to CHARLES RIVER MEDIA, INC., 10 Downer Avenue, Hingham, Massachusetts 02043. CRM's sole obligation to the purchaser is to replace the disc, based on defective materials or faulty workmanship, but not on the operation or functionality of the product.

To my wonderful and loving wife, Leslie.
Your support and constant giving go far beyond what I could
describe here . . . I will forever strive to continue earning it.

Contents

Acknowledgments   **xxi**

Introduction   **xxiii**
    About Macromedia   xxiii
    Purpose of This Book   xxiv
    Scope of This Book   xxiv
    Summary   xxv

1 An Introduction to the Web Server Process and the Design Cycle **1**
    What Is Server Side?   1
    What Is Client Side?   2
    Fitting It Together   2
    Web Protocols   4
    What Happens to the Request?   6
    Macromedia Studio MX 2004 and the Design Cycle   7
        Plan—Brainstorming and Feedback   7
        Design—Fireworks and Flash   8
        Build—Dreamweaver   8
        Test—Browsers and People   8
        Maintain—Dreamweaver, Fireworks, Flash   9
    Summary   9

2 Taking the Macromedia FreeHand MX Tour   **11**
    Wireframes and Storyboards   12
    Raster Graphics   13

Vector Graphics	14
Raster or Vector Graphics—Which Should You Use?	15
Exploring the Interface	17
The Tools Panel	19
Creating Paths	19
Selecting Your Initial Line and Fill Colors	21
Creating Paths with Sharp Corners	21
Creating Paths with Smooth Curves	22
Creating Multiple Curves Going the Same Direction	24
Combining Styles to Create a Shape	24
Using the Pointer, Subselect, and Lasso Tools to Modify Points	27
Using the Bezigon Tool	30
Creating Freeform Paths with the Pencil Tool	32
The Variable Stroke and Calligraphic Pen Tools	34
The Line, Arc, and Spiral Tools	35
Creating Shapes with FreeHand MX	36
Creating Rounded Shapes with the Ellipse Tool	36
Creating and Modifying Rectangles	38
Creating Polygons and Stars	40
Creating and Manipulating Text	42
Path Manipulation Tools	45
The Scale Tools	45
Using Transform Handles	47
Path Transform Tools	47
The Eraser and Knife Tools	48
Summary	49
3 Exploring the Object Panel and Looking at More Effects	**51**
The Object Panel	51
Editing External Content	52
Using Fills	54
Custom Fills	54
Gradient Fills	54

Lens Fill   57

Textured, Pattern, and PostScript Fills   58

Tiled Fills   58

Using Strokes   **60**

Basic Strokes   61

Brush Strokes   62

Calligraphic Strokes   65

Other Strokes   65

Live Effects   **66**

Strokes and Fills   **69**

Effects Tools   **71**

Perspective   71

3D Rotation   73

Fisheye Lens   73

Extrude   74

Smudge and Shadow   76

Trace   77

Blend   79

Mirror   79

Graphic Hose   81

Chart   83

Action   84

Connector   84

Path Operations   **84**

Creating Flash Animations   **86**

Exporting HTML   **87**

Assets   **87**

Swatches and the Color Mixer Panel   87

Styles   87

Symbols   88

Library   88

Summary   **89**

4   Designing Frameworks in FreeHand MX   **91**

   Creating a Wireframe   91

      Creating Symbols   91

      The Align and Transform Panel   96

      Scaling and Placing the Box Symbols   98

      Arranging the Folder Symbols   99

      Adding Text to the Wireframe   100

      Creating More Icons   101

      Using the Connector Tool   104

   Publishing in FreeHand   107

      Sharing Content with Flash   107

      Creating Flash Animations   107

   Pages and Layers in FreeHand   112

      Pages   112

      Layers   114

   Exporting Images   115

   Publish as HTML   115

      HTML Output Assistant   116

   Summary   117

5   Introduction to Macromedia Flash MX 2004   **119**

   A Brief History of Flash   119

   Looking at the Interface   121

   The Timeline   123

      Looking at Layers   126

   The Tools Panel   127

   The Property Inspector   128

   Panel Sets   130

   Contextual Menus   134

   Using the Tools Panel   134

      The Line, Arrow, and Subselection Tools   135

      The Pen Tool   137

      Text Tool   140

Check Spelling   145
Oval Tool   145
Rectangle Tool   145
PolyStar Tool   146
Pencil Tool   148
Brush Tool   148
Free Transform Tool   149
Fill Transform Tool and Color Mixer Panel   151
Ink Bottle Tool   153
Paint Bucket Tool   153
Eyedropper Tool   154
Eraser Tool   154
View Tools   155
Colors Tools   156
Object Overlap Considerations   156
Find and Replace Tool   157
Summary   157

6   Tweens and Layers   159
Frame-by-Frame Animation   159
Motion Tweening   162
Motion Tween: First Example   163
Motion Tween: Second Example   165
Watch Your Modes   166
Adding Motion Guides   168
Using Layer Folders   172
Finishing the Movie   173
Refining Motion Tweens   175
Using Shape Tweens   181
Using Shape Hints   181
Working with Mask Layers   184
Guide Layers   187
Layer Options   188
Summary   190

7   Symbols, Timeline Effects, and Interactivity   **191**

   Graphic Symbols   191

   Movie Clips   197

   Buttons   205

   Timeline Effects   208

   Adding Interactivity with Behaviors   210

      Behavior Choices   213

      Custom Behaviors   215

      Creating a Custom Behavior   218

   Summary   221

8   Introduction to ActionScript and Programming Concepts   **223**

   The Actions Panel   223

   Code Comments   225

   Variables   226

      Literals and Variables   226

      Variable Types   229

      Variable Scope   230

      Global Variables   232

      Strict Data Typing   232

      Variable Conversion   232

      Arrays   233

      Associative and Multidimensional Arrays   234

      Array Methods   235

   Operators   236

      Basic Arithmetical Operators   236

      Other Arithmetical Operators   238

      Assignment Operators   239

   Conditionals   240

      if   240

      Comparison Operators   240

      Truth Tables   241

      if/else   242

`if/else if/else`	242
`switch`	243
The Conditional Operator	243
Loops	**244**
`while`	244
`for`	245
`for . . . in`	246
`break/continue`	246
`do`	247
Functions	**248**
Basic Functions	248
Arguments and Parameters	248
Functions that Return a Value	249
Objects	**250**
External Variables	**252**
Events	**254**
Timeline Events	254
`on` Handler	255
`onClipEvent` Handler	257
Event Handler Properties	259
Button, Movie Clip, and Text Field Properties	**262**
Common Properties of Buttons, Movie Clips, and Text Fields	262
Common Properties of Buttons and Movie Clips	263
Movie Clip Properties	263
Text Field Properties	263
Movie Clip Methods	**264**
Code Hinting with Object Names	**264**
Applying ActionScript	**265**
Possible Improvements	276
Summary	**277**
9 Saving Flash Movies and Creating Flash Web Sites	**279**
Making a Flash Web Site	280
Adding Navigation to a Flash Movie	280

Publish Settings   287

   Flash (.swf) Format Publishing Settings   287

   HTML Publishing Settings   290

   GIF Format Settings   293

   JPEG Image Settings   293

   PNG Image Settings   293

   Windows Projector   293

   Macintosh Projector   294

   QuickTime Settings   294

Optimization with the Bandwidth Profiler   294

Summary   296

10 Exploring Macromedia Fireworks MX 2004   **297**

Creating a New Document   297

   Saving in Macintosh   304

Saving in Windows   306

Exploring the Tools   308

Strokes   308

Fills   309

Select Tools   311

Vector Tools   312

   Line Tool   312

   Pen Tool   312

   Vector Path and Redraw Path Tools   312

   Rectangle Tool   313

   Ellipse Tool   313

   Polygon Tool   314

   Auto Shapes Tool   315

   Assets Panel Shapes Tab   317

   Text Tool   319

   Freeform Tool   320

   Reshape Area Tool   321

   Path Scrubber Tools—Additive and Subtractive   321

Knife Tool   321

Bitmap Tools   **321**

Marquee and Oval Marquee Tools   321

Lasso and Polygon Lasso Tools   323

Magic Wand Tool   325

Brush Tool   326

Pencil Tool   326

Eraser Tool   326

Blur Tool   326

Sharpen Tool   326

Dodge and Burn Tools   326

Smudge Tool   327

Rubber Stamp Tool   327

Replace Color Tool   328

Red Eye Removal Tool   329

Eyedropper Tool   329

Paint Bucket Tool   329

Gradient Tool   330

Live Effects   **331**

Fireworks MX 2004 or FreeHand MX?   **332**

Summary   **332**

11   Creating Content with Fireworks MX 2004   **333**

Creating the Layout   334

Adding Hotspots   338

Adding More Content   340

Creating Buttons, Pop-Up Menus, and Other Behaviors   341

Creating a Button   341

Adding an Over State to Buttons   343

Finishing the Button States   345

Editing Button Instances   347

Adding Buttons to the Page Layout   350

More Masking Methods   352

Creating Pop-Up Menus   356

Finishing the Layout   360

Summary   **363**

12   Exporting, Optimizing, and More Effects in Fireworks MX 2004   365

All About Slices   **366**

Creating a Swap Image   371

Removing Behaviors   373

Adding a Status Bar Message   374

The Behaviors Panel   374

Animations in Fireworks MX 2004   **376**

The Frames Panel   376

Frame-by-Frame Animations   377

Using Distribute to Frames   379

Using Tweens and Graphic Symbols   381

Creating Animation Symbols   382

Importing Graphics   **385**

Optimizing   **386**

The Preview Buttons and Optimize Panel   387

Optimizing the Logo as a GIF   389

Optimizing the Buttons as JPEGs   392

Optimizing Selective JPEGs   394

Batch-Processing Images   397

Exporting HTML   **399**

Summary   **402**

13   An HTML Primer   **403**

History of HTML   **403**

GML and SGML—The Origin   403

On to HTML and the WWW   404

HTML Structure   **404**

Core Tags   405

White Space, Comments, and Case   406

Block-Level Tags   407

Introducing Attributes 410

The `<div>` Tag 411

Line-level Elements 411

The `<img>` Tag 414

Anchor Tags and Hyperlinks 416

A Look at Lists 418

A Look at Tables 422

Exploring Forms 425

HTML Special Characters 429

Within the `<head>` Tag 430

The DOCTYPE Declaration 432

The Future with XML and XHTML **432**

XML 432

XHTML 434

Summary **435**

14 **Exploring Dreamweaver MX 2004** **437**

Exploring the Workspace **438**

The Insert Toolbar 441

The Document Toolbar 444

Panel Groups 445

The Property Inspector 447

Creating Your Site **448**

Summary **455**

15 **Creating Pages with Dreamweaver MX 2004** **457**

Roundtrip HTML **457**

Roundtripping with Fireworks MX 2004 458

Roundtripping with Macromedia Flash MX 2004 463

Setting Up Page Properties **467**

Adding Head Content **469**

Adding Text and Images to Your Page **470**

Adding Text 470

Using Lists 472

Adding Images   475

Flash Text and Buttons   479

Using Tables   482

Inserting a Basic Table   482

Using a Basic Table for Layout   484

Adjusting Table Properties   486

Using the Layout Mode for Tables   490

Assets in Dreamweaver MX 2004   495

Summary   496

16   Site Management and More Dreamweaver Features   497

Using Templates   497

Cascading Style Sheets (CSS)   504

Using Layers   510

Adding Behaviors   514

Server Behaviors   517

Creating Forms   518

Creating a Jump Menu   522

Cleaning Up HTML   523

Site Management   524

The Files Panel   524

The Results Panel Group   526

Summary   528

A   Other Resources   529

Macromedia Products   529

Macromedia FreeHand   529

Macromedia Flash   530

Macromedia Fireworks   530

Macromedia Dreamweaver   530

General Web Development   531

Programming Resources   531

B   About the CD-ROM   **533**

   System Requirements   533

      CRWeb   533

   Installation   535

C   Open Source Licenses   **537**

   Apache Software License (Apache and mod_perl)   537

   PHP Software License   538

   MySQL License   540

Index   **549**

Acknowledgments

Cynthia Frank- Without your "eagle-eye" and wonderful insight, this book would be wanting.

Michael Griffith- For showing me some of the true wonders of integration and providing inspiration with instruction.

Jerry and Beverly Hunley- For your support and patience in this challenging endeavor.

Larry and Kitty Smail- For your constant and unwavering care.

Jim Walsh- You have provided a vast supply of guidance and wisdom leading me down the correct path.

Bryan Davidson- For assisting me in putting it all together.

David Pallai- For giving me the opportunity to write on this subject.

Gareth Downes-Powell- Your input and suggestions were invaluable.

Introduction

ABOUT MACROMEDIA

Throughout its history, Macromedia® has embraced creativity. What started out as a merger of three companies—MacroMind, Paracomp, and Authorware®—has become a dominant player in the Internet technology field.

It all started with the creation of Macromedia Dreamweaver® and the acquisition of FutureWave Software, the original creators of FutureSplash Animator, now Macromedia Flash™. Previously, most Macromedia products were focused on CD-ROM creation. Then they divested themselves of numerous products and, seemingly overnight, were reinvented as a player in the Web market. As their market share grew, creating client-side applications, they took the bold step of acquiring Allaire®, the makers of ColdFusion®. This move propelled them to be not just a client-side Web technology company but a full solution provider with both client and server products.

The company is agile in a tough marketplace, and their focus has shifted again. Their focus is now not primarily on the products themselves (although they are still very committed to development) but on *solutions*. Macromedia Studio MX 2004 is a prime example of this change in focus. The package comprises a bundle of applications designed to integrate with each other completely in a nearly seamless manner.

You can now use Macromedia FreeHand® MX to create graphic content that can be saved in a number of formats for use both in print and on the Web. You can import that same content directly into Macromedia Flash MX 2004 and add it to your movies. You can also bring it directly into Macromedia Fireworks® MX 2004 and combine it with images and HTML for stunningly designed pages. From there, you can merge everything into Dreamweaver MX 2004, your central Web site management tool, and publish it to the Internet.

PURPOSE OF THIS BOOK

This book initiates you in the four core applications of Macromedia Studio MX 2004—Flash MX 2004, FreeHand MX, Fireworks MX 2004, and Dreamweaver MX 2004. Countless books on each separate product (especially for Macromedia Flash MX 2004) are available, but few cover using the entire suite.

This book is intended to make you comfortable with all of the products in the bundle. It is written with the idea that you might not be familiar with these products and, most important, that you might not be a graphic artist. If you are a graphic artist, you shouldn't feel excluded—you can take this material and really set fire to the world. This book focuses on us mortals.

ON THE CD

The exercises in this book can be accomplished comfortably. They are created to teach you the tools, not show off the author's work. Many books provide pre-created content that you must use to complete exercises—a method that starves you of the actual creation process. By being forced to actually create the content in this book, you use every step in the process and can learn more. Although you are expected to create all content, a completed version of nearly every example is included on the CD-ROM for you to compare with what you have made. Also, for exercises that require photographs and the like, the materials are provided.

Some of the work in this book is based on an actual Web site, *http://www. jdukesphoto.com/*. Refer to the Web site to see the principles covered in the text actually applied in a real environment and not just on a vanity section of the author's Web site.

SCOPE OF THIS BOOK

This book provides an introduction to Studio MX 2004. For the purposes of clarity and approachability—not to mention *size*—not all of the features in the applications are covered. Instead, the book covers the core concepts to get you designing a site quickly. After reading this book, you will feel comfortable with all of the products and be able to produce material immediately, as well as possess enough knowledge to learn advanced concepts later.

Applications are introduced in the order in which you would use them when designing a Web site. You start out with FreeHand MX, looking at the tools within the application and creating a site plan or framework. From there, you learn the wonders of Flash MX 2004, the basics of animation, and how Flash sites are created. Next, you tackle Fireworks MX 2004. Many don't know that Fireworks MX 2004 is used not just to doctor photos, but to create Web pages. When used in combination with Dreamweaver MX 2004, it is a streamlined dream for Web page creation and updating. Then you continue with full site control using Dreamweaver MX 2004. The power of this tool is that it allows you to not only create Web pages but to maintain Web sites.

As a progressive learning tool, the book is written in a linear manner—each part builds on the previous. You can feel free to jump around, but you may find yourself having to refer to a supporting concept covered earlier.

A certain degree of comfort with your operating system is assumed. Although the book is an introduction to Studio MX 2004, you should already be comfortable with basic computer tasks like mousing, working with menus, and working within most application windows as a whole.

SUMMARY

You have learned a bit of Macromedia history and looked at how the applications are covered in this book. You are fully involved in the process and will learn by doing.

As you can see, we have five programs to cover—we better get started! We will start with "An Introduction to the Web Server Process and the Design Cycle."

1 An Introduction to the Web Server Process and the Design Cycle

Once you wipe away the complex infrastructure of cables, routers, switches, and the like, the Internet is based on just two simple parts: the client and the server.

WHAT IS SERVER SIDE?

Many different types of servers are used. The first servers, file-and-print servers, had the express purposes of sharing files among a workgroup and allowing many users to share one printer. Printers used to cost a fortune—the money saved on buying just one printer could fund an entire local area network (LAN). Like everything else in technology, servers have evolved to include Web servers for generating Web pages, database servers for offering connectivity with company information, and many other application servers.

This book focuses on Web servers. The definition of a Web server may surprise you. A Web server is nothing more than any device (not just a computer) that is on a network and that runs special software in the background. This software constantly monitors for any HTTP (HyperText Transfer Protocol) requests for services coming into the device.

The server side of the house is all of the back-end technology that the user never sees. It's the connectivity of the vendor's products or services with the user's credit card. If this part of the technology did not take place on the server, potentially anyone could view it. Most users don't want their credit card numbers or other personal information broadcast over the Internet.

The laundry list of server-side technologies includes Perl™, PHP, ASP, Python, ColdFusion (Macromedia's own entry in middleware), Java, and myriad databases.

This list is not all-inclusive. Just going through all of the names can be a bit over-whelming, but rest assured, they don't have to be used all together. These technologies often present an either/or situation.

WHAT IS CLIENT SIDE?

The client is the end user, the recipient of all the wonderful information, products, or services a company or individual wants to share. The client side of the technology is the user experience. It may not sound as earth shattering as writing lines of code out of thin air, but you could argue that the client side is the most important part of the process. If a user cannot navigate a Web site, his visit will be quite brief and usually interrupted by the Back button. If the user can't find where to buy your glorious goods, other sites will happily serve him. And if the user finds the site to be clunky and ugly, he will leave.

The Web designer is often the person in charge. The Web developer may even work for the designer. A Web designer controls how the Web site interfaces with the user. If there is no user, there is no job. The Web developer is usually responding to requests from the designer, such as "The scripts are running slow," "The generated format isn't clear," or "The user needs an e-mail message to verify the order."

Client-side technology is everything that runs directly on the client computer, including the display of text and graphics and some scripting, like JavaScript™. Any technology that can run on the client is invaluable. The server processes potentially thousands of requests a second, and any extra work bogs it down. The user winds up waiting for the page to load and quickly finds the Back button. The results of any processing done on the client side, however, are nearly instantaneous and make the experience more complete. For example, you may fill out a form and wait a while for it to be processed. Right when the processing seems to be done, you find out that the server is sending back an error because you forgot to fill out a field. A client-side script on the Web page to validate the form would have informed you of the error instantly.

FITTING IT TOGETHER

But how does it all fit together? Well, to start with, the client issues a request to the Web server. This request is not just a straight-out "do you have . . . ?" The client

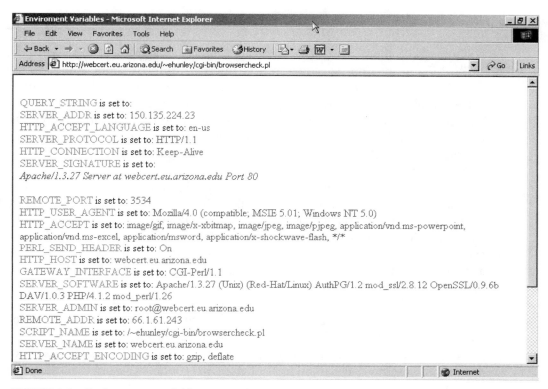

FIGURE 1.1   Environment variables.

computer is actually sending a bunch of information of its own. Figure 1.1 shows some of the information pulled from a Perl script using the environment variables hash.

Notice how the REMOTE_ADDR (client Internet Protocol address) shows up here, along with HTTP_USER_AGENT (client browser and operating system)? This isn't Big Brother activity, but rather information that must be sent for the Web server to do its job. Where is the return IP address? If you send a letter, you need a return address if you expect a reply. What browser is being used? On what platform is the computer running? What plug-ins can the computer handle? This information is extremely important, because the server now knows where to send the data. By using this information, Web designers and developers can enhance an end user's experience.

WEB PROTOCOLS

It all starts with the IP address. IP (Internet Protocol) is a protocol that lives in the TCP/IP (Transmission Control Protocol/Internet Protocol) suite. Protocols are agreed-upon modes of communication between devices, like languages. The Internet was built on TCP/IP. All devices on the Internet or any other network using TCP/IP have what is known as an IP address. The IP address comprises two parts, the network and the host. This address is what devices use to communicate with one another. The IP address, using what is known as dotted-decimal notation, is shown in Figure 1.2.

Four parts of the address are visible, containing numbers from 0 to 255. These parts are known as 8-bit parts. On the surface, the IP address may make little sense to us, but computers see all numbers as binary. Binary numbers use only bits, which are either 1 or 0. This system works well in an electronic environment because it translates to either "on" or "off." The IP address seen by the computer is also made up of four parts with 8 bits in each. Figure 1.3 shows how a computer views an IP address.

Fortunately, you don't have to type in either of these addresses to access a Web site—just type in the domain name. This shortcut is thanks to a service in the TCP/IP stack called DNS (Domain Name System), shown in Figure 1.4.

DNS is a hierarchal structure of databases that maps domain names to IP addresses. For example, the IP address of the URL (uniform resource locator) for *http://www.charlesriver.com/* is 209.15.176.206.

The domain names all start with the root—that's the "dot," as in "charlesriver-dot-com"—followed by the top-level domain name, such as .com, .net, .org, .edu, .gov, and .mil, as well as multiple two-letter country codes, like .us for the United States, .de for Germany, or .ca for Canada.

Each of the available extensions was originally created for a type of organization. You will want to note this information when you purchase a domain name. Originally, you had to purchase a domain name through Network Solutions, but now several companies can sell domain names. Most Web hosting companies offer domain names as part of their service packages.

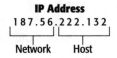

FIGURE 1.2   An IP address from a human's point of view.

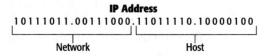

FIGURE 1.3   An IP address from a computer's point of view.

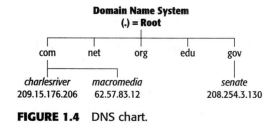

FIGURE 1.4 DNS chart.

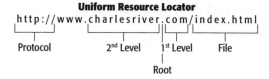

FIGURE 1.5 Breakdown of the Charles River Media URL.

A partial top-level domain name list follows:

.com: Denotes a commercial business that sells products.

.net: Originally created for Internet service providers (ISPs); that practice stopped being followed as less .coms were available for purchase.

.org: Denotes nonprofit organizations, such as churches and charities.

.edu: Denotes educational institutions, such as universities and colleges.

.gov: Denotes a U.S. federal or state government entity.

.mil: Denotes a U.S. military entity.

.xx: Represents the two-letter country code. Most countries have one.

New extensions include .tv, .biz, .info, and .pro.

The address's extension, or everything to the left of the slash (/) in a URL, is the physical address of the server. Everything to the right of the slash is the file system. This is where things get critical. When you type to the left of the slash, case never matters—*WWW.CHARLESRIVER.COM* works just as well as *www.charlesriver.com*. But to the right of the slash, case can matter and frequently does. Many (actually the majority) Web servers on the Internet run either Unix or Linux, which are case-sensitive operating systems. If you type the wrong case, you will receive a "file not found" (404) error. As a Web designer, you must consider this limitation and ensure that the names of all of your Web pages are lowercase with no spaces. Let's break down the Charles River Media URL in Figure 1.5.

To the left of *companyname.com*, you will usually see *http://www*. The *www* means that the document is on the World Wide Web. Most browsers assume this, but it is still often required. To the left of *www* is *http://*. These characters signify that what follows is a Web request using the HTTP in the TCP/IP stack. Other options include *ftp://* for FTP (File Transfer Protocol), *news:* for newsgroups, and *mailto:* for sending an e-mail message.

WHAT HAPPENS TO THE REQUEST?

Now that we know about Web servers and how to find them, let's look at what happens in the process.

The Web server sits on the network, constantly listening to traffic. If it hears a request come into port 80 (the port for HTTP), it starts to look at what file or page was requested. The Web server does one thing well: it generates HTML code and sends it to the client so the browser can display a Web page. The actual processing of the viewable Web page happens on the user's computer.

If the server looks at a requested page and sees that it is straight HTML, it generates the markup code and sends the information to the client. If there is more involved with the page, however, like a CGI script, the Web server cannot process the code immediately because it doesn't understand it. Fortunately, the Web server knows where the external program to process the code lives, and sends the code to the external program (such as Perl). The external program in turn processes the script, moves the data according to the request, and then sends back HTML code with the results. The Web server now passes the modified code to the client. Figures 1.6 and 1.7 show the client-server model and the server perspective.

The overall process follows:

1. The client sends a request to the Web server, usually through port 80 (the HTTP protocol).
2. The Web server software looks at the information in the HTML document stored on the server.
3. If the information is pure HTML, the server generates the code and sends it to the user for display. If the information is a request for a server-side script or external access, the Web server looks at and then passes the information to the appropriate program for processing.

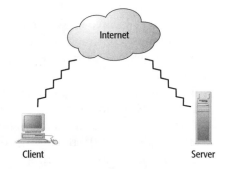

FIGURE 1.6   The client-server model.

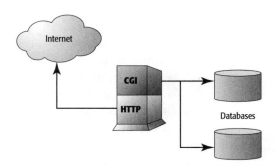

FIGURE 1.7   The components of the server.

4. The appropriate program parses the information required and then instructs the Web server what HTML must be written.
5. The Web server generates the new HTML document and sends it to the client.

MACROMEDIA STUDIO MX 2004 AND THE DESIGN CYCLE

Now that we have seen the overall process of how documents are moved around the Internet, let's look at basic design cycle diagram, shown in Figure 1.8. How do we break it down?

It's like a clock: the hands inevitably travel the same path again and again. The design cycle can be seen as both a source of aggravation and job security, depending on your outlook. Either way, the path will be traveled.

Plan–Brainstorming and Feedback

The planning stage often starts with a pencil, paper, questionnaires, and reports.

- What products or services do we offer?
- Do we need a Web site? The knee-jerk reaction is "Yes!" but it may not always be the case. What about a feed store in a rural area with a customer base that doesn't even own computers? Shipping would be cost prohibitive, and few

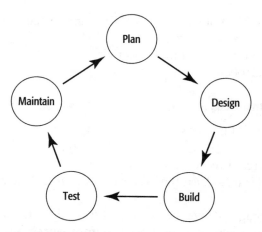

FIGURE 1.8 The design cycle.

would visit the site. The feed store would be better served to use another medium.

- Who is our target audience?
- What kind of technologies will they have?
- How will our customers use our Web site? Will it be primarily on computers, or perhaps mobile phones or other devices?
- What are our competitors doing with their Web sites?
- How will the Web site fit into our business model?

Design—Fireworks and Flash

Use more pencils and paper to draw a basic sketch of how the Web site should look.

- What will the user see when arriving?
- How will one page flow into another?
- How will the Web site be organized? This question is extremely important because Web sites tend to grow out of control quickly without proper planning.
- Do we have any existing marketing materials? Should the Web site resemble our brochures and mailings?
- Do we have artwork that can be reused?
- Can we create the site for file storage?
- Can we create and optimize all images and graphics?

Build—Dreamweaver

This stage involves putting all of our pages together.

- Import all of our Fireworks HTML and images into Dreamweaver.
- Add all text and core content.
- Set up any server-side connectivity.
- Upload all content.

Test—Browsers and People

Now let's see if it works.

- Use Dreamweaver to verify all links.
- Alpha Stage—Visit the Web site yourself and have your team members do the same.
- Beta Stage—Have the client and trusted business partners view the Web site. Does it work for them? Can it be improved?

- Test it again—not just the links and mechanics, but the overall feel. Is it easy to navigate? Is it a sound design? Is it too barren? Too busy? Now is the time to really see if the Web site is serving its purpose.
- Release stage—Let the public see it. Make certain a feedback point is easily accessible for users. Users are the final link as to whether or not the Web site is a success.
- Accessibility—Make certain that all users, even those with disabilities, can view the content.
- Test it yet again.

Maintain–Dreamweaver, Fireworks, Flash

Now you repeat the whole cycle in an ongoing process of Web site maintenance.

- Plan—What is the focus now? A Web site is dynamic and should always reflect updates in terms of business strategy, new products, and services, or just to keep it fresh.
- Design—Put all of our new art together.
- Build—Post all of our changes. Dispose of out-of-date documents and unnecessary graphics to keep the site from becoming too difficult to control.
- Test—Does everything still work?

SUMMARY

Now that you have an understanding of how documents are moved about the Internet and how a design cycle can be applied using Macromedia Studio MX 2004, it's time to start digging into the tools. Next we will be "Taking the FreeHand MX Tour."

2 | Taking the Macromedia FreeHand MX Tour

As the 11th release of the program, FreeHand MX is a mature graphic illustration program with quite a history behind it. FreeHand was developed by a company called Altsys in the late 1980s. Altsys in turn licensed the product to Aldus for distribution, and it was known as Aldus FreeHand for four versions. Then things got a little bit crazy. Aldus merged with Adobe. Adobe then started to distribute FreeHand temporarily, and Altsys sued Aldus over the fate of FreeHand. Aldus settled with Altsys by agreeing to release the rights to the software at the end of their contract period in the mid-1990s. At that point, FreeHand was back with Altsys, briefly. In 1995, Macromedia bought Altsys and brought Free-Hand into the Macromedia product family with version 5 and has owned it ever since.

FreeHand was initially designed to create graphics for print, and this remains its strongest application today. With Macromedia's excursion into Web development and the integration of its products, many Web features have been added to FreeHand. It is an especially powerful partner with Macromedia Flash MX 2004. Although Flash has some great drawing tools of its own, it was initially designed as an animation package and lacks the pure illustrative power of FreeHand. When used together, FreeHand and Flash allow you to create some truly beautiful movies.

FreeHand also enhances Fireworks in a similar manner. Fireworks creates vector graphics and works with bitmap images, but it does not have the depth of vector tools available in FreeHand. You can leverage FreeHand for specialized vector portions in your Web graphics, combine them in Fireworks, and export it all to Dreamweaver.

This tour of FreeHand MX and its core drawing tools will be fast paced so you can get up and running immediately. FreeHand is a complex application with many nuances that can equate to a full-time job. (Many graphic artists use FreeHand as their primary tool every day.) This expertise is not the goal of this book. We need to get our hands dirty and learn how we can create basic content for use on the Web. With its added Web functionality, FreeHand is a great tool to launch a Web site. Because this book is geared toward Web design, FreeHand print capabilities are not covered in depth.

WIREFRAMES AND STORYBOARDS

A popular use of FreeHand in Web design is for creating a site's *frameworks*. Frameworks are essentially a collection of *wireframes* or *storyboards*. Each term's meaning varies, depending on whom you ask. Some say that a storyboard is the overall flowchart of a Web site and that a wireframe is a mockup of a Web page stripped of all graphics. Many point to the practices of Hollywood as an example of this theory, but this example doesn't quite support the argument. In Hollywood, a storyboard comprises drawn-out pictures of actual scenes, which leans more toward the mockup side of the equation.

Ultimately, storyboards and wireframes could be considered the same thing. They are a combination of a visual site-flow diagram and individual page mockups, as shown in Figure 2.1. You will create storyboards with FreeHand later in this

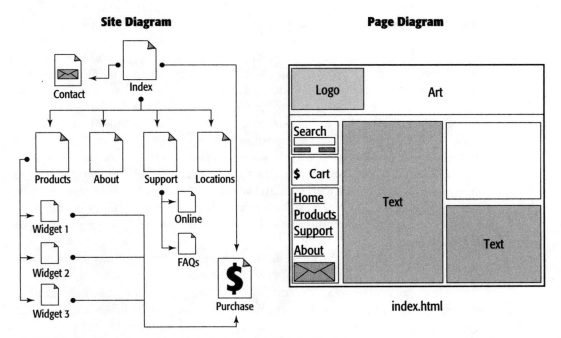

FIGURE 2.1   The two main types of wireframes or storyboards.

chapter. With the added Web functionality, FreeHand is a great tool to launch the site. Due to the fact this book is geared toward Web design, FreeHand print capabilities will not be covered in depth.

FreeHand is a vector graphics tool, so let's start with the obligatory introduction to graphics formats. This introduction may seem to be boring technical stuff, but it is important to understand the difference between vector and raster graphics.

RASTER GRAPHICS

Raster graphics, also called "bitmap" images, are the standard pictures that you see all over the Internet. *Bitmap* is a tricky term; it can refer either to the Windows .bmp picture format or to a generic term for raster graphics (much like how many people refer to any cola product as Coke).

NOTE

The term bitmap *initially referred to a collection of binary data representing what should be displayed on a monitor. Now it also refers to an image itself.*

If you have a digital camera or a scanner (if you don't, it is highly recommended that you get one), you have seen these images. They are a pixel-by-pixel representation of a picture. Pixels are tiny physical points that are displayed by the computer—a kind of modern-day pointillism. Thousands to millions of tiny dots (on a computer they are represented as squares) combine to display a picture.

For example, see Figures 2.2 and 2.3.

FIGURE 2.2 A blown-up raster image.

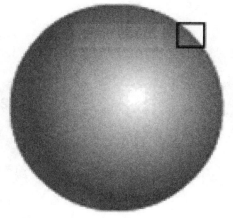

FIGURE 2.3 The raster image from Figure 2.2 shown at normal size.

Figure 2.2 shows the pixelated image from Figure 2.3. Notice how pixels are represented as squares. You may have seen this type of image when you have increased the size of a picture to edit it.

Now that we understand the basics of raster graphics, let's look at vector graphics.

VECTOR GRAPHICS

Vector graphics are often used as an alternative method to create computer graphics. Unlike raster graphics, with their pixel-by-pixel representations, vector graphics are instructions. If you take your image as a grid, as shown in Figure 2.4, you can see how the placement will work.

Two points connected to one another directly will, by default, create a straight line. Figure 2.4 shows the simplest of vector designs. Point 1 is connected to Point 2; a straight line is created between the points.

A vector graphic consists of two parts, lines and fills. Lines, also referred to as *paths*, are the connections of points at coordinates. *Fills* are created by a closed group of lines having color added within. For example, a rectangle comprises four connected lines. If you want the rectangle to be colored, you apply a fill in the middle. To achieve complex colors, vector graphics work with *gradients*. A gradient starts with one color and merges into another by displaying a series of shades, or *gradations*, in between.

By giving the computer instructions, we decrease the file size immensely. For example, a 3770-byte raster graphic would be approximately 69 bytes if rendered as

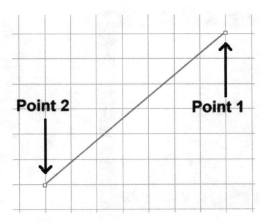

FIGURE 2.4   The image as a grid.

a vector graphic—just 2 percent of the raster graphic's size. Representing the diagram in Figure 2.4 as a raster graphic takes 394 pixels, and that's just the line. Every bit of white space also counts as a pixel. It takes far less storage to tell the computer, "Give me a canvas that is 137 pixels wide by 120 pixels high with a white background. And go ahead and draw a line from Point 1 at this coordinate to Point 2 at that coordinate." Another distinct advantage of vectors is that resolution is never lost. Because they are simply instructions, the computer's CPU redraws them at a larger size, preserving the image quality.

As you can see in Figures 2.5 and 2.6, the resolution is distinctly different between the types of image as their size increases.

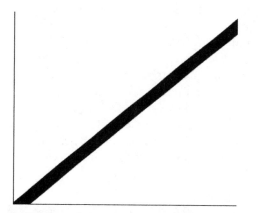

FIGURE 2.5 The line as a vector graphic at 2000%.

FIGURE 2.6 The line as a raster graphic at 1600%.

Vector graphics were the earliest method of displaying graphics on a monitor. This practice dates back to the use of punch cards. The process was initially used with monitors, but they could not refresh fast enough for the graphics to display clearly. Now, most monitors display in a raster graphics format. The images are bitmapped and then shown on the monitor, meaning that even when you use vector graphics, the monitor is physically displaying them as rasterized.

RASTER OR VECTOR GRAPHICS—WHICH SHOULD YOU USE?

At first glance, it would seem that vector graphics should always be used on the Web and that raster graphics should be dying out. As with everything, however, you should consider certain factors:

How complex is the graphic? When choosing between vector and raster graphics, complexity of the image is a serious consideration. While giving the computer instructions for an image, it is best if the image does not contain too many varying shapes and textures.

How many colors? The more colors added to a vector graphic, the more instructions are needed.

How many shades? This is similar to the color question. A merge from one color to another is called a gradient. The number of gradients an image contains adds to its overall complexity.

When you add in these factors, you find that the vector graphic's file size is not substantially decreased, and the image is so complex that it is incredibly taxing on the computer and can wind up taking longer to load. The complexity of the image may force a computer (especially an older one) to actually lock up while trying to render it. Plus, when a vector graphic image contains too many textures, colors, and gradients, it not only looks just as poor in quality as a raster image when it is enlarged, but it also has a large file size. With these added factors, you should use vector graphics for line drawings and basic computerized art, and raster images for photographs and extremely detailed images. Figures 2.7 and 2.8 demonstrate the difference between a photograph rendered in raster graphics and in vector graphics.

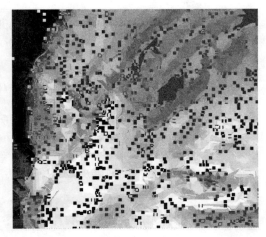

FIGURE 2.7   A 190 KB rasterized photograph without compression.

FIGURE 2.8   A vector graphics version of Figure 2.7. This image is 2.76 MB and takes several minutes to render.

EXPLORING THE INTERFACE

At its core, FreeHand MX resembles the rest of the Macromedia MX line in terms of the interface, but it is not quite as close in terms of a common interface as Dreamweaver MX 2004, Macromedia Flash MX 2004, and Fireworks MX 2004. This inconsistency is partly due to the program's age and print heritage. Let's create a new document and look at it. To create a new page, select File > New, or press the keyboard shortcut Ctrl + N (Command + N on a Macintosh).

The FreeHand interface is divided into four main parts, as shown in Figures 2.9 and 2.10.

> **Main menu:** Common across most applications, the main menu bar contains the overall functions of the program, file operations (open, save, and so on), editing functions, advanced settings, and access to interface appearance controls.

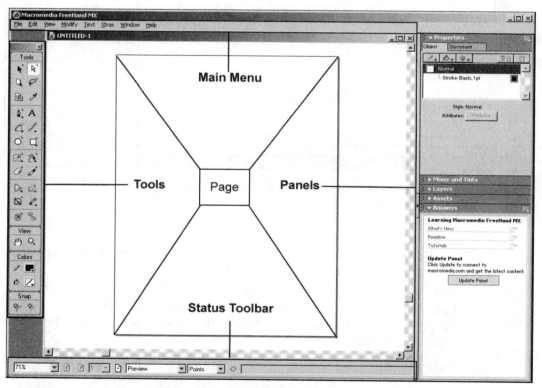

FIGURE 2.9   The FreeHand MX interface in Windows 2000.

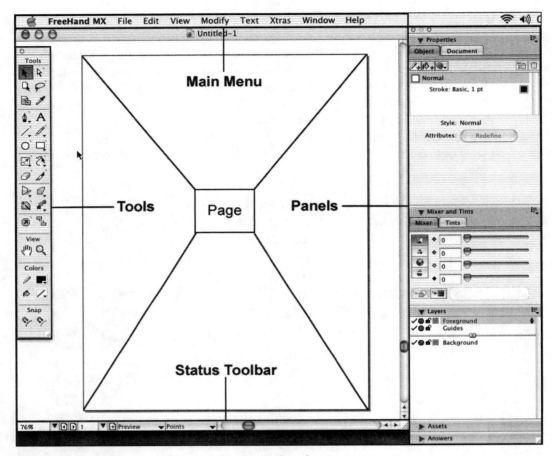

FIGURE 2.10   The FreeHand MX interface in Macintosh OS 10.2.

Tools Panel: This area is the meat-and-potatoes portion of the application. The most often used drawing tools are located here.

Panels: Your *panels* and *inspectors* are found here. They essentially are the same thing but were given different names throughout version history. They refine the properties of objects you create with the Tools Panel as well as the documents themselves.

Status Toolbar: This section provides overall information about the document as far as what mode you are in, how much of the document is seen, and what ruler units are displayed. With Windows, the Status Toolbar also enables you to see the status of a running operation. (You can press Cancel to end the operation.) On Macintosh platforms, this bar is built in and cannot be moved.

THE TOOLS PANEL

The Tools Panel is where you literally put the pencil to the page. It is divided into four main parts:

Tools: Contains the main drawing tools, such as the Pointer, Pen, Text, and Shape Tools. These tools not only draw but also modify what has been drawn.

View: Includes the Zoom Tool and Hand Tool. The Zoom Tool literally zooms in. (Press Alt + Option and click to zoom out.) The Hand Tool is a great tool that enables you to move the page around so you can get different views. To temporarily invoke the Hand Tool while you are working, press the spacebar on your keyboard. When you have finished moving the page, release the spacebar. The control returns focus to whichever tool you were using before invoking the Hand Tool.

Colors: Provides quick colors for initial stroke and fill creation.

Snap: Snaps whatever object you are creating to another object or to a specific point in an object. The main difference between the options is that with Snap to Object your new creation snaps to any line or vector point in the object when it gets close enough, whereas Snap to Point snaps the object only to an actual vector point.

CREATING PATHS

In this section, we create paths using the predominant vector illustration tool, the Pen Tool. The Pen Tool is based on using Bézier handles. Pierre Bézier was a French mechanical engineer and mathematician who came up with the mathematical formula to create curves out of points. The basic principle behind the process is of string or wire art. If you take a box and hang a wire loosely off the edges, you have a curve. See image 1 in Figure 2.11. Now imagine that you have handles and pull the wire tighter. This action would give you image 2. Then, if you took the ends, pushed them together, and rotated until the wire was facing up, you would have image 3.

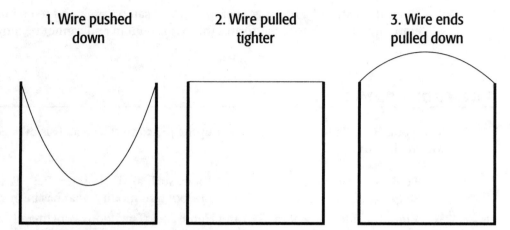

FIGURE 2.11   Wires in a box that demonstrate the Bézier principle.

We now begin to put some content together by looking at the Pen Tool and how it is used. The Pen Tool is an ingenious principle but can be challenging to master. The Pen Tool is used in FreeHand, Flash, and Fireworks, as well as in numerous illustration, 3D, and CAD (computer-aided design) applications. Figure 2.12 shows the two basic forms that are created by the Pen Tool, curves and corners.

Notice that when dealing with sharp corners, no handles appear on the Bézier curves. Pushing a handle all the way into a point causes the line between points to be straight. The longer the handle is when you pull, the longer the curve that is created. This process can seem almost contrary, so let's practice making Bézier paths. Figure 2.13 displays a basic shape made with no curves.

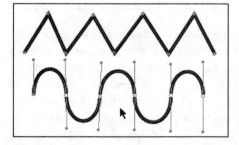

FIGURE 2.12   Curves and corners, the two basic Bézier-guided paths.

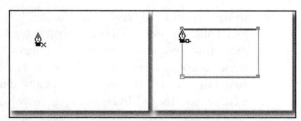

FIGURE 2.13   Creating a simple path with corners.

Selecting Your Initial Line and Fill Colors

Before you draw any line or shape, select your line colors. If a stroke has no color, you create a path, but no line appears on the page. The tools to assist you can be found in two places—the Colors portion of the Tools Panel or the newly updated Object Panel, shown in Figure 2.14.

The Object Panel is an important update in FreeHand MX because it enables you to create and edit your strokes, fills, and text in a single location. In FreeHand 10, you have to work with the Stroke, Fill, and Text Inspectors separately. Again, for a stroke to appear on a page, you must select a color in either the Tools Panel (by clicking the color swatch next to the pencil icon and selecting a color) or by checking the Object Panel and verifying that a Stroke is listed. (If it is not listed, click the pencil icon in the top-left corner of the panel to create a stroke.) Use Figure 2.15 to explore the steps necessary to create a basic shape. Each step corresponds with the number in the figure.

Creating Paths with Sharp Corners

1. Select the Pen Tool. Check to see that you have a stroke color selected if you want the path to appear on the page. When you mouse over an area with the Pen Tool, you initially see an "x", as shown in step 1 in Figure 2.15, indicating that FreeHand will create the first point in your path. (X marks

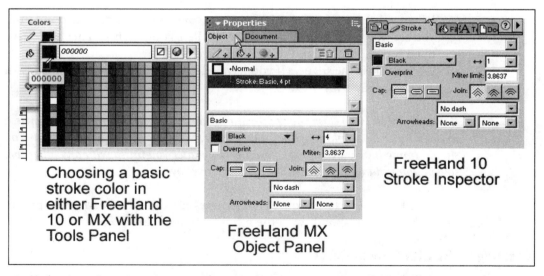

FIGURE 2.14 The Colors Group in the Tools Panel, the FreeHand MX Object Panel, and the FreeHand 10 Stroke Inspector.

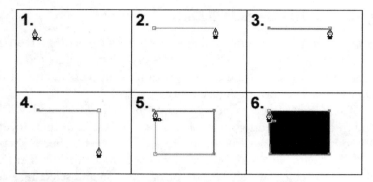

FIGURE 2.15 Creating paths and shapes with sharp corners.

the spot.) As you move your mouse to the next location, you see a "rubber band" preview of what the line will look like. Click and immediately release to create the point. Do not drag the mouse while pressing the mouse button or you will start a curve.

2. Move the pen to the spot where you would like the next point, as shown in step 2.
3. Click and immediately release to create the point, as shown in step 3.
4. For each following point, click and release the mouse button, as shown in steps 3 and 4.
5. When you are ready to close the shape, hover over your starting point until you see the open box appear next to the Pen Tool, as shown in step 5. This open box indicates that the path will be closed.
6. Click to close the shape. (If you have selected a fill, the shape is filled with a color or pattern.)

If you do not want to close your path, after you have placed your last point, switch to the Pointer Tool (black arrow). You can press the V or 0 key as a shortcut. You should immediately switch to the Pointer Tool after you finish with any other tool so you don't inadvertently leave artifacts on the page.

Now use Figure 2.16 to explore the steps necessary to create a path with smooth curves. Each step corresponds with the number in the figure.

Creating Paths with Smooth Curves

1. Select the Pen Tool, and check to see that you have a stroke color selected if you want the path to appear on the page. When you mouse over an area

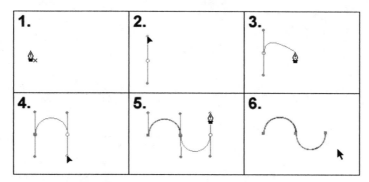

FIGURE 2.16   Creating smooth curves on a path.

with the Pen Tool, you see an "x", as shown in step 1 of Figure 2.16, indicating that FreeHand will create your first point.

2. Click and drag, without releasing your mouse button, in the direction you want the curve to appear, as shown in step 2. Notice how two vector handles now appear.

3. Release the mouse button, and move to where you want your second point to appear, as shown in step 3.

4. Click and drag, without releasing the mouse button, in the opposite direction of the first curve, as shown in step 4. The vector handles reappear again. Release the mouse button after the vector handles are at the desired length. (You can match your current and previous handle length to create a curve of the same shape.)

5. Repeat steps 3 and 4 to create however many more curves you want.

6. When you are ready to end your path, select the Pointer Tool. (You can also press the keyboard shortcut V or 0 to quickly switch to it.) The completed path is selected, as shown in step 6. Notice that this path has no fill. If a path is not closed, no fill appears.

NOTE

If you want to create many paths in a sequence, you can temporarily invoke the Pointer Tool by pressing the Ctrl key (Command on a Macintosh) and clicking a blank spot on the page to deselect the current path. After you click and release (while holding the Ctrl or Command key), the Pen Tool is available to create a new path and does not continue the previous path.

Now use Figure 2.17 to explore the steps necessary to create a path with multiple curves going in the same direction. Each step corresponds with the number in the figure.

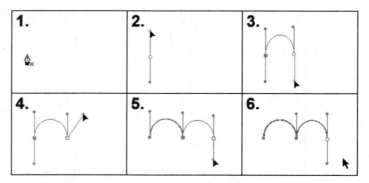

FIGURE 2.17 Creating curves running in the same direction.

Creating Multiple Curves Going the Same Direction

1. Select the Pen Tool, and check to see that a stroke color is selected. Select where you would like to place your first point, as shown in step 1 in Figure 2.17.
2. Click and hold the mouse button. Drag a handle in the direction you would like the first curve to appear, as shown in step 2.
3. Click to create your next point, and drag your handle in the opposite direction of your first curve, as shown in step 3.
4. While still holding down the mouse button, press and hold the Alt or Option key. Pull your handle around and up, as shown in step 4. Keep pulling the handle until you have it lined up with the top handle, and then release the mouse button and Alt or Option key.
5. Click where you want to place your next point, hold down the mouse button, and drag the handle in the opposite direction of your previous curve, as shown in step 5. Repeat step 4 if you want to create another curve.
6. When you have finished making your curves, change back to the Pointer Tool. You have a completed path, as shown in step 6.

Combining Styles to Create a Shape

This task demonstrates that using the Pen Tool can prove to be a real challenge. The first few times you create complex shapes, you may feel that you are performing gymnastics with your fingers. Let's create the saguaro cactus, shown in Figure 2.18, to mix and match curves and corners. Before we start, select a fill color from the Colors portion of the Tools Panel (seen in Figure 2.14). Click the color next to the paint bucket and select a shade of green.

1. Select where you would like to place your first point.
2. Click and hold down the mouse button. Drag the handle upward to set yourself up for your first curve, then release the mouse button. Drag a little bit because the top of the cactus has a long curve.
3. Click and hold down the mouse button where you want to place your second point. Drag your handle straight downward to pull out your curve, then hold down the Alt or Option key. While holding down the Alt or Option key, pull your handle around and up to approximately 2 o'clock, as shown in step 3 in Figure 2.18. Release the mouse button and then the Alt or Option key.
4. Click and hold down the mouse button to place the anchor point for the first arm. Drag out a handle to the right to give it a nice curve, as shown in step 4.
5. Click and hold down the mouse button where the arm reconnects to the body. It may look like the stroke is too close to the upper stroke in the arm, but this is normal. We will be pulling out the curve with our handle. Pull out the handle to form a nice contour, continuing to hold down the mouse button, as shown in step 5.
6. Still holding down the mouse button, click and hold the Alt or Option key. Drag the handle straight down, as shown in step 6, and release both the mouse button and the Alt or Option key. This action cues the straight line going down the trunk of the cactus.
7. Move the mouse down to create the bottom-right corner. Click and release the mouse button immediately. Do not drag the mouse.
8. Click to create the bottom-left corner, as shown in step 8. Again, release immediately without dragging.
9. Click and release again to create the point where the left arm comes out, as shown in step 9.
10. Click and hold down the mouse button at the point of the second arm. Pull out the handle, as shown in step 10, to create a nice curve for the arm coming up, then release the mouse button.
11. To simplify creating the arm on the left, click on the other side of the arm and drag the handle in the opposite direction of the current curve to achieve a rounded end. This action is shown in step 11.
12. Finally, click the original point to close the shape. The fill automatically happens because the path is closed. The cactus may not look exact, but no worries—you can adjust the points and vector handles to tweak it.

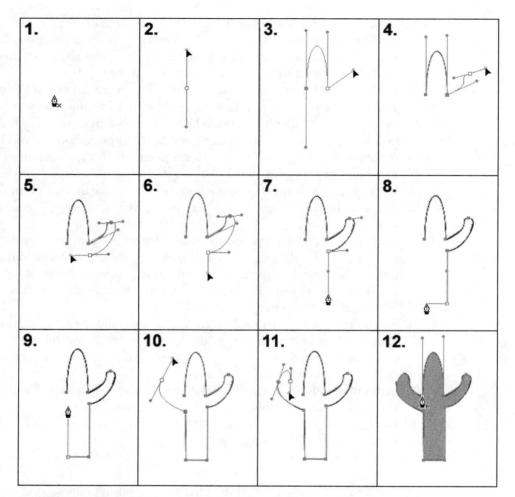

FIGURE 2.18 Combining corners and curves to make a shape.

The Pen Tool is not the easiest tool to use. Even professionals who have been doing graphic design for years still struggle with it. Just realize that, with practice and prayer, it will become easier over time. Don't stop creating with just the cactus shape; create several images on your own to get a better feel for the tool. If the objects are a little bit off, you can further refine them with all of your selection tools, including the Pointer, Subselect, and Lasso Tools. These tools are covered in the next section.

If you want to add points to an object that you have already created, you can use the Pen Tool. Simply hover the Pen Tool over the path until you see a plus sign (+) next to the cursor, then click to add the new point.

Using the Pointer, Subselect, and Lasso Tools to Modify Points

The main tools used in FreeHand to move paths and modify points are the Pointer (black arrow) and Subselect (white arrow) tools. Both tools are used in a similar manner within FreeHand, but you can use the Subselect Tool to select points and objects, even in a group. The Subselect Tool can also pull point handles out of a straight corner for modification into a curve. You use the Lasso Tool to select a freeform area of objects or a shape within an individual object.

Let's take a look at these tools using the saguaro cactus we created, starting with the Pointer Tool, as shown in Figure 2.19.

1. To move an entire object, click it using the Pointer Tool and begin to move it. Your cursor turns into a four-pointed arrow, shown in step 1 in Figure 2.19. Remember, if you have no fill in the object, you must click directly on the stroke to move it.

2. If you want to move a single point, click directly on it and move it as shown in steps 2 and 3. The selected point becomes hollow. If you cannot see any points, select the entire object (this makes all the points visible), then click the point. If you hold down the mouse button before moving it, your cursor turns into a four-pointed arrow as you move the point.

3. To shape a curve, you must click one of the point handles that appears after you select your point, as shown in step 4. If you want a longer curve, pull the handle in the direction of the curve. Conversely, if you want a straight line, push the handle all the way into the point.

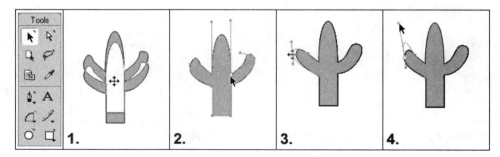

FIGURE 2.19   Using the Pointer Tool to manipulate an object.

If you want to move objects in a precise manner, don't use the mouse; use the directional arrows on the keyboard. The directional arrows assist you in exact placement with less room for error. If you press only the left key, for example, the object moves only left (with a mouse it may wander) one pixel per press. To move an object more quickly, hold down the Shift key and tap the arrow.

Now let's look at the Subselect Tool. The Subselect Tool is useful for working with points; that is its core purpose. This tool is the predominant tool for point manipulation in most vector illustration programs and, with FreeHand, it has the additional power to select points even when an object is locked in a group. Let's look at it in Figure 2.20:

1. Like the Pointer Tool, the Subselect Tool can select and move the entire object, as shown in step 1 in Figure 2.20. Also like the Pointer Tool, you must click directly on the stroke if the object has no fill.
2. Selecting points is what sets this tool apart. When you get in close to a point, notice that the white arrow loses its stem, as shown in step 2.
3. At this point, one of two things can happen. If you are slightly outside the vector point, you pull out a handle, as shown in step 3. If you are directly on the point, however, you move the entire point as shown in step 4.

The Subselect Tool is your primary point manipulation tool in Flash and Fireworks, so you might want to consider using it for all of your point manipulation tasks.

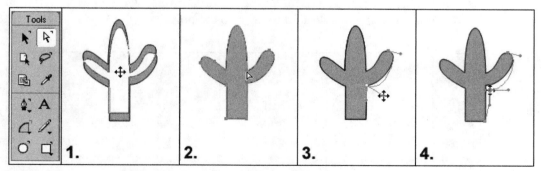

FIGURE 2.20   Using the Subselect Tool for object manipulation.

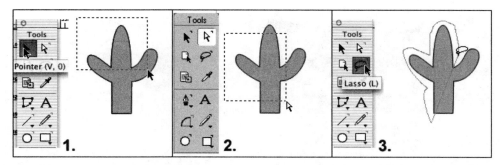

FIGURE 2.21 Using the Pointer, Subselect, and Lasso Tools to select parts of an object.

To select multiple points within an object, you can use the Pointer and Subselect Tools to draw a marquee (a rectangle with dotted lines), as shown in steps 1 and 2 in Figure 2.21, or you can use the Lasso Tool, as shown in step 3. The Lasso Tool allows you to select a more freeform shape. Simply click and draw a shape with the mouse. The selected area stays closed the entire time, as shown in step 3 in Figure 2.21.

An alternative method of selecting more than one point is to press Shift + click on each point adding it to the previously selected points. To deselect a point, keep holding down Shift and click the point you want to deselect.

Another consideration when using your pointer and selection tools is how you want the points to appear. By default, when a point is selected in FreeHand, the point appears hollow, which is different from many graphic design tools, including both Fireworks and Flash. To change the default behavior to show selected points as solid instead, change the setting in the Preferences dialog box, shown in Figure 2.22. You can access the Preferences dialog box by selecting Edit > Preferences or by using the keyboard shortcut of Ctrl + U (Command + U for Macintosh).

You can also change the behavior of your pointer tools by double-clicking either the Pointer or Subselect Tool and making it Contact Sensitive (changing this setting under either tool modifies both of them), as shown in Figure 2.22. When you select Contact Sensitive for the pointer tools, they select points near where you drew the marquee. If the points are not within the marquee area but are near, they are still selected.

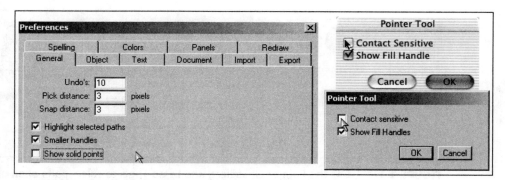

FIGURE 2.22   Adjusting General and Pointer Preferences.

Using the Bezigon Tool

Because many people find the Pen Tool intimidating, some use the Bezigon Tool as an alternative. It can be found underneath the Pen Tool by clicking and holding the mouse button on the Pen Tool button, as shown in Figure 2.23.

The Bezigon Tool operates in a similar manner to the Pen Tool but is much more limited. You can use it to place points. It lacks the capability to shape them as they are created.

Like the Pen Tool, you can use the Bezigon Tool to create one of two types of path—straight lines and curves. (Use the Alt or Option key for a curved line.) You must use the point handles after creation to shape your objects. The Bezigon Tool is great to use if you have a shape with primarily straight edges. If you are going to use curves, however, this tool adds significantly to your workload. Let's look at creating the cactus with the Bezigon Tool, as shown in Figure 2.24.

1. Hold down the Alt or Option key to make the first point of a curve for the top of the cactus, as shown in step 1 of Figure 2.24. You will notice a difference from the Pen Tool immediately. As you hold down the Alt or Option key, a point handle does not appear; you are able to move only where

FIGURE 2.23   The Bezigon Tool.

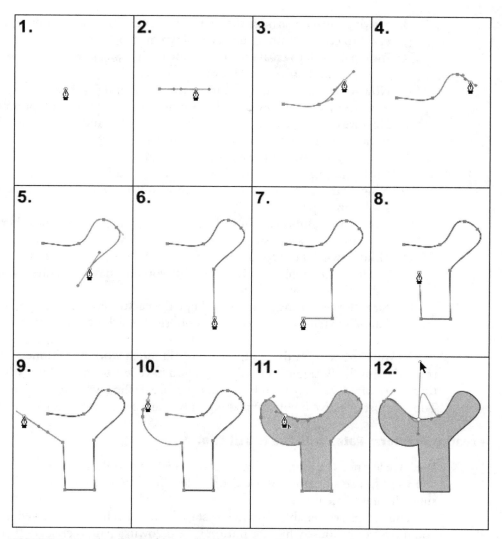

FIGURE 2.24   Creating a shape with the Bezigon Tool.

the point is placed. (When using the Pen Tool, when you drag the mouse as you are placing a point, you pull out handles.) Click and release both the mouse button and the Alt or Option key.

2. Hold down the Alt or Option key and select the other side of what will be the top of the cactus, as shown in step 2. Click and release the mouse and the Alt or Option key.

3. Moving onto the arm of the cactus, you must press the Alt or Option key again to create another curve, as shown in step 3.
4. In step 4, click to create the other side of the cactus arm, which is another curve, so hold down the Alt or Option key.
5. Now we move back to the trunk of the cactus and finish your last curve for now. (As you probably guessed, you need to use the Alt or Option key.)
6. Now we create the line for the body of the cactus and just simply click and release for the next point, as shown in step 6.
7. Click and release for the bottom-left corner.
8. Click and release where the left arm will protrude.
9. Now, you use the Alt or Option key again to create a curve in the arm, as shown in step 9.
10. Hold Alt or Option again and click to place the point for the other side of the arm as shown in step 10.
11. Hold down Alt or Option one last time while you connect to your starting point, as shown in step 11. Notice that you now have a headless cactus; you still have some work to do.
12. Start to pull on the handles to shape the cactus. For the top, pull out long handles (as shown in step 12) on both sides to achieve the long curve shape.

As you can see from the result, there is still much work to be done. This is the tradeoff with the Bezigon Tool. Although you have less to think about when plotting your points, you pay for it later when you are dealing with curves. The Bezigon Tool is most effective if you are making only sharp corners and exact curves.

Creating Freeform Paths with the Pencil Tool

We have learned the highly technical tools, the Pen and Bezigon Tools, but what if you want to use a freeform illustration style? That is where the Pencil Tool and its subordinates come into action.

The Pencil Tool enables you to just start drawing. When it is selected, wherever you move your mouse while the button is held down, a path is created. If you want the line to be straight, simply hold down the Alt or Option key while you draw. FreeHand fills in all the necessary points to create your path. Let's look at creating the cactus using the Pencil Tool, as shown in Figure 2.25.

1. To create your shape, just click where you want to start and begin drawing, as shown in step 1 in Figure 2.25.

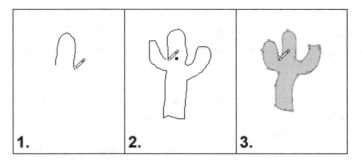

FIGURE 2.25 Creating a shape using the Pencil Tool.

2. Just like with the Pen and Bezigon Tools, when you hover over your starting point, FreeHand changes the cursor to reflect that you are closing your shape. In this case, it shows a square next to the cursor.

3. If a fill has been selected, when the shape is closed, it will automatically be filled, as shown in step 3. Notice how the vector points appear when the object is complete. After it is complete, the shape is slightly smoother than the shape you drew.

When using the Pencil Tool, keep in mind that FreeHand adds points where it thinks they need to be placed. It will frequently add more points than are necessary, and you want to dispose of these extra points because they add needless complexity to your graphic. To delete extra points, select a point and press Delete. An alternative is to have FreeHand simplify the shape for you. You can find Simplify under Xtras > Clean Up on the main tool bar or by right-clicking (Windows only) the shape and selecting Xtras > Clean Up > Simplify. This action opens the Simplify dialog box, shown in Figure 2.26.

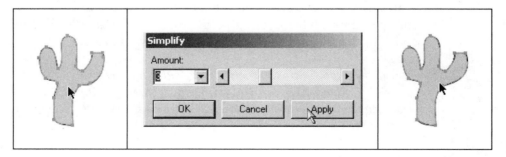

FIGURE 2.26 Using Simplify. With the setting of 3, three points were removed from the cactus—two on the arm to the right and one on the arm to the left.

When using Simplify, you choose the number of points you want to remove from your shape. FreeHand removes the points while maintaining the overall integrity of the design. This option is helpful if you are uncertain which points you can remove safely.

When you are using the Pencil Tool to create your strokes, you may notice that they don't appear as crisp as when created with the Pen Tool. You can resolve this problem by selecting the object, then reselecting your stroke in the Object Panel. You can also select a thicker stroke than you currently have to make it appear bolder.

The Variable Stroke and Calligraphic Pen Tools

Nested underneath the Pencil Tool are two tools that make your designs more expressive—the Variable Stroke and Calligraphic Pen Tools. Select them by clicking and holding down the mouse button on the Pencil Tool, then selecting the tool you want, as shown in Figure 2.27.

The Variable Stroke Pen Tool is most effectively used with a digitizer tablet. FreeHand responds to the pressure you place on the pen. If you are not using a digitizer tablet, you can still get a similar result by pressing your left and right arrows on the keyboard to make the stroke lighter or thicker. You can also use the left and right brackets ([and]). You can further modify the settings by double-clicking the selected tool and changing its properties (shown in Figure 2.27). The Precision value controls the amount of sensitivity to pressure, with a higher number being more sensitive. Selecting Draw dotted line changes your preview to a dotted line, which can be useful for speeding up path creation. Selecting Auto remove overlap removes extra paths when you overlap your lines. The Width values constrain how wide or narrow the path can be.

The Calligraphic Pen Tool is similar to the Variable Stroke Tool in that it creates paths with varying degrees of width, but it is designed to look more like a calligraphy pen stroke. It has all of the properties of the Variable Stroke Tool, plus the capability to change the angle of the stroke, as shown in Figure 2.27.

To call these tools "Stroke" Tools is a bit misleading. They are not creating strokes but rather vector shapes, as you can see in Figure 2.27. If you want the shape to look cleaner and more like a stroke, do not set a stroke color. Work with just a fill color.

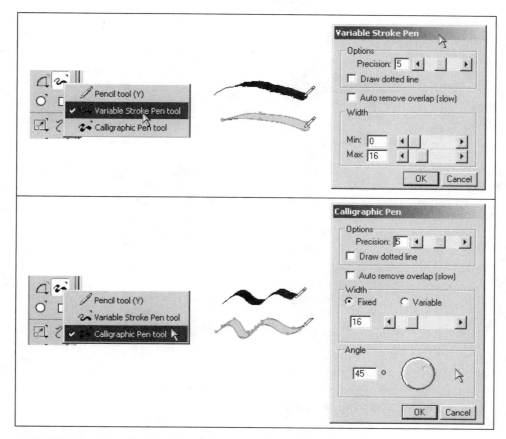

FIGURE 2.27   Using the Variable Stoke and Calligraphic Pen Tools.

The Line, Arc, and Spiral Tools

The Line, Arc, and Spiral Tools are used for creating different types of strokes. The Line Tool creates a simple two-point straight line. The Arc Tool also creates a basic two-point line, but it creates it as a curve and provides more options when you double-click the tool. You can create an open or closed arc (completing the shape), or you can make it concave or convex. The Spiral Tool—well, it makes spirals. You can choose how many rotations the curve has, how much it expands for each rotation, and in which direction you would like the spiral to travel. Figure 2.28 shows the Arc and Spiral Tools and their properties.

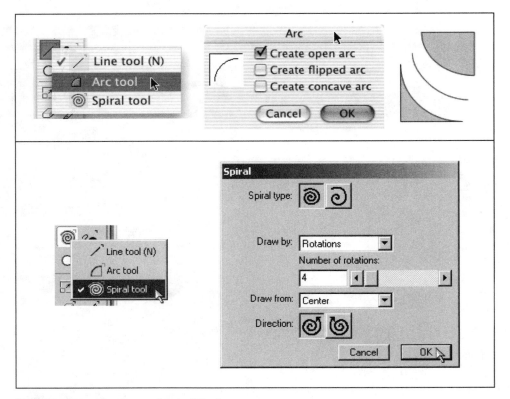

FIGURE 2.28 The Arc and Spiral Tools.

CREATING SHAPES WITH FREEHAND MX

With FreeHand, you are not limited to drawing shapes manually. You also have the ability to create some standard shapes, like circles, rectangles, and polygons. Like the Pen, Pencil, and Pointer Tools, the various shape tools can be found in the Tools Panel. Let's look at creating some shapes and then work with the Object Panel to further manipulate them.

Creating Rounded Shapes with the Ellipse Tool

We use the Ellipse Tool to create oval and circular shapes, either filled or hollow. This tool is fairly straightforward, and not much manipulation is available.

If you want to create a circle or oval, simply click where you plan to place the top-left portion of the shape and drag out the shape. If you want the shape to be a perfect circle, hold down the Shift key while you drag. As you create the circle, your cursor appears as a plus sign (+), as shown in step 1 in Figure 2.29. You can also start the shape from the center. In this case, hold down the Alt or Option key while drawing the circle. When you hold down the Alt or Option key, your cursor changes from the plus sign to a plus sign with a circle combined, as shown in step 2 in Figure 2.29. If you have a fill selected before you make your shape, the object is created with a fill, as shown in step 3.

You can also use the Object Panel to manipulate the properties of your ellipse. Let's do a quick exercise and look at this in Figure 2.30.

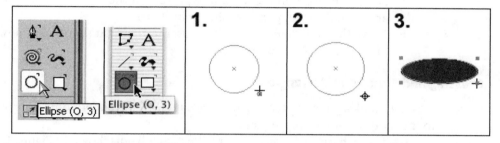

FIGURE 2.29   The Ellipse Tool.

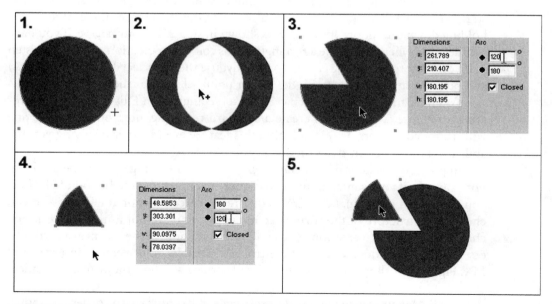

FIGURE 2.30   Using the Ellipse Tool and Object Panel to create and modify circles.

1. Select a basic fill and line for your circle.
2. Click your Ellipse Tool to select it and drag out a shape while holding the Shift key to constrain the shape into a perfect circle, as shown in step 1 in Figure 2.30.
3. Change to the Pointer Tool and select your new shape. Hold down the Alt or Option key and drag to your left. This action is a shortcut for making a copy of your first object, as shown in step 2. When you have two circles side by side, release both your mouse and the Alt or Option key.
4. Select the circle to the right, and then type 120° in the top text box in the Arc area in the Object panel, as shown in step 3.
5. Select the circle on the left and type 120° in the lower text box in the Arc area in the Object panel, as shown in step 4.
6. Move the new shape on the left closer to the right shape. You now have a piece of pie cut from the circle.

Creating and Modifying Rectangles

Now let's look at creating rectangles. FreeHand MX has added some improvements to the modification of rectangles.

To create a basic rectangle, select the Rectangle Tool (shown in Figure 2.31), and click and drag out your shape, as shown in step 1 in Figure 2.31. Like the Ellipse Tool, if you hold down the Shift key while creating a rectangle, the shape is constrained as a perfect square. You can also create the shape from the center out by holding down the Alt or Option key, as shown in step 2. Like any shape, if you have a fill selected when you create a rectangle, it has color after creation, as shown in step 3. If you want to round the corners on the fly, use the Subselect Tool (white arrow) and push toward the center with the corner point selected, as shown in step 4.

You have more options when creating a rectangle than Ellipse Tool when creating an ellipse. Yes, you can create a standard rectangle, but you may want one with rounded corners. FreeHand takes this feature even further by giving you the ability to have different styles on different corners.

In previous versions of FreeHand, all corners in a rectangle had to be uniform. For example, if you wanted a rounded corner, all corners had to be rounded. Now, you can round individual corners by different degrees, or not at all. You also can change the structure of the corners at any point. You are not limited to declaring changes only prior to creation. You can even have some corners concave with others convex. This added degree of control is a sizeable improvement in FreeHand MX. Figure 2.32 shows the different types of corners and how they can be modified.

1. By default, when you create a rectangle, it has four sharp corners, as shown in step 1 in Figure 2.32.

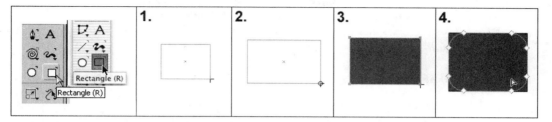

FIGURE 2.31 The Rectangle Tool.

2. If you leave the Uniform checkbox selected and change the corner radius to a number (the higher the number, the sharper the curve), all four corners are rounded by the same amount, as shown in step 2.

3. The ability to select which corners are curved, as shown in step 3, is where FreeHand MX stands out, even over FreeHand 10.

4. In addition to being able to select which corners are rounded, you also have the option of making them concave, as shown in step 4.

With the added improvements, FreeHand MX shows some real growth with the Rectangle Tool. You still have the ability to double-click the Rectangle Tool and select your corner radius before drawing the shape, as in FreeHand 10, but the real power of FreeHand MX is in the Object Panel.

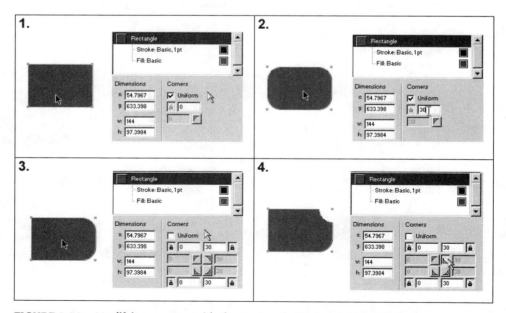

FIGURE 2.32 Modifying corners with the Rectangle Tool and Object Panel.

When creating any vector shape, you can modify the placement of the shape by pressing the space bar while drawing the shape and moving it to wherever you would like on the screen.

Creating Polygons and Stars

With FreeHand, you can get a bit more complex with your shapes by creating polygons and stars with the Polygon Tool. This tool is located underneath the Rectangle Tool, as shown in Figure 2.33.

The Polygon Tool offers many variations, as is the nature of polygons. How many sides? Is it a star? What kind of corners do you want? You can adjust the number of sides and whether the shape is a star or polygon in the Polygon Tool dialog box, which you can access by double-clicking the Polygon Tool in the Tools Panel, as shown in Figure 2.33. If you select Star, more options are available, including whether the angles are acute (sharp) or obtuse (more rounded), also shown in Figure 2.33. If you change the acute or obtuse values, the Star Points options automatically change to have Manual selected. You use these properties to change the value *before* shape creation.

The properties available before creation are the same as they were in FreeHand 10. Where FreeHand MX begins to flex is in what you can do *after* creation. The newly revised Object Panel provides an incredible amount of flexibility in modifying polygons and stars. Let's create and manipulate some polygons in Figure 2.34. Each step corresponds with the number in the figure.

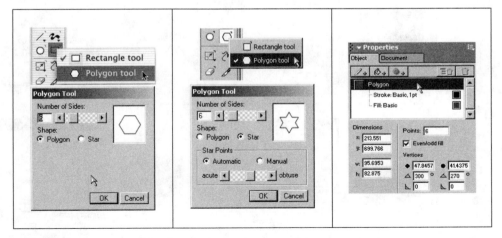

FIGURE 2.33   The Polygon Tool, its properties, and the Object Panel.

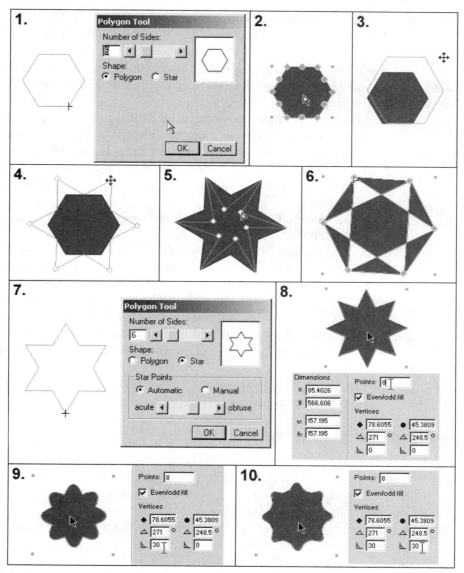

FIGURE 2.34 Manipulating polygons.

1. Select the Polygon Tool. Double-click the tool to access the tool properties and make sure that the number of sides is set to 6 and the shape is Polygon. Create your polygon.

2. With your Subselect Tool chosen, you can see manipulation points on your polygon. The squares in each corner are for sizing, the diamonds represent peaks, and the circles represent valleys.

3. To resize your polygon, choose one of the tiny squares in the four corners with the Subselect Tool. (Hold down the Shift key if you want to constrain the shape.)

4. This is where things get interesting. If you pull out one of the diamond shapes, you no longer have a polygon but a star. The two shapes are actually the same—the polygons just have flat peaks and valleys.

5. If you pull in one of the circle points, you increase the depth of the valley. If you don't want to create an angle, hold down the Shift key to constrain the shape.

6. If you continue to pull on a circle past the center point, you create an inverted star.

7. Now let's create a basic star. Double-click the Polygon Tool and make sure that Star is selected with 6 points and that the points are set to Automatic. Create your shape.

8. After you have created your shape, select it with your Pointer or Subselect Tool and modify it even further in the Object Panel. This feature is new to FreeHand MX. Change the number of points to 8.

9. You can also modify the roundness of your points. Type 30 to round off the peaks.

10. Type 30 to round off the valleys. The shape has now taken on completely new dimensions.

Creating and Manipulating Text

With its roots in the print world, FreeHand offers many options to create and manipulate text. Let's look at some of its capabilities. Not every available feature is covered, just enough to get you up and running. As you get deeper into projects, you can explore all the alternative features.

At its most basic, select the Text Tool in the Tools Panel, click where you want the text to start on the screen, and start typing. This procedure creates what is known as an auto-expanding text box. If you want to create a text box that constrains the text within, click and drag a rectangle to the size you need. Figure 2.35 shows the two types of text box.

You have several options available to change the properties of text. Text is so important to FreeHand that it has its own toolbar, which can be found under Window > Toolbars. The Windows and Macintosh versions of FreeHand have slightly different toolbars by default. The Macintosh version has the same buttons as the Windows version, with the addition of Find Text, Increase Leading, Decrease Leading, Increase Baseline Shift, and Decrease Baseline Shift. You can change the properties of text using the Text Toolbar, the Text menu command, or the Object Panel. The revised Object Panel breaks text editing into several areas, as shown in Figure 2.36.

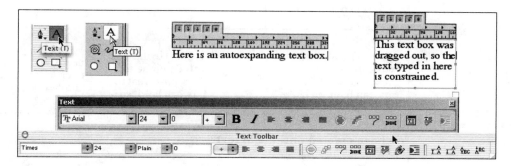

FIGURE 2.35 The Text Tool, Toolbar, and text boxes.

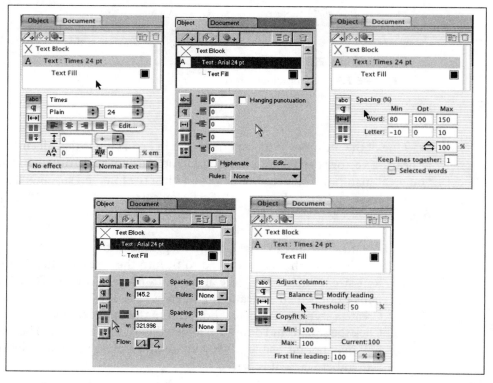

FIGURE 2.36 The numerous text-editing options in the Object Panel.

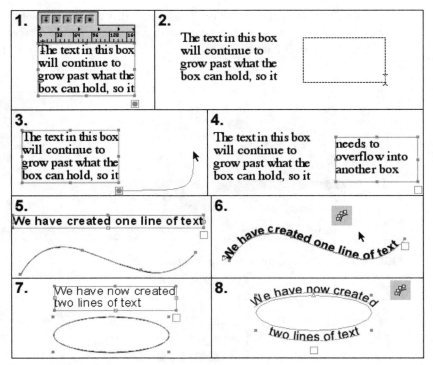

FIGURE 2.37 Manipulating text.

One of the most powerful aspects of text in FreeHand is that all characters are, at heart, a vector shape. This enables extreme clarity when printed and also gives you great manipulation possibilities beyond just the font and spacing. Let's look at some of these options in Figure 2.37. Each step corresponds with the number in the figure.

1. Create a text box by clicking and dragging it into a shape. Then type some text. Too much text was typed to fit into the box with the type's current font size. Notice the square at the bottom-right corner. The square contains a dot, which indicates that there is excess text.
2. Create a second, empty text box next to the first text box.
3. Click the square and drag an arrow to the second text box. (The second text box may not be visible while you are dragging the arrow, so be certain to remember where it is placed.)

4. Release the mouse button. The second text box now holds the overflow text from the first text box. This principle is useful for having text flowing from one area of a page to another or even across multiple pages.

5. A line of text has been created, along with a vector path. Both the text and the path have been selected using Shift + click.

6. With both the text and the vector path still selected, the Attach to Path button on the Text Toolbar was pressed. The text has now attached itself to the path and is flowing in the same manner.

7. What if you want an oval shape with text on the top and bottom? FreeHand can do this, too. Select the Text Tool, click the screen (don't draw your text box), and type the first line. Then press Enter or Return (you must use a hard return for this procedure to work) and type the second line. Underneath the text (or anywhere you want on the page), create an oval.

8. Select both the oval and the text by pressing Shift + click and pressing the Attach to Path button on the Text Toolbar (or clicking select Text > Attach to Path on the main menu bar). You now have a line above and below the path.

You can get really creative with text and paths in FreeHand. Instead of having your text flowing from one text box to another, you can have it flowing from inside one shape to another.

PATH MANIPULATION TOOLS

Now that we have created various paths and shapes using FreeHand, let's look at modifying them a bit. FreeHand provides several ways to change and modify the shapes you create. We have seen some methods using the Pointer Tools and changing properties in the Object Panel, but several other tools are dedicated to object and path manipulation. Let's start off with four that live in the Tools Panel.

The Scale Tools

The Scale Tool provides four different tools: the Scale Tool itself, the Rotate Tool, the Reflect Tool, and the Skew Tool, all shown in Figure 2.38. You can also invoke the Transform Panel (also shown in the figure) to use numeric transformations when you want to be more exact. Figure 2.38 shows all of these tools. Each step corresponds with the numbers in the figure.

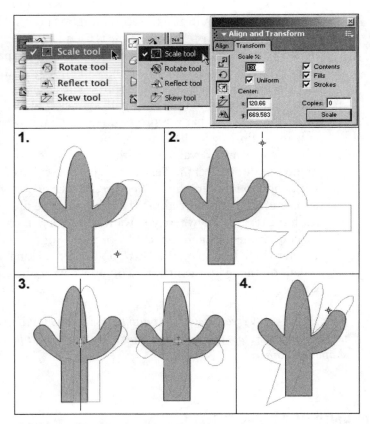

FIGURE 2.38 Using the Scale Tools.

1. Scaling is fairly straightforward. By using the Scale Tool, you can size an object by changing its width or height or both. If you want to constrain its proportions, hold the Shift key.
2. With the Rotate Tool you can rotate objects. A great feature of this tool is that the pivot point is placed wherever you click on the object.
3. The Mirror Tool allows you to flip an object. Move the mouse to determine if you want a horizontal or vertical flip. The bisecting line reflects in which direction the object will flip.
4. The Skew Tool gives objects a different perspective. If you are looking at an object sideways, it appears to get smaller at the distant end. Use this Skew Tool to give your objects some depth.

Using Transform Handles

Sometimes, you want to quickly size, rotate, or skew your object without digging out a bunch of tools. FreeHand gives you this ability with the simplest action possible. Just double-click your object to make transform handles available. (You may have done this by accident already.)

If you want to resize the object, move the cursor to one of the squares. When the cursor changes to a double arrow, pull in the direction you want to size. To rotate the object, hold the cursor outside the object until it becomes a curved double arrow. If you want to rotate from a different pivot point, click and drag the circle in the middle of the object to where you want to place a new pivot. To skew the object's perspective, hold your mouse near an edge of the transform handles, and click and drag the mouse when two half-arrows going the opposite direction appear. The use of transform handles is shown in Figure 2.39. To return to normal mode, double-click again.

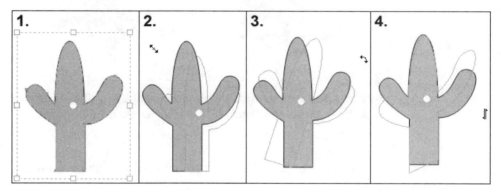

FIGURE 2.39   Using Transform handles.

Path Transform Tools

Next to the Scale Tools are some path transformation tools, including the Freeform Tool, the Roughen Tool, and the Bend Tool. These tools are shown in Figure 2.40.

The Freeform Tool is considered a lifesaver by those who really struggle with the Pen and Bezigon Tools. This tool allows you to modify an object in a freeform manner, like modeling clay. It also responds to the pressure sensitivity of a digitizer tablet or the left and right arrows on the keyboard. By double-clicking the tool, you can choose whether the tool works in Push/Pull setting—push out a path or pull on a path to reshape it, as shown in steps 1 and 2 in Figure 2.40. You can also use the Reshape Area Freeform Tool. Reshape Area is similar to pushing, except as you

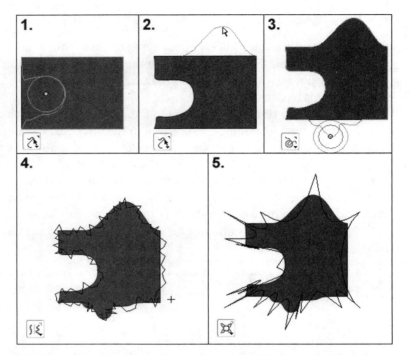

FIGURE 2.40   Path transform tools including the Push/Pull Freeform Tool, the Reshape Area Freeform Tool, the Roughen Tool, and the Bend Tool.

move away from the object, the area gets smaller, creating a point instead of a rounded path. This tool is shown in step 3.

The Roughen and Bend Tools are similar. With the Roughen Tool, you can click an object and drag it out, giving the object a ragged appearance, as shown in step 4. Double-click the Roughen Tool to adjust its properties, such as to achieve a hand-drawn effect. The Bend Tool distorts an object with sharp angles, as shown in step 5. You can adjust the amount of distortion by double-clicking the tool.

The Eraser and Knife Tools

The Eraser and Knife Tools, shown in Figure 2.41, were designed for modifying paths. The Eraser Tool erases strokes and fills. FreeHand fills in a new path where this tool has traveled. Think of the Eraser Tool as a Variable Stroke Pen Tool in reverse. It doesn't add a new path; it cuts one out of an existing object. It is also responsive to a digitizer tablet and left and right arrow keys, like the Variable Stroke Pen Tool. You can adjust its properties by double-clicking the tool.

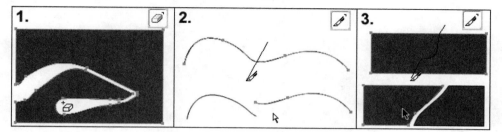

FIGURE 2.41   The Eraser and Knife Tools.

The Knife Tool's sole purpose is to cut paths into pieces. You can adjust it to be freeform or straight by double-clicking the tool. You also have the option of closing your path when finished, as shown in step 3 in Figure 2.41. This feature is useful if you want to cut a shape in half.

SUMMARY

Your whirlwind tour of the core drawing tools in FreeHand MX is now complete. Let's continue with FreeHand by "Exploring the Object Panel and Looking at More Effects."

3 Exploring the Object Panel and Looking at More Effects

THE OBJECT PANEL

Now that we have a basic handle on FreeHand tools, we can apply some extra effects to our creations. FreeHand MX has significantly revised the Object Panel, shown in Figure 3.1.

The Object Panel replaces four separate Property Inspectors—the Object Inspector, the Fill Inspector, the Stroke Inspector, and the Text Inspector. FreeHand MX not only rolls these inspectors into one condensed panel but also adds additional features, which constitutes a major upgrade to the interface and allows you to do more with your creations in one location.

This new Object Panel also adds the capabilities to provide Macromedia Live Effects™. Live Effects combines vector effects like transform (scale, skew, distort, and rotate) with traditional raster effects like drop shadows. These effects were previously available only in Fireworks and now have been added to FreeHand. Macromedia frequently shares tools from one application to another to enhance each program's capabilities. This practice works great for better integration and a superior workflow.

The real magic of Live Effects is that when an effect is applied, it does not change the original object in any way. When you print or export the file, the effect is seen, but the core file maintains its vector capability. In other words, the file is resolution independent. If you resize the documents in any way, FreeHand reapplies the effects to the new resolution, overcoming any pixelation issues—hence the word *Live*.

These effects can be applied to any vector creation you make, including text. (Remember, text is still a vector graphic in FreeHand.) They can also be applied to imported raster graphics, enabling you to mix photos with crystal clear text and vector graphics suitable for both print and the Web. Using FreeHand, you can

51

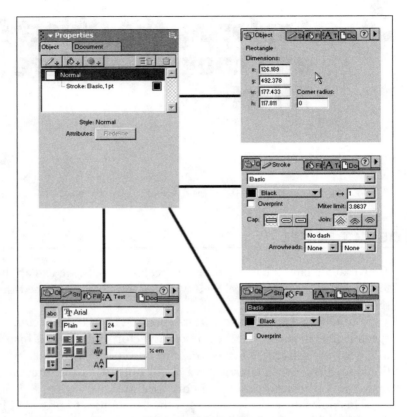

FIGURE 3.1 The new Object Panel and the four inspectors from FreeHand 10 that it replaces.

make a brochure and graphics for your Web site at the *same time*. Thanks to its marriage to Fireworks MX 2004, you can even import a raster graphic into a Free-Hand document. If the graphic needs to be further refined, you can open it in Fire-works directly from FreeHand to edit it. Guess where you can do this—the Object Panel. You can also accomplish the same task with a Flash.swf file.

Editing External Content

When you export a file to FreeHand from either Flash or Fireworks, the Object Panel reflects the original application when the object is selected, as shown in Figure 3.2.

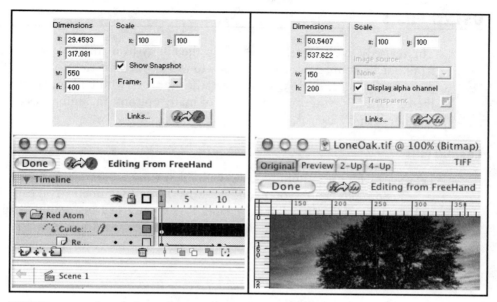

FIGURE 3.2   Using Flash or Fireworks content in FreeHand.

Clicking the button in the Object Panel opens an instance of either Flash or Fireworks. When the program is first opened, it prompts you for the original file, if applicable. After you either select the original file or decline, the program opens with a differently formatted window. At the top of the interface, the line *Editing From FreeHand* appears and a button labeled *Done* appears, also shown in Figure 3.2.

When you have finished making your changes, press Done. At this point, either Flash or Fireworks saves all changes to the original file, publishes these changes to the output file, and then closes. You are then returned to FreeHand with all of the changes reflected in the file.

This integration is an incredible time-saver. Without it, you would have to perform several steps. First, you would have to open the appropriate application. Then, while the application is open, you would have to open the original file. Next, you would make your changes. After your changes are complete, you would need to save the file and republish it. Then you could close the application, if you choose, and return to FreeHand. Once back in FreeHand, you would have to delete the object and reimport it. After you reimport it, you would have to move it around to place it correctly.

As you can see, a lot of work is done for you with the inclusion of one simple button. Features like these are well worth the price of admission.

USING FILLS

The revised Object Panel provides you the ability to manipulate strokes and fills from one location, as well as the ability to work with *multiple* strokes and fills. You can select either the stroke or fill you want to work with and manipulate it from there. With fills, you can choose one of many options, including Basic, Textures, Gradients, and Patterns.

Custom Fills

Let's start with the custom fills, shown in Figure 3.3.

Custom fills enable you to add patterns to your document. You can select any of the custom fills offered in FreeHand. When you use a custom fill, it appears as tiled "Cs" in your shape. The fill appears only when the drawing is exported into another application or printed.

Gradient Fills

You can also use gradient fills, as shown in Figure 3.4.

1. Start by creating a star shape with six points using the Polygon Tool. Feel free to adjust how acute or obtuse you want the angles.
2. If a fill is not already selected, click the Add Fill button in the Object Panel.
3. Select Gradient from the drop-down menu. (The default is Basic.)

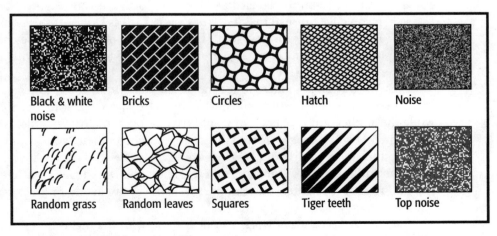

FIGURE 3.3   Available custom fills.

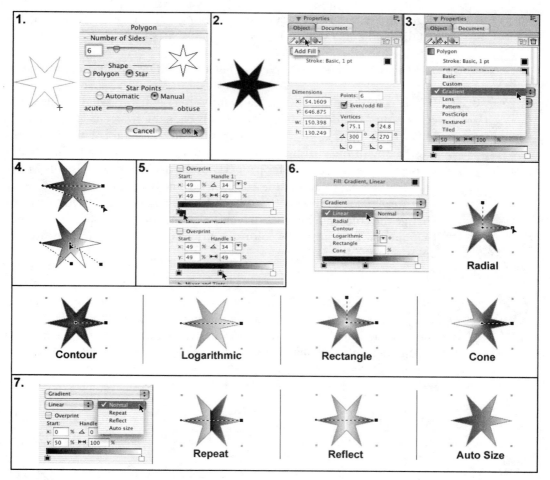

FIGURE 3.4   Working with gradient fills.

4. After you select a fill, while using the Pointer or Subselect Tool, you will see a brand-new feature in FreeHand MX—gradient fill handles. Gradient fill handles were previously available in both Flash and Fireworks and have now found their way into FreeHand. In previous versions of FreeHand, you had to use a dial to adjust the angle of the gradient and slide the swatches to change the gradient size. Now, you have either one or two handles, depending on the type of gradient you choose. The default linear gradient has one handle. With this handle, you can change the center point,

angle, and length of the gradation. The longer the handle, the more gradual the gradient; a shorter handle creates a sharper blend.

You must select the Pointer or Subselect Tool for the gradient fill handles to appear.

5. When you select the fill, you can adjust the colors on what is called the color ramp. To add another color, simply click the swatch under either the left or right of the color ramp and drag toward the center. This action creates a copy of the currently selected swatch. This copy can be handy because it shares the same color property of the original color. Use the Mixer and Tints Panel to adjust the color based on the original or create your own new shade and drag the swatch to the color ramp. If you want to change the color, click the swatch and pick a new color from the swatches that appear, or drag a new color directly into the swatch underneath the color ramp.

You can also change colors by dragging a color swatch directly onto a shape. If you press and hold the Alt or Option key while dragging the new color into the center of the object, not only does the center color change but also the point of origin according to where you place the swatch. Remember that you have to begin dragging the swatch out before you hold the Alt key or this procedure will not work.

Several gradients other than Linear are available.

Radial: The gradient is laid out in a circular manner. Two handles are available. You can use them to reflect the width and height of the gradient and the angle of the fill.

Contour: Contour is a unique gradient that follows the outline of a shape. This gradient is useful for providing a 3D appearance to an object. It has one gradient fill handle.

Logarithmic: The Logarithmic gradient is similar to a Linear gradient in that it travels in a straight line as it gradates. The difference is that whereas a Linear gradient has even bands traveling, Logarithmic gradient bands grow wider as they move from the index point.

Rectangle: The Rectangle gradient is similar to the Radial gradient but is rectangular in shape. It has two handles.

Cone: The Cone gradient has a center point with the gradient cascading out, almost like a starburst. It has one handle.

You can further refine these gradient options with the following options:

Normal: Displays the default view.

Repeat: Causes the gradient to repeat more than once. You can set how many times you want it to repeat by typing a new value under Count, which appears after you select this option.

Reflect: Similar to the Repeat option, Reflect causes the gradients to reflect off one another. You also have a Count option with this selection.

Auto size: Causes the gradient fill handles to disappear because you are no longer manually sizing the gradient. Your only option is to move the center point.

Lens Fill

The next fill is the lens fill. The lens fill options are shown in Figure 3.5.

When you select this fill, the dialog box shown in step 1 in Figure 3.5 may open. It is not an error but an informational box saying that what you see through

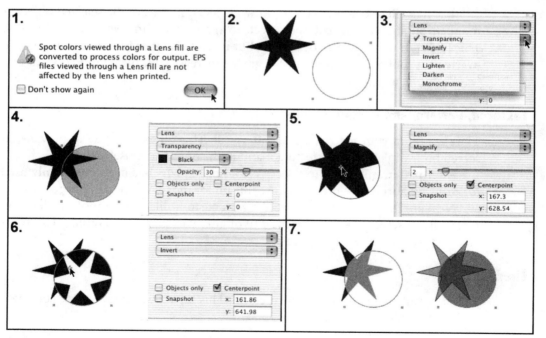

FIGURE 3.5   Using the lens fill.

the lens will be converted into colors when printed but will not be affected in an EPS (Encapsulated PostScript) file.

1. First create a star shape with a fill and an ellipse, as shown in step 2.
2. There are several lens options to choose from—let's start with Transparency, as shown in step 3. If you select Lens > Transparency to add a fill to the ellipse, we will be able to see the shape underneath the object. The opacity (amount of color) is set to 30, as shown in step 4.
3. You can adjust not only the magnification of the fill but the center point as well. In step 5, the center point has been moved toward the center of the star. Moving the center point changes the perspective of what is displayed in the shape. This method can be effective to magnify another point on the document or to simply show another part of the document, creating the illusion that the user is viewing the scene through a window.
4. The Invert option, shown in step 6, inverts the colors to their exact opposite on the color wheel. This option also gives you a center point.
5. The Lighten and Darken options darken or lighten the area of a selected shape, as shown in step 7.

The lens fill also allows you to show objects underneath the selected object as monochromatic, causing colored objects to appear black and white under the lens. This fill is not used often in designing, but it can be a lot of fun. Remember not to overuse the tool because doing so can greatly increase your file size and does not always result in an image that prints well.

Textured, Pattern, and PostScript Fills

The next fill in your arsenal is the pattern fill. This fill enables you to preview on screen both while you are selecting it and in the objects themselves.

After pattern fill, you can select PostScript fill, which is most commonly used for printing purposes. You can ignore this fill for most Web design purposes.

Next are the textured fills. Just like with custom fills, you cannot preview textured fills on screen; they appear in print or after you export the graphic. The available textures are shown in Figure 3.6.

Tiled Fills

The last available fill option is the tiled fill. This fill allows you to create your own design. This fill is shown in Figure 3.7.

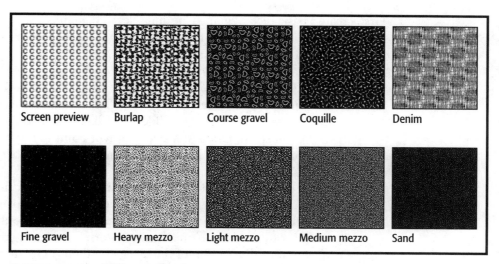

FIGURE 3.6   Available texture fills.

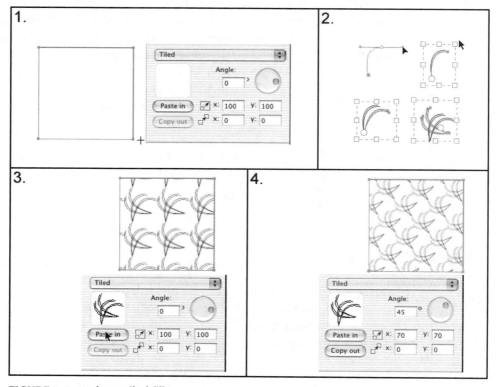

FIGURE 3.7   Using a tiled fill.

1. First, create a basic rectangular shape and select a tiled fill, as shown in step 1 in Figure 3.7. Notice that no fill appears at first because we haven't created anything to use for our tiling.
2. Step 2 is divided into four parts:
   a. First, we use the Pen Tool to create a simple curved line.
   b. Next, copy and paste the line onto the stage. Then move the new line directly on top of the first line and, while it is still selected, double-click it to open the transform handles. Move the pivot point to the bottom of the line and then rotate the line slightly to the right. Remember to double-click again to return to normal mode.
   c. Next, select both lines by either pressing Shift + clicking, or drawing a marquee with the Pointer or Subselect Tool. Copy the lines, paste them, and move them on top of the original two lines. Then double-click while the lines are selected to open the transform handles. Again, move the pivot point to the bottom of the lines, and then rotate them to the right.
   d. Now select all of our lines, copy, paste, and then rotate them to the left until they cross the original lines.
3. Now that we have our creation for use as a fill, let's select all of the lines and click Edit > Cut, Ctrl or Command + X, or right-click > Cut. Select the rectangle, select Fill: Tiled, and press Paste in. You object is now tiled inside our rectangle, as shown in step 3.
4. You can modify the tile fill further. In step 4, the tile fill is scaled to 70 percent on both the x and y planes (width and height) and the fill is rotated 45 percent.

Tiled fill is a powerful tool that allows you to customize your input. When using it, however, keep in mind that you cannot paste in an image (like a .jpg or .gif that has been imported) to be tiled.

USING STROKES

As you can see, numerous options are available with fills. It should come as no surprise that many options for strokes are also available. FreeHand really starts to show its power in this category. A stroke by itself is simple—it is a line used to place a border around something or to draw objects. However, there is more to it than that. How a stroke looks can seriously change the flavor of a creation. Sometimes a subtle change can have a strong impact in the overall graphic.

Basic Strokes

The name *basic strokes* is a bit misleading. They are your general-purpose tools, but you have many options with which to adjust them. Let's start by looking at caps and joins. Caps and joins are how the lines are finished in terms of ends of the lines and corner joints. Figure 3.8 shows how they look when applied.

1. Start by looking at the default of Butt for the cap, as shown in step 1 in Figure 3.8. The Butt is the point at the exact end of the stroke. The Miter join is used; it causes the corner joint to have a sharp point.
2. The Round cap is used in step 2. This option rounds off the end points.
3. The Square cap, shown in step 3, is similar to the Round cap, but it adds a square buffer past the point.
4. In step 4 are two other Join options: Round and Beveled. Round Join causes the corner to have a rounded edge, and Beveled Join causes the corner to have the sharp point that is squared off.

You have a lot of options for the stroke itself. You can choose from several types for the line: solid, dashed, dotted, thatched, or even a combination. For the ends, you can select from five styles of arrowheads as well as two other ends. You can choose which end has what arrowhead using the Arrowheads drop-down menu. This flexibility adds some neat capabilities for creating diagrams. The line types and arrowheads are shown in Figure 3.9.

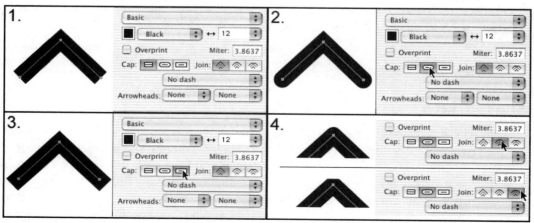

FIGURE 3.8 Working with caps and joins.

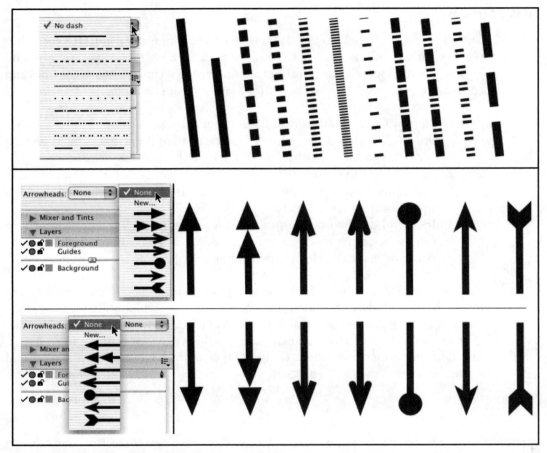

FIGURE 3.9 Options available with basic strokes.

Brush Strokes

The next stroke type available from the drop-down menu is Brush. The Brush stroke offers some wild examples of strokes, which are shown in Figure 3.10.

Not only can you use any of the strokes you have seen, but you can customize them further using multiple options. The first option is apparent when you use the brush—you can choose how wide the brush is. This option is especially useful for a brush like Palm Trees, because the strokes tend to be quite large. Setting a new width value decreases the actual size of the graphics.

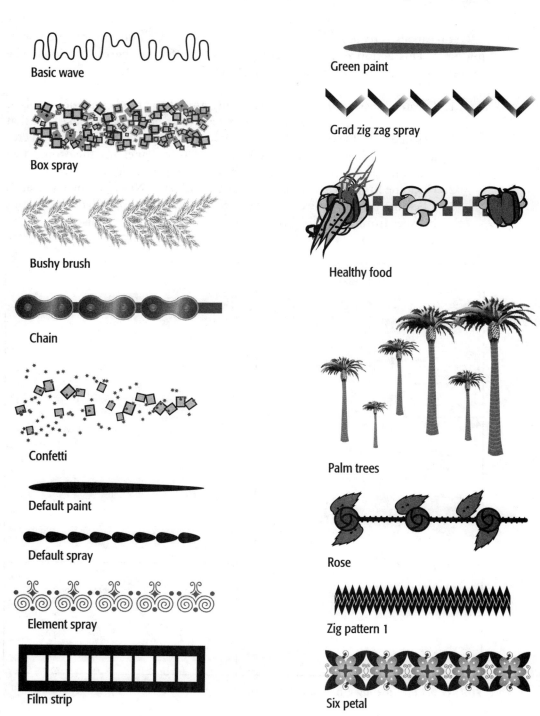

Basic wave

Box spray

Bushy brush

Chain

Confetti

Default paint

Default spray

Element spray

Film strip

Green paint

Grad zig zag spray

Healthy food

Palm trees

Rose

Zig pattern 1

Six petal

FIGURE 3.10   Brush stroke options.

You can also create your own brush by clicking the Options button and selecting New. This action opens a new window that offers numerous options. The process of creating a new brush stroke is shown in Figure 3.11.

1. Create a basic path on the stage using any of the stroke creation tools—Pencil, Line, or Pen/Bezigon. After you have created a path, make sure that a stroke is visible in the Object Panel. If one is not, click Add Stroke to create one. With your stroke selected in the Object Panel, use the drop-down menu to select a Brush stroke, as shown in step 1 in Figure 3.11.
2. Click the Brush Wave drop-down menu and select New, as shown in step 2.
3. Click the plus sign next to Include Symbols. A list opens with numerous brushes from which to choose, as shown in step 3. Select Bush Left.

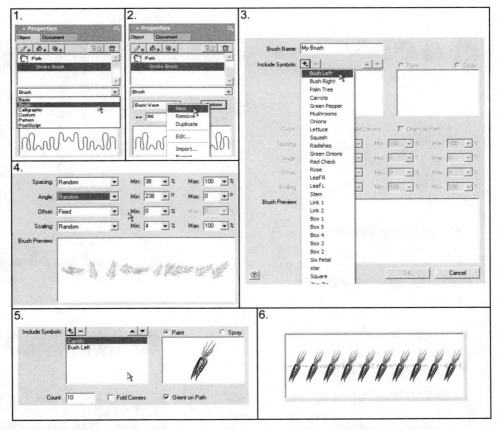

FIGURE 3.11   Creating a new brush stroke.

4. Use the following settings:
   - **Spacing**: Random; Min: 38%; Max: 100%
   - **Angle**: Random; Min: 238°; Max: 100°
   - **Offset**: Fixed; Min: 0%; Max: 0%
   - **Scaling**: Random; Min: 4%; Max: 100%
5. Click the plus sign next to Include Symbols and select Carrots. Adjust the scale to the desired size, as shown in step 5.
6. The result, shown in step 6, is a custom brush with carrots and bush leaves.

Calligraphic Strokes

The next stroke is the Calligraphic stroke. This stroke allows you to create lines that have a ribbon quality, like you find in calligraphy. This stroke is shown in Figure 3.12.

When making a Calligraphic stroke, you are provided a default oval shape that creates rounded edges. You can adjust the width and height of your base shape as well as the angle. If you want a custom stroke, draw a small shape on the stage, click Edit > Cut, and then, with the stroke selected, press the Paste in button in the Object Panel.

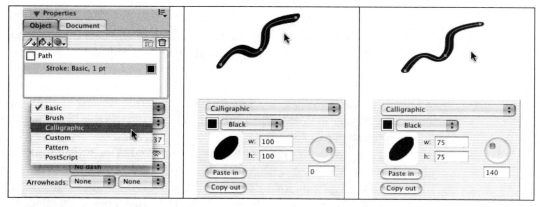

FIGURE 3.12 A Calligraphic stroke.

Other Strokes

Other stroke options in FreeHand are Custom, Pattern, and PostScript strokes. Custom strokes allow you to choose from 23 predefined shapes to make your path. Keep in mind that you cannot see the result until you print the document.

You can also select Pattern strokes. Pattern stroke gives the stroke a texture, such as checkerboard, dots, bricks, and thread. These strokes are not intended for printing to high-resolution printers and may not have a crisp resolution.

The last option is PostScript. This stroke is used for printing to high-resolution PostScript printers. PostScript is a programming language beyond the scope of this book.

LIVE EFFECTS

One of the new features of FreeHand MX is the inclusion of Live Effects, which were previously available only in Fireworks. This feature enables you not only to apply vector effects like Bend and Transform but also raster effects like Bevel and Drop Shadow to objects in FreeHand.

Applying raster effects to vector shapes really opens up your creative capability. Another bonus is that when you apply a raster effect to vectors in FreeHand, they are reapplied when you scale an object; therefore, you will not have pixelation, giving you the best of both worlds.

Some of the available effects are shown in Figure 3.13.

1. **Add Effect Button popup menu:** To add a Live Effect, select the shape and then click the Add Effect (plus sign) button in the Object Panel. A dropdown menu opens, with vector effects in the top portion of the menu and raster effects and their submenus in the lower portion. You also can apply a Live Effect exclusively to a fill or stroke by selecting the stroke individually and pressing the Add Effect button, which restricts the Live Effect to the selected stroke or fill.

2. **Bend:** Causes the path on an object to be distorted. You move points on the path either closer or farther from the center point. The center point is also movable. Options include size and the x- and y-coordinates of the center point. The size ranges from −100 to 100, with 0 being no effect. Either adjust the center point by typing in its x- and y-coordinates or by dragging it within the shape.

3. **Duet:** Creates clones of a selected object. Use this effect to create more complex shapes. When you choose Reflect, a duplicate of the object that acts as a mirror image is created. You can move the center point to rotate the reflection, as shown in item 3 of Figure 3.13. You can also choose Rotate, which allows you to determine how many clones to create of an object. The clones will be created in even increments, according to how many

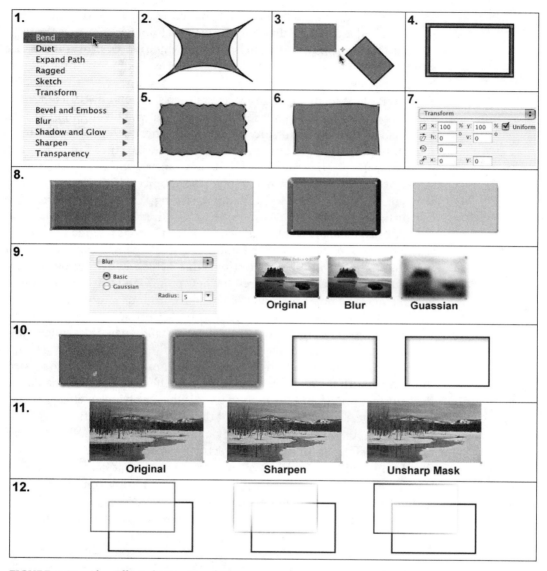

FIGURE 3.13 Live Effects in FreeHand MX.

copies you create. You can then move the center point to move the objects to the desired location. Other options include Join, which causes the original path to connect with its copies; Closed, which closes strokes if they are empty; and Choose Even/Odd fill, which alternates the color of any overlapping clones.

4. **Expand Path:** Widens a path in a shape. It then surrounds the altered shape with an outline. You can choose the direction in which you want the path to be widened (Inside, Outside, or Both). Another option is Width (from 1 to 50 pixels). You can also choose Cap, Join, and Miter Limit, like any normal stroke. Keep in mind that if you have an arrowhead applied to your stroke, it will be removed when you apply this effect.

5. **Ragged:** Adds new points to your paths, creating a ragged appearance. You can further refine the result by choosing a desired size to dictate how far from the original path to place the new points. Options include Frequency, which determines how many new points appear; Copies, which clones your path by a chosen number; Selecting Edge, which allows smoothing or straightening of the paths between the new points; and Selecting Uniform, which places the new points an even distance from one another.

6. **Sketch:** Makes a stroke appear hand drawn. You can set the amount of distortion and number of copies. This effect is handy when drawing something like hair on a cartoon character.

7. **Transform:** Allows you to scale, rotate, skew, move, and copy the object the same as with the normal transform tools. The difference between using the transform effect and the regular tools is that applying an effect changes only the appearance of the object, not the object itself. The effect can be removed without affecting the integrity of the original shape. When you use regular transformation tools, the effects are permanent.

8. **Bevel and Emboss:** The first of the raster effects that can be applied to both vector and raster objects within FreeHand. Multiple options are available within each effect. Four effects are available in Bevel and Emboss.

   a. **Inner Bevel:** This effect provides several choices for refinement:
      i. Width—How wide do you want the bevel to appear?
      ii. Contrast—How sharp of a contrast do you want between the high points and shadowing?
      iii. Softness—How smooth should the bevel be?
      iv. Angle—What is the direction of the light source?
      v. Bevel Shape—Several predefined shapes are available, providing different bevel appearances.
      vi. Button Effect—Provides premade modifications to bevel appearance that you can use as a quick way to show a button state change.

b. **Inset Emboss:** As with bevels, you have options to refine the emboss:
   i. Width—How wide do you want the emboss?
   ii. Contrast—What is the range between highlights and shadows?
   iii. Softness—How smooth should the emboss appears?
c. **Outer Bevel:** This effect creates a beveling effect outside of the shape. It has all options available to Inner Bevels, in addition to the option to change the color of the Outer Bevel.
d. **Raised Emboss:** This effect offers the same refinement choices as Inset Emboss.
9. **Blur:** Provides two options—Blur and Gaussian Blur. Whereas Blur makes an object appear unfocused, Gaussian Blur makes an object appear as if it is seen through fog.
10. **Sharpen:** Modifies the contrast of pixels to make an image appear sharper. This effect offers two options—Sharpen and Unsharp Mask. Sharpen affects the entire object, and Unsharp Mask adjusts only the edges of the object, as shown in item 11 in Figure 3.13.
11. **Transparency:** Adjusts the alpha settings of the objects to make them appear transparent. This effect offers three options for refinement:
    a. **Basic:** Adjusts the alpha of the entire shape, both fill and stroke.
    b. **Feather:** Causes edges to fade.
    c. **Gradient Mask:** Causes the transparency to gradate, according to the gradient you choose. This option can be used with any available gradient.

STROKES AND FILLS

In FreeHand, you now have the ability to apply multiple strokes and fills to the same object. Previously, you had to create another shape, then merge the two shapes together in your document. Figure 3.14 shows this tool in use.

1. Create a four-pointed star by double-clicking your Polygon Tool, typing 4 for Number of Sides, and selecting Star for the Shape, as shown in step 1 of Figure 3.14. You may want to adjust the Star Points settings to be more acute than the default.
2. Now add a fill in the Object Panel and modify it to be a Contour Gradient, as shown in step 2.
3. After you have completed your shape, add another stroke and fill. Notice that your Contour Gradient is no longer visible, as shown in step 3. This is

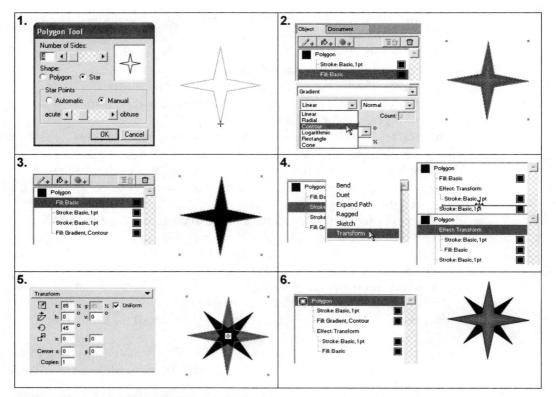

FIGURE 3.14 Using multiple fills and strokes in the same object.

because your new stroke and fill are on top of your original shape. We will adjust in upcoming steps.

4. Select the newest stroke you created, click the Add Effect button, and choose Transform from the pop-up menu. After you have added the effect, you must pull your newer fill into it so it is also affected. Click Fill Basic and drag the fill underneath both Effect Transform and Stroke Basic 1 pt. You must drag the fill with your mouse toward the right for it to be within the effect. You should see a blue line denoting where it will be placed, as shown in step 4.

5. Now adjust the Transform effect. Click Effect Transform to open its menu, and type 85 for x. (Make sure Uniform is checked.) Also type 45 for Rotate. Your result should resemble the image shown in step 5.

6. The last step is to put the new stroke and fill in the back, so drag your original stroke and fill above Effect: Transform. You should have created the compass shape shown in step 6.

EFFECTS TOOLS

Now that we have made our way through the Object Panel, it's a good time to start looking at more effects, available in the Tools Panel. These effects build on all of your original tools and give you more power. Let's look at the first set of tools, located in the section after the Eraser and Knife Tools.

Many of the tools you will learn can also be found on their own toolbar, the Xtra Tools Toolbar, accessed by clicking Window > Toolbars > Xtra Tools.

Perspective

Although FreeHand is primarily a 2D drawing tool, some tools have been added to help you give more depth to an illustration by emulating 3D. The first of these tools is the Perspective Tool. It allows you to place shapes on a grid that makes them appear as if they are turned away from you. Think of this feature as an assisted skew. This tool is shown in Figure 3.15.

1. When you want to use the Perspective Tool, you should make the Perspective grid visible. This setting is not required, but it assists you in placing objects. To make the grid visible, click View > Perspective Grid > Show to open the most recently opened grid on the document. To define your Perspective grid, click View > Perspective Grid > Define Grids. In the Define Grids dialog box, you can define the number of vanishing points to use—1, 2, or 3 (as shown in step 1 of Figure 3.15). You can click on grid edges and disappearing points to modify the shape and placement of the grids.
2. Click View > Perspective Grid > Show, then define the grid to have two vanishing points. To experiment, draw a rectangle that covers nearly the entire canvas. Give the rectangle a black stroke and gray fill, as shown in step 2.
3. Select the Perspective Tool, then click the rectangle while you are over the left side of the grid. While you are clicking the rectangle, press the left arrow key on your keyboard. This keystroke snaps the rectangle to the left grid, as shown in step 3.

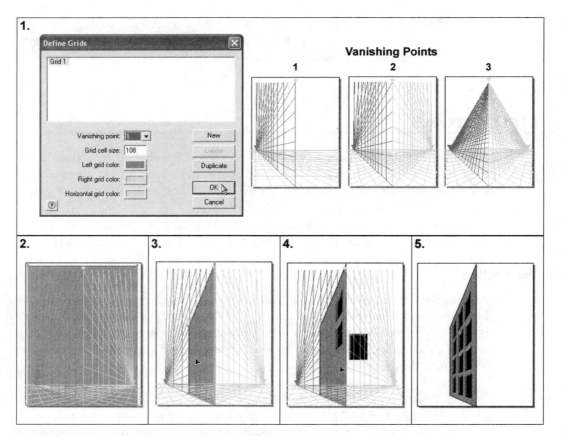

FIGURE 3.15 Using the Perspective Tool and grids.

4. Now we can place other items into the picture. Create a rectangle with a stroke and fill of black, and add an Inner Bevel effect. Then, select the rectangle, and copy and paste it on the canvas so you have a couple of copies with which to work. Select the Perspective Tool, and drag a rectangle over to the left side of the picture. While over the left side, press the left arrow key on your keyboard to place the rectangle into the left grid and move it into place, as shown in step 4. Repeat this procedure until you fill the image.

5. Your result should resemble what is shown in step 5. Save this image as *building*; We will revisit it later.

3D Rotation

The next available tool is the 3D Rotation Tool. It can be accessed by clicking and holding down the Perspective Tool until a pop-up menu appears. You use this tool to rotate a shape on the stage in a 3D fashion. It automatically skews an object as you move it to modify its perspective.

Fisheye Lens

The Fisheye Lens Tool causes a distortion in shapes that gives the illusion that the content is being viewed up close through a strong lens. One of the popular ways to use this effect is on text, as explored in Figure 3.16.

1. Using the Text Tool, type your name on the screen. Make it a strong font, such as Impact with the size of 72, shown in step 1 of Figure 3.16.
2. To apply an effect to text, you must convert it to vector paths. Click Text > Convert To Paths.
3. Now for the fun part. Select the Fisheye Lens Tool Perspective Tool by clicking and holding the Perspective Tool (or 3D Rotation Tool, if you still have that selected). Use the Alt or Option key (to draw out a shape from

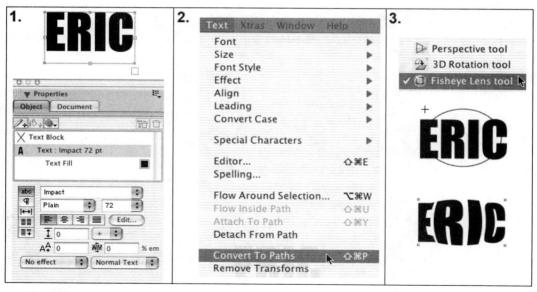

FIGURE 3.16 Using the Fisheye Lens Tool.

the center of where you click the mouse), and draw out an oval shape. You then see how the Fisheye Lens Tool distorts your text, as shown in step 3.

You can adjust how the Fisheye Lens effect is applied by double-clicking the tool in the Tools Panel. This action opens the Fisheye Lens dialog box where you can make the effect more convex or concave.

Extrude

The Extrude Tool is brand new to FreeHand MX. It gives you the capacity to turn a 2D shape into a 3D object. Unlike previously described effects, the Extrude Tool actually adds 3D functionality to the program. Although it is created for an illustration program, it has a surprising degree of control. Let's look at this wonderful addition to FreeHand MX in Figure 3.17.

1. To start, draw a rectangle with a gray fill. After you draw the rectangle, choose the Extrude Tool and give the object depth by dragging the vanish-

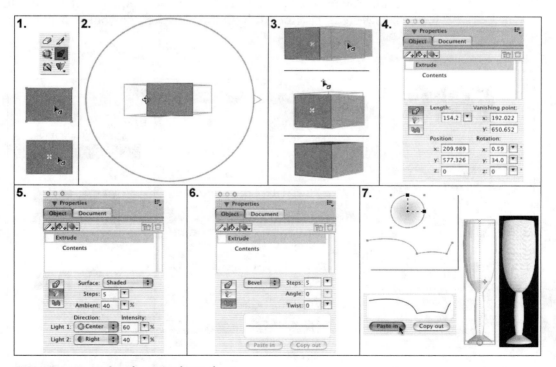

FIGURE 3.17   Using the Extrude Tool.

ing point, which resembles a solid circle with an x inside, away from the center, as shown in step 1 of Figure 3.17.

2. After you have created an extrusion, you can further edit the extrusion by double-clicking your object with the Extrude Tool. This action puts your object into 3D space, shown in step 2, where you can rotate the object and edit it further. Notice that when you rotate that object, it may have more depth than you desire. Double-click the shape to access the control points.

3. To modify the depth of the object, drag the Depth Control point—the open circle shown in step 3—closer to the object center point (the x on the face of the shape). You can also adjust the vanishing point (four tiny diamonds resembling a plus sign) by dragging it away from the shape. This action causes the shape to cant and allows you to adjust which part of the extrusion is visible.

4. If the Object PanelExtrude button in the Object Panel is chosen, you can specify the Length, Vanishing point, Position, and Rotation explicitly by typing numeric values, as shown in step 4. Notice that the z plane is among the available coordinates. When looking at 3D space, x is the horizontal plane, y is vertical, and z is for depth—just remember z as "zoom."

5. When you press the Surface button in the Object Panel, the following new options become available:

   Surface: Changes the type of rendering FreeHand uses. Shaded (default) shows the object completely rendered with shading applied to the extrusion, giving the object depth. Flat uses the same color on the face and sides of the object. Wireframe shows the object as strokes with no fills. Mesh breaks the shape into polygons, representing the way it will be formed using only strokes. Hidden Mesh shows polygons and the fill of an object.

   Steps: Controls how many steps are used to complete the extrusion. The more steps, the smoother the object appears. Keep in mind that the higher the number of steps, the longer the drawing time required. In fact, it may seem as if FreeHand MX has locked up.

   Ambient: Controls the overall light on an object. Use this setting to adjust the brightness of the object. The higher the number, the brighter the object appears.

   Light 1 and **Light 2:** Provide directional lights. You can use them to adjust the direction from which the light comes and its intensity.

6. The Profile option, shown in step 6, controls the appearance of the extrusion using the following options:

   Profile Attributes: Using none, the default, causes a shape to extrude in straight lines to the vanishing point. Bevel gives you some very interesting options. Use it to create a different profile on an object. (This option is explored in step 7.) Static is similar to Bevel, but instead of changing the profile of an object, it modifies the path of an extrusion.

Steps: This option works in the same manner as Steps for the surface. The more steps used, the smoother the profile path.

Angle: Used with a Static profile, this option determines the angle the profile takes when traveling away from the face.

Twist: This option twists the profile as it heads to the vanishing point.

7. Now let's examine the Bevel Tool in FreeHand MX. Traditional 3D programs have two commonly used tools, Extrude and Lathe. You are familiar with the Extrude Tool; it simply extends a path away from the face of an object. Lathe, on the other hand, spins a profile shape to create a rounded profile. Using the Bevel profile, available in the Extrude Tool, you can emulate a lathe to create some interesting objects. The following steps, shown in step 7, break down this process:

    a. First create two shapes: use the Ellipse Tool to create an open circle with a width and height of 60 and a Radial gradient fill. Use the Ellipse Tool and the Pen Tool to create an open path.

    b. Next apply the Extrude Tool to the circle. Within the Object Panel, set the Extrude length to 250. Set the x rotation to 270 and the y rotation to 90.

    c. Click the Profile button and choose Bevel from the drop-down menu.

    d. Click Edit > Cut to move the open path to the clipboard, then click the Paste in button. This command applies the profile to the object. The shape now resembles a wine glass.

    e. Set the number of steps to 20 in both Profile and Surface so the glass becomes much smoother. Place your glass in front of a dark shape to see it more clearly.

Smudge and Shadow

The Smudge and Shadow Tools allow you to add a degree of depth to objects. These tools are shown in Figure 3.18.

The Smudge Tool creates a shadow effect by creating grouped copies of the same item. You can adjust the fill and stroke of the copies by double-clicking the tool before using it. The copies gradate until the final fill and stroke color are reached.

The Shadow Tool creates a single copy of the initial object by default. You can adjust the settings by double-clicking the Shadow Tool. One shortfall of the

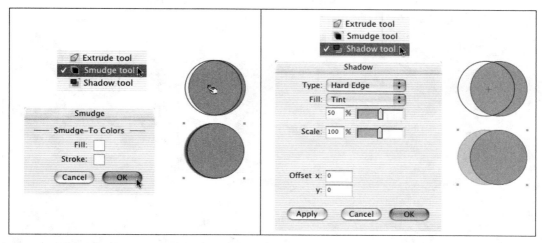

FIGURE 3.18   Smudge and Shadow Tools.

Shadow Tool is that it does not work on text or grouped objects. To apply a shadow to these objects, you must use the revised Object Panel and Live Effects.

Trace

Sometimes you want to transform a raster image into vector art. This could be for any number of reasons, including using a shape found in nature or something you wish to emulate. The Trace Tool can assist you in some of these cases. It attempts to find the edges in a bitmapped image and duplicate them with vector paths. The Trace Tool contains numerous settings. Its general functionality is shown in Figure 3.19.

This wheel is the study of two attempts at tracing. The top row shows the original digital photograph imported into FreeHand, whereas the bottom row was cleaned of its background in Fireworks.

In the top row, the object was traced by selecting the Trace Tool and double-clicking the preferred area to trace. When prompted with the Wand Options dialog box, Trace Selection was chosen. You can see the complexity of the result by the number of vector points.

Next, the area was traced, but instead of Trace Selection, Convert Selection Edge was used. This option resulted in a cleaner image than the previous example, but it still requires touch-up.

In the bottom row, the image was cleaned up in Fireworks. Doing this extra step is useful because less of the image is left for the Trace Tool to sort out. When

FIGURE 3.19   Effects of the Trace Tool.

you plan to trace an image, you may want to consider stripping all unnecessary pixels from it.

When Trace Selection was chosen in the Wand Options dialog box for the bottom image, the result was better than the original image offered. However, it is still complex. When Convert Selection Edge was chosen instead, the result is very good—it is nowhere near as complex, and there is little to clean up.

The Trace Tool is a useful tool for cases when you are stuck with a bitmap and need the scalability of vectors, but it does have limitations. It is not very effective for translating actual photos of anything organic or complex; so many vectors will result that your Trace Tool is effectively useless. Trace works best with line art or solid shapes in raster images. Anything else may prove too difficult to work with.

You also should consider if the Trace Tool will even save you time. Often it is quicker to just import an image and manually trace it using your Pen and Shape Tools. The time saved in cleaning up the Trace result can make these other tools a better alternative. Flash also offers a Trace Bitmap capability, but it is even weaker than that of FreeHand.

Blend

The Blend Tool blends one shape into another, making them appear as if they are going through a metamorphosis. It is also used to create effects for display in an exported .swf. Creating Flash animations with FreeHand is covered later in the book.

The basic steps of blending one object into another is to click the object you want to start blending, and drag to the object into which you want it to morph. This process is shown in Figure 3.20.

A gray circle and black star are shown in the top row of the figure. When you click the star first, it goes to the back of the blend, and the gray circle is the final outcome of the process.

In the bottom example, the colors of the shapes were reversed for a clearer contrast. If we used the same colors going the opposite direction, the black of the star would blend into the effect and not stand out. The start and finish points of the blend are also reversed, and you can see the star is now the focus.

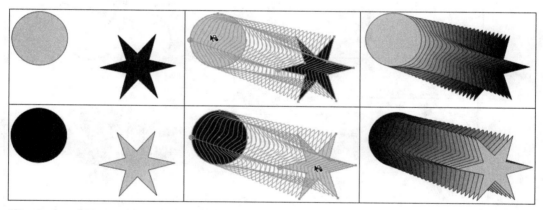

FIGURE 3.20   The Blend Tool.

Mirror

The Mirror Tool is a lot of fun and can be helpful on some occasions. It serves as a quick, easy way to duplicate objects in an illustration. Two ways it can be used are shown in Figure 3.21.

1. Open the shapes created using the Perspective Tool (saved as *building*). After opening the file, select all of the shapes and group them by clicking Modify > Group. Now apply the Mirror Tool with its initial setting of Ver-

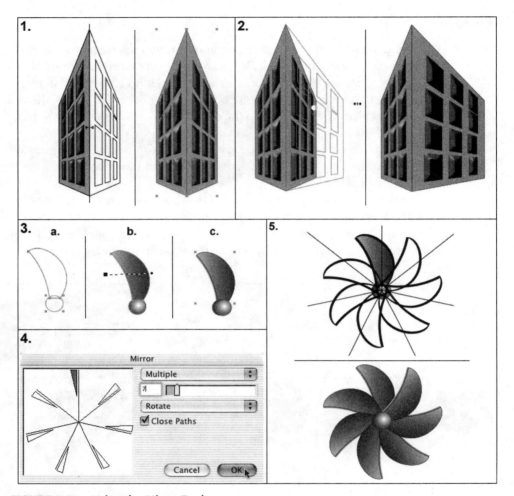

FIGURE 3.21   Using the Mirror Tool.

tical. With the tool selected, simply click the shape to be mirrored, and drag the preview of its clone to the new location. When you release the mouse button, a new shape is created, perfectly mirroring our initial object, as shown in step 1 of Figure 3.21.

2. In its current state, although mirrored, the shapes still don't quite resemble a building. This is where creativity can help. Double-click the shape on the right to open the Free Transformation option. Move your mouse over the right edge until your cursor becomes a double arrow, then drag to the right to widen the shape. Now the shapes resemble a building, as shown in

step 2. Remember that your original shape and its clone are two separate shapes. You can group them by selecting both and again applying Modify > Group so you can move them as a unit in the future.

3. In step 3, a more advanced type of mirroring—Multiple with Rotate—is covered. This option can be a real time-saver to create objects like flowers and other shapes that have a constant, evenly distributed series of shapes in a circle.

   a. Start with two shapes: one will be the blade of a propeller, and the other the center sprocket. To create the propeller blade, use the Pen Tool to draw your basic blade shape, then apply a linear gradient with black and white as a fill. For the sprocket, create a circle with the Ellipse Tool with a height and width of 28. Add a radial gradient fill.

   b. When the gradient is created, swap the black and white swatches in the Object Panel to reverse its pattern. After doing this, select the Pointer Tool, making sure the gradient is selected in the Object Panel. This gradient causes the Fill Transform handles to appear. Use them to manipulate the gradient, as shown in step b. Do the same thing with the circle to move the radial gradient center point to slightly upper-right of center.

   c. Now add some depth to the shapes. For the blade, use the Smudge Tool to drag out a small shadow to the left. Select both the blade and its smudge, and click Modify > Group to keep them together. For the sprocket, use the Extrude Tool and specify a length of 20 and y-rotation of 348.

4. Now we are ready to use the Mirror Tool. Select the blade group and double-click the Mirror Tool to open its dialog box. From the drop-down menu, choose Multiple. Next, type 7 to define the number of copies of the blade. Then choose Rotate from the drop-down menu. Then select Close Paths. Press OK to save your settings.

5. Click your blade with the Mirror Tool, and drag the mouse until you see all seven new blades in the proper position within the preview window. Select all of the blades by pressing Shift + click. Click Modify > Arrange > Send To Back to place them behind your sprocket. You now have a completed fan. You may want to group it so it is locked as one object.

Graphic Hose

The Graphic Hose Tool enables you to spatter random shapes around a document. You can use one of the predefined hoses, import a new one, or create your own with up to 10 shapes in each. The results of predefined hoses and a newly created one are shown in Figure 3.22.

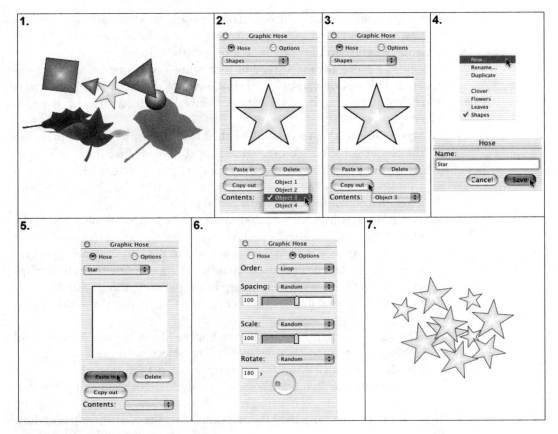

FIGURE 3.22   The Graphic Hose Tool.

1. In step 1 of Figure 3.22, two FreeHand predefined hoses—Leaves and Shapes—are shown. To change which one is selected, double-click the Graphic Hose Tool.
2. Now we will create your own Graphic Hose Tool using the star available within Shapes. Double-click the Graphic Hose Tool to open its dialog box and choose Shapes from the drop-down menu. With Shapes selected, choose Object 3 from the drop-down menu next to Contents, as shown in step 2.
3. Press the Copy out button to save a copy to the clipboard.
4. Choose New from the drop-down menu, type the name Star, and click Save.
5. Click Paste in to make your star shape appear.

6. Click the Options button, and set Spacing, Scale, and Rotate to Random. Type 180 in the Rotate text box.
7. Use your new hose.

Chart

The Chart Tool is a handy feature. With the economy being in such a state of rapid flux, charts have proven extremely popular because they are effective for displaying "the bottom line" for a business and will continue to be seen on both presentations and Web sites. Figure 3.23 shows the basic steps for chart creation in FreeHand.

1. First, select the Chart Tool and draw out a rectangular shape to specify where and how large the chart will be.

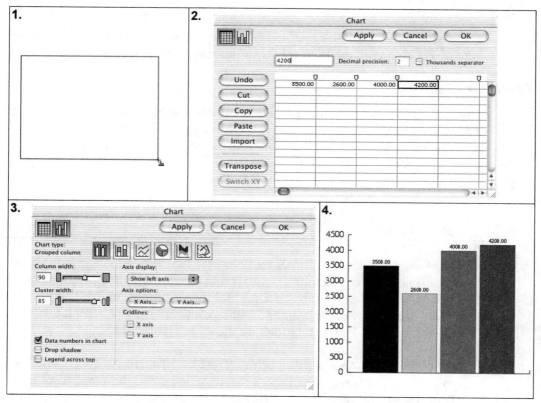

FIGURE 3.23   Creating a chart in FreeHand.

2. After you release the mouse button, the Chart dialog box opens, as shown in step 2 of Figure 3.23. Here, you can either manually enter figures or import them from a tab-delineated data source, such as a spreadsheet program. When you create the chart, the area on the data form with a black rectangle is considered the active cell. Whenever using a pie chart, the first cell of data is the one that is broken out.

3. After you have entered your data, you have a choice of several types of chart. Use the default, a bar chart.

4. Press Apply or OK. Our results are displayed in the document in grayscale. If you want to change the colors or fonts, use the Subselect Tool to modify properties inside without breaking the chart. The Subselect Tool can make changes within a group, unlike the Pointer Tool. If you want to edit your chart after you create it, click Xtras > Chart > Edit to reopen the Chart dialog box.

Action

The Action Tool is new to FreeHand MX. It allows you to put basic Flash actions onto objects. You will use this tool for connecting pages in the next chapter.

Connector

The Connector Tool is yet another new feature in FreeHand MX. It was created to help users create flowcharts and diagrams and is especially useful for creating wireframe mockups of a Web site flow. This tool is covered in the next chapter when we create a site map.

PATH OPERATIONS

This exploration of FreeHand MX features wraps up with a look at Path Operations, the skills necessary to round out all you have learned. Path Operations can be accessed in one of two ways: by clicking Modify > Combine and Modify > Alter Path or by using the Xtra Operations Toolbar found at Window > Toolbars > Xtra Operations. Some of Path Operations are shown in Figure 3.24.

Blend: We have seen this effect before. The Blend Tool in the Tools Panel gives you a bit more control than this version. When using the Blend Tool in the Tools Panel, you can define which way you want the blend to travel by which object you select first. However, when you use Blend in either the Xtra Opera-

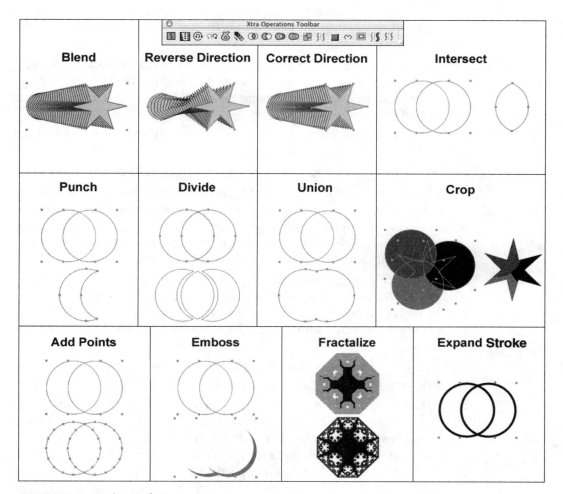

FIGURE 3.24 Using Path Operations.

tions Toolbar or through Modify > Combine > Blend, you are constrained by whichever object is made last. The object made last winds up on the top of the blend. You can modify this behavior by clicking Modify > Arrange and changing the order of each shape.

Reverse Direction: This tool is handy to use with blends. When applied, it causes the blend to have a 180 degree twist.

Correct Direction: This tool changes the direction back to normal if you have applied Reverse Direction.

Intersect: When you have multiple shapes selected, this tool causes the overlap to become the final shape.

Punch: This tool causes the shape made last to punch out its shape from a previously made object. If you want to change the behavior, click Modify > Align and either send the later-created shape backward or the earlier-created object forward before applying the tool.

Divide: This tool causes the overlap area between shapes and the rest of the shapes themselves to become separate shapes.

Union: When applied, this tool joins overlapping shapes into one shape.

Crop: Commonly used for a mask effect, this tool causes all overlapping objects to be cropped into the uppermost shape. Keep in mind that all areas without overlapping are cropped as well. If you want to fill an entire shape with other shapes, the objects to be cropped must be larger than the cropping shape. Note that if you want to mask photographs, Fireworks is the tool of choice.

Add Points: You sometimes must add points to an object to make a more complex shape. This tool adds points to an object, spreading them evenly throughout the object. Although you can use the Pen Tool to do this, it is difficult to spread the points evenly with the Pen Tool. Figure 3.24 shows Add Points applied twice.

Emboss: This tool creates an embossing effect with your shape. Unlike using Live Effects in the Object Panel, this tool changes the properties of the object.

Fractalize: Though not commonly used, the Fractalize tool creates rather complex square-based patterns. Keep in mind the word *complex*. Each application of this tool nearly doubles your points and, if applied too many times, can lock up your computer. The example shown in Figure 3.24 started as a square with a black fill and had the command applied 11 times. Notice how, in the first view, the large number of vector points make the object seem almost solid. The points increase almost exponentially when the tool is applied multiple times.

Expand Stroke: This tool makes strokes appear wider. Figure 3.24 shows the stroke expanded to a value of 5.

CREATING FLASH ANIMATIONS

FreeHand enables you to create not only static illustrations but also rudimentary Flash Animations. This feature is more important if you are using FreeHand as a standalone product and do not have Flash.

This book covers the entire Studio MX 2004 suite and so it focuses on creating Flash Animations in Macromedia Flash MX 2004. FreeHand MX offers basic animations as a product enhancement, but their functionality is nowhere near that of Flash MX 2004. You use FreeHand MX to create animations primarily if you want to create a simple chunk of content to show a client. This will be covered in the next chapter.

EXPORTING HTML

Just as FreeHand allows output into a Flash Animation, it also exports HTML. This capability is helpful if you want to add some actions to art created in FreeHand and then later import it into Dreamweaver. This feature is covered in the next chapter.

ASSETS

Swatches and the Color Mixer Panel

Swatches and the Color Mixer Panel work hand in hand to assist you with custom colors. When you create a particular shade you want to use throughout an illustration, you may find it tedious to constantly recreate it. This is where Swatches comes in.

When you create a shade you like in the Color Mixer Panel, click the Add to Swatches button. The color then appears in the Swatches Panel, ready for use when you need it again.

To apply a swatch, select an object and click the swatch you want. The object fill then is transformed. You can also drag the color square from the Swatches Panel to wherever you want to apply the color. For example, if you are using a gradient, you can drag the color square into the gradient to apply it.

Styles

Styles are similar to Swatches in principle, but they affect more than just color. With Styles, you can set not only a fill color but also any Live Effects you have applied to an object. For example, if you have created a particular color and are using a drop shadow, you can apply the same fill and drop shadow to numerous objects in your document. Simply select the object and then click New in the Styles Panel. All effects and colors you have used are combined into a style that can be applied to future objects. Figure 3.25 demonstrates using styles.

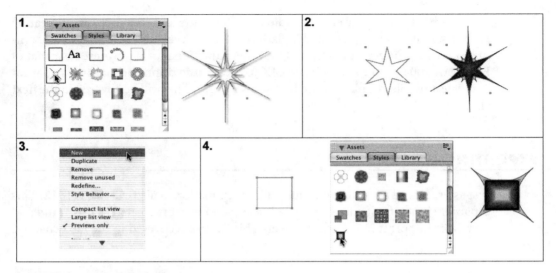

FIGURE 3.25   Applying Styles.

1. Create a basic star shape. Then select the star shape and click the predefined style within the Styles Panel, as shown in step 1 of Figure 3.25.
2. Next, create another star shape. This time, apply a contour gradient and Bend effect to the shape using Live Effects, as shown in step 2.
3. With the new star selected, click New from the Styles Panel Options menu to add the new style to the panel.
4. Create a new rectangle, then click the custom style to apply it. You can see in step 4 how the rectangle was modified.

Symbols

Symbols with FreeHand are used for graphics that you want to appear multiple times within a document. Their use keeps the file's size down. Symbols are introduced in the next chapter.

Library

The Library is where you store symbols and Master pages in a FreeHand MX file. The parent copy of each symbol is stored in the Library. Any changes made to the parent copy of a symbol affects all instances of the symbol in the document.

SUMMARY

Step two of the tour of FreeHand MX is now complete. As you can see, it is a powerful application. You haven't learned all there is; to do so would take a few hundred more pages. What has been covered will get you well on your way to creating some effective graphics to use on your Web site and in Macromedia Flash MX 2004. Now let's move on to an important chapter for designing our site, "Designing Frameworks in FreeHand MX."

4 Designing Frameworks in FreeHand MX

The previous two chapters explored many of the tools available in FreeHand MX. Now it is time to see the program applied. This book focuses on the development cycle of Design, Build, Test, and Maintain; FreeHand assists in the Design phase. This chapter describes how to create a wireframe to revise *http://www.jdukesphoto.com* using FreeHand.

CREATING A WIREFRAME

A wireframe shows the navigational flow of a Web site, similar to a flow chart. Instead of representing a business procedure, it shows what decisions users will have before them.

It is important to provide guidance while developing a Web site. Without planning, development time and costs can skyrocket, and you may find yourself losing both money and clients. Wireframes are also useful for selling a concept without having to go through the work of creating a prototype that the client may not purchase. The completed wireframe site map is shown in Figure 4.1.

Creating Symbols

Now that we have seen the final result, let's break it down into easily digestible chunks. Notice that two shapes are used consistently throughout the document: a rounded rectangle to symbolize a computer screen and an open folder to represent files.

We create these two shapes first. After creating them, we convert them into a symbol so you can reuse them without increasing the file size significantly. Let's start with the rounded rectangle shown in Figure 4.2.

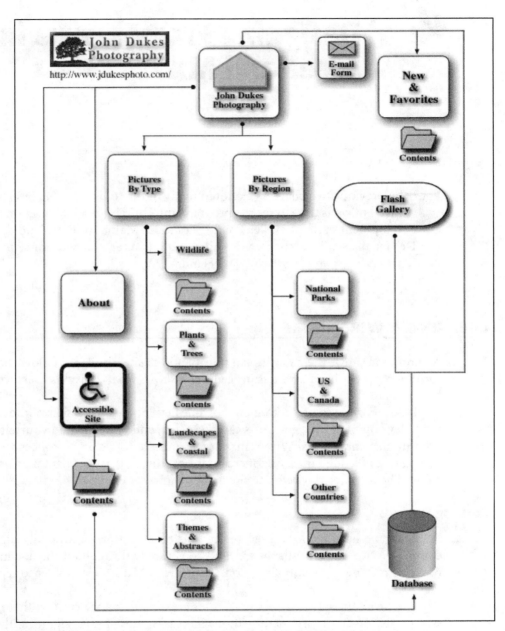

FIGURE 4.1 The completed *www.jdukesphoto.com* wireframe.

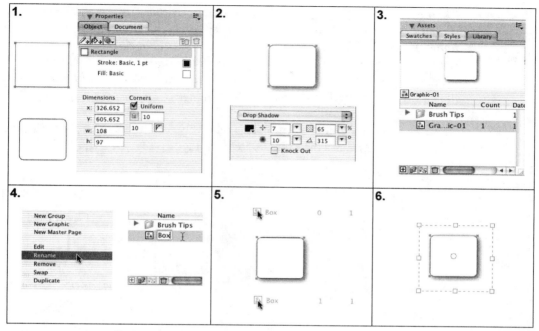

FIGURE 4.2   Creating the screen symbol.

1. Create a rectangle using your Rectangle Tool. Set the width to 108, height to 97, stroke 1-point black, fill white, and corner radius 10.
2. In the Object Panel, add a Drop Shadow effect with the default settings of 7 for Offset and 10 for Softness.
3. With the object selected, click Modify > Symbol > Convert to Symbol (or press the F8 key on your keyboard). The rectangle appears in the Library. You can open the Library by clicking Window > Library. The symbol is given the default name of Graphic-*n* (where n is the number of the graphic symbol created).
4. Choose Rename from the menu in the top-right corner of the Library Panel and type the new name *Box*.
5. You can now drag multiple instances of the object onto the stage. As you are dragging them, you can see a faint description with the Graphic Symbol icon, the name, and the number.
6. Once your symbol is on the stage, activate the Transform Tool by double-clicking an instance to modify its scale, rotation, and skew. These modifications will not affect any other instance that may be on the stage.

Although you can modify instances on stage without other instances being changed, all instances are affected if you make modifications from the Library Panel. If you double-click an instance in the Library Panel, FreeHand opens the symbol in a separate editing window. Any changes made here are reflected in all instances. This capability is convenient when you must modify multiple instances in one sweep, such as if your company logo changes.

Next, we create the folder symbol. It is relatively easy to make but has a couple more steps than the rounded rectangle. Refer to Figure 4.3.

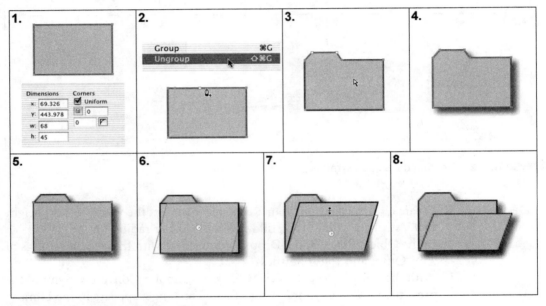

FIGURE 4.3 Creating the folder symbol.

1. To start, create two rectangles with a stroke of 1 and a fill of gray (#CCC-CCC). The width and height must be set as 68 and 45, respectively.
2. To make changes to paths within rectangles, you must first ungroup them by clicking Modify > Ungroup. After we ungroup the rectangle, we can add three extra vector points using the Pen Tool. Select the Pen Tool, and add a point slightly in from the left edge on the top path. Add a second point approximately twice the distance of the first to the right. Then add one more point slightly to the right of your second, as shown in step 2 of Figure 4.3.
3. Now you can move your points. Use Shift + click to select the first and second points you created. While they are selected, use your up arrow key to

move the points upward. Do not use the mouse because it is not as accurate or easy to control. Keep pressing the up arrow until your tab is revealed, as shown in step 3.

4. Add a Drop Shadow effect to your shape using the default settings.
5. Now we work with the second rectangle. Line it up with the bottom edge of the completed folder back, as shown in step 5. If it disappears behind the back of the folder, select the back of the folder and click Modify > Arrange > Send To Back.
6. Double-click the new rectangle to open the Free Transform Tool and skew the new rectangle to the right, as shown in step 6.
7. Align the bottom corners of the front rectangle with the bottom corners of the back of the folder. Notice that the front rectangle is too tall. Scale its height using the Free Transform Tool.
8. Apply another Drop Shadow effect to the new shape using the default settings. You now have a folder. Select both shapes, click Modify > Symbol > Convert to Symbol, and name it *Folder* in the Library.

Now you start placing the symbols in the document. We must go through the process of placing and then scaling all of the images to balance the page. Start with the rounded rectangles, shown in Figure 4.4.

1. First, drag instances of Box from the Library Panel onto the stage. You will need 14 instances for the wireframe.
2. Arrange the Box instances so they loosely resemble what is shown in step 2 of Figure 4.4.
3. Now open the Align and Transform Panel to adjust the scale of the two bottom-right vertical rows. You can open this panel by clicking either

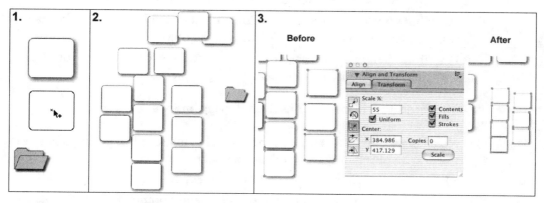

FIGURE 4.4   Resizing symbols with the Align and Transform Panel.

Window > Align, or Window > Transform. Change back and forth between Align and Transform by clicking the tabs in the Panel. We will use Transform > Scale, so make sure the Transform tab and the Scale button (third down on the left) is selected. Press Shift + click to select all seven instances that make up the two vertical rows on the bottom right, and type 55 under Scale %: in the panel. You must ensure that Uniform is checked so the objects scale easily.

The Align and Transform Panel

We have just used the Align and Transform Panel. This panel is one of the most useful tools available in FreeHand, so it warrants further discussion. The panel contains two tabs, aptly named Align and Transform. Align assists you with the placement of objects on the stage; Transform offers numeric precision for moving, rotating, scaling, skewing, and reflecting objects on the stage.

Starting with the Align Panel, you have several options on the horizontal and vertical planes. The horizontal (x) plane offers the following options:

No change: Causes no effect on the horizontal plane. Use this option if you want to affect an object only using the vertical plane.

Align top: Aligns the tops of multiple objects.

Align center: Aligns the centers of multiple objects.

Align bottoms: Aligns the bottoms of multiple objects.

Distribute tops: Disperses multiple objects evenly either on the stage or with one another based on the tops of the objects.

Distribute centers: Disperses multiple objects evenly either on the stage or with one another based on the centers of the objects.

Distribute bottoms: Disperses multiple objects evenly either on the stage or with one another based on the bottoms of the objects.

Distribute heights: Disperses multiple objects evenly either on the stage or with one another based on the heights of the objects.

The vertical (y) plane contains the following options:

No change: Causes no effect on the vertical plane. Use this option if you want to affect an object only using the horizontal plane.

Align left: Aligns objects based on their left edges.

Align center: Aligns objects based on their center points.

Align right: Aligns objects based on their right edges.

Distribute lefts: Disperses multiple objects evenly either on the stage or with one another based on the left edges of the objects.

Distribute centers: Disperses multiple objects evenly either on the stage or with one another based on the center points of the objects.

Distribute rights: Disperses multiple objects evenly either on the stage or with one another based on the right edges of the objects.

Distribute widths: Disperses multiple objects evenly either on the stage or with one another based on the widths of the objects.

Other options when using the Align Panel are the To Stage checkbox, which causes all alignments to be based on object placement on the stage instead of on one another, and the Lock command. The Lock command, accessed by clicking Modify > Lock (or pressing Ctrl or Command + L) locks a selected object in place, forcing other objects to align to it. Click Modify > Unlock if you want to make the object.

The Transform Panel gives you granular control when you transform objects. It is important if you are working toward precision. Several categories are available from which to choose, with each represented by a button in the panel.

Move: Allows you to explicitly type how far and in what direction you want an object moved. If you type a number within the Copies text box, FreeHand adds a new copy of the object every time it reaches the specified distance. The originally selected object or objects stays in place. The following steps provide a quick demonstration of this tool by creating a checkerboard:

a.   Create a square with a height and width of 40. Add a black fill, and place it in the upper-left corner of the stage.

b.   Press the Move button in the Transform Panel and enter 80 within the x text box. Type 3 in the Copies text box, and click the Move button. You have created your first row.

c.   Select the entire row of objects. Within the Transform Panel, clear the x text box, and type –80 within the y text box. Leave 3 in the Copies text box, and click Move.

d.   Now select all of the squares, and change x to 40 and y to –40. Change Copies to 1, and click Move.

e.   To complete the checkerboard, select all of the squares and group them. After they are grouped, you can see in the Object Panel the width and height of the group is 320. Create a new square with a height and width of 320 (but don't create a fill). Select the grouped squares and lock them in place. Press Shift + click to select both the new rectangle and the group, and switch to the Align Panel. Making sure that To stage is cleared, choose Align centers in both the Horizontal and Vertical drop-down menus. Press the Align button. You now have a checkerboard.

Rotate: Defines the numeric values for the rotation. You can also create copies while you are rotating.

Scale: Allows numeric values for scaling and copy creation.

Skew: Defines the numeric values for the skew.

Reflect: Flips an object. When you type a number for Copies, the new clones reflect the original object in an alternating fashion.

Scaling and Placing the Box Symbols

Now that we have explored the Align and Transform Panel, it's time to apply its options. We need to align the newly scaled rows and scale all of the Box instances. This procedure is shown in Figure 4.5.

First, select the left vertical row, and open the Align Panel. In the Align Panel, choose Align center and press the Align button to align the row. Repeat this procedure with the right vertical row.

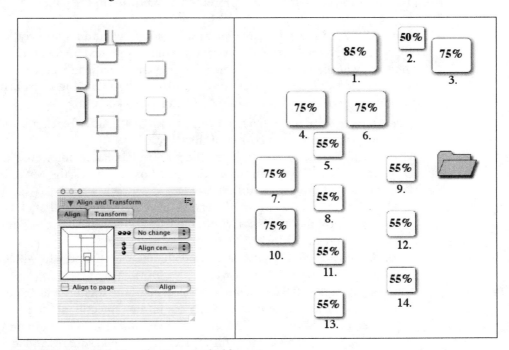

FIGURE 4.5   Finishing the Box symbol layout.

After you have aligned the rows, scale all the other Box instances within your diagram. The correct scale for each object is shown in Figure 4.5.

If you are concerned about having the exact placement of each object, the x-, y-, and scale sizes coordinating with the numbers in Figure 4.5 are listed in Table 4.1.

TABLE 4.1   Values for Placement of Objects

Object	Scale	X	Y
1.	85%	246	622
2.	50%	383	669
3.	75%	452	622
4.	75%	151	506
5.	55%	207	439
6.	75%	275	506
7.	75%	087	366
8.	55%	207	326
9.	55%	358	387
10.	75%	087	255
11.	55%	207	210
12.	55%	358	270
13.	55%	207	098
14.	55%	358	150

NOTE

You also need to modify the two boxes on the far left of the document. Both boxes should be squares, so change the current width to match the height using the Object Panel. You also need to add a black stroke with a size of 5 to the bottom box. This stroke is used to make Accessible Site stand out.

Arranging the Folder Symbols

Now it's time to arrange the folders. This process is shown in Figure 4.6 and is described the following steps:

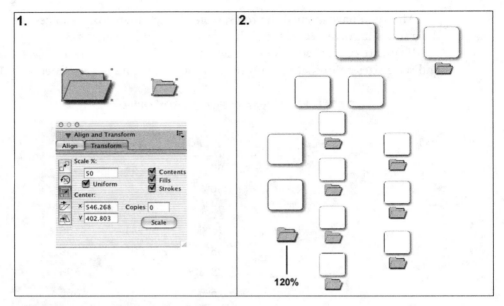

FIGURE 4.6 Placing the folder symbols.

1. Using the Transform Panel, scale the Folder instance to 50%.
2. After you have scaled the instance, make nine copies of it on the stage. A shortcut for copying is to press Alt + click and drag eight copies. This shortcut saves you from having to scale each copy. Place all the copies as shown in step 2 of Figure 4.6. You must modify the Folder instance in the bottom-left of the document to 120%, as shown.

Adding Text to the Wireframe

Now you are ready to add text to the wireframe to describe what each item is. We could have added text to each item when we created it, but doing so would have added significantly to the file size and your workload. By choosing symbols, we can reuse the Folder and Box instances not only in the current document but also in future diagrams.

Let's add some text, as shown in Figure 4.7.

As shown in Figure 4.7, text has been added to every Box and the word *Contents* under each Folder instance. The text has a font of Times New Roman, Bold, and a size of 11 for most instances, with the following font size exceptions:

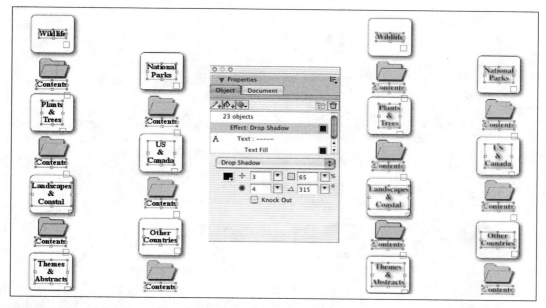

FIGURE 4.7   Adding text with a Drop Shadow effect.

- About and New & Favorites is 14 points.
- E-mail Form is 10 points.
- Contents on the bottom left is 12 points.

After you have placed all of the text, add a Drop Shadow effect. Press Shift + click to select all of the text and add a Drop Shadow effect. Change the Offset to 3.

Creating More Icons

To add some flair to the document, create some extra icons. You don't need to create these as symbols, because you will be using each of them only once. If you want to add them to other documents, you can convert them to symbols for greater portability.

Each of these icons is a visual cue representing something in the document. You will build a house shape to represent the home page on the Web site; the universally recognized wheelchair to address accessibility in our design; an envelope for the e-mail form; and a canister, one of the most commonly used symbols to represent a database. The icons are shown in Figure 4.8.

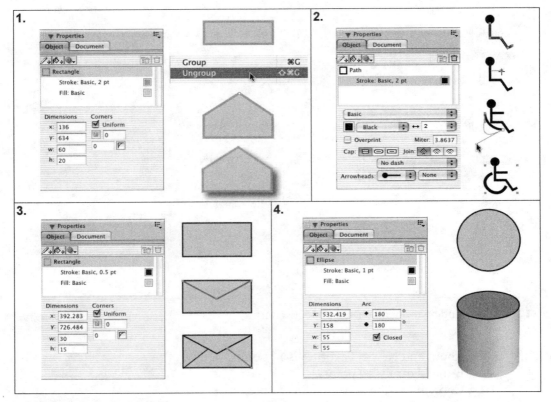

FIGURE 4.8 Creating the icons.

1. Start by creating the House icon, the easiest of all the icons.
   a. Build a rectangle with a width of 60 and a height of 20. Add a gray (#CCCCCC) fill.
   b. After you complete it, ungroup it so it can be modified, and add a single point to the center of the top edge using the Pen Tool.
   c. After you add the point, shift it up. Now you have a house.
   d. Add a Drop Shadow effect with the default settings, and move it into place.
2. The wheelchair icon is a little trickier but still very approachable.
   a. Use the Pen Tool to lay out the profile of the person.
   b. Change the stroke to 2 points and black, and add a left arrowhead with the disc shape.
   c. Use the Line Tool to draw a straight 2-point black stroke out from the body.

d. Now use the Arc tool (found underneath the Line Tool) to draw a basic arc that begins behind the person's arms and finishes just under the knees.

e. Use the Pointer or Subselect Tool to modify the path by pulling and moving the vector handles on each point.

f. Group the paths, and add a Drop Shadow effect with an Offset of 3. Move the icon into place.

3. Now create the envelope, another easy icon.

a. Create a rectangle with a black stroke of .5 and a gray (#CCCCCC) fill. Set its width to 50 and height to 25.

b. Next, use the Line Tool to create a straight line that matches the width of the rectangle. Set its stroke to .5 and black.

c. Use the Pen Tool to place a point in the center of the new line. Move the point down using the down arrow key.

d. Create two more lines on each side that come up from the bottom corners to approximately two-thirds of the distance down the flap on the envelope. Set their strokes to black and .5.

e. Group the envelope, add a Drop Shadow effect with an Offset of 3, and move it into place.

4. Now we make the canister icon for the database using the Extrude and Ellipse Tools.

a. Create a circle with a width and height of 55.

b. Activate the Extrude Tool and click the circle.

c. In the Object Panel, set the length to 60 and the x-rotation to 300. You also need to set Steps to 20 in the Surface properties.

d. Add a Drop Shadow effect, and move the icon into place (at x-value of 489 and y-value of 116).

e. Add the text *Database* underneath the icon in 12-point bold Times New Roman with a Drop Shadow effect with an Offset of 3.

f. Group the container icon with the text.

You're not off the hook yet—you have one more object to create to symbolize the possibility of a future Flash Gallery on the Web site.

Create a rectangle 130 pixels wide by 50 pixels high. Give it a black stroke of 1.5 and a white fill. Round the corners to 30, and use a Drop Shadow effect with the default Offset and Softness. On the new rectangle, add the text *Flash Gallery* on two lines using 12-point bold Times New Roman. Also add a Drop Shadow effect to the text with an Offset of 3. Group the new shape after creating it so it is easier to move.

Using the Connector Tool

FreeHand MX introduces the Connector Tool. This tool is handy when creating flow diagrams. It is located next to the Action Tool in the Tools Panel. Although it may seem to be an oversight that it was not discussed previously, it is most appropriate to apply it for the wireframe. The following procedure is shown in Figure 4.9.

1. The basic behavior of the Connector Tool is straightforward. Click the parent shape first, then the child. This order causes a stroke with a disc and arrowhead to appear indicating that the first object links to the second.

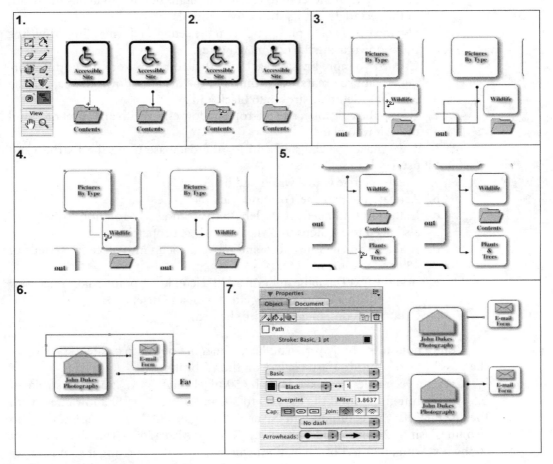

FIGURE 4.9 Using the Connector Tool.

2. Although the objects aligned satisfactorily, you may notice, as shown in step 2 of Figure 4.9, that the disc is quite a distance from the Accessible Site square. This distance results from the Drop Shadow effect. FreeHand calculates this while determining the placement. To place it closer, you can connect from the text instead of the Box instance. You can also change the Start Offset difference within the Object Panel. (You must have the connector line selected to do this.)

3. In step 3, you see potentially undesirable behavior. If two objects are too close, the Connector Tool may create a looping stroke.

4. To correct this connector behavior, delete the connector line and Move Pictures By Type to the left. You should use your arrow keys for accuracy. This action causes the connector line to be closer to normal.

5. One great feature of the Connector Tool is that when it is used on multiple aligned objects, the connector lines lie on top of one another. This feature gives the diagram a clean appearance.

6. Step 6 shows again the issue of the Connector Tool creating a loop. This time, we don't want to move any objects, so you must explore another method.

7. Using the Line Tool, create a stroke between John Dukes Photography and E-mail Form. Set the stroke to 1 and add a left arrowhead with a disc and a right arrowhead of an arrow.

You have now used the Connector Tool to create a diagram. Flow diagrams used to be created using this tool. It is handy to understand the Connector Tool and this alternative method. There are times, however, when it is quicker to just add a stroke rather than fight the Connector Tool.

Continue using the Connector Tool to connect all of the instances on the stage. You must also create some of the connector lines using the stroke method just mentioned. Your results should resemble the diagram shown in Figure 4.10.

ON THE CD
You now have a completed wireframe. All that you need to do for the client is add their logo. Click File > Import and navigating the CD-ROM that came with the book to *FreeHand\Chapter 04\JDPLogo.tif*.

When the image is ready to be placed, your cursor resembles an upside-down L. Use the L to specify where the top-left corner of the image is placed. Once you find your desired location, click your mouse button, and the graphic appears.

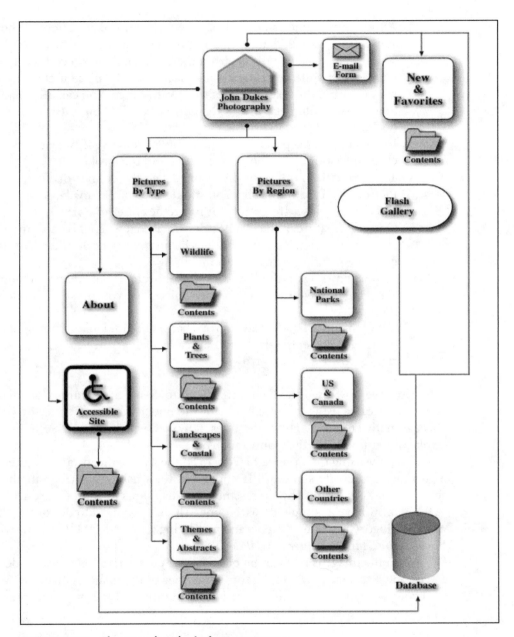

FIGURE 4.10 The completed wireframe structure.

PUBLISHING IN FREEHAND

Many of the basic tools in FreeHand have been covered, and you have created some content, so now it's time to look at publishing. Because FreeHand is such a mature tool with strong print roots, a myriad of publishing and export options are available. The next sections cover some of the most popular while focusing on the Web aspects of using the options.

Sharing Content with Flash

An output file format that gets many designers excited is .swf. This format works well if you are using FreeHand to create vector art that you want to use in Flash.

Although Flash can create vector art, it lacks the advanced capabilities of Free-Hand. Often designers create complex graphics in FreeHand and then export them into Flash to add interactivity.

Multiple methods of bringing FreeHand content into Flash are available. The first is to simply copy the contents off your FreeHand document and paste them onto the Flash stage. This process is shown in Figure 4.11.

1. Step 1 of Figure 4.11 shows a star shape made in FreeHand using a Contour gradient, which is not available in Flash. This shape was copied and pasted into Flash. Whenever objects are pasted from FreeHand to Flash, they appear in the Library. Flash treats them as graphic symbols, so they can be duplicated without adding file size. They are also constrained to being symbols because they are created using a series of masks and groups that would be easy to break apart inadvertently.

2. Another method of turning FreeHand content into content that can be displayed in the Flash player or authoring tool is to export the content as a .swf file. This method opens a dialog box that gives you several options. You can choose how many layers in which you would like the movie to be published, select how many FreeHand pages are used for the output, define Flash Movie properties, and determine how the movie is optimized.

3. Yet another way to get FreeHand content into Flash is to import the content directly from Flash by clicking File > Import. Flash MX and later can directly import a FreeHand document.

4. All content imported from FreeHand appears in the Flash Library.

Creating Flash Animations

In addition to sharing content with Flash, FreeHand can create rudimentary Flash Animations itself. Figure 4.12 demonstrates some of these methods.

You can create a Flash Animation in FreeHand using several methods. Although these methods work, they are not as intuitive or as flexible as using Flash. The animation shown in Figure 4.12 was created using the Blend Tool.

1. Create a star shape with a black and red gradient fill. Copy the shape to another area on the stage, and scale the clone with a 90-degree rotation.
2. Use the Blend Tool to merge the two shapes.
3. After blending the shapes, click Xtras > Animate > Release to Layers.
4. Clicking Release to Layers opens a dialog box offering the following options, of which you select Sequence:
   Sequence: Creates the illusion of movement by playing each layer created, one after another.

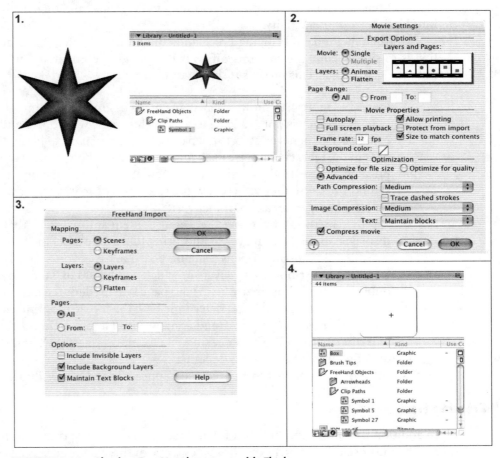

FIGURE 4.11   Sharing FreeHand content with Flash.

Build: Causes each layer to build on the last. This method is interesting when you use it to make text seem to write itself across the screen or an object seem to draw itself. You must attach the text to a path or convert it to layers before you click Xtras > Animate > Release to Layers.

Drop: Causes objects to seem as if they are appearing in place.

Trail: Similar to Sequence, except as you move the next layer, the previous layer or layers remain, depending on the number you enter in the Trail By setting.

Trail By: Specifies how many layers remain on screen as the animation progresses. This option is available only with the Trail option.

Reverse direction: Reverses the direction of an animation.

Use existing layers: Adds new content to existing layers. If you are adding to an animation and do not want new content displayed on the current layers, deselect this option.

Send to back: Available with Use existing layers. If you want to have new content released to layers, select this option to send the new content to the back of the current layer stack.

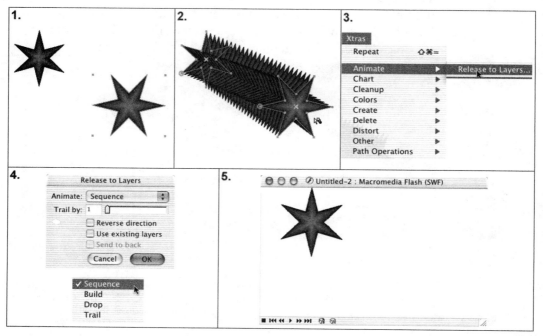

FIGURE 4.12 Creating Flash Animations.

5. Once you have completed Release to Layers, you can test your movie by clicking Window > Movie > Test or by pressing Ctrl or Command + Enter. Navigation controls are located across the bottom of the window that opens. To the left are the standard playback controls and to the right are two icons with the Flash icon. The icon on the left publishes your .swf file according to what the previous settings were; the icon on the right opens the Movie Settings Panel (shown in step 2 of Figure 4.11).

Now we can add action to the Flash Animation. Notice that when you test the movie a play button is available; the user won't see this button. You must add a component for the user to initiate the movie or create a way for the movie to self-initiate. Now is when your Actions Tool and Navigation Inspector come in handy. These tools are explored in Figure 4.13.

1. Create a circle with a red and black gradient fill using the Ellipse Tool. Add the word *Play* on the face of the circle. Select the Actions Tool, click the new circle, and drag your mouse off the circle, releasing the mouse button over the canvas. This action causes a curved path to appear underneath the circle with a box containing an arrow, as shown in step 1 of Figure 4.13.
2. The default action, Go To and Stop, is pointed at Page 1. This setting will not initiate the movie, so you must adjust it. Open the Navigation Inspector either by double-clicking the arrow icon within the Actions stroke or by clicking Window > Navigation.

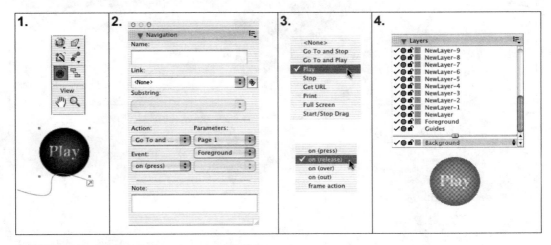

FIGURE 4.13   Adding Actions to an animation.

3. In the Navigation Inspector, change Actions to Play and Event to on (release). Actions represents what will happen when an event occurs and Event specifies the event. Several options are provided from which to choose:

■ Actions

<none>: Applies no action.

Go To and Stop: Goes to a particular page and stops on that page. You define which page in the Parameters menus.

Go To and Play: Initiate playback on the specified target. Works similar to Go To and Stop.

Play: Starts playing from the current page.

Stop: Stops the movie.

Get URL: Loads a new Web page in the browser window. Choose one of the following options to define where the Web page opens:

■ _self—Loads the new page in the current window.
■ _blank—Loads the new page in a new window.
■ _parent—Loads the new page into a parent frame, if you are using frames.
■ _top—Loads the new page in the current window and discards all current frames.

Print: Initiates a print. Parameters can determine what in the selected page is to be printed from the Flash player.

Full Screen: Displays the movie as Full Screen.

■ Events

on (press): Denotes when the object is clicked.

on (release): Requires the user to press and release the mouse button while the pointer is over the object. This choice is good because users are accustomed to this behavior on Web sites. It allows them to change their minds by moving the mouse away from the object before releasing the mouse button.

on (over): Denotes an event when a cursor passes over the object.

on (out): Denotes when the cursor has passed over the object and is moving away from it. This option is usually used in conjunction with the on (over) option to create a rollover effect.

frame action: Doesn't involve the user at all. It is initiated when the playhead enters the frame/layer.

4. When you have released objects to layers, you can see all of the new layers created in the Layers Panel. Click Window > Layers, if it is not available in your panel set. If you test the movie right now, you see that the button appears only at the end of the movie for a brief second. This is not what we are looking for. For an object to be seen in a movie, no matter which frame or layer the playhead is on, the object must be created on a nonprinting background layer. If you look at your Layers Panel, you see a thick gray dividing line. This line separates the foreground from the background. Anything on the background layer does not print. Move the button to the background layer by selecting all objects that make up your button and then clicking the background layer. It should appear to be faded on the stage, as shown in step 4 of Figure 4.13.

If an object doesn't move from one layer to another, choose Move Objects to the current layer from the pop-up menu in the top-right corner of the Layers Panel. This command causes selected objects to be moved to the layer with the Pen icon showing.

This procedure completes the basic overview of Flash Animations in FreeHand. This section didn't travel too deep into the subject because you will create animations in Flash in the next several chapters.

PAGES AND LAYERS IN FREEHAND

You may have noticed that in the previous sections, pages and layers were mentioned briefly. These two concepts are important in FreeHand and in most other graphic programs, so they are explored more in this section.

Pages

It is important to acknowledge that FreeHand as a product was created primarily for the print world. Its capabilities have expanded over time, but it remains true to its roots. Numerous graphic studios use FreeHand almost exclusively for print purposes, so the program should continue to maintain this focus.

As a tool of the print world, FreeHand is often used to create brochures, pamphlets, and the like. To accommodate these uses, a way to generate multiple pages in one document must be available. This is where the concept of pages enters.

When you create a new document in FreeHand, a single page appears on the screen. You can add more documents by pressing the plus sign (+) at the bottom of the window or by opening the Document Panel next to the Object Panel in Properties. This Panel and the pages created are shown in Figure 4.14.

1. The Document Panel offers a look at all the parameters of the pages on the screen. Within the miniature pasteboard, you can see the single page in your document. Underneath the page, you can choose what kind of view you want; within the page, you can choose which document has focus. To the right you can choose what size and in which direction (portrait or landscape) you want the currently selected page displayed. Under Printer resolution, you can define how many pixels- or dots-per-inch the document will print. (If you are aiming for the Web, choose 72 dpi.)

2. To add a new page to your document, choose Add pages from the Document Panel Options menu or click the Add Page icon at the bottom of the main window. You can also press Alt or Option and drag a new document from a current page with the Page Tool in the main window.

3. After adding a page you can zoom out to see multiple pages within the main window, as shown in step 3 in Figure 4.14.

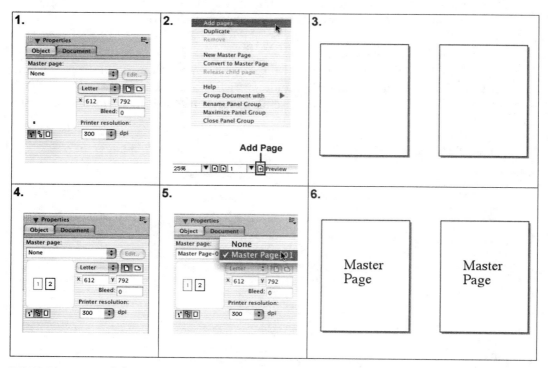

FIGURE 4.14 Working with the Document Panel and pages in FreeHand.

4. The pages are also displayed in the miniature pasteboard in the Document Panel, shown in step 4.

5. Master pages are used to place content (like a company logo) consistently throughout all pages based on the template. Type the words *Master Page* on the first page in the main window and choose Convert to Master Page from the Document Panel Options window. After you have done this, change your focus to the second page using the miniature pasteboard and choose Master Page-01 from the Master Page drop-down list. You can edit the master page by clicking the Edit button next to the drop-down list. The Master Page opens in a new editing window.

6. As shown in step 6, both pages are based on the Master Page.

Layers

Layers in FreeHand provide a way of organizing objects within a document. You already have the capability of using Modify > Arrange, but layers take this principle to another level. You can put multiple items on one or more layers and then lock or hide the layers for protection. You can also bring items onto the background layer in FreeHand. Doing so assists in layout by having the background layer contents visible but not printable. Layers are shown in Figure 4.15.

This figure is split into two parts: The Layers Panel and Adding a Layer. First, let's look at the panel itself.

The Layers Panel is split into two parts. All layers on the top of the gray bar are printable (with the exception of Guides, which is covered in a moment) and all layers below are not. This feature is useful if you want to have content, such as a pro-

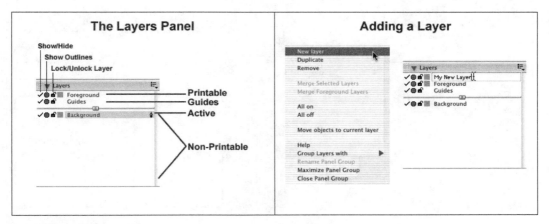

FIGURE 4.15   Using Layers in FreeHand.

duction note or even a layout design you use to structure the page, on a layer below the line that will not be in the output. The Guides layer is another nonprintable layer that facilitates the ability to add custom guides to help with an illustration.

Other features in the Layers Panel to assist you are the icons to the left on each layer displayed in the figure.

Show/Hide: Makes all the contents of the layer invisible while you are editing.

Show Outlines: Hides all fills but leaves a basic outline of the contents. This option is helpful if you have a complex illustration and want to base new content location on the previous layer, but the fills are distracting.

Lock/Unlock Layers: Prevents content on the layer from being selected when the padlock is closed.

To add a layer, select New Layer from the Option menu. After you add a new layer you can drag it to another location, within the Panel, to change its level. To name the layer, double-click the name and type a new name.

EXPORTING IMAGES

FreeHand can export files as many different formats. Some of these formats are for sharing with users of a different program, such as Adobe Illustrator, and others are for final viewing. A list of all available formats is displayed in the Format drop-down menu shown when you click File > Export.

If you want to publish output that is still editable in different vector-drawing applications, choose from any of the Adobe Illustrator or EPS (Encapsulated Post Script) file types.

If you are going to be outputting the file as a final export, use either .swf or one of the many image formats. These image formats are explored more in the Fireworks chapters.

PUBLISH AS HTML

The last topic covered in the FreeHand chapters is publishing to HTML. FreeHand can create basic HTML from your document. FreeHand has nowhere near the control of Dreamweaver or even Fireworks when publishing to HTML. This feature is useful mostly if you have a simple mockup that you just want to spit out without opening another application. The HTML Output and Setup screens are shown in Figure 4.16.

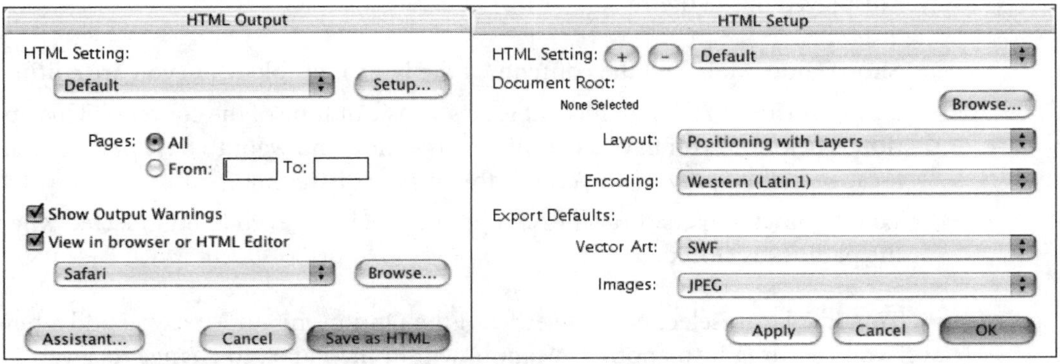

FIGURE 4.16   Publishing document as HTML using FreeHand.

When you click File > Publish as HTML, the HTML dialog box opens, offering several options.

First, you can use Default or press the Setup button (shown in Figure 4.16) to modify your settings. Within HTML Setup, you can change the Document Root, Layout, Encoding, and what image formats you want to use.

Next, you can choose which pages you want published. You can choose all or a series of pages.

If you select Show Output Warnings, FreeHand alerts you to issues that come up during the export process. Be sure to look at the final result because you may be warned about something only to find your output is fine.

The next option is what browser you want to use for viewing the HTML content. This option associates the file with the particular browser, which opens when you double-click the file.

The last option is the Assistant button. This option gives you clear directions while you are making choices.

HTML Output Assistant

This tool was created to step you through publication of HTML. Seven screens are available:

First screen: Introduces what the tool is for and what it can do for you.

Second screen: Allows you to choose how the layout is positioned on the final HTML document. You have two options: Positioning with Layers and Positioning with Tables. Using layers offers the most accurate layout and helps if you have overlapping content, but you can have issues with browser compatibility. On the other hand, tables are nearly universally compatible, but you cannot have any overlapping content.

Third screen: Allows you to choose what image format you would like to use for your vector graphics in the final HTML file. You can choose from SWF, GIF, JPEG, and PNG.

Fourth screen: Allows you to choose what format should be used for bitmap images. As with the third screen, you can choose from SWF, GIF, JPEG, and PNG.

Fifth screen: Defines where the HTML files are stored. If you don't want to use the default location, you can browse to a new folder. Images are stored in a subfolder called images.

Sixth screen: Allows you to save all the settings you have chosen under a name of your choice. This way, you don't have to use the HTML Output Assistant or HTML Setup every time in the future.

Seventh screen: Applies the settings when you click Finish.

SUMMARY

This chapter completes your exploration of FreeHand MX. This application is an invaluable tool for creating vector graphics for both print and Web work. The nuts and bolts of the application have been covered, so you can be well on your way to creating graphical content. Once you get a handle on what was covered here, you may want to read one of the many books dedicated to FreeHand as a product. You will find that the application contains much depth.

Now that we have been exploring vector graphics, it's time to make them move. We will do this with an "Introduction to Macromedia Flash MX 2004."

5 Introduction to Macromedia Flash MX 2004

A BRIEF HISTORY OF FLASH

Flash, like FreeHand, comes with its own bit of history. It can be seen as one of the applications that helped shape the Internet. It started as a drawing program called SmartSketch, created by a company called FutureWave Software. SmartSketch was initially created in 1993, for what, at the time, was a futuristic operating system made by a company named Go. This operating system was made for the purposes of pen computing (using a pen on the screen instead of a keyboard as a computer interface). Go was bought by AT&T, and the operating system was subsequently cancelled in 1994. Interestingly enough, tablet PCs have become the rage—10 years later. With its operating system scrapped, SmartSketch had to be ported to Macintosh and Microsoft Windows, where it faced formidable competition from Illustrator and FreeHand.

By the summer of 1996, SmartSketch was reinvented as FutureWave Splash, a program used to create animations for the Web. Macromedia, with a new focus on animation and the Web, bought FutureWave Software and released the program as Macromedia Flash 1.0. The application was enhanced to deliver high-impact, but small-size, animations that could be comfortably viewed over small bandwidth connections like modems. The files output by Flash have the .swf extension. There are different views as to what *swf* stands for. Some claim it means *Shockwave Flash*; others say it stands for *small Web file*. Either one works. The .swf files are read by the Flash Player, a free application bundled with most browsers and computers. It can also be downloaded from *www.macromedia.com/software/flashplayer/*.

The magic behind making the files small—ideal for low bandwidth connections— is a combination of vector graphics and streaming. As we have learned from the chapters covering FreeHand MX, vector graphics are great for illustrations because they are scaleable yet resolution independent. These characteristics make the file size small because they are instructions instead of physical pieces of data. The second part of the equation is streaming. Streaming is the process of enabling a file to start playing even before the entire file has been downloaded. You may be familiar with streaming data already; it is used with most video players on the Internet. The power of Flash streaming is the added factor of the vector graphics. The file is not only streaming, but it is quite small to begin with, so the user sees far fewer hiccups in the movie playback. If the movie is well designed, the user may not even experience any pause or interruption.

Now, six versions later, the Flash Player not only is synonymous with Web animation but also could be arguably the most frequently distributed software on the Internet. More copies of the Macromedia Flash Player are running on computers than even Microsoft® Internet Explorer or Netscape Navigator. It is bundled with nearly every new computer sold and is available for numerous operating systems, including Microsoft Windows®, Macintosh®, Linux, IBM OS/2®, Sun Solaris™, HP HP-UX, and SGI® IRIX®. With this kind of saturation, it's not surprising that its use is a fairly comfortable choice to deliver dynamic content to Web sites.

With the widespread acceptance of Flash, numerous developers have adopted it and used it in unique ways. It started out as an efficient animation package, but Macromedia added some basic programming capabilities. With this added functionality, something odd happened. Web developers started to use the program in innovative ways and created content that was far more powerful than even Macromedia had imagined. The company added scripting commands to Flash to make it interactive, and developers created complete games.

These new uses for Flash took Macromedia by surprise, and they responded by adding more and more programming capability. In version 5, they rewrote ActionScript from the ground up. It is based on ECMAScript, the ECMA-262 (formerly the European Computer Manufacturers Association, as of 1994, ECMA International—European association for standardizing information and communication systems) standard. JavaScript is also based on this standard, so developers who were familiar with JavaScript could easily adapt to ActionScript.

Macromedia Flash MX 2004 has grown way beyond its original scope. Over the past few years, it has made serious inroads into a whole new front—*embedded devices*. Embedded devices are small computing systems that are specially created for a particular function. One of the most popular examples is the palm-size personal data assistants (PDAs) running Microsoft Pocket PC. These devices are now even bundled as cell phones. What makes this advance in technology important is that a developer can create one Flash interface that can be scaled for either a desktop or a PDA.

Imagine an individual, like a contractor on a construction site, who needs to order some building materials. He could fire up his cell phone, pull up the Flash interface, and punch in the needed materials. Meanwhile, because he is connected to the same database using the same interface that accountants use in the main office, the purchases can be properly reflected in the overall company database without any extra work. This same model can be applied to any number of businesses with a roving workforce.

Flash is ideal for embedded devices because its roots are in small file sizes. It didn't need much reengineering to be compatible with these devices. Two things that most embedded devices usually lack are a decent amount of memory and a large bandwidth connection. Flash applications can now be found in numerous places, including cell phones, automated teller machines, and even video game consoles. With the releases of Flash MX 2004 and Flash MX 2004 Professional, Macromedia has pushed development to a whole new level by revising ActionScript into version 2. Flash now has even more traditional programming capabilities, causing it to resemble Java™ and other compiled languages, rather than just scripting languages like JavaScript™.

LOOKING AT THE INTERFACE

New to Flash MX 2004 and other MX 2004 products is the Start page. This tool provides a quick snapshot of what is available to you upon launch. It is shown in Figure 5.1.

Looking at the Start Page from left to right, you see that it begins with the most recently opened files. This view can be convenient as we often may have several projects running simultaneously and saved in multiple locations on the hard drive. At

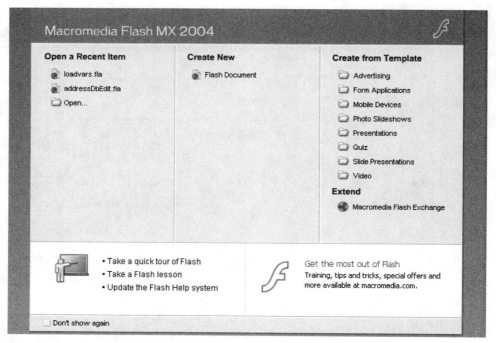

FIGURE 5.1   The new Start page for Macromedia Flash MX 2004.

the bottom of the list the Open button allows you to browse for a file if the file you want is not on the list.

Moving to the right you see the Create New area, which enables you to open a standard new 2004 .fla 550x400-pixel file. To the right of that area is a brand-new option—Create from Template. This area contains several preformatted sizes and shapes to assist you for specified mediums.

Below the Create from Template area is the Extend area. This area provides you with a link to the Macromedia Flash Exchange, a great location for extensions (similar to plug-ins) developed by Macromedia, independent developers, and companies to enhance Flash. Many of these extensions are free, and others are shareware. It is a great place to look if you want to enhance your movies.

In the bottom half of the Start Page, three links are available: Take a quick tour of Flash, Take a Flash lesson, and Update the Flash Help system. The last option is valuable. Macromedia Flash MX 2004 has grown so complex that the help files likely will be frequently revised and appended.

If you don't want to see the Start page every time you open the program, click Don't show again. (You can change this setting by clicking Edit > Preferences > General on Windows or Flash > Preferences > General on Macintosh.)

Because Flash was created as an animation package, its heritage is reflected in the interface, shown in Figures 5.2 and 5.3.

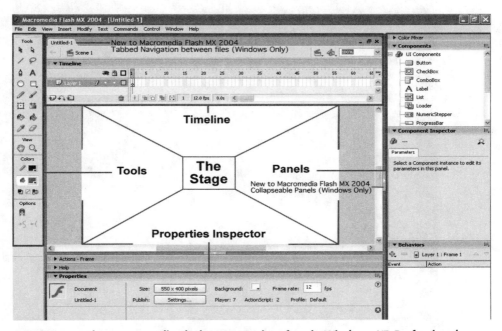

FIGURE 5.2   The Macromedia Flash MX 2004 interface in Windows XP Professional.

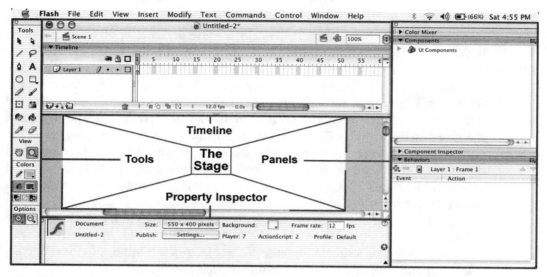

FIGURE 5.3   The Macromedia Flash MX 2004 interface in Macintosh OS 10.2.6.

The key item especially unique to the Macromedia Flash MX 2004 interface is the timeline at the top of the screen. This area is where you will be working with the flow of your movies. It contains visual references of both time, as it elapses, and layers.

THE TIMELINE

Everything created using the basic nature of the program is based on the timeline. This should always be in your mind. Let's take a closer look at it in Figure 5.4.

Essentially, you should view the timeline in two directions—left to right and up and down. Frames are shown from left to right. Each frame represents a piece of time, which is controlled by the document settings. By default, a movie is 12 frames

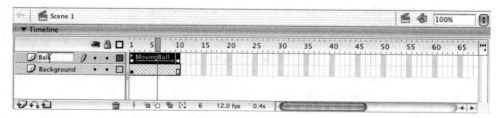

FIGURE 5.4   The Macromedia Flash MX 2004 timeline.

per second (fps). This setting is a compromise between the smoothness of animation versus CPU utilization on the system. To give perspective on the issue, video in the United States usually runs at the NTSC (National Television Standards Committee) standard of 30 fps. A Flash animation, at 12 fps, is not as smooth as what you would see on a videotape, but it still shows animation clearly. If you set the frame rate higher than the default, your users may pay a penalty. The higher the frame rate, the larger the file (it takes more frames to cover the time passage) and the more taxing on the CPU. Remember, because Flash is a vector medium, the CPU must draw every single frame. If you are developing animation for embedded devices, you may want to consider dropping the frame rate even lower, to around 10 fps, because the CPUs in these devices are not as powerful as those in desktops and notebooks.

Another important point to consider is that the timings in the Flash Player are not precise. These settings depend on the end user's CPU speed, and bandwidth can cause some issues on a stream. Because of these factors, it is important to really consider your audience and to test according to their conditions.

Three basic types of frame are found on the timeline: frames, keyframes, and blank keyframes. Keyframes are created for the purpose of a significant change in the flow of the program. A keyframe is automatically created when you draw or drag an object onto the stage in a frame. You also insert a keyframe to reflect change, such as an object being added, modified, or moved to another location on the stage. You can insert a keyframe anywhere in the movie, but it is advisable to insert them only where the scene changes. Any extraneous keyframes serve no purpose and increase the file size needlessly because the computer has to draw every one. A blank keyframe is slightly different from a keyframe. Although it has no content on the stage, it still carries significance. It is used for script placement and for labeling, or named anchors, to aid user navigation. Last, we have frames. Frames are the simplest of the three types. They are basically placeholders either to cover a period of time during which you maintain the same content or to be filled by Flash automatically. For example, if you have a background image that never changes, you would use a keyframe to introduce the content and then use frames (not keyframes) for the rest of the movie. By using frames, the CPU doesn't have to redraw the image as it would with a keyframe.

When looking at the timeline, as shown in Figure 5.5, you can see the different frame types. A keyframe is represented by a small filled circle inside of a frame. A blank keyframe shows an empty circle inside of a frame. Frames are represented with a vertical rectangle. Above the symbol on keyframes or blank keyframes, you can see if either a frame label, named anchor, or comment has been added. If a frame label has been added, you see a flag above the circle (hollow or filled) with

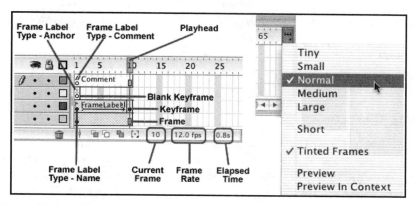

FIGURE 5.5   Timeline components.

text to the right describing what it is. If a named anchor has been added, you see an image of an anchor above the frame identifier. New to Macromedia Flash MX 2004, frame comments are delineated by a double slash in the same manner that they are used in ActionScript and many other programming languages.

Named anchors were new to Macromedia Flash MX and solved an issue many users had with Flash movies when viewing them in a browser. Previously, when a user was on a Web page that had a .swf embedded in it, he could not use the standard Web browser navigation buttons, such as back and forward. If he used the back button, for example, he would not be taken back in the movie but back to the previous Web page. This behavior caused great confusion among users and is now overcome with the use of the named anchors. Now, when the user presses the back or forward button, he is taken to the nearest named anchor frame (forward or backward) and not out of the entire .swf and Web page.

On the top of the timeline, you see the numbers identifying the frames below. Resting on the numbers is the playhead with a line that crosses all the frames. The playhead sets the stage content to what frame number you want to see and can be used for what is known as scrubbing the timeline. *Scrubbing* is the process of dragging the playhead left and right and watching the stage content changing below.

Underneath the timeline is the current frame on which the playhead is resting. To the right of the current frame, you see what the frame rate for the movie is, and to the right of that, how much time has elapsed up to the current frame.

On the far right of the timeline is a symbol that looks like two Hs combined. If you click this, you can change the size of your frames—large to make them easier to see, or smaller if you have a large timeline.

A frame slot that hasn't had anything created in it is sometimes referred to as a protoframe, or a placeholder.

Looking at Layers

The same way that the timeline works from left to right, layers work up and down. Layers are similar to stacked, clear sheets of papers. Each item drawn underneath on another layer is clear from above, unless content is directly above it on a higher layer. Layers are stacked from the bottom to the top, with the highest-level layer visible first. Figure 5.6 shows two layers. One is named Rectangle and has a black rectangle as its content; the other is named Star with a white filled star. Because the white star is on the layer above the black rectangle, its content is visible. If the layer order were reversed, the star would not be visible.

Layers provide a great way to display your content in an organized manner. Multiple types of layer are available, including masks, or guide layers. As of the release of Macromedia Flash MX, you can create layer folders, which enable you to organize your content even further. We will work with layers more in a later section.

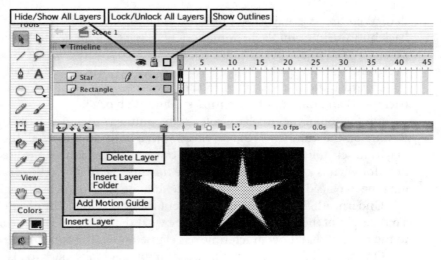

FIGURE 5.6 A look at layers.

THE TOOLS PANEL

The Tools Panel is located in the same location in all of the graphics programs in Macromedia Studio MX 2004. In addition, the tools themselves, although not always having the same specific functionality from one application to the other, are very similar.

The Tools Panel is divided into four main areas: the main or vector-creation tools (remember, Flash graphics at heart are vectors), view tools, colors, and options.

The main tools allow you to create vector graphics and text for use in Flash movies. These tools are similar to the layout in Macromedia Flash MX but have received a cosmetic upgrade and include the new PolyStar Tool. The following tools make up the Flash MX 2004 main tools:

Arrow Tool: Your main tool for moving objects and manipulating shapes. It is similar to the Pointer Tool found in both FreeHand MX and Fireworks MX 2004 but with its own spin. You can actually manipulate vectors while pushing and pulling lines (strokes).

Subselection Tool: The standard vector point manipulation tool for artists who want to manipulate vector points directly. Its functionality is similar to the same tool in FreeHand MX and Fireworks MX 2004.

Line Tool: Makes a basic two-point line. You can hold down the Shift key to constrain it to 45 degree angles much the same as in FreeHand MX and Fireworks MX 2004.

Lasso Tool: Allows you to select freeform areas of objects on the stage.

Pen Tool: Allows you to directly plot vector points in creation of objects. This tool is similar in functionality to the Pen Tool in FreeHand MX and Fireworks MX 2004. This tool was added after many requests from illustrators who use it for vector graphic creation.

Text Tool: Adds text to Flash movies. Flash has different types of text that can be added, including Static, Dynamic, and Input. Static text is general text that is not subject to change when the movie is played. Dynamic text is text that changes as the movie is playing to reflect things that happen programmatically. Input text allows the user to interact with the movie.

Oval Tool: Allows you to create basic ovals on the page. It is similar in functionality to the Ellipse tools in FreeHand MX and Fireworks MX 2004.

Rectangle Tool: Allows you to create normal and rounded rectangles, similar to the tool in FreeHand MX and Fireworks MX 2004.

PolyStar Tool: Allows you to create both polygons and star shapes. This tool is new to Macromedia Flash MX 2004.

Pencil Tool: Creates freeform lines. The vector points are created in reaction to what you draw. It also has some other options that are covered later.

Brush Tool: Allows you to create freeform fills.

Free Transform Tool: Allows you to change the shape and scale of objects in a freeform manner.

Fill Transform Tool: Changes the direction of a fill and its basic properties dynamically using handles.

Ink Bottle Tool: Applies a different color to lines.

Paint Bucket Tool: Applies a different color to fill.

Eyedropper Tool: Pulls one color from one shape to be applied to another. When a color is pulled from a line, the tool turns into the Ink Bottle Tool. If a color is pulled from a fill, the tool becomes the Paint Bucket Tool.

Eraser Tool: Cuts material from lines or fills. This tool works similarly to the Brush Tool but in reverse. It can be applied to lines and fills and has settings to constrain what it actually changes as it is used.

The View tools are useful for navigating the interface. The Hand Tool allows you to move the stage for a better view without affecting object placement. The Zoom Tool is used like a camera lens to provide a better view.

The Colors tools are for selecting basic stroke and fill colors when you create a shape. They have been around for multiple versions and are maintained primarily for backward compatibility. The newly added Property Inspector provides a better place to pick your colors with Macromedia Flash MX 2004.

The last section in the Tools Panel is Options. Options are not tools themselves but modifications of the currently selected tool. For example, if the Zoom Tool is selected, options appear allowing you to zoom in or zoom out with each mouseclick.

The Tools Panel is shown in Figure 5.10. We will explore each tool more in depth later in this chapter.

THE PROPERTY INSPECTOR

New to Macromedia Flash MX and Fireworks MX, the Property Inspector is a central source for much of the manipulation you do in a movie. It was initially introduced in Dreamweaver 4 and proved so popular that it was added to the interfaces of Macromedia Flash MX and Fireworks MX.

The exciting aspect of the Property Inspector is its versatility. Whatever you have selected on the stage—the stage itself or frames—now is editable in one convenient location. You now have a form of one-stop shopping. Be sure to look within the Property Inspector to note what object you have actually selected.

Figure 5.7 shows five different views of the Property Inspector. The first view is of the stage itself, where you can change the properties of the document, such as Size, Background color, Frame rate, and version of the Flash Player to which the movie will be published. The second view is of a shape selected on the stage. You can change the shape's stroke color, fill color, stroke thickness, line type, width, height, and position on the stage. The third view has a frame selected. Here, you can add a frame label, determine if you want a named anchor, select a Tween, adjust sound, add a sound effect, choose sound sync options, and define whether the sound will loop. The next view shows the Text Tool selected, allowing you to choose the properties of the text before you insert it on the stage. And last is a view of a movie clip selected on stage. This view provides other offerings, such as naming, width and height, placement (x and y), and color options.

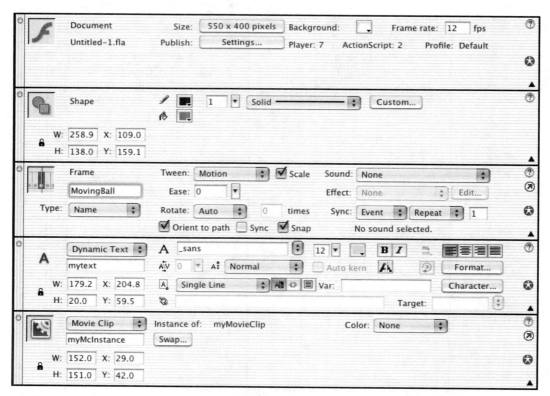

FIGURE 5.7 Different views of the Property Inspector.

PANEL SETS

Panels give you the ability to manipulate your movie to a finer degree. After you install the program, you can choose between two premade Panel sets and three different resolutions to match your current desktop size (1024x768, 1280x1024, and 1600x1200). It is common for designers to have their desktop resolution set as high as possible to see as much as possible on the screen.

The premade Panel sets are located at Window > Panel Sets and include Default (automatically set on installation) and Training. Training is essentially the Help menu by itself. Figure 5.8 shows the two main Panel set layouts and where they are selected.

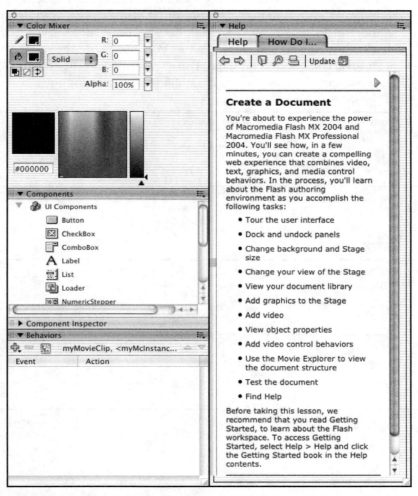

FIGURE 5.8   The two preconfigured Panel set layouts—Default and Training.

You can expand or collapse panels by clicking the triangle on the top left of the panel, next to the panel's name. You can also pull a panel out of a set by clicking the little dots in the panel's title bar. Add a panel to a set by clicking the same dotted area in the title bar and dragging the panel into the panel set. A black shaded area appears in the panel set as you drag the panel over to the set, indicating where the panel will be placed. When you release the mouse button, the panel appears in the new location.

You can add panels to your workspace by selecting them under the Window menu on the main menu bar. After you have added all the panels you want use on a regular basis, save your layout by clicking Window > Save Panel Layout. This action opens the Save Panel Layout window where you can name your custom panel set.

You can also collapse and expand the timeline and Property Inspector (Windows only), which helps to free up screen real estate.

Panels have been expanded in Macromedia Flash MX 2004. They are located under both the Window and Help menus, and many of them are subdivided into submenus, as shown in Figure 5.9.

In addition to the Tools Panel (sometimes called the toolbox), the Property Inspector, and the Timeline, which can all technically be considered panels, Flash includes the following panels:

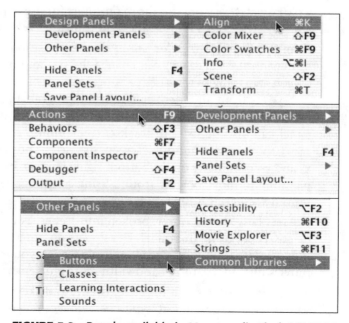

FIGURE 5.9 Panels available in Macromedia Flash MX 2004.

Help: Contains tutorials and links to references for learning Macromedia Flash MX 2004. You can access this panel either by clicking Help > Help or pressing the F1 key. It was previously called Answers.

ActionScript Dictionary: Looks up functions, properties, and other scripting keyword parameters used in ActionScript. You can access this panel by clicking Help > Help or by clicking the F1 key and choosing the ActionScript Dictionary within the table of contents on the left of the Help Panel.

Library: Contains all symbols, movie clips, sounds, bitmaps, and buttons. This panel enables you to have instances of objects rather than multiple copies, which keeps the movie size down and enables you to share assets with other Flash movies.

Design Panels

Align: Aligns content on the stage. You can align objects not only to one another but also to the stage itself. Additionally, you can use it to distribute objects in an even manner. You can also match the size of objects on the stage. These options are all huge time-savers.

Color Mixer: Enables you to mix custom colors. After you have created a color, you can add it as a swatch, which appears in the Colors section of the Tools Panel, Property Inspector, and Color Swatches Panel. You can also change the type of fill you are using, including gradients and bitmap fills.

Color Swatches: Contains the main colors for use in the program. You can add or delete colors in the panel and choose a Web-safe 216-color palette.

Info: Provides information about the size, position, and color of selected objects on the stage. You can change the size and position of the selected objects by typing new values or coordinates. This panel is a bit of a legacy (carryover from an older version of the program) panel because you can use the Property Inspector to change and view all these properties. This panel can also be used to track current mouse coordinates. When you move the mouse around the screen, its current position is reflected in the x- and y-coordinates on the bottom right. This can be helpful when you are planning to move objects around using scripting, by allowing you to determine actual coordinates on the stage.

Scene: Flash Movies can be broken into scenes. You can add, duplicate, or delete scenes using this panel. Developers do not always use the panel: if a movie is large enough to need multiple scenes, you can use multiple small movies instead to utilize bandwidth more efficiently.

Transform: Allows you to resize, rotate, and skew objects by typing new values. To resize an object, type a percentage. You have the option of constraining the object while resizing it. You type degrees for rotating and skewing selected objects.

Development Panels

Actions: Manipulate movies with the Macromedia Flash MX 2004 scripting language ActionScript.

Behaviors: Allows for basic interactions to be applied to frames and objects with precreated ActionScript. This panel is new to Macromedia Flash MX 2004.

Components: Replaces Smart Clips, which were used in older versions of Flash. Components are premade movie clips that a designer or developer can use and adjust in movies. Thirteen basic components are included by default, including TextInput, CheckBox, ComboBox, List, Button, RadioButton, TextArea, ProgressBar, and ScrollPane among others. These components are well suited for creating Flash applications that include interfaces like forms. With these components, you have an alternative to creating forms with HTML. Other components can be downloaded for free from the Macromedia Exchange located under Help > Exchange.

Component Inspector: Adjusts what is reflected in the currently selected component. These options are also available in the Property Inspector. This panel was formerly called Component Parameters.

Debugger: Debugs scripts that have been written in your movie.

Output: Displays errors that occur when running a movie with scripts or statements that are put in scripts deliberately.

Other Panels

Accessibility: Determines if an object is accessible and how it is described. The Accessibility Panel was introduced in Flash MX and is expanded upon with Flash MX 2004. It allows you to reach a bigger audience and show care for the disabled. This panel can also be opened directly from the Property Inspector.

History: Allows you to select multiple steps and replay them to automate some of the work. New to Flash MX 2004, this panel can also be found in Fireworks MX 2004 and Dreamweaver MX 2004. It is a useful tool for keeping track of steps you have taken during object creation. You can also save your steps to a command and then access the saved command under Command > <commandname> To delete or rename previously created commands, click Command > Manage Saved Commands. A panel opens in which you can choose individual saved commands and modify them.

Note that when you see a red X next to any step in the History Panel, that step cannot be replayed.

Movie Explorer: Allows you to view your movie in an organized manner. This panel is one of the best but often overlooked in Macromedia Flash MX 2004. You can open a listing of all parts of your movie, including text; ActionScripts; movie clips, graphics, and buttons; sounds, video, and bitmaps; and frames and layers.

Strings: Allows you to set any language as the default. This panel, new to Flash MX 2004, allows designers and developers to reach an international audience. Once you set your preferences, you can select a Dynamic or Input text field on the stage. Then type a unique ID and some text for the text field on the stage. Below your input boxes in the panel, all the languages you have chosen are shown. You can manually enter translations for the text in each language and see how they display by toggling them. At runtime, the Flash Player reviews an XML document that contains all of the language information enabling it to adjust to the target audience. The method with the external XML files provides options to translators. They can translate the .fla file (working Flash document) or XML document directly or run the XML file through translation software.

Common Libraries: Opens a submenu that contains sample libraries with objects you can use in your movies.

CONTEXTUAL MENUS

Sometimes, when you want to manipulate objects or frames, you can use Contextual menus. They are accessed by right-clicking (Control + click on a Macintosh) the item. You have many editing options, like Copy and Paste, along with other features, such as adding frames and creating Motion Tweens. Contextual menus as well as other panels are covered later.

USING THE TOOLS PANEL

Now let's use some of Macromedia Flash MX 2004 tools, starting with the Tools Panel. This panel is similar to the Tools Panel in both FreeHand MX and Fireworks MX 2004 but trimmed down. Although it may not offer as many options in terms of tools, that is not always a bad thing. You still have plenty of room to be creative, and there are some neat spins on how some of the tools are used. In many ways, Macromedia Flash MX 2004 has an elegant interface that really allows creativity to flourish. Let's go ahead and look at the Tools Panel, as shown in Figure 5.10.

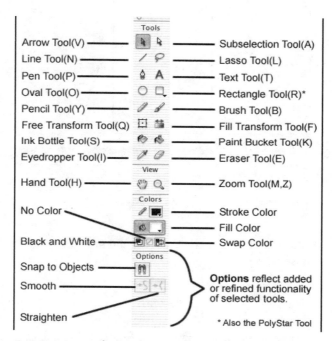

FIGURE 5.10   The Tools Panel and keyboard shortcuts.

At the top of the panel are the two main selection and manipulation tools, the Arrow Tool and Subselection Tool. Because nothing is currently selected, they are difficult to use at this point, so let's jump down a bit and first look at the Line Tool and then use the selection tools to manipulate it.

The Line, Arrow, and Subselection Tools

The Line Tool is a very basic tool. It creates a line by placing two vector points on the stage with the line connecting them. What is unique about Macromedia Flash MX 2004 is how you can use the Arrow Tool to manipulate this line. When you select the Line Tool, you can use the Property Inspector to define the color, thickness, and type of line. Follow the steps shown in Figure 5.11.

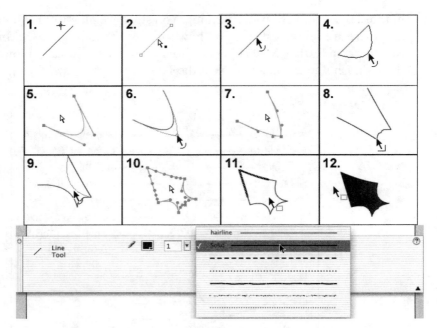

FIGURE 5.11 Using the Line Tool and modifying with the Arrow and Subselection Tools.

1. Start by creating a line with the Line Tool. Holding down the Shift key while creating the line causes it to be constrained to the closest 45 degree angle, as shown in panel 1 of Figure 5.11. The cursor is away from the end of the line because of this constraint. The line is placed at the 45 degree angle nearest the cursor.
2. In Panel 2, select the entire line using the Subselection Tool. This tool allows you to see the vector points in the line. Also, we can move the line around the stage while the whole line is selected. If you want to move only one point, click again on the vector point you want to move. The point becomes solid, indicating that it is selected. You can now manipulate it.
3. Macromedia Flash MX 2004 has a unique feature in the Arrow Tool. In FreeHand MX, the Pointer Tool (black arrow) can be used to move points and objects. With Fireworks MX 2004, the Pointer Tool can only select, size, and move objects. With Flash MX 2004, you can change the shape of the line simply by pulling it. When you hover over the line with your mouse, a semicircle appears behind the pointer, indicating that it will create a curve in the line.

4. Click near the center of the line, drag out a curve, and then release the mouse button. The line becomes a curve.
5. By clicking the line using the Subselection Tool, you can see that it still has only two vector points, but the handles are now pulled out.
6. Now pull on the curve with the Ctrl key (Command on a Macintosh) pressed. The cursor still shows a semicircle, but we are actually pulling out a corner.
7. By clicking the shape using the Subselection Tool, you can see that an extra vector point has been added to form a new corner.
8. We have now used the Arrow Tool to pull two more corners out of the path. (Remember to hold down Ctrl/Command while performing this task.)
9. In panel 9, you push the curves toward the center of the shape using the Arrow Tool.
10. In panel 10, you pull out a new corner on each side of the shape with the Arrow Tool and then push the stray ends together. When you push two points together, it closes the shape. You don't have to perform any other steps because of this unique method of creating shapes.
11. The Arrow Tool was used in panel 11 to select a portion of the new shape. By clicking a blank area of the stage and drawing out a rectangle, you perform a marquee selection. This action is the same as that in FreeHand MX and Fireworks MX 2004.
12. Because the shape is closed, we can easily add a fill.

Macromedia Flash MX 2004 has a unique way of creating strokes and fills. They are treated as separate objects after creation. For example, if you select only a fill and move it, the stroke stays in place. This behavior can cause an unintentional, undesired result. If you want to select an entire shape (both stroke and fill), double-click the fill of the object. If you double-click the stroke, only the stroke is selected. You can also draw a marquee around the shape using the Arrow Tool. Start in a blank area outside of the object, then drag a rectangular shape large enough to surround the object.

The Pen Tool

The Pen Tool in Flash MX 2004 has similar functionality as the Pen Tool in Free-Hand MX and Fireworks MX 2004, but it is not as robust. It plots vector points on the screen. This tool was brought into Flash in version 5 due to requests from many graphic artists who felt it was needed in a graphics program for them to fully adopt it. The Pen Tool works as follows:

1. To create a point, with the tool selected, click on the stage.
2. The Pen Tool has five icons that appear next to it to display your current activity:
   - **x:** Shows that the tool is over the stage and ready to place a point.
   - **+:** Shows that you are going to add a point to your working path.
   - **–:** Shows that you have the option to remove the point over which you are currently hovering. You can also select a point with the Subselection Tool (white arrow) and press the Delete key on your keyboard.
   - **^:** Shows that you can change the current point over which you are hovering to a corner point.
   - **o:** Appears if you hover over the first point in a path and are about to close the shape.
3. To have corners, click and release immediately after placing a point, or you may inadvertently create a curved path.
4. To create curves, drag in the direction in which you want the curve to be. With the Pen Tool in Macromedia Flash MX 2004, you do not have the option of pressing the Alt or Option key to change the direction of your curve as you can in FreeHand MX and Fireworks MX 2004. You must change it after the path is completed using the Subselection Tool. Then you can use the Alt or Option key to change a path direction.
5. To place the last point, either close the path by selecting the first point, or double-click to place the last point, if you want an open path.
6. To preview the path while creating it, you can modify your preferences. The Pen Preferences are accessed by clicking Edit > Preferences (Flash > Preferences on Macintosh). Click the Editing tab and select Show Pen Preview. You can also select Show Precise Points, which turns your Pen icon into crosshairs for greater accuracy.
7. Like the Line Tool, if you press the Shift key, the Pen Tool is constrained to a 45 degree angle between points.

We have already practiced with the Pen Tool in FreeHand MX, but let's try the tool in Flash. You can never practice too much with this tool. Follow the steps shown in Figure 5.12 to create a coyote.

1. Start with the top of the coyote's nose by clicking and creating a short path, as shown in panel 1 of Figure 5.12.
2. Add a second piece to the path and pull out a new, slightly curved line for the back of the head and ear.

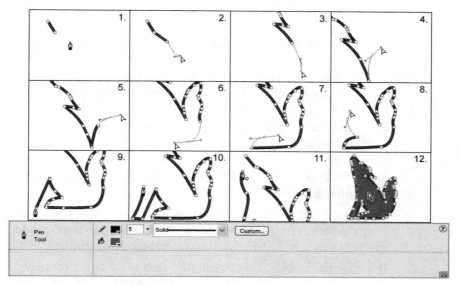

FIGURE 5.12   Creating a coyote with the Pen Tool.

3. Complete the ear by placing a point at a sharp angle from the last point. Then add a curved point for the center of the back, and place another curved point to complete the back.
4. Pull out a curved point to start the coyote's tail.
5. Place another curved point to finish the top of the tail.
6. Place three more curved points to complete the tail.
7. Place a corner point to the left to represent the extent of the rear leg and foot. Pull a curved point to complete the foot.
8. Pull another curved point to complete the stomach.
9. Place a new point for a corner for the rear of the front leg.
10. Completed the front foot with a corner point and place another point to complete the front leg.
11. Now pull up a curved path to start the bottom of the head.
12. Place the last curved point. You now have a complete shape that can be refined with the Subselection Tool. Because the coyote is a closed shape, you can add a fill.
13. Click File > Save, and save your new coyote graphic as *coyote.fla*. You will use it later.

Text Tool

The Text Tool, on the surface, seems the same as many other tools in Macromedia Studio MX 2004, but there's more here than meets the eye. The standard Text Tool, which you see across many applications, allows you to define options such as font, weight (bold), style (italic), kerning (space between letters), leading (space between lines), direction of the text, and alignment.

What sets the Text Tool in Macromedia Flash MX 2004 apart is the three types of text available: Static, Dynamic, and Input.

Static Text: Text that is not likely to change. Use it for overall text, such as title labels on the stage.

Dynamic Text: Text that will change. It is most commonly used with Action-Script to reflect results from a script. It is not always populated with text when you first create it, because you may be using programming.

Input Text: Enables users to interact with the movie as it plays. It is also used with ActionScript, often in conjunction with Dynamic Text. For example, you may have a Flash movie that can calculate a mortgage for the user. The user inputs the price of the property, the interest rate, and the term of the loan. The script calculates the result and displays it in the form of Dynamic Text.

If you wish to add accessibility to Flash movies for screen readers, you can use only Dynamic and Input Text fields. The Accessibility Panel is accessed by clicking the blue circle that contains a white, star-shaped human figure on the bottom-right corner of an expanded Dynamic or Input text field Property Inspector.

All three types of text can be formatted in terms of font, size, color weight, and so on. Figure 5.13 shows the Text Tool in different forms. The first view shows the

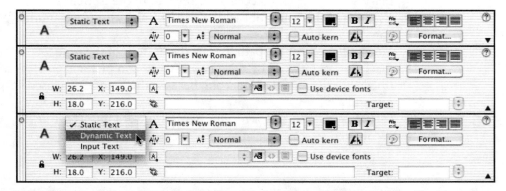

FIGURE 5.13 Different views of the Property Inspector while the Text Tool is selected.

Property Inspector collapsed to the smallest display level while the Text Tool is selected. On the bottom-right corner of the Property Inspector, you can see an arrowhead pointed downward. Clicking the arrowhead expands the Property Inspector to reveal the second view. The third view shows you where you choose the type of text to use. Dynamic and Input Text are covered more in the Action-Script section. For now, let's look at Static Text.

When you use Static Text in a Flash movie, you are actually working with vector shapes that have been grouped, which gives you more power in creation. You can break apart the text into shapes and manipulate them into a more customized look, which is especially helpful for creating a logo or new design. Note that when you do break apart the text into vector shapes, you cannot go back. This process is shown in Figure 5.14.

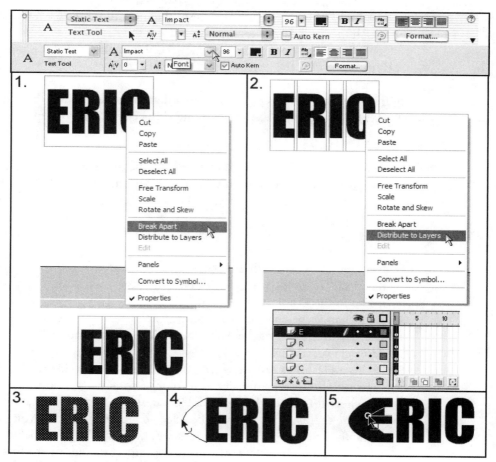

FIGURE 5.14   Using the Text Tool.

1. For the text used in the figure, the font is Impact, the color is black, and the size is 96 points. Type the word *ERIC*, and click Break Apart in the shortcut menu, accessed by right-clicking (Control + Click for Macintosh). This command causes each letter to be a separate text box.
2. Selecting Distribute to Layers from the shortcut menu will cause each letter to be on its own layer. Notice how Flash names each layer automatically according to the letter it holds. This feature was new to Macromedia Flash MX and has proven itself a handy utility, allowing quick, easy placement for animation.
3. Select Break Apart again to turn each letter into a vector shape. Because the word *ERIC* was part of one text block, you must select Break Apart twice to change it into vector shapes. If you are selecting text that has only one letter, you only need to select Break Apart once.
4. In panel 4 of Figure 5.14, you can see that now the letter *E* is a vector shape, which means it can be manipulated using the Arrow Tool. You can use either the Arrow Tool or Subselection Tool to manipulate the shapes.
5. Further modify the letter *E*.

Figure 5.15 shows another examples that demonstrates the fun that can be had with the Text Tool. For this exercise, you need the coyote we created with the Pen Tool.

1. Select the Text Tool and choose the font Webdings and a size of 400. (The Font Size slider bar goes only to 96, so you must type in the size.) On the stage, type a capital *E*. This should create a desert scene, as shown in panel 1 of Figure 5.15.
2. Now that we have a desert scene, select it and choose Break Apart on either the Modify menu or shortcut menu.
3. Next, deselect everything by clicking a blank area of the stage. Then click the circle in the sky, which will be your moon. Pick a new color for the moon in the Property Inspector.
4. Let's change the color on the cactus. Click it, and notice that it is selected along with the rest of the background. This is not quite what we want, so deselect everything.
5. Because Flash has separate strokes and fills, you can dissect the shape by drawing a line (pick an easily seen color) across the very bottom of the cactus where it touches the ground. Now deselect everything again, and then click the cactus. It should now be selected alone. If it is not, you may have made the line too short. Simply deselect everything again, click the line to select it, and press Delete on your keyboard. Then redraw the line.

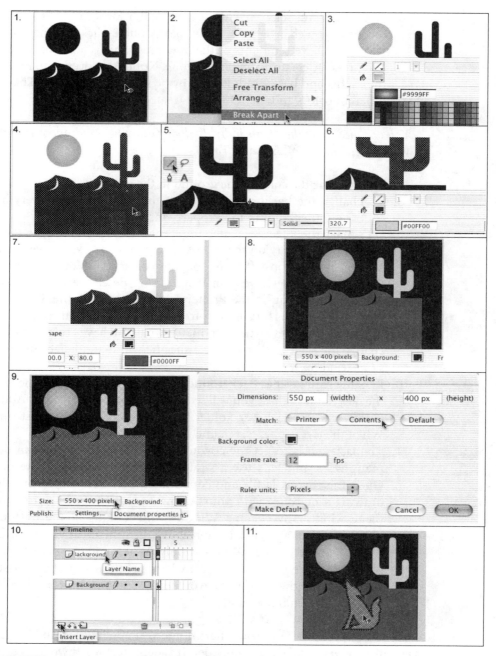

FIGURE 5.15   More fun with the Text Tool.

6. With the cactus selected, choose a new color for it in the Property Inspector. After you change the cactus's color, double-click the line and delete it. If you still have remnants of the line, press Shift + click on each of them and press Delete until they are all gone. Notice that even with the line gone, the cactus and background can now be selected separately. They are now different colors and, therefore, are treated as separate shapes.

You can also select the cactus individually by drawing a marquee around it using your pointer or one of the Lasso Tools.

7. Now change the color of the ground in the picture.
8. To change the background color of the stage, deselect everything and choose another color in the Property Inspector.
9. Let's make the stage size match the scene. Select everything on the stage by pressing Ctrl + A (Command + A on Macintosh). When everything is selected, align the top-left corner of your content with the top-left corner of the stage. Once you have aligned everything, deselect everything so you can see the Size button in the Property Inspector. Click the Size button and press the Contents button next to Match. These options provide a convenient way to size everything to match what you have created. You can also change the stage size by typing a specific width and height in the Dimensions text box.
10. Rename your layer as Background by double-clicking the name and typing the new name. Below, you will see three buttons: Insert Layer, Add Motion Guide, and Insert Layer Folder. Click Insert Layer, the first one listed. When the layer appears, rename it as Coyote.
11. The last step is to get the coyote we created earlier. You can do this in many ways, but let's use a straightforward Copy and Paste operation. Open the coyote.fla file and copy the coyote. You can easily select it by drawing a marquee with your Arrow Tool. Change back to your desert scene window by clicking Window and looking at the bottom of the menu. You can also click the tab above the timeline if you are using Windows. Tabs are, sadly, Windows only. When you are back to the desert scene, click the coyote layer to make sure it is selected and paste in the coyote. Move it wherever you would like. You now have a complete desert scene, as shown in panel 11.

As you can see, the Text Tool offers numerous possibilities, and by using your imagination, you can take it even further. It is definitely worthwhile to experiment because you can come up with many unique concepts.

Check Spelling

Macromedia Flash MX 2004 has introduced what is bound to be a welcome feature—spell-checking. It can be found on the main menu bar under the Text menu. It works in a similar manner to the tool you find in word processors, but it adds the capability to also check spelling within strings created in ActionScript.

When you run the Check Spelling tool, all text fields are examined throughout the document. Text areas can be on any frame or layer and still be checked. This is useful because, previously, users had no other option than to check their text in another application by copying and pasting; it is very difficult to keep track of where all text is when you manually go through a large movie.

Oval Tool

The Oval Tool is straightforward. You can create ovals and circles, either with or without fills and lines. (You must use either a fill or a line, but you are not required to have both.) If you want to constrain your shape to a perfect circle, hold the Shift key while using the Oval Tool. You select the stroke and fill colors either in the Color portion of the Tools Panel or within the Property Inspector. By using the Properties inspector you have the added ability to select the thickness of the stroke in addition to the type of line, as shown in Figure 5.16.

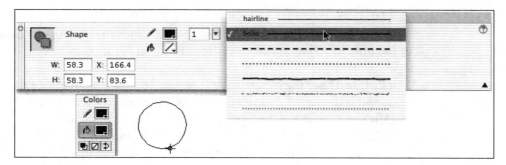

FIGURE 5.16   Using the Oval Tool.

Rectangle Tool

Using the Rectangle Tool you can to create rectangles, squares, and rounded rectangles. This tool acts in a similar manner to the Oval Tool, but it has the added option for rounded rectangles. When you create a rectangle, you can constrain it to have sharp corners by holding the Shift key during creation. If you wish to create a rounded rectangle, select the rounded rectangle button found under Options. This action opens a dialog box in which you can select how many points you want the corner to be, as shown in Figure 5.17.

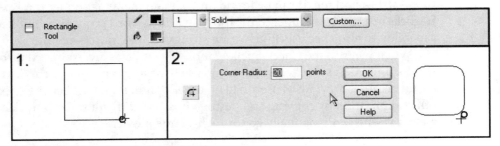

FIGURE 5.17   Using the Rectangle Tool.

When you want to create a rounded rectangle, you have to select the option before you create the shape. You cannot turn back after creation. Unlike in FreeHand MX where you can change the corner radius any time you wish, in Flash MX 2004 you must delete the shape and re-create it.

PolyStar Tool

New to Flash MX 2004 is the useful PolyStar Tool. With this tool, you can make both Polygons and Star shapes, which can prove tedious to construct by hand. Let's look at the PolyStar Tool in the procedure shown in Figure 5.18.

1. Click and hold the mouse button on the Rectangle Tool until a drop-down menu is displayed. Release the mouse button and select the PolyStar Tool. After you select the tool, you can see it reflected in the Property Inspector. Click the Options button, which opens the Tool Settings dialog box. Here you can choose the style (polygon or star), number of sides, and star point size (only available with stars).
2. Select Polygon and 5 sides. Drag the shape on the stage. As you create the shape, you can drag your mouse in any direction to rotate and size the shape during creation. When you release the mouse button, the new polygon appears on the stage, complete with the stroke and fill you had chosen.
3. Now you create a star. First, select the PolyStar Tool, and click Options in the Property Inspector. This time, you want to create a star with shorter points so set the Star point size to .70. Draw the shape on the stage.
4. Repeat the same steps shown in panel 3, but this time choose the number .30 to have much sharper points on the star.

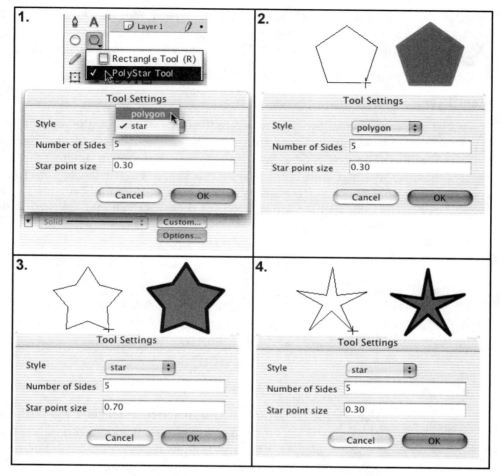

FIGURE 5.18   Using the PolyStar Tool.

Essentially, a star and a polygon are the same thing in terms of drawing on a computer—it is all peaks and valleys. The peaks are the outer points, and valleys are the areas closest to the center of a star.

When looking at a polygon shape and its sides, imagine another point in the center of each side. Now, imagine if you push that point evenly on each side toward the center. This action creates a star. Available sizes of points are determined by the height of the valley. The options range from .01 (as close to the center as the program allows) to 100, which puts you close to the height of the peaks, causing very shallow star points.

Unlike FreeHand MX, when you create a polygon or star in Flash, no further adjustments, such as number of points or sizes, are available. If you want to change the number of points or the pitch, you must delete the original shape and re-create it.

Pencil Tool

The Pencil Tool allows you to create freeform strokes on the page. It, like other drawing tools in Flash, has some neat features. You can select from three modes in Options. The first is Straighten, which modifies your input to reflect corners. Smooth modifies your input to reflect more curves. The last option, Ink, reflects your stroke as accurately as possible. As with the other tools, use the Property Inspector to choose the color and style of the stroke. The three Pencil options are shown in Figure 5.19.

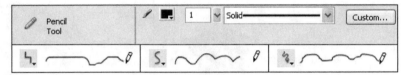

FIGURE 5.19   Using the Pencil Tool.

Brush Tool

The Brush Tool is similar to the Pencil Tool in terms of making freeform paths, but the Brush Tool creates a fill instead of a stroke. By working with fills, you not only have every color available from a stroke, but you can use gradients and bitmap fills (imported pictures) as your basis. Some prebuilt gradients are available in the Swatches Panel. The Swatches Panel is reflected in the panel itself, in the Fill Color option in the Tools Panel, and also in the Property Inspector. The gradients are shown in the bottom row of the panel shown in Figure 5.20.

Several options are available with the Brush Tool. You can pick not only what brush size and brush shape you are using but also how you want the fill applied. You can choose from 10 brush sizes and nine brush shapes. The default is the circle shape, but you can choose square or different angles, which give the brush tool an almost calligraphic effect. You can also use a graphics tablet with Flash, which causes the brush size to reflect the pressure on the tablet. The last option available is the Lock Fill option. Lock Fill causes a gradient to be applied across multiple objects rather than in each individual object. This option is shown in the bottom-right corner of Figure 5.20, along with its various options. The Brush Mode options follow:

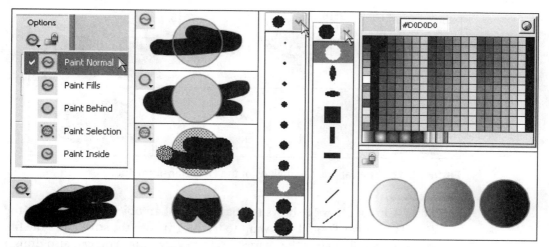

FIGURE 5.20   The Brush Tool options.

Paint Normal: Paints over everything, disregarding lines, fills, and selected shapes.

Paint Fills: Places the brushstroke (actually a freeform fill that acts like a stroke) over only fills and the stage.

Paint Behind: Paints behind all objects on the stage.

Paint Selection: Paints only within what has been selected on the stage. It can be one object, multiple objects, or even just an area within an object selected with the Lasso Tool or Arrow Tool.

Paint Inside: Paints only within the first object in which the brushstroke was started. If the brushstroke does not start within an object, it acts like Paint Behind.

Free Transform Tool

Use the Free Transform Tool to scale, rotate, and manipulate selected shapes on the stage. It is a convenient tool for manipulating objects. It was available with fewer options in Flash 5 but was buried underneath the Arrow Tool. Now with Flash MX 2004, it has been brought to the forefront with its own spot in the Tools Panel and with two extra options, Distort and Envelope. One of the best features of this tool are the actions that can be performed without selecting an extra option. Without selecting an extra option you can perform approximately 75 percent of all available options, including scaling, rotating, skewing, and distorting. The procedure for using this tool is shown in Figure 5.21.

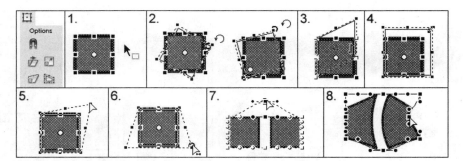

FIGURE 5.21 The various capabilities of the Free Transform Tool.

1. Panel 1 in Figure 5.21 shows the basic look of an object selected with the Free Transform Tool. If you want to transform both the stroke and the fill, you must double-click the shape to select everything. You can also draw a marquee around the object using either the Arrow Tool before choosing the Free Transform Tool, or by using the Free Transform Tool itself.

2. Rotating can be achieved whether or not the actual Rotate and Skew option is selected. If you do not have the Rotate and Skew option selected, you can rotate the object by hovering just outside a corner on the object until you see the pointer become a circular arrow. When the cursor has changed, click and move your mouse in the direction you would like the object to rotate. The principle works the same when you select the Rotate and Skew options. The only difference is that you are restricted to only rotating and skewing an object when the options are selected. A great feature of the Free Transform Tool is that when you have an object selected, you can move the pivot point of the object by moving the open circle in the center of the object. When the pivot point is moved, the object rotates around its new location.

3. Skewing can also be achieved with or without the Rotate and Skew option selected. Skewing emulates how an object appears at a slant. It is useful for creating perspectives. To skew an object, with or without the Rotate and Skew option selected, hover over a line until you see the pointer become two arrows facing in opposite directions. Drag in the direction you want the object skewed.

4. Scaling can be performed in one of two ways. If you have the Free Transform Tool with no options selected, pull on one of the square handles to size the object in the direction you move your mouse. To constrain the shape of the object as you are sizing it, hold down the Shift key. The second method is to use the Scale option. The only differences between the meth-

ods are if the Scale option is chosen, the only action you can perform is sizing, and the Shift option no longer is used to constrain. Use handles on the corners of the selected object to maintain the shape as it is resized.

5. Distorting an object is a new option in Flash MX 2004. This option allows you to perform a distortion based on one point, or a tapering effect where one end of a shape is wider than the other. Distortion can be performed with the Distort option or with modifier keys. To perform a basic distortion, either select the Distort option and pull the point you want to distort, or hold down the Ctrl key (Command on a Macintosh) with no options selected.

6. To cause a tapered effect, select either the Distort option and hold down the Shift key while pulling your point, or hold down both the Ctrl (Command on Macintosh) and Shift keys.

7. The last available option is Envelope. Envelope is a rather unique modifier. It can be used on a single object or on multiple objects. You pull on two areas. You can either adjust a point (represented by a square) or a tangent handle (represented by a circle). By pulling a point, you are physically moving a portion of the object or objects. When you adjust the tangent handle, you are changing the curve path.

8. Using the Envelope option, you can also hold down the Alt key when pulling on a tangent handle to cause the handle to be split into two. This way you can adjust only one side or the other.

Notice that when a point is moved, not only is the point affected but the entire shape or shapes are adjusted, which is useful for a more balanced deformation. It saves the time of having to pull each point.

Fill Transform Tool and Color Mixer Panel

To get a feel for the Fill Transform Tool, let's look at the Color Mixer Panel and the Library Panel. The purpose of the Fill Transform Tool is to manipulate gradient or bitmap fills. Where do we find gradient and bitmap fills? They are in two primary locations, the Color Swatches Panel and the Color Mixer Panel.

The Color Swatches Panel is simply a repository for commonly used colors and gradients. You have the options not only to use the basic colors and gradients that appear by default but to add your own, or even to change your color palette. Two types of gradient fill are available in Flash MX 2004—radial and linear. A linear gradient works in a straight line, combining colors from the left to the right or the reverse. A radial gradient has gradations coming from the center of an object in a circular pattern. Without other options, gradients would be very restrictive.

This is where the Fill Transform Tool comes in. It allows you to modify the gradients in an intuitive manner—you pull handles. Figure 5.22 shows the Fill Transform Tool used with both a radial and a linear gradient. Some of the adjustment capabilities of the tool follow:

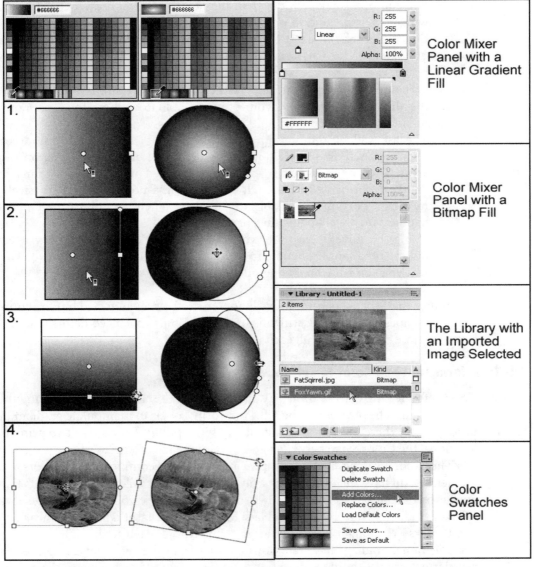

FIGURE 5.22 A look at the Fill Transform Tool, the Color Mixer Panel, the Color Swatches Panel, and the Library Panel.

1. To modify a gradient fill, you can select only an object that was not previously selected. If you have an object selected, click a blank area of the stage with the Arrow Tool (or press the Ctrl key in Windows or Command on a Macintosh to temporarily invoke it) to deselect everything. Then click the fill you want to modify with the Fill Transform Tool.
2. You can move the center point on your fill to change how the gradient flows across the image.
3. By selecting the bottom-right handle, you can rotate the direction of the gradient. This option is helpful for giving a more personalized touch to gradients. The square handle on the side of the bounding box allows you to size the gradient.
4. The effects that can be applied to a bitmap fill are similar to what can be accomplished with gradient fills with the addition of scaling and skewing the bitmap. These actions size the fill but not the object itself. If you scale the image smaller than the shape, it tiles the image.

To use a bitmap fill, you must have the image you want to work with available in the Library Panel. To get an image into the Library, click File > Import to Library. You can also use Import, but this causes a copy of the image to be placed on the stage, which may not be desirable. You can view the contents of the Library by opening the Library Panel found under the Window menu.

To apply the bitmap fill, select your current fill, then in the Color Mixer Panel select Bitmap Fill. All images currently available in the Library appear in the bottom of the panel. Use the Eyedropper Tool to select the image you want to use for the fill.

Ink Bottle Tool

The Ink Bottle Tool applies new properties to strokes. Whatever properties you have selected, including the Color, Thickness, and Style, are applied to any stroke you click. It can also be used to add a stroke to a shape that currently has only a fill. If the object was selected before you choose the Ink Bottle Tool, the new stroke is not applied. Conversely, if you don't select the object and apply the Ink Bottle Tool, it functions as expected.

Paint Bucket Tool

As the Ink Bottle Tool applies new properties to strokes, the Paint Bucket Tool applies new fills to shapes. It either changes the fill currently in the shape or adds a fill if there is none. Unlike the Ink Bottle Tool, you can change a fill on an object that is currently selected.

You can also use the added options of Don't Close Gaps, which disallows a fill to be applied to a shape that does not have a stroke completely closed; Close Small Gaps; Close Medium Gaps; and Close Large Gaps, which allow you to have gaps in the shape closed and the fill to be applied, regardless.

Eyedropper Tool

The Eyedropper Tool allows you to select a stroke or fill properties to apply to other shapes. Let's look at this tool in Figure 5.23.

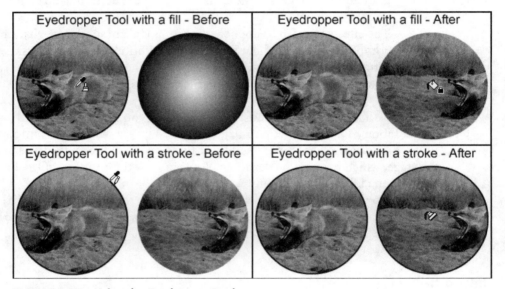

FIGURE 5.23   Using the Eyedropper Tool.

When you use the Eyedropper Tool and select a fill on an object, the icon changes into the Paint Bucket Tool. You can then apply the fill properties you have selected to another object using the Paint Bucket Tool. The Eyedropper Tool works in the same manner when a stroke is selected, except it turns into the Ink Bottle Tool instead.

Eraser Tool

The Eraser Tool works much like the Brush Tool but in reverse. Instead of adding color to a page, it takes it away from shapes on the stage.

You can choose from multiple shapes and sizes for the Eraser Tool. These options are shown in Figure 5.24.

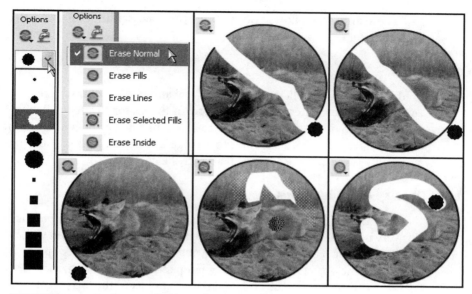

FIGURE 5.24 Options available with the Eraser Tool.

The Faucet: Completely erases a selected stroke or fill. This tool can be handy when applied to a stroke. By default, when you select a portion of a stroke with the Arrow Tool, if the stroke is not around an oval, it selects only the segment. You must double-click the stroke to select it all. With the Faucet tool, just click the stroke and it all disappears.

Erase Normal: Erases fills and strokes indiscriminately.

Erase Fills: Erases only fills.

Erase Lines: Erases only lines.

Erase Selected Fills: Erases a fill or a section of a fill that has been selected with the Arrow Tool or Lasso Tool.

Erase Inside: Erases only inside the object that was first selected.

View Tools

The View Tools include the Zoom Tool and Hand Tool. The Zoom Tool zooms in and out of the stage. You can use it in multiple ways. If you draw a rectangle around the selection with the Zoom Tool, the area fills the viewable area. When the Zoom Tool is selected, you can choose from the Enlarge and Reduce options. You can also press the Alt or Option key to switch to the opposite function temporarily.

The Hand Tool allows you to move the stage without affecting the placement of objects on the stage.

Colors Tools

Within the Tools Panel, you can select a fill and stroke color for creation and application to objects. These colors come from the Color Swatches Panel. The Colors tools also provide some options within the panel. You can change the colors to black and white, press a shortcut to change a selection to none, and press another shortcut to reverse the current fill and stroke colors.

Object Overlap Considerations

One last topic that must be considered in Flash is how it treats shapes that are created; it is very unusual in this matter. In Fireworks, every object created will, by default, be on its own layer. This arrangement prevents any issues with overlapping of objects. In FreeHand, the objects are completely independent. With Flash, each stroke and fill is treated as a different object, and if you overlap objects, the top object cuts out the underlying object. Let's look at the way shapes are handled in Figure 5.25.

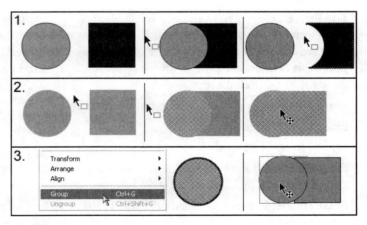

FIGURE 5.25   Shape issues with Flash.

1. In panel 1 of Figure 5.25, you have created two shapes, a circle and a square. Next we move the circle over the square and deselected everything by clicking a blank area of the stage with the Arrow Tool. Now, move the circle back off of the square. You can see that the square has a piece cut out of it. Notice how the stroke has also been cut. Whichever shape is selected is the cutting shape.

2. In panel 2, we have deleted the strokes on both objects and changed the fills to the same shade of gray. Next, move the circle over the square. Then, deselect everything and click the shape. Notice how the shapes have been combined? This is a feature with Flash MX 2004. If fills are the same color, they are combined into one object when overlapped.

3. Convert the circle shape into a group by clicking Modify > Group or Ctrl + G (Command + G on Macintosh). When an object or objects have been grouped, they do not affect other objects and are not affected themselves. This characteristic also applies to text. You can recognize a group by the light blue rectangle around it and its identification in the Property Inspector when it is selected.

Find and Replace Tool

Flash MX 2004 introduces a powerful enhancement with the Find and Replace Tool. This incredible tool can really make life easier. What if the vice president, whose name is listed all over your Flash movie, is replaced? With the Find and Replace Tool, you can rectify the situation using just one tool.

The Find and Replace Tool is found under Edit on the main menu bar. It offers numerous options. You can find and replace not only text but also fonts, colors, symbols, sounds, and even videos and bitmaps.

You have many choices as to how you search. You can look for whole words, words that match the case of your search term, and regular expressions. These options filter the search to a great degree. For example, you may need to replace Smith with Jones at the Smithsonian. By choosing Whole Words, you replace only Smith and don't wind up with the Jonessonian.

The one consideration when using this tool is its power. Performing a Replace operation without really checking your parameters can cause serious issues. For example, let's say someone used the letter *o* to act as open bullets. You copy what you think to be a bullet character and choose to replace it with nothing. This action would cause every word in the document with an *o* to be changed.

SUMMARY

We have now explored some of the history of Macromedia Flash MX 2004. It has grown from software used to create small animations on the Internet to a full-fledged application builder that creates a dominant file format. And with the introduction of Flash MX 2004, it can now be used as a full-blown IDE (Integrated Development Environment), putting designers and developers together again.

Designers can focus on the look and feel of an application while developers handle the backend, all in the same application.

We have also explored the use of the Tools Panel and can see that you have numerous ways to draw with the program. Although some of the tools may be trimmed down, it by no means limits creativity.

Now that we know how to use the basic drawing tools, you can start to learn how to create animations by working with "Tweens and Layers."

6 Tweens and Layers

Now that we have gotten a feel for the drawing tools, let's explore animation with Macromedia Flash MX 2004. With animation, we see the Timeline broken down yet again into frames and layers. Frames represent time passage, and layers represent content placement. This becomes especially blurry when dealing with animation: when we talk about moving an object on the stage, we are speaking of something created on the stage, yet we still must focus on the frames to show the passage of time for the animation itself.

The very root of animation is frame-by-frame animation. You may be familiar with this already and not realize it. Children frequently decorate the top corner of a book with doodles to create a cartoon. On each page is a drawing similar to the previous one but with slight modifications. These modifications create the appearance of movement when the book pages are flipped. Margin doodles are essentially a frame-by-frame animation, the root of all animation. This principle is examined in the following section.

FRAME-BY-FRAME ANIMATION

In this style of animation, each film cell is drawn showing movement as it is played. The example of a bouncing ball is shown in Figure 6.1.

1. First, name the layer *ball* by double-clicking Layer 1.
2. Next, create a circle shape (by holding down the Shift key and using the Oval Tool) on the stage with a black outline and red fill. A keyframe is created automatically when we create content on the frame.
3. Now select the next frame and create a keyframe. You can do this in three ways: right-click (Control + click on Macintosh) and select Insert keyframe; click Insert > Timeline > keyframe; or press the F6 key. Any of these methods creates a keyframe in the movie.

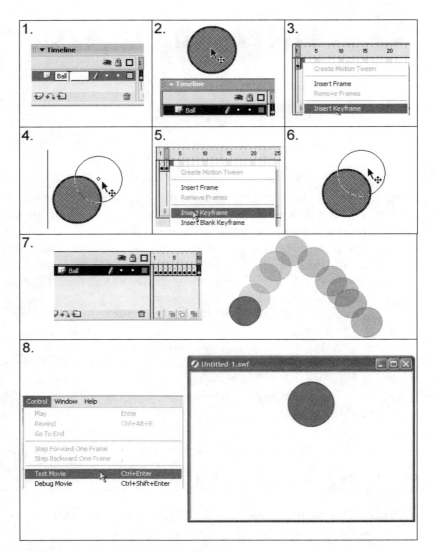

FIGURE 6.1 Frame-by-frame animation.

4. Now move the object to the next location, above and to the right of the original location. Remember, we must double-click the shape to select both the stroke and fill before moving it.
5. Insert another keyframe, this time at Frame 3.
6. Move the object again.

7. Continue creating keyframes and moving the object until we have 10 keyframes showing the movement from the bottom-left of the stage up to the top-center, and back down to the bottom-right. This series of frames simulates a bouncing ball.

8. When you complete the animation, click Control > Test Movie or Ctrl + Enter (Command + Return on Macintosh) to view the movie in the Flash Player. If you are using a Macintosh, you may need to save the movie before you play it. Windows does not require that you save the movie.

You have now created your first frame-by-frame animation, a practice with over 100 years of history. One of the first individuals credited with creating animation was Winsor McCay with his breakthrough film *Gertie the Dinosaur*. He created this film by drawing an image on a chalkboard, taking a picture of it, and then changing the drawing before taking another picture. You will notice that this is a very time-intensive procedure. Not only that, but it appears somewhat choppy when it is played. In the first animations, everything was drawn over and over again. If you look at most animations, not everything in the movie is moving at all times. For example, if you have a house and a cat, as shown in Figure 6.2, you can

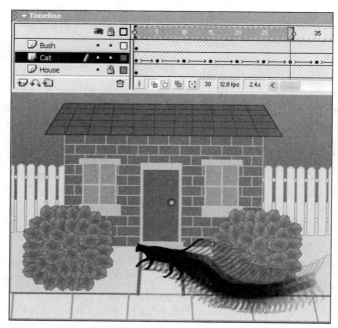

FIGURE 6.1   A look at movement in an animation and layers.

see that the house and yard are not moving while the cat is moving. Using the original frame-by-frame animation method, the animator is drawing not only the cat but also the background over and over.

The next innovation in the world of animation, cel animation, was invented by Earl Hurd. This technique involves painting characters or moveable objects on clear sheets of plastic and then laying the sheets carefully over a prepainted background before photographing them. This method is like using layers in Flash. Layers are stacked on top of one another, representing the order of visibility of the objects seen. This practice enables you to create movies using cel animation concepts.

Using layers when creating animations still proves tedious and increases your file size tremendously. If you use frame-by-frame animation, the objects on the stage must be completely created as the playhead hits the keyframe. This may seem to be a minor problem, but consider that this happens 12 times a second at the default frame rate. Imagine a higher frame rate. Flash helps you deal with this challenge by offering the method of motion tweening.

MOTION TWEENING

Flash uses a process known as motion tweening to add smooth motion and small file size to movement in an animation. The concept of tweening has its roots in animation history as a cost-cutting method.

As costs began to rise and animations grew in length, some sort of assembly line procedure had to take place to turn out productions at a quicker rate. This issue was essentially handled by building animation teams. The teams had lead animators and several junior animators. The lead animators drew the principle content in the form of keyframes.

A keyframe would be something significant, such as a pose or the entrance of a character. For example, if a character is moving across a room, the lead animators would draw the character at different stages in its travels but would not cover what happened between those points. The junior animators then drew all the frames in between the keyframes. This practice led to the nickname of tweeners for the junior animators, as well as cost savings for the studios.

With tweening in Flash, the program becomes your cheap labor pool, and you are the lead animator. Two forms of tweening can be used in Flash: Motion and Shape. A Motion tween involves creating a symbol, group, or text block on one keyframe and moving it to the next location in another keyframe several frames away. Flash then creates the frames in between. Multiple ways are available to create a Motion tween.

Motion Tween: First Example

The most commonly used method of Motion tweening is shown in Figure 6.3.

1. Create a new Flash movie by clicking File > New or by pressing Ctrl + N (Command + N on Macintosh). Remember to save the movie if you are using a Macintosh. Next, name the layer *BlueBall* by double-clicking Layer 1. (Layer 1 is created by default when a new movie is opened.) Then pick a

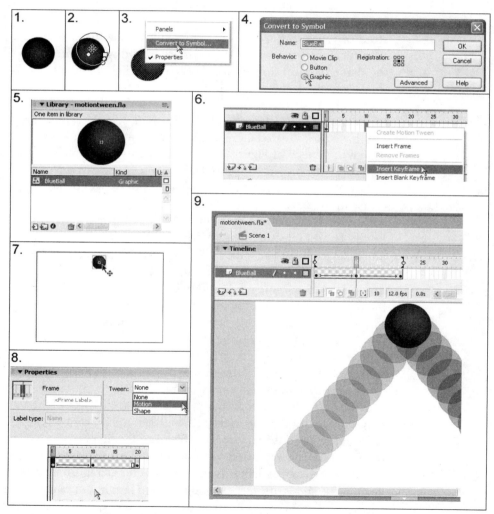

FIGURE 6.3 First example of creating a Motion tween.

black line and the default blue-to-black gradient available in the Colors portion of the Tool Panel. Last, create a perfect circle by selecting the Oval Tool and holding down the Shift key while drawing the circle.

2. Because we are creating a ball, we want to adjust the gradient to make it appear more three-dimensional. To do this, select the Fill Transform Tool and move the gradient up and to the right to make it appear as if a light source is present.

3. To create a Motion tween, the shape must be a symbol (such as a movie clip, button, or graphic), or a grouped object. Turning the shape into a symbol allows Flash to move the same symbol throughout the frames instead of redrawing the object, which allows the file size to remain small. You can convert a shape into a symbol in two ways. You can double-click the shape to select the stroke and fill, right-click (Control + click on Macintosh), and select Convert to Symbol. You can also click Insert > Convert to Symbol, which opens the Convert to Symbol dialog box.

4. In the dialog box, name the object *BlueBall*, select Graphic, and click OK.

5. You have now created a graphic symbol that is available in the Library, as shown in panel 5 of Figure 6.3. When a symbol is created, it is available in the Library for use in your movie. Each occurrence of a symbol is called an instance. You can add multiple instances of a symbol with very little increase in file size.

6. Next, create a keyframe by right-clicking (Control + click on Macintosh) Frame 10 and selecting Insert keyframe. You can also click Insert > Timeline > keyframe or press the F6 key. Remember, keyframes are where a significant change occurs, be it an introduction or a significant change. You must place a keyframe on Frame 10 to reflect the ball in its second location, the top of the stage, and again on Frame 20 for its final location.

7. Move the BlueBall graphic symbol to reflect the changes in the movie. First, select the keyframe on Frame 10 by clicking it, and move the symbol to the top-center of the stage. Next, select the keyframe on Frame 20, and move it to the bottom-right of the stage.

8. You have now completed your work as the lead animator and need to give an assignment to the junior animator, Flash. First, click any of the frames in the first sequence of the ball in its path between the bottom-left and top-center areas of the stage. When we have a frame or the first keyframe selected, go to the Property Inspector and select Motion from the drop-down menu that appears next to the label Tween. This action creates an arrow between keyframe 1 and keyframe 10 showing that Flash has drawn all the frames in between. Repeat the same procedure between keyframe 10 and keyframe 20 (or on the keyframes themselves), which gives you your second arrow.

9. The animation is now complete. You can now view it working on the stage itself by pressing the Enter or Return key, or you can view it in the Flash Player by pressing Ctrl + Enter (Command + Return on a Macintosh). You can also select these options on the Control menu by clicking Control > Play to see it on the stage, or Control > Test Movie to view it in the Flash Player. Viewing the animation in the Flash Player gives you the advantage of seeing it looped (repeated continuously) by default. If you want to see it looped when it plays on the stage, select Control > Loop Playback and press the Esc key to stop playback when you are finished.

Motion Tween: Second Example

In the first example, not only did you not have to create every frame, the playback was much smoother. In addition to these advantages, the file size is much smaller. However, you do have an alternate method to creating a Motion tween that can actually be considered more efficient in many cases. The process of creating the same Motion tween using the new method is shown in Figure 6.4.

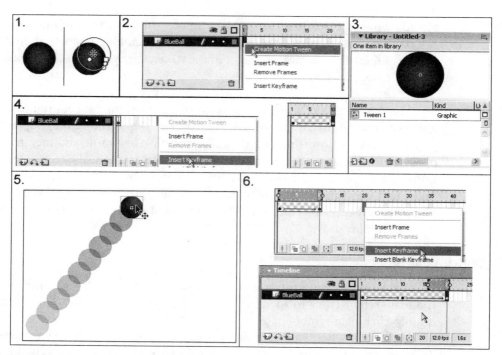

FIGURE 6.4 Another method to create a Motion tween.

1. Create a new movie by clicking File > New or by pressing Ctrl + N (Command + N on Macintosh). Again, remember to save the movie if you are using a Macintosh. Again, create a perfect circle with a black line and blue gradient fill, and move the gradient to make the ball look more three-dimensional. Name the layer *BlueBall*.
2. This time, we are not going to create a graphic symbol; we are going to let Flash do it for you. Right-click (Control + click on Macintosh) the automatically created keyframe on Frame 1. You can also use the option Insert > Create Motion Tween on the main menu. However, you *cannot* use the Property Inspector to create a Motion tween using this method.
3. Flash must have a symbol to create a Motion tween. A shape cannot be tweened. Because we have not created a symbol, the program creates it for us calling it Tween 1. (Each automatically created graphic symbol from a Motion tween is named Tween <n>). The symbol can now be seen in the Library. You can change its name, for clarity, by double-clicking the name of the object in the Library and typing the new name.
4. Now, we are going to insert a new keyframe on Frame 10. After we have done this, an arrow appears between the keyframes on Frame 1 and Frame 10.
5. Move the ball to its second location on the top-center of the screen.
6. Finish the animation by inserting a keyframe on Frame 20 and moving BlueBall to the bottom-right of the stage. After you have completed this action, test the movie.

The advantages of this procedure over the previous procedure are the speed and ease of creation. In this procedure, you can skip creating the graphic symbol yourself, and the flow is more logical. By creating a keyframe and then moving the object before creating the next keyframe, you can more easily keep track of locations. If you create all the keyframes first, you must move the object from its origin in the first keyframe. When you create, move, and create again, you are moving the object from its previous location. This movement is sometimes easier to keep track of in a complex movie.

Watch Your Modes

One of the most common problems that happens to users new to the program is the inadvertent entry to the Symbol- or Group-Editing mode. This is caused by double-clicking a symbol or grouped object.

By default, when a shape's fill is clicked, only the fill is selected, not the stroke. To overcome this, double-clicking the fill in a shape causes both the fill and the stroke to be selected. As a result, designers are in the habit of double-clicking shapes to move them around the stage.

Where the trouble comes is if an object is either a symbol or group. When this is the case, not only is the item selected but you enter a whole new window—Symbol-Editing mode. You can still see everything on the stage, which has faded in the background, but you are on a whole different timeline. This situation is shown in Figure 6.4, using the previously created bouncing ball Motion tween.

If you look at the main timeline view in Figure 6.4, you see the BlueBall symbol is selected. The easy way to recognize that it is a symbol is the blue square around it. (Graphic is also displayed in the Property Inspector.) The timeline shows all of the frames in addition to the arrows symbolizing the tween. The layer name is also correct in showing BlueBall.

Now, look at the Symbol-Editing view in Figure 6.5, and see what happened when BlueBall was double-clicked. Instead of a blue square around BlueBall, it is covered with tiny dots. All of the frames seem to have vanished, and the layer name is now Layer 1. You are in a different place than you were before.

At the top of the timeline, you see a breadcrumb with a Graphic Symbol icon and BlueBall label. This breadcrumb is where Flash tells you your current location within the movie. If you are in Symbol-Editing mode by mistake, click the breadcrumb labeled Scene 1, and you will return to the main timeline.

Always watch where you are in the movie. Being in the wrong location while creating effects and graphics can cause a great deal of confusion.

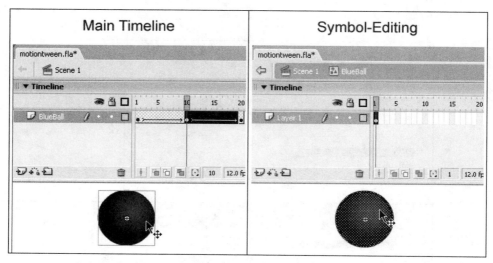

FIGURE 6.5   Accidentally entering the Symbol-Editing mode.

Adding Motion Guides

So far, we have created Motion tweens that move a graphic symbol from one location to another. The only problem with what we have learned so far is that your objects must move in a straight path. This is an issue because objects don't always travel in a straight path. Life is just not that way. Flash uses motion guides to help with this issue. When you create a layer with a motion guide, your object in the tween can be constrained to the path.

You will create another animation, this time using motions guides to control the paths, as shown in Figure 6.6.

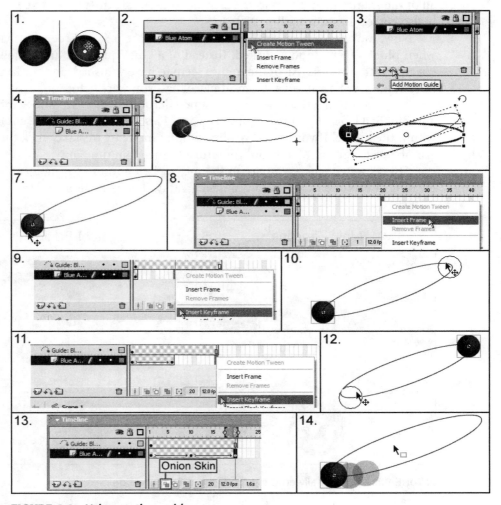

FIGURE 6.6   Using motion guides.

1. Create a new movie and save it as *atoms.fla*. Rename the layer to *Blue Atom*. Now create another perfect circle with the blue radial gradient fill but with no stroke. Shift the gradient up and to the right again.

2. Now, we need to create your tween. Use the second method for speed. Right-click the keyframe on Frame 1 and select Create Motion Tween. It is a good idea to name your graphic symbol now; call it *Blue Atom*.

3. Now you need to add a motion guide because Blue Atom should move along an elliptical path. To add a motion guide, you must make sure you have selected the layer that has the tween to be affected. After it is selected, add a motion guide by pressing the Add Motion Guide button underneath the layers.

4. After you have created a motion guide, a new layer is created above the current layer with a new icon. The label Guide: Blue Atom is also added. The Blue Atom layer itself has been indented, showing it is influenced by the new Motion Guide layer.

5. Now that we have created the guide layer, you must create the motion guide itself. In this case, it is going to be an elliptical path, so use the Oval Tool to create an ellipse.

6. You want Blue Atom to travel on an elliptical path, but the whole path should be at an angle. Use the Free Transform Tool to rotate the oval to an angle.

7. With the path created, notice that when you click your graphic symbol, it snaps to the path by default.

8. Before we insert the next keyframe for your tweened layer, you must resolve an issue with the Guide layer. When you insert another keyframe in the tweened layer, the guide disappears because you are at a new point in time. You must tell the program that the guide will be present in the movie and for how long, and you do this through frames. You are going to have a 20-frame animation. You need the guide to be there for all frames, but we don't need the guide to be drawn more than once. Putting a keyframe on Frame 20 to cover the spread would be a waste because Flash would have to draw your oval twice. Although this is a minor problem with a small movie, it adds up over the long run in terms of file size. What we do is insert a frame by right-clicking (Control + click on Macintosh) on Frame 20 and selecting Insert Frame. This command essentially tells Flash to continue showing the oval through Frame 20 but to not redraw it.

9. Now we can start moving the Blue Atom around its axis. Insert a keyframe on Frame 10 for the first half of the path.

10. Move the Blue Atom around the guide to the halfway point.

11. Insert a keyframe for the final destination in the animation at Frame 20.

12. Now move the Blue Atom to just shy of the starting point. You don't want to have it stopped before the starting point because that causes a brief pause on playback of the movie when Blue Atom doesn't move for two frames.
13. Now to check that the Blue Atom is moving correctly on the path (clockwise in this case) you use a process called onion skinning to preview what is happening in adjacent frames. Two types of onion skins are available for use: onion skins that look like faded objects on other frames, and onion skin outlines that show only the outline.
14. You can now see what the animation looks like with onion skins—it is moving in the correct direction. If the onion skins were coming from the other direction, we could move the Blue Atom closer to its previous point until we see the onion skins reflect the correct direction. Do the same procedure with the keyframe on Frame 10 to check the halfway point.

Although this Flash movie is titled atoms.fla, *it is by no means an accurate representation of atoms found in nature. You are just making it for fun.*

NOTE

When we play the movie by clicking Control > Test Movie (or Ctrl + Enter or Command + Return), you see Blue Atom traveling in an elliptical path. Notice the guide does not appear; it is a guide, not an object to be seen. This animation is going well, but, in the case of a stylized atom, we want to see the axis. You must add one, which is shown Figure 6.7.

1. Because we want to add a visible axis to the movie but cannot have any other object on a layer where a tween occurs, you must add another layer by selecting the Guide: Blue Atom layer and clicking the New Layer button. Name this new layer *Blue Axis*. Notice how Flash automatically creates a keyframe on Frame 1 and a frame on Frame 20 for you. This occurs because the rest of the movie is 20 frames long, and Flash creates new layers to span the length of the movie.
2. Now that we have a new layer that covers the whole length of the movie, you must have a visible axis. You want it to appear as if Blue Atom is traveling around an actual axis so it must be the exact same size and placement as the guide. Rather than trying to create a perfect duplicate, just copy the guide itself by right-clicking (Control + click on Macintosh) the guide. You can also use the Edit menu or Ctrl + C (Command + C on Macintosh).
3. Now move to the new layer and select the empty keyframe by clicking it. After you select the empty keyframe, paste your content on the stage. It is very important when you move the mouse to the stage area that you don't

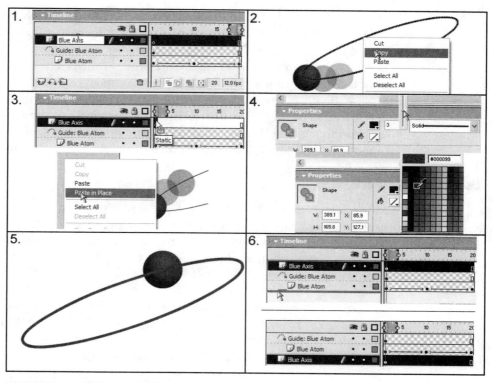

FIGURE 6.7   Adding a visible axis to the animation.

accidentally click any object, including the stage. If you do, you inadvertently change to the layer of the object you have clicked and can potentially break the animation by pasting into the wrong layer. It is a good idea to move the mouse just off the stage, right-click (Control + click on Macintosh), and select Paste in Place. Be certain to select Paste in Place, not just Paste. Paste does not place the oval in the same location. Be certain to double-check your keyframe when you are done. It should become a solid circle in the frame. If it does not, repeat the process.

If you really struggle in keeping the current layer selected, use Edit > Paste in Place instead of right-clicking (Control + click on Macintosh) to overcome the issue.

TIP

4. Now we are going to modify the axis to make it fit better in the movie. Change the thickness of the stroke to 5, and the color to a deep blue (RGB #000099).

5. When we test the movie in the Flash Player, we can see that the axis is visible and looks in proportion to Blue Atom, but there is still an issue. The top of Blue Atom doesn't look right.

6. Solve the overlap issue by changing the order of the layers. Click the Blue Axis layer and drag it to just below the Blue Atom layer. You must move the mouse slightly to the left as you are moving it down or you will place it as a layer affected by the Guide: Blue Atom layer when it should be an equal, not a subordinate, layer. If you accidentally wind up with it indented, just drag it to the left to move it back out. Now you can save and test the movie.

Using Layer Folders

A new feature available in Flash MX 2004 is the ability to use layer folders. As movies grow in complexity, you can wind up with a lot of layers. It is not unheard of to have 50-plus layers. This number of layers makes it difficult to see exactly what you are doing as you scroll up and down to find the layer you need. Let's insert a Layer folder into the project, as shown in Figure 6.8.

1. Underneath the layers, press the Insert Layer Folder button. You can also click Insert > Layer Folder, or right-click (Control + click on Macintosh) and select Insert Folder.

2. After you have inserted the folder, double-click the name and rename it *Blue Atom*.

3. Now drag your layers into the folder. Click a layer, hold down your mouse button, and drag over the folder until you see a shadowed Folder icon appear. When you see the icon appear, release the mouse button to drop the layer.

If you want to move a layer that is controlled by a motion guide, move the motion guide layer itself, which moves both layers at the same time. If you move the guided layer instead, you can break the association, which might lead to undesired results.

TIP

4. When you have moved all layers into the folder, collapse the folder by clicking the downward-facing triangle.

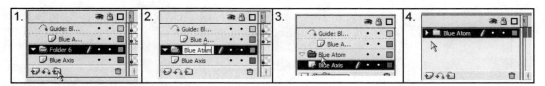

FIGURE 6.8 Inserting a Layer folder.

Finishing the Movie

Now we have your movie with a basic Blue Atom spinning along an elliptical path. You can modify the movie some more by creating a Red Atom traveling in the other direction, as shown in Figure 6.9.

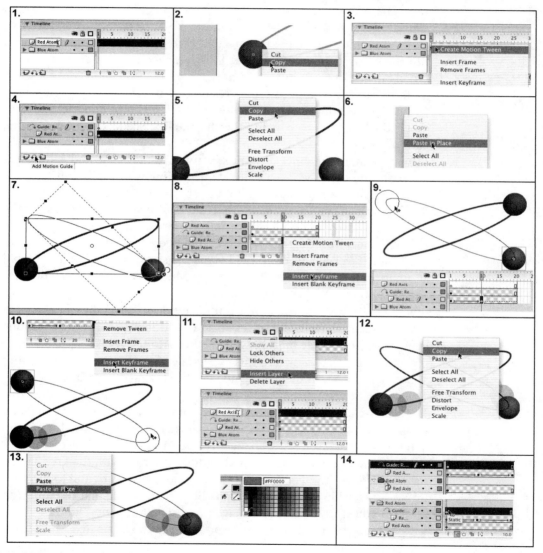

FIGURE 6.9   Finishing the movie.

1. Create a new layer by selecting the Blue Atom folder and clicking the Insert New Layer button. Name the new layer *Red Atom.*
2. For this layer you need a red circle shape identical in size and shape to the Blue Atom. Fortunately, you can copy the contents of the Blue Atom to be the basis of Red Atom. You cannot copy the Blue Atom graphic symbol; you must have the shape it was created from so we can change the color later. The way we can get this is by double-clicking Blue Atom, which opens the object in Symbol-Editing mode. You can see that you are in this mode by looking above the timeline. Next to Scene 1, you see Blue Atom with the graphic symbol icon next to it. This icon indicates that you are actually inside of the symbol and have left your scene. Now, double-click the Blue Atom shape to select it. Then copy the shape by right-clicking (Control + click on Macintosh), pressing Ctrl or Command + C, or clicking Edit > Copy. After copying the shape, click Scene 1 to return to the main timeline.
3. Within the main timeline, click the empty keyframe in the Red Atom layer and paste the shape you have just copied. Now, while it is still selected, choose the Red radial gradient fill on the bottom of the available colors in the fill colors in the Properties inspector. You now have the basis for the Red Atom; now you just need to make it move. Right-click (Control + click on a Macintosh) on keyframe 1 on the Red Atom layer and select Create Motion Tween. This command turns the shape into a graphic symbol automatically and prepares the layer for a Motion tween. You can now rename the object as *Red Atom* in the Library.
4. As with the Blue Atom, you need a motion guide to reflect the elliptical path on which the Red Atom will travel, so add a Motion Guide layer by clicking the Add Motion Guide button while the Red Atom layer is selected.
5. Now, we need a guide to use that is in scale with the current Blue Atom guide. Just click the Blue Atom guide on the stage and copy it.
6. Now select the empty keyframe in the Guide: Red Atom layer. Just off-stage, right-click (Control + click on a Macintosh) and select Paste in Place. Again, make certain that you watch what layer is selected. If you have issues with the selected layer being changed, click Edit > Paste in Place instead.
7. While the new guide is still selected, modify its angle with the Free Transform Tool. Select the Tool and rotate the guide downward and to the right until it is placed in a position with the Blue Atom guide that resembles an *X.* When you click the Red Atom, it should snap to the new guide.
8. Because the guide is in place, we are prepared to move the Red Atom itself. Insert a keyframe at Frame 10.

9. Move the Red Atom to approximately halfway around the guide. This time we want the movement to be counterclockwise so it won't appear to collide with Blue Atom. You may want to turn on the onion skins to be certain of the path.
10. Insert a keyframe at Frame 20 and move the Red Atom to just shy of the starting point.
11. Now we need to add the last item to the stage, the visible Red Axis. Remember, the guide is not visible after publication. Make sure the Guide: Red Atom layer is selected, then create a new layer using the Insert Layer button. Rename the layer as *Red Axis*.
12. We will copy the guide we are using for the Red Atom as our basis for a new axis.
13. Now make sure the empty keyframe on the Red Axis layer is selected and Paste in Place. After the guide is pasted (the keyframe will display a solid circle), you must change the properties of the axis. Give the axis a stroke height of 5 and color of red (you choose the shade) in the Property Inspector.
14. The last step is to create a second Layer folder by using the Insert Layer Folder button. Rename the folder as *Red Atom* and drag the layers related to Red Atom into the folder. If you drag in the Red Axis folder first and then the Guide: Red Atom layer, you do not need to worry about the layer order; it will resolve itself. Now save and test the movie.

Refining Motion Tweens

Many options are available with a Motion tween. Figure 6.10 shows the use of text as a Motion tween. If you want to use multiple characters individually, click Edit > Break Apart followed by Edit > Distribute to Layers. Let's make the Motion tween shown in Figure 6.10.

1. First create a letter. In the figure, *E* is used, but you can use any letter you like. Select a sans serif font, a size of 96, and the color black. Name this layer *Letter*.
2. Now that we have created the letter, change the layer to reflect a Motion tween by selecting the keyframe and choosing Motion from the Tween drop-down menu in the Property Inspector.
3. Next, click the Insert Motion Guide button to create the Guide: Letter layer.
4. On the new Motion Guide layer, use the Pen Tool to add a path for the letter to follow.
5. For the guide to be visible for the entire animation, insert a frame on Frame 20.

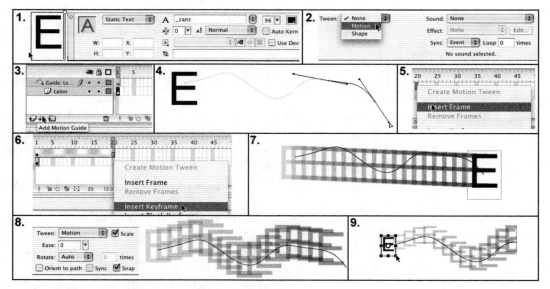

FIGURE 6.10 Modifying Motion tween attributes.

6. Now add a keyframe to Frame 20 on the Letter layer.
7. Within the keyframe on Frame 20, move the letter to the end point of the path. If you test the movie now, you will see that the letter just travels in a straight line from start to finish; it is not following the guide.
8. For the letter to follow the guide, select the keyframe on Frame 1 and click Snap in the Property Inspector. This option causes the item being tweened to snap to the path. Repeat the procedure with the keyframe on Frame 20.
9. You are not limited to only movement with a Motion tween; you can also scale, rotate, skew, and even change color of an item (only with symbols). In this step, use the Free Transform Tool and select the letter in the keyframe on Frame 1. Scale the letter down to a much smaller size. You can see that the letter get larger as it moves across the screen when tested.

In Figure 6.11, a movie involving a sled is shown. You are going to use a Motion tween, with further options to assist you with its path of travel. Let's create the first half of the movie in Figure 6.11.

1. We first draw the sled. It is made up of two red lines with a stroke thickness of 10, one on top and the other on the bottom. Add eight black lines with a stroke thickness of 5 to act as the supports in the middle. After completing our sled, select the entire shape and name the layer *Sled*.

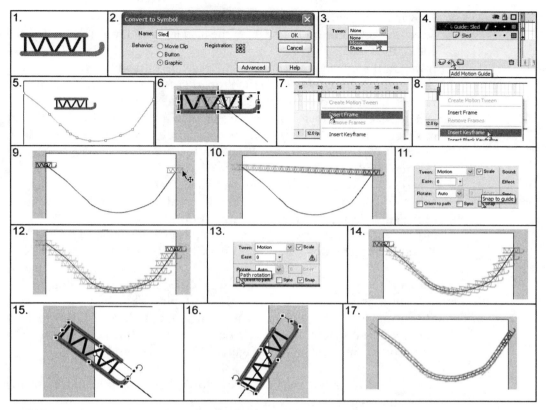

FIGURE 6.11 Creating a sled movie using a Motion tween.

2. You now convert the sled into a symbol either by right-clicking (Control + click on a Macintosh) and selecting Convert to Symbol, or clicking Insert > Convert to Symbol. In the Convert to Symbol dialog box, name the symbol *Sled* and click Graphic before clicking OK.

3. Now select the keyframe in Frame 1 and click Motion from the drop-down menu in the Property Inspector.

4. With the keyframe selected, click the Add Motion Guide button.

5. Within the keyframe on Frame 1 of the Guide: Sled layer, draw the guide to look like a slope that comes from the upper-left corner of the stage and dips and rises to the upper-right corner of the stage.

6. Use the Free Transform Tool to scale down the sled. This action makes the sled more in proportion to the hill.

7. The guide must be available for all 20 frames of the movie, so insert a frame on Frame 20 on the Guide: Sled layer.

8. Now insert a keyframe on Frame 20 on the Sled layer.
9. Select the keyframe on Frame 20 in the Sled layer and move the sled to the end of the guide.
10. If we test the movie now, the sled will travel in a straight line.
11. By selecting the Snap option in the Property Inspector for the keyframes on Frames 1 and 20, you cause the sled to travel along the guide.
12. When we test the movie now, you see that the sled does travel the path, but it is facing in the same direction the entire time, which doesn't look right.
13. Select Orient to Path in the Property Inspector for the keyframes on Frames 1 and 20.
14. The sled is now starting to orient itself to the path but needs some help.
15. Select the sled in the keyframe on Frame 1 and rotate it to match the angle of the guide using the Free Transform Tool.
16. Now select the keyframe on Frame 20 and rotate the sled again.
17. When we test the movie now, we can see that the sled follows the guide.

In Figure 6.11, we created a sled and then modified its movement along a motion guide. It now appears to be traveling along a typical sledding path. You now will modify the movie to complete the scene. You must complete the hill so that the sled appears less like a spacecraft. You also must further refine the movement to make it more convincing. Let's look at Figure 6.12 to see the process.

1. You first need the line visible so it can form the basis of the hill. Copy the stroke that is forming the guide.
2. While the Guide: Sled layer is still selected, click the Insert Layer button to create a new layer. Name this layer *Hill*.
3. While the empty keyframe on Frame 1 of the Hill layer is selected, position the pointer just off the stage, right-click (Control + click on a Macintosh), and select Paste in Place.
4. After you paste the stroke to the Hill layer, change its attributes to have a stroke thickness of 5 and a color of pale gray or white.
5. Next, you need to have a fill for the hill. Use the Line Tool to create a line going from the top-right of the hill to the bottom-right corner of the stage. Continue the line from the bottom-right corner to the bottom-left corner of the stage, making certain that the lines are actually connected. Then draw a third line that connects the bottom-left corner of the stage to the top-left of the hill.

Start on the right side of the stage to prevent inadvertently clicking the sled and dropping the line on the wrong layer.

TIP

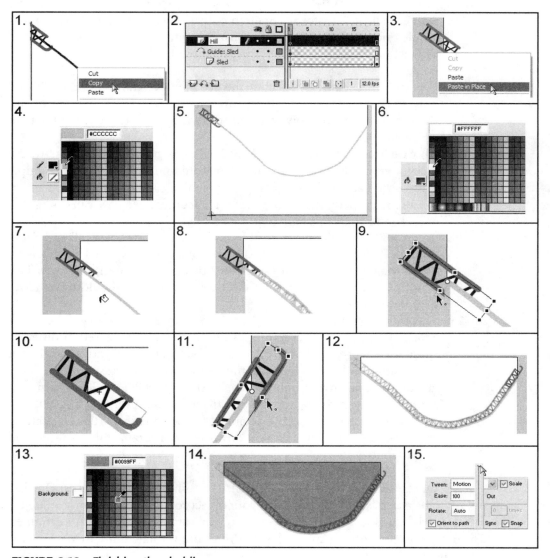

FIGURE 6.12   Finishing the sledding scene.

6. When the lines are complete, choose the Paint Bucket Tool and select a white color.
7. Apply the tool to create a fill inside the hill shape.
8. With our hill complete, notice that the sled is only half visible. This is because the sled is following the guide with its center point.

9. Select the Free Transform Tool to modify the center point. Click the now-visible center point and drag it to just below the runner.

10. This action causes the sled to travel just above the hill, but it still follows the guide.

11. Repeat the procedure by selecting the sled in the keyframe on Frame 20 and moving the center point to just below the runner.

12. If you test the movie now, you can see that the sled is following the path very well.

13. Now we need to create the sky. This time, to keep the file size down, we are not going to create another fill—that would be overkill. Instead, simply change the stage color by clicking on a blank area off the stage. This action causes the Property Inspector to reflect Document. Now we can change the background color to a light blue for the sky.

14. When we test the movie now, it looks really good. It has a hill and background. It also looks as if the sled is traveling along the hill. The only issue is that the sled travels at the same speed throughout the entire movie. This is not quite realistic. When the sled goes downhill, it should travel faster than it does uphill.

15. Select the keyframe on Frame 1 in the Sled layer and change Ease in the Property Inspector. This setting causes the animation to reflect different speeds at either the start or the end. If the value is a negative number, it starts slow and speeds up as the animation progresses to the next keyframe. A positive number makes it start quickly and slow down as it approaches the next keyframe. You can choose the level of easing between −100 to 100, with 0 being the default. Choose an Ease of 100. This setting causes the sled to drastically slow down as it goes up the hill. Now test and save the movie.

As you can see, you have several options for refining Motion tweens. One last option to be noted is the ability to have your object rotate. You can cause an object to rotate while it is in a Motion tween simply by rotating manually at keyframes. The only problem with this method is that you cannot rotate more than one revolution using this cycle.

Flash gives you another method for rotation that can be used in addition to the manual rotation, or alone. While selecting a keyframe in a Motion tween, you can select either CW or CCW from the Rotation drop-down menu in the Property Inspector. You can then select the number of times you want the shape to rotate.

USING SHAPE TWEENS

You have learned one of the methods of tweening—Motion tweens. Now, we are going to look at another version—Shape tweens. Although Motion tweens can be used to scale, rotate, and move objects, they cannot actually change the structure of the object.

Shape tweens allow you to accomplish everything a Motion tween can, but they also give you the ability to morph your objects from one shape into another. When creating Shape tweens, Flash automatically draws intermediate paths from the first shape into the second. Let's look at a very basic Shape tween, shown in Figure 6.13.

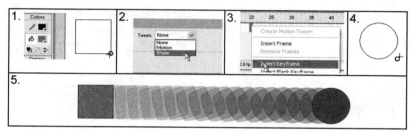

FIGURE 6.13   A basic Shape tween.

1. First, create a square using the Rectangle Tool and holding the Shift key while drawing. The square has a black stroke and a red fill.
2. Click the keyframe in 1 and select Shape from the Tween drop-down menu in the Property Inspector.
3. Now let's insert a keyframe on 20.
4. In the keyframe on Frame 20, create a circle shape with a black stroke and no fill.
5. Now preview the movie. You can vary how the results look in many ways. If you leave the original square on the screen, it appears as if the circle is being spawned from it. If you don't want the original shape to stay on the screen throughout the movie, you can delete it after you create the destination object. You must delete it after, not before, creating your new shape or you break the tween. Another option is if you want it to stay in place. If this is the case, create your new object and delete your first object. Then move the new object to the now-vacant space where the first object existed.

Using Shape Hints

Sometimes when you use Shape tweens in Flash, you get a result that does not resemble what you intended. You must realize that the program is at best *guessing* what it is that you want and fills the rest in between keyframes. To help you overcome this obstacle, Flash allows the use of shape hints. Shape hints are additional information you give the program to clarify how you want the process to happen. Let's experiment with shape hints, as shown in Figure 6.14.

1. In the blank keyframe on Frame 1, type the letter *Z*.
2. Because this is text and part of a group, you must break it apart to use a Shape tween. This situation shows how a Shape tween is the opposite of a

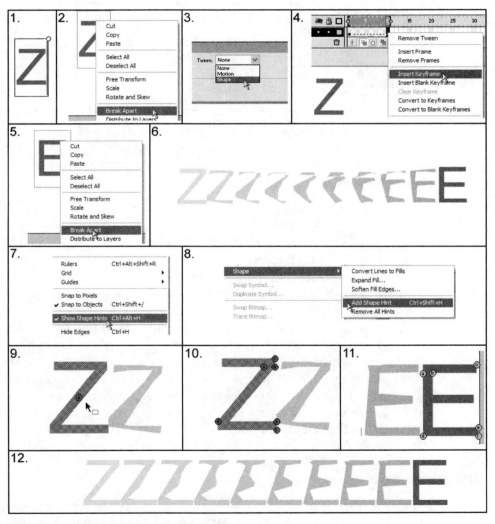

FIGURE 6.14 Using shape hints.

Motion tween. A Motion tween must use symbols, groups, or text blocks for the process to work. A Shape tween, however, must have the shapes broken down to be fully editable. Right-click (Control + click on a Macintosh) the letter and select Break Apart. Because you are using only one letter, we need to do this only once.

3. Now select the keyframe on Frame 1 and, in the Property Inspector, select Shape from the Tween drop-down menu.
4. Insert a keyframe at Frame 10.
5. Type the letter *E* in the new keyframe using the Text Tool and then break it apart. After breaking it apart, delete the *Z* in this keyframe.
6. When we test the movie, we can see that the shape really gets mutilated during the tween.
7. Under the View menu, make sure that Show Shape Hints option is enabled (has a check mark next to it). If it is not enabled, click it to enable it at this time.
8. You can now put in your first shape hint. You can either put in a shape hint by clicking Modify > Shape > Add Shape Hint or by pressing Ctrl or Command + Shift + H.
9. When you add a shape hint, it appears as a red circle with a letter inside in the center of your object.
10. Insert more shape hints until you reach the letter *F*. Then start dragging them to the positions shown in panel 10 of Figure 6.14.
11. Now move to your keyframe at Frame 10 and move your shape hints. It appears that only one shape hint exists, but they are all there, just stacked on top of one another. Move the shape hints to the positions shown in panel 11. Be careful that you place them exactly on a line or a corner. If you have placed them correctly, they turn green. If not, they remain red. If you continue having trouble with a point not changing color, go back to your earlier keyframe and make certain that you have the original shape hint exactly on a line or corner. If both keyframes have the shape hint placed exactly, they appear yellow in this keyframe.
12. Now when testing the movie, you can see that the transition from the first shape to the second is much smoother.

When looking at Shape tweens, you can see that they really add a great deal of punch to animations. You may even ask, because they can do everything that a Motion tween can plus more, why not just use Shape tweens instead? There are two very valid reasons not to do this. One, when using a Shape tween, your files can get large quickly. The reason for this significant growth is that every frame in the tween has to be drawn. So instead of just one symbol repeated, Flash has to actually create each shape. The other issue with using Shape tweens is the toll they can take on the CPUs. Remember, it must draw every shape it receives. At multiple frames per second, even a short animation can be taxing. If you are developing for older computers or embedded devices, use Shape tweens only sparingly, if at all.

WORKING WITH MASK LAYERS

Just like FreeHand MX and Fireworks MX 2004, Flash MX 2004 enables you to work with masks. Masks can really add flair to an animation and enable you to create effects that may not be possible otherwise. Let's create a mask and look at some of the effects that can be achieved, as shown in Figure 6.15.

1. First, type your name in the empty keyframe at Frame 1. You can make your name larger than the largest default setting of 96 by typing a larger number in the Property Inspector. In panel 1 of Figure 6.15, the font size is 200. After creating the text, you must break it down into vectors. Either right-click (Control + click on a Macintosh) or click Modify > Break Apart. Because this is a text block with more than one character, you must break it apart twice. Give this layer the title of *Name*.
2. Now create a new layer by clicking the Insert Layer button while the Name layer is highlighted. Give this one the name of *Name Mask*.

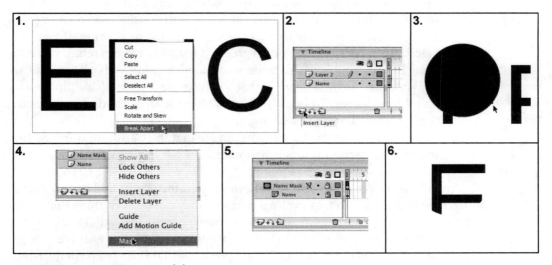

FIGURE 6.15 Creating a Mask layer.

3. Select the empty keyframe at Frame 1 in your new Name Mask layer, and create a circle with your Oval Tool. Make sure that you have a fill. The fill color does not matter.

4. All that is left is to change your Name Mask layer into a mask. You can do this easily by right-clicking (Control + click on a Macintosh) the layer and selecting Mask.

5. Notice now that the Name Mask layer has a new Mask icon, along with the Name layer. The Name Mask Layer icon stands for Mask, because this is the layer that is doing the actual masking, whereas the Name layer is the layer that is being masked. Also note that both layers are now locked. If the layers are not locked, you cannot see the effects of the mask on the main stage.

6. When you test the movie, you see that only the portion of text within the circle shape is now visible.

As you can see from this example, creating a mask is easy. What is great about using a mask in Flash is that you can combine it with other effects to do some really interesting things. Let's continue with the current mask and enhance it, as shown in Figure 6.16.

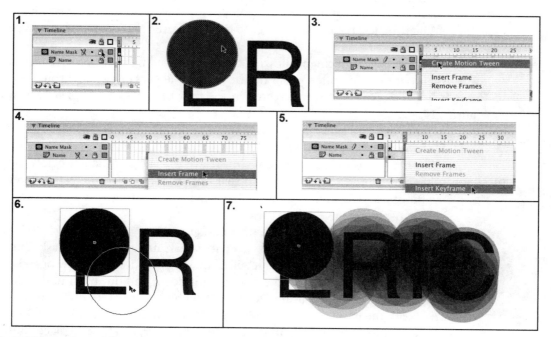

FIGURE 6.16 Adding some movement to the mask.

1. First, unlock the Name Mask layer so we can edit the circle by clicking the Padlock icon near the layer name.

Macromedia Flash MX 2004 locks both the mask and masked layers in a movie to display the effect while authoring. When you want to see the effect turned back on in your authoring view, you must relock the layers by clicking the Padlock icon.

2. Because you have unlocked the layer, the shape is now selectable.
3. Now right-click (Control + click on a Macintosh) the keyframe at Frame 1 in the Name Mask layer and select Create Motion Tween.
4. This movie must contain enough frames to accommodate however long your name is. The idea is for the circle to go up and down from the left to the right and back. Because Eric has only four letters, a frame on Frame 50 is needed in the Name layer. A longer name may require more frames.
5. Now create a keyframe at Frame 5 on the Name Mask layer.
6. Move the circle symbol down to the opposite side of the text.
7. Continue this process throughout the movie. After five frames, insert a keyframe, then move the circle to the top or bottom of the text opposite of the current placement. Once you reach the end of the text on the right, follow it back five frames at a time until you are just shy of the starting placement. When you test the movie, you see that this time, the mask moves around.

It is great to have movement showing the mask unveiling portions of letters as the movie progresses, but often you want the letters to always be visible throughout the movie. Let's revise the move created in the previous procedure, as shown in Figure 6.17.

1. First unlock the Name layer so it can be edited.
2. You may want to hide the Name Mask layer by clicking the dot below the eye icon. Doing so allows you to select all of the text on the Name layer without accidentally clicking the circle symbol, putting you on the same layer. After you have the text selected, copy it.
3. Now create a new layer and name it *Background*.
4. When creating the Background Layer, it appears underneath the mask. This placement must be changed or it will be masked out, destroying the purpose of this exercise. Click the layer and drag it down and out from under the mask. Make certain you drag to the left slightly so it comes out from underneath the mask. It should look like that shown in panel 4 of Figure 6.18.
5. Now that we have pulled out the Background layer, it is time to place your content. Click the empty keyframe at Frame 1. Just off stage, right-click

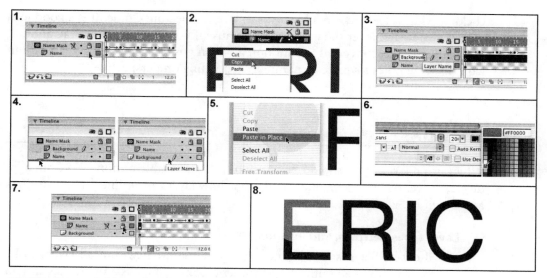

FIGURE 6.17 Finishing the animation with a visible text block.

(Control + click on a Macintosh) and select Paste in Place. Be sure to watch your layers. If your layer accidentally is unselected when you paste, undo the action (Edit > Undo or Ctrl/Command + Z) and repeat the procedure, this time using Edit > Paste in Place.

6. Now that you have pasted the text, click somewhere off the stage to deselect everything, and then select the text on the stage. This text will be the text in the Name layer. Change the fill color to red to make it appear as if a red highlight is traveling over the text.

7. Lock the Name layer again.

8. You can now see that a portion of the text is now showing up as red. Save and test your movie.

GUIDE LAYERS

Not only do they share a similar name to motion guide layers, guide layers also serve a similar purpose. Whereas motion guides are used to help you constrain movement to a guided path without being published themselves, guide layers are used to help you place content on the stage more easily. They also are not published with the final movie. You can create a guide layer by simply creating a layer, right-clicking (Control + click on a Macintosh) it, and selecting Guide. It is a good idea to make your first layer the guide layer because if you inadvertently drag another layer under it, it is converted to a motion guide. A guide layer is recognizable by an icon that resembles a square or hammer, depending on perspective.

LAYER OPTIONS

When using layers, you should be aware of other available options. You can add, delete, move, rename, lock, hide, and even show layers as outlines. These options are shown in Figure 6.18.

Layer types, settings, and buttons

Show All Layers as Outlines: Causes all content within all layers to be shown only as an outline. The content looks as if it has only strokes and no fills. If you click the square within this column on a layer, it affects only the individual layer. By having outlines available, you can draw new shapes on a layer, based on the placement of objects on another, without being distracted by its content.

Lock/Unlock All Layers: Causes all layers to be locked, or unlocked if they are currently locked. When a layer is locked, all content is visible but cannot be edited. If you click the dot within this column on a layer, it affects only the individual layer. Locking layers you don't want to change protects

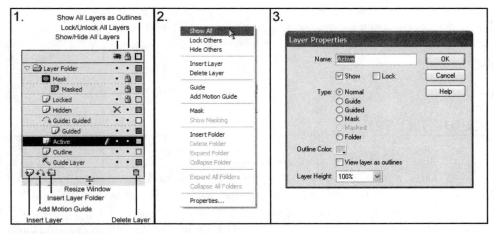

FIGURE 6.18 Layer options.

them and prevents you from accidentally clicking items in the layer and causing your new drawings to be in the wrong layer.

Show/Hide All Layers: Similar to locking but takes it a step further. The content of the layers is not only uneditable but also invisible. If you click the dot within this column on a layer, it affects only the individual layer. This option can be useful if the content on the selected layer is in the way of content you want to work with.

Insert Layer: Allows you to insert a new layer.

Add Motion Guide: Adds a motion guide layer. You can use this option to constrain your tween path.

Insert Layer Folder: Allows you to organize your layers into collapsible folders.

Delete Layer: Deletes a layer and all content in all frames on it.

The Layer Context Menu: Accessed by right-clicking (Control + clicking on a Macintosh) on a layer title. The following options are available in this menu:

Show All: Shows and unlocks all layers in your movie.

Lock Others: Locks all layers except the selected layer.

Hide Others: Hides all layers except the selected layer.

Insert Layer: Adds a new layer.

Delete Layer: Deletes the selected layer.

Guide: Transforms the selected layer into a guide.

Add Motion Guide: Inserts a new motion guide layer above the selected layer.

Mask: Transforms the selected layer into a mask and causes the layer directly underneath to be affected by the mask.

Show Masking: Causes the mask layer and masked layer to be locked if they are currently unlocked.

Insert Folder: Adds a Layer folder.

Delete Folder: Deletes the selected folder.

Expand Folder: Expands the selected folder.

Collapse Folder: Collapses the current folder.

Expand All Folders: Expands all folders in the scene.

Collapse All Folders: Collapses all folders in the scene.

Properties: Opens the properties for the selected layer.

Properties: Provides options to refine the selected layer.

Name: Allows you to edit the layer name.

Show/Lock: Contains checkboxes to define whether the layer is hidden or locked.

Types: Allows you to change the current layer type.

Outline Color: Allows you to change the current outline color.

View layer as outlines: Makes the layer appear as outlines.

Layer Height: Allows you to change how high the layer is displayed.

SUMMARY

In this chapter, you learned about the timeline and layers and had a chance to start animating. You can see by now that Macromedia Flash MX 2004 really gives you some options for creativity.

You worked with Motion tweens, motion guides, Shape tweens, masks, and more. You also created graphic symbols but didn't look at them in depth. In the next chapter, we will learn about "Symbols, Timeline Effects, and Interactivity."

7 Symbols, Timeline Effects, and Interactivity

In the previous chapters, we have looked at the Macromedia Flash MX 2004 interface and then started to animate. This chapter covers the three symbols available in the program and interactivity.

Macromedia Flash MX 2004 offers three types of symbol: movie clip, graphic, and button. By using symbols, you can fully empower your movies. Symbols, at their most basic, are designs that are created once and used many times. By creating content as symbols, the end file needs to keep only one copy of the symbol. When your movie is played, an instance of the symbol is placed wherever you want it to be shown. This practice drastically decreases the size of the file because the program only needs a few instructions to place the symbol.

Both FreeHand and Fireworks use symbols to shrink file size and share images, but Flash takes their use to a higher level. Not only can graphics be reused, but with Flash these symbols can be full animations or even movies within themselves, complete with scripting. Much of the interactivity in Flash is directly tied to symbols. We will learn about symbols, starting with graphic symbols.

GRAPHIC SYMBOLS

Graphic symbols are the most basic of available symbols. They are usually used for simple objects, but they have more capabilities and are not always static. Within a graphic symbol, you can have an animation. However, this feature is not commonly used because a graphic symbol does not have an independent timeline. Graphic symbols are best used for objects that are created for reuse.

When you are using a graphic symbol, any change you make within the original symbol applies to all instances of the symbol in your movie. You can also scale, rotate, skew, and change the alpha (transparency) and even the tint of an individual instance. This ability to modify the symbol can prove handy when you need to

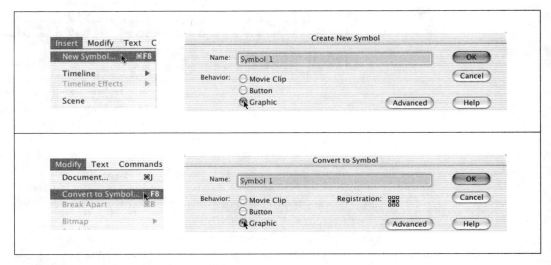

FIGURE 7.1 Creating a graphic symbol.

make a sweeping change, such as for a revised logo. Let's start exploring graphic symbols in Figure 7.1.

You can create a graphic symbol in many ways: by clicking Insert > New Symbol; by pressing Control/Command + the F8 key; by selecting an object on the stage and clicking Modify > Covert to Symbol; or by pressing the F8 key or right-clicking/Control + clicking on the object or objects and selecting Convert to Symbol. This procedure is a change from previous versions of Flash where you would find Convert to Symbol under the Insert menu.

It can often be useful to create your object first and then convert it, because you can create it based on the content on the stage. If you just create a new symbol, you cannot see what is on the stage and must use your best guess.

Once a graphic symbol is created, you can editing it in Symbol-Editing mode. You access Symbol-Editing mode in multiple ways. You can double-click the symbol's icon (not the name, which is for renaming) in the Library. You can also double-click an instance on the stage, or select the Edit Symbols drop-down menu to the right of the Edit Scene button, just above the Timeline. When you are in Symbol-Editing mode, your screen resembles that shown in Figure 7.2.

When looking at Figure 7.2, you can see that we are in Symbol-Editing mode. We entered this mode by double-clicking a symbol instance on the stage. This mode can be advantageous because we can edit our current symbol while seeing the rest of the items on the stage faded in the background. When you double-click a

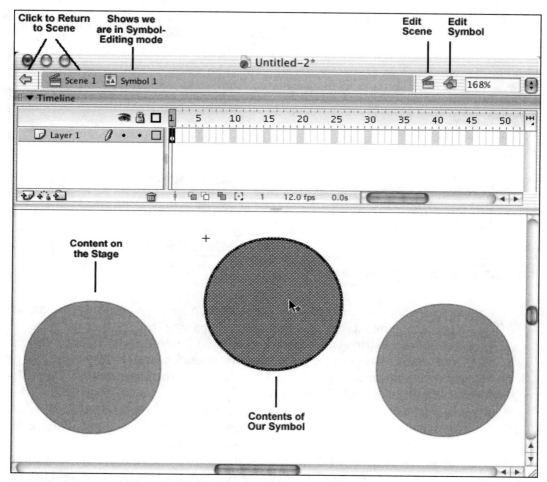

FIGURE 7.2   The Symbol-Editing mode interface.

symbol in the Library, you enter Symbol-Editing mode independent of the stage, so you can't see what else is on the stage while you edit.

Let's now look at creating a graphic symbol in Flash and placing instances of the symbol on the stage, as shown in Figure 7.3.

First, make a circle with a black stroke and red fill and convert it to a symbol. Next, name it *Red Circle with the Behavior of Graphic*. Then drag another instance of the symbol from the Library. (If it is not open, click Window > Library.) When you drag a symbol out of the Library, you see a square icon appear behind your cursor.

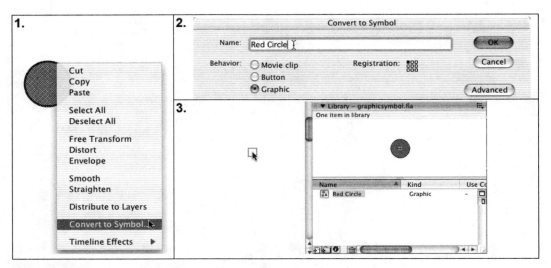

FIGURE 7.3 Creating a graphic symbol.

You can place as many symbols as you want on the stage simply by dragging an instance out of the Library or by copying and pasting instances on the stage. (A great shortcut is to press Alt/Option + click on an instance and drag out a copy.)

Now that we have created a basic graphic symbol, we can look at some editing options. Graphic symbols can be edited within or on the instance itself. Figure 7.4 shows how graphic symbols can be edited.

1. First, add another copy of the symbol on the stage, then double-click the instance in the center to enter Symbol-Editing mode.
2. While in Symbol-Editing mode, change the fill color of the circle to white.
3. You can see how all instances of the same symbol change to white. Click the Scene One reference to return to the main timeline. Remember, be careful when clicking. Sometimes you may accidentally double-click a symbol on the stage, which brings you into the Symbol-Editing mode.
4. Now that we are out of Symbol-Editing mode, we can use the Free Transform Tool to scale an instance. Notice that only one instance is changed.
5. We can also rotate and skew instances. However, you cannot use the Envelope or Distort options because they modify the actual vector points.
6. If you have an instance selected, within the Property Inspector you have new options available. In this case, we are changing the tint of the center instance to black. You can control how much of the tint you to apply to the object—choose between 0 percent and 100 percent. The higher the num-

ber chosen, the more of the color is applied, with 100 percent changing the color completely.

7. Now let's move the symbol on the right until it overlaps the modified symbol in the middle. If it does not appear on top of the center symbol, click Modify > Arrange > Bring to Front while the symbol on the right is selected.

8. Another option you can select with symbols is Alpha. Within the Property Inspector, select Alpha in the Color drop-down menu and set it to 50

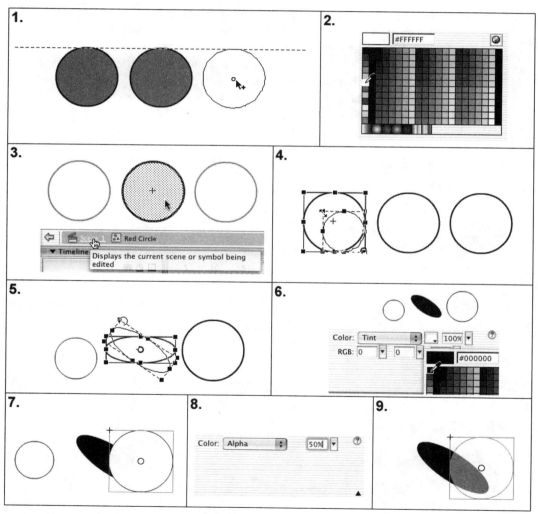

FIGURE 7.4   The effects of editing graphic symbols.

percent. This setting causes the symbol to be half-transparent (the lower the alpha, the more transparent), letting you see the instance, now tinted black, underneath.

Let's look at how we can animate graphic symbols within their own timelines and how their timelines are dependent on the main timeline. We will continue working with our current graphic symbol instances, as shown in Figure 7.5.

1. First, enter the Symbol-Editing mode by double-clicking an instance. We are going to use a Motion tween for our animation, so we must turn the shape into a group. You can group objects by clicking Modify > Group or by pressing Ctrl/Command + G. We could convert the shape into another symbol, but that would be redundant.
2. Once we have the shape grouped, select the keyframe on Frame 1 and, within the Property Inspector, choose Motion from the Tween drop-down menu.
3. Now, add a keyframe on Frame 5 and move your grouped object to another position. In this case, we move it downward. Also turn on onion skins so we can see the animation path.

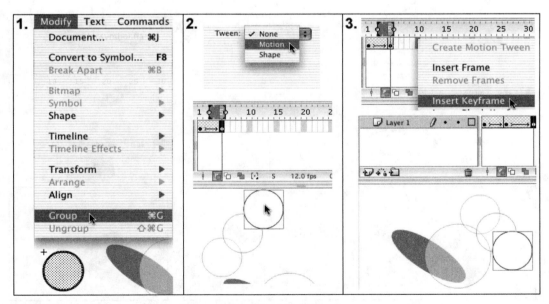

FIGURE 7.5 Creating an animation within a graphic symbol.

We complete your movement by inserting another keyframe on Frame 10 and moving your grouped object back to just shy of where it started. If you press Enter/Return now, you can see the animation play in the Symbol-Editing mode.

Even though you can see that the object is animated, when you test the actual movie you will find that your symbols don't move. This is because graphic symbols do not have an independent timeline and are completely reliant on the main timeline.

Insert a new frame on Frame 10 in the main timeline so that it has enough frames to cover the animation. We don't need to use a keyframe because the frame is nothing more than a marker to extend the number of frames to accommodate the animation within the graphic symbol. Although you can create a tween or animation within a graphic symbol, it does not have its own timeline. If you do not have enough frames on the main timeline to accommodate an animation, it will not play.

Graphic symbols are fantastic for images that you want to reuse in your movie but are not the best choice for animation. They also cannot have any scripting attached them. This limitation prevents them from being used for interactive features. If you want to use animations and have interactivity with symbols, you need to use movie clips and buttons.

MOVIE CLIPS

Movie clips are extremely powerful symbols used within the Flash authoring environment. Like graphic symbols, movie clips can be used multiple times throughout the movie by using instances. They also can contain animations. But they go much further than that. They can contain anything developed in a Flash movie, including graphic symbols, buttons, video, sounds, and even other movie clips. As a matter of fact, the main timeline is actually a movie clip. It can be considered the root movie clip.

The magic of the movie clip is that it has its own independent timeline. This means you can have a movie with interactivity and animation that takes up only one frame on the main timeline. It is common to find one-frame movies. Movie clips, along with other symbols, can also be shared between different Flash movies. The only limitation of a movie clip is that it is constrained to the overall frame rate of the Flash movie.

Now open the file we created in the previous chapter called *atoms.fla* and refer to the procedure shown in Figure 7.6.

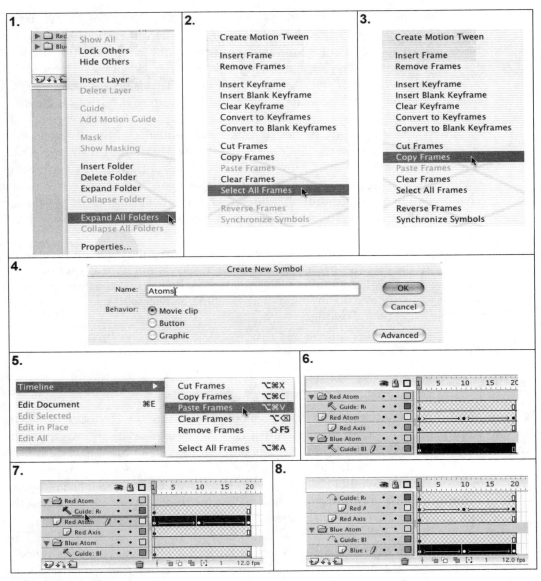

FIGURE 7.6   Creating a new movie clip with content from another Flash document.

1. First, open the *atoms.fla* document to access the data inside. After you open it, select Expand All Folders by right-clicking (Control + click on a Macintosh) one of the layers. You must expand all folders to be certain you can copy their content.

2. Now right-click (Control + click on a Macintosh) or click Edit > Timeline > Select All Frames on the first frame.

3. Now, select Copy Frames by using either the shortcut menu or by clicking Edit > Timeline > Menu. It is very important to choose Copy Frames, not just Copy.

4. Create a new Flash movie. After you have the movie open, click Insert > New Symbol, or press Ctrl/Command + F8. Name this symbol *Atoms with the Behavior of Movie Clip.*

5. Now that we are inside the new movie clip, we need to select the empty keyframe on Frame 1. Right-click (Control + click on a Macintosh) and choose Paste Frames, or click Edit > Timeline > Paste Frames. You must choose Paste Frames, not just Paste. When this step is complete, you will see that the layers have been populated in your movie clip.

The previous two steps resolve an issue that may occur when you perform this process.

6. You may notice that when you paste your frames, your motion guides have now reverted to regular guides, which will not work with this procedure. You must convert your guides into motion guides. Drag the Red Atom layer into the Red Atom Guide layer to resolve the guide layer issue.

7. Repeat this same procedure with the Blue Atom layer. Your movie clip should resemble those shown in panel 8 of Figure 7.6.

Now that you have created your movie clip, you want to use it in your new Flash document. The movie clip is available in your Library for use throughout your movie. Let's see at how we can pull instances onto the main timeline and demonstrate a one-frame movie. This procedure is shown in Figure 7.7.

1. The first thing we need to do is exit Symbol-Editing mode and return to the main timeline by pressing the Scene button or the left-pointing arrow.

2. When we look at the Library (click Window > Library, if it is not currently open), the Atoms movie clip is visible. In addition, the two graphic symbols that make up the tween within the Atoms movie clip are also present. If you look in the top-right corner of the preview window, you see play and stop buttons. If you press play, it previews the animation in the window.

3. Because the stage is empty, drag an instance of the Atoms movie clip onto it. When we test the movie, the animation will work, even with only one frame in the movie, because the movie clip has its own independent timeline.

4. Scale down your current instance of the movie clip on the stage with the Free Transform Tool.

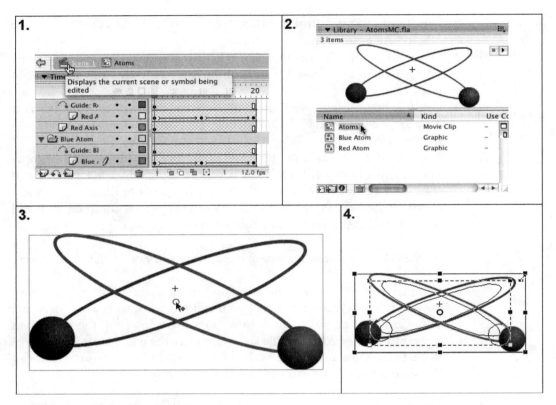

FIGURE 7.7   Scaling movie clip instances.

You must click on a solid part of a symbol to select it. If you click on a blank area within the movie clip instance, you cannot select it.

Drag out two more instances of the movie clip, and scale them to fit around each other. You can use all available editing options with graphic symbol instances on movie clips.

Now that we have created your first movie clip using content that we previously had, let's look at creating one from scratch. This movie clip consists of only one square and one circle, but even with that simplicity, it can be something fun. This process is shown in Figure 7.8.

1. First, create a new movie and click Insert > New Symbol (or Ctrl/Command + F8). Within the Create New Symbol dialog box, use the name *Die* and select the Movie Clip behavior.

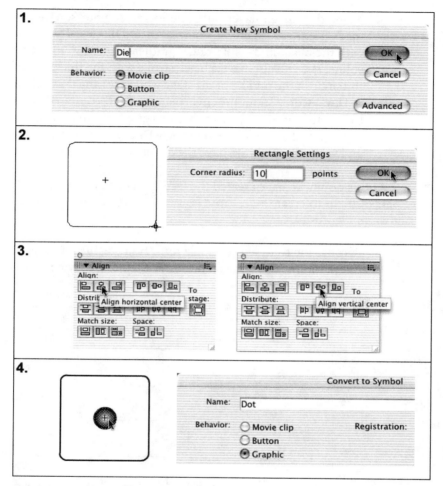

FIGURE 7.8   Creating a movie clip from scratch.

2. In Symbol-Editing mode, create a rounded rectangle with a corner radius of 10 points, a black stroke with a thickness of 2, and a white fill. Hold down the Shift key to force the rectangle to be square. Size doesn't matter, but make it large enough to be visible.

3. To help place your content more easily, open the Align Panel by clicking Window > Design Panels > Align. Double-click the square, if it is not already selected. In the Align Panel, make sure To stage is selected. This option causes your alignment choices to be relative to the stage. You can align objects either to the stage or to each other. Select Align horizontal center, as shown in panel 3 of Figure 7.8. Also choose Align vertical center.

4. Name the current layer *Back* and lock it so your square won't be selected inadvertently. Also create a new layer and name it *Dot*. Now create a circle with the black-and-white radial gradient, found in the bottom of your fill colors. We will also have a black stroke with the thickness of 1. Now, draw the circle in the middle of the stage while pressing the Shift key to constrain it. Don't worry about the circle being perfectly centered at this point. While the circle is selected, convert it into a graphic symbol with the name of *Dot*. Using the Align Panel, align the new Dot symbol instance both horizontally and vertically. Now we have the number one on the die.

At this point, we have created the face for a basic die. Ultimately, we will have a pair of them to create a dice movie. We will create the rest of the faces next, as shown in Figure 7.9.

1. Because the rounded rectangle must be available for all six faces of the die, insert a frame in Frame 6 on the Back layer. It only needs to be a frame because the Back layer never changes.

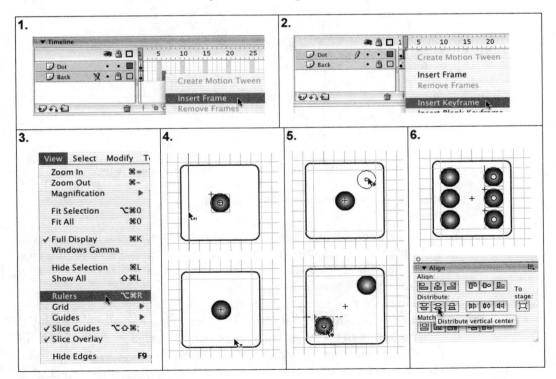

FIGURE 7.9   Completing the die.

2. Insert a keyframe in Frame 2.
3. Now you need to figure out a way to place all of the dots in a precise manner. This situation is where rulers and the grid can rescue you . Click View > Rulers, then click View > Grid > Show Grid.
4. To help you align everything, place guidelines on the stage. Click in the center of the ruler on the left edge of the document window, and drag out a ruler just inside of the left edge of the die shape. Pull three more guides for the top, bottom, and right side of the die. It should resemble what is shown in panel 4 of Figure 7.9. Use the grid to help you judge a uniform distance from every edge.
5. Make a copy of the Dot instance to form your next face on the die—the number two. A convenient method is to press Alt/Option + click the symbol, drag out a copy, release the mouse button, and then release the Alt/Option key. Then place both symbols to form the number two on the die. Continue to insert keyframes and create the numbers for each face. Use your arrow keys on the keyboard to align the dots. Don't align the dots themselves with the guides; instead align the blue box surrounding them to be more precise.
6. Repeat the process for numbers three through six. On the faces for three and five, you can place the center dot correctly by using the Align Panel and selecting To stage. Because the Back layer is aligned to the center of the stage, you know that when you align the dot, it will be perfectly centered. To align the rows on each side for the number-six face, press Shift + click. Click the Distribute vertical center button. This option looks at the top and bottom objects and distributes everything in between evenly.

We now have your Die movie clip created and available for use within your movie. It is especially advantageous to use movie clips for this movie because doings so enables you to have more than one die on the stage while only having to create it once. Plus, by being movie clips, they are animated and still give you the option to add scripts for interaction.

Now you continue working with the Die movie by bringing two dice onto the stage and having them roll across the stage, as shown in Figure 7.10.

1. First, click the Edit Scene button above the timeline to return to the main timeline. Notice that nothing is on the stage. This is to be expected because we used the Insert > New Symbol method. You must have the Library open to pull out instances. If it's not currently open, click Window > Library.
2. Name your first layer *LDie* and create a second layer named *RDie*. Drag an instance of the die for the LDie layer, and scale it down to be relative in size to the stage.

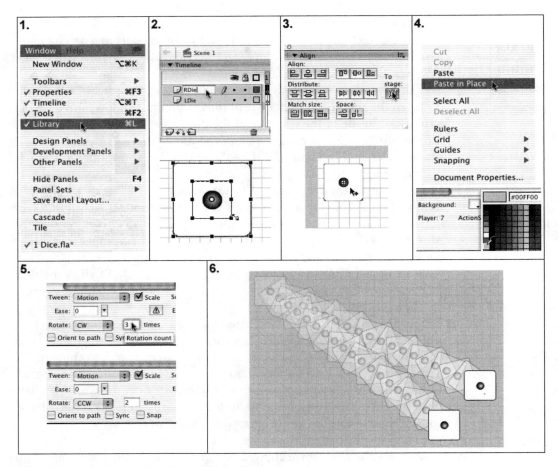

FIGURE 7.10 Bringing the dice onto the stage.

3. When you have your die instance scaled down, open the Align Panel, make sure the To stage button is selected, and press the Align left edge and Align top edge buttons. These options place the die instance on the top-left corner of the stage. With the die is still selected, hold the Shift key and press your right and down arrows on the keyboard, one time each.

4. Copy your die instance, and select the RDie layer. Click Edit > Paste in Place. We now have a die on each layer. Select a green background color for the stage to make the dice more visible and create the appearance of a craps table.

5. Select the keyframe on Frame 1 in each layer, and select Motion from the Tween drop-down menu in the Property Inspector. Also select Rotate CW

and set the value for Times at 3 for the RDie layer, and Rotate CCW 2 Times for the LDie layer. These settings cause the dice to appear as if they are being rolled on a table.

When you choose Rotate with a tweened object, take into account the number of frames in your movie. If you do not have enough frames to account for the number of rotations you select, Flash will not rotate them.

6. Enter a keyframe in Frame 20 on each layer. On the new keyframes, move the dice to the bottom-right corner of the stage so they are still visible. When you test the movie, you should see them traveling the path shown.

Now when you test the movie, you see that the dice travel across the stage. The numbers changing give the illusion of rolling dice. You can see that even something as simple as a circle and a square can lead to an interesting animation. If you have not done so already, save your movie as *Dice.fla* and close it. We will revisit this file when we explore ActionScript later.

BUTTONS

The last type of symbol is the button. Buttons are a unique type of symbol. Like the other two symbols, it has its own timeline. Similar to a graphic symbol, a button is dependent on its parent object, whether it is the main timeline or a movie clip. This is where the similarities end, however.

Unlike graphic symbols and movie clips, buttons only have four frames available. Each frame represents a state: Up, Over, Down, and Hit. The Up state is the initial state, which is what appears whenever the frame it lives on loads. The Over state shows up when the pointer is hovering over it. The Down state appears when the button is selected. The Hit state shows what the active hittable area is. The Hit state is commonly used with invisible buttons (similar to hotspots in Fireworks and Dreamweaver) or to make an object easier to select by increasing the clickable area. Let's look at creating a button, as shown in Figure 7.11.

1. Just like graphic symbols and movie clips, to make a button, start by creating a shape on the stage and then convert it to a button. We are going to use a rounded rectangle with the corner radius set to 70 points, a black stroke with a thickness of 1, and the blue radial gradient fill available in your fill colors. You can use the Fill Transform Tool to refine your gradient.

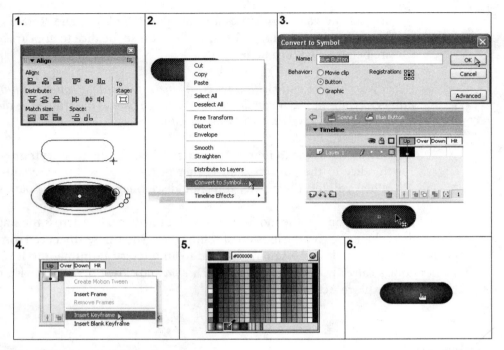

FIGURE 7.11 Creating a button.

2. Now double-click the shape to select it and convert it to a symbol. Name it *Blue Button* and define it as a Button. Double-click the instance to go into Symbol-Editing mode. Here you see that the button has only four frames.

3. Select the Over state and insert a keyframe. In the Over state keyframe, change the color of the button fill to the red radial gradient found on the bottom of your fill colors. If you want, you can repeat the procedure and select another color for the Down state.

4. When you test the movie you see that the button changes color as you mouse over it.

Now that we have created a basic button, continue by examining what is used for the Hit state in Figure 7.12.

1. First, return to the main timeline, select the Text Tool, and type *My Link* at a font size of 100. Right-click (control + click on a Macintosh) the new text and choose Break Apart twice to turn it into vectors.

2. Now that you have broken it apart into vectors, make sure it is all selected and convert it into a symbol with the Behavior of Button and name of *Text*.

3. Test your movie by pressing Ctrl + Enter (Command + Return on a Macintosh). Notice that your mouse changes into a hand only if you are directly over a letter; it does not change if you select an empty area, which can prove difficult for users.

4. Close the Flash Player window and insert a keyframe on Hit. We will draw a rectangle over the text, but you need to change the corner radius back to 0 points.

5. Draw a rectangle large enough to cover the text. Make sure it has a fill. (Color doesn't matter here.) You now see the text covered completely by a rectangle. This rectangle will not be seen when the movie is published. Think of this as a type of mask, only this time you are masking the clickable area.

6. When you test your movie, you will see that you can now click anywhere in your text.

The Hit state is an invaluable tool to place hotspots anywhere on the stage. It is also great to use in conjunction with normal buttons.

When you work with buttons, don't just stop with straight color-changing rollovers like we just created; experiment with them. You can have an Over state showing items elsewhere on the stage. For example, you can have text appear in the

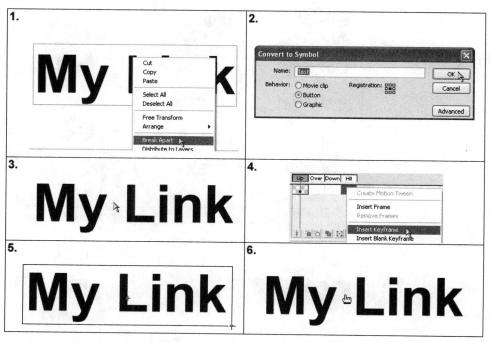

FIGURE 7.12 Using the Hit state.

center of the stage when your buttons are in the Over state. You are also not limited to only static content in your states. You could put a movie clip in the Over state, which makes the rollovers even more dynamic.

TIMELINE EFFECTS

Timeline effects are new to Macromedia Flash MX 2004. They were added in response to users who wanted precompiled effects that could be quickly used to turn out an animation with some basic adjustment capabilities. Timeline effects are located under Insert > Timeline Effects or on the shortcut menu, accessed by right-clicking (Control + click on a Macintosh). Timeline effects can be applied to nearly anything, which makes them very robust. They are effective with text, graphics (from shapes and groups to graphic symbols), bitmaps, and buttons. Available timeline effects are broken into three categories, as shown in Figure 7.13.

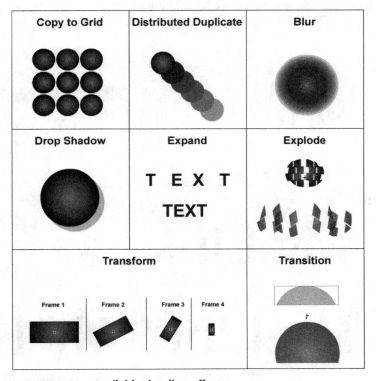

FIGURE 7.13   Available timeline effects.

If you create a symbol in FreeHand and try to apply a timeline effect to it, it may fail. The resolution to the issue is to ungroup the object before applying the effect. You also may have to double-click to edit the object and adjust your placement by clicking Modify > Arrange.

Assistants

Copy to Grid: Duplicates an object and places all of the copies in a grid. You can choose how many rows and columns and the distance between each.

Distributed Duplicate: Adds a second copy of the initial shape with a different color and alpha. It fills the area between the shapes with other instances at different alphas. This option is similar to the effect of the Blend Tool found in FreeHand MX.

Effects

Blur: Causes an object to grow outward in selectable directions. It comprises numerous layers of different Motion tweens using scale and alpha.

Drop Shadow: Creates a Drop Shadow effect. You can adjust the direction of light, distance away from the original object, tint, and alpha of the shadow.

Expand: Causes the objects to move away from one another over time. You can also choose Squeeze, which causes the object distance to collapse. This option works best with multiple objects, such as text.

Explode: Cuts an object into pieces and creates an explosion effect. You can adjust direction, fragment size, and time, as well as other settings.

Transform/Transition

Transform: Represents essentially a premade Motion tween. You can choose to use nearly all effects available for Motion tweens.

Transition: Allows the user to have a filmlike transition on an object of Fade or Wipe. You can fade in or out and change the direction of the wipe, the number of frames used, and the speed at the start and finish of the clip.

Any timeline effect is adjusted using its preview window. Figure 7.14 shows the preview window used for the Explode effect.

In any preview window, preview to the right shows how the effect will look. On the left side of the screen are the settings for the timeline effect. Anytime you adjust the settings for an effect, you can press the Update Preview button to see how the effect will look with the new settings.

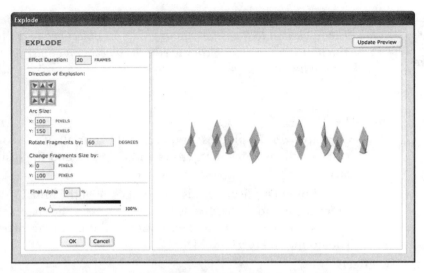

FIGURE 7.14 The preview window for the Explode timeline effect.

ADDING INTERACTIVITY WITH BEHAVIORS

Now that we have created buttons and movie clips, let's look at adding interactivity with behaviors. Behaviors, like timeline effects, are new to Macromedia Flash MX 2004. Also like timeline effects, they are added to the program to act as an easier way to create effects. They already existed in Dreamweaver and Fireworks, and bringing them into Macromedia Flash MX 2004 added another common feature between the programs.

Behaviors are actually nothing more than precreated ActionScript segments with parameters available for you to set in a dialog box. This way, users can add interactivity to the movie without having to look at one bit of code. Let's explore adding some actions using behaviors, as shown in Figure 7.15. We will use your *sled.fla* file.

1. The first thing you do is create a new layer named *Actions* by clicking the Hill layer and pressing the Insert Layer button. This is a good practice to help with organization. By creating a separate layer and placing all of your frame actions on it, you need to look in only one place to find them. Even though we are using behaviors for your actions, the actions are still ultimately written in ActionScript.
2. Insert a keyframe at Frame 20.

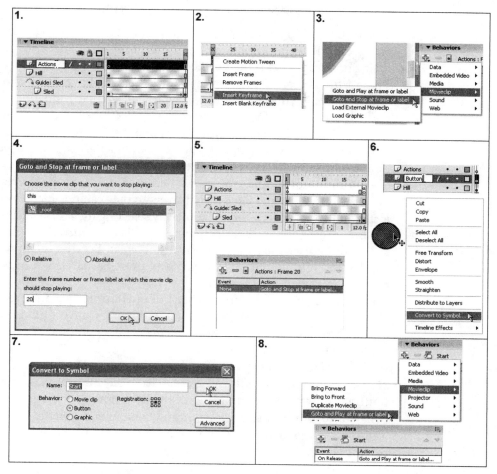

FIGURE 7.15 Adding interactivity using behaviors.

3. Once the new keyframe has been created, select the empty keyframe on Frame 1 and click the + (plus sign) in the Behaviors Panel. Notice that the Behaviors Panel reflects Actions: Frame 1. Navigate through the drop-down menu to Movieclip > Goto and Stop at frame or label. Even though the menu says Movieclip, it is still correct because the main timeline is literally the root movie clip in Flash.

4. The Goto and Stop at frame or label dialog box opens, showing you a navigational structure of your movie. Because this is a basic movie with all elements on the main timeline, it is not deep. It has the keyword of *this*, which means "This object that you have selected." That keyword is what

you want here. The Enter the frame number or frame label at which the movie clip should stop playing text box should contain 1. Leave this value and press OK. Repeat the same process on Frame 20, only enter 20 in the dialog box that asks for the frame.

5. These settings cause the empty keyframes to have a lowercase *a* above each empty circle. If you test the movie, you will see that it now has the sled parked at the start of the scene. Also, if you select a keyframe with an action in it, you will see in the Behaviors Panel that it appears on the list as Event: None and Action: Goto and Stop at frame or label. If you want to edit this, double-click the action to open the dialog box again.

6. The user can now initiate the movie because we have stopped everything. Lock the Hill, Sled, and Guide: Sled layers so they can't be inadvertently selected. Add another layer to the movie by selecting the Hill layer and pressing the Insert Layer button. Name the new layer *Button*. We selected the Hill layer to place the new layer directly above it. Because the Button layer will have a button with interactivity and must be visible above the other content, this placement is ideal.

7. Select the empty keyframe on Frame 1 of the Button layer and create a circle on the bottom-left side of the stage with a fill. Convert this button to a symbol with the name of *Start and Behavior of Button*. If you want a rollover effect, double-click the new button instance and insert a keyframe in the Up state, changing the fill color to another color.

8. Now return to the main timeline and select your button on the stage. The button is now reflected in the top of the Behaviors Panel. This time, use a behavior to create what is known as an On handler. Click the + (plus sign) again, and navigate to Movieclip > Goto and Play a frame or label. Leave it set to 1 and click OK. Test your movie.

In the previous exercise, we assigned your last action to a button. If you look in the Behaviors Panel with the button selected, you see that Flash added the On handler for you. An On handler is a set of code that dictates actions to happen when an event occurs, much like your car will not accelerate unless you press the gas pedal. Think of your gas pedal as the handler and your foot pressing down as the event.

The events are listed in the left column. If you click where is reads On Release, a drop-down menu of available events appears, as shown in Figure 7.16.

Press: Reacts to the mouse button being pressed while over the object.

Release: Allows an action to occur when a mouse button is pressed and released while over an object.

FIGURE 7.16   Events available for a button in the Behaviors Panel.

Release Outside: Occurs when the button is pressed while over an object, but released after the mouse has moved away from the button.

Key Press: Happens when a key on the keyboard is pressed. You can define which key.

Roll Over: Occurs when the mouse hovers over an object.

Roll Out: Happens when the mouse hovering over an object moves away from the object.

Drag Over: Occurs when the mouse button is down and dragged over an object.

Drag Out: Occurs when the mouse button is down while moving off of an object.

Select Release to cause the user to complete the entire cycle of pressing and releasing the mouse on the button. If the user changes his mind and moves away from the button before releasing, the action will not be initiated.

Behavior Choices

As you have seen, you have several behaviors from which to choose. They are easy to use by having the programming built into them, but they may not seem to be organized in an intuitive manner. Let's look at all of the categories and behaviors Flash offers.

Data

Trigger Data Source: Works with outside data, especially XML. This behavior was introduced in Flash MX Professional.

Embedded Video: Allows interaction with embedded or imported video in your Flash movie. This behavior is usually applied to buttons.

Fast Forward: Speeds up video playback. You can choose how many frames at a time you want it to advance.

Hide: Hides a video so other content can be seen. Hide works well with a button.

Pause: Pauses the video clip.

Play: Starts or continues playback of the video clip.

Rewind: Works as the reverse of Fast Forward. Again, you can choose how many frames at a time you would want it to move.

Show: Works in the opposite manner of Hide. You can have two buttons available, one to hide and the other to show.

Stop: Stops video playback.

Media: Further refines interactivity with video. This behavior is new to Flash MX 2004 Professional.

Associate Controller
Associate Display
Labeled Frame CuePoint Navigation
Slide CuePoint Navigation

Movieclip: Allows for basic navigation to frames and for loading external SWFs and JPEGs.

Goto and Play at frame or label: Tells the target where to start the playhead. It can be the main timeline (_root) or any movie clip.

Goto and Stop at frame or label: Same as Goto and Play, but when the playhead hits the target frame, it stops.

Load External Movieclip: Loads an external .swf file into either the main timeline at a level or into a movie clip on the stage.

Load Graphic: Loads an external JPEG. Standard .jpg files (not progressive) are the only image format you can load into a Flash movie at runtime.

Projector: Appears only if a button or a movie clip is selected.

Toggle Full Screen Mode: Toggles the view on the screen. This behavior works with your Flash movie if you have published it as a projector (standalone executable file).

Sound: Manipulates sounds in your Flash movie.

Load Sound from Library: Loads a sound file into the document. You must have the sound set up for linkage ahead of time by right-clicking (Control + clicking on a Macintosh) the sound in the Library and choosing Linkage. Within the Linkage dialog box, select Export for ActionScript and give it an Identifier.

Load streaming MP3 file: Allows you to type a URL to an MP3 file and gives it an identifier for later reference.

Play Sound: Plays the sound you have specified in the Identifier field.

Stop All Sounds: Stops all currently playing sounds. This behavior can be useful as an action on a mute button.

Stop Sound: Stops the sound you specify in the identifier.

Web: For opening Web pages.

Go to Web Page: Opens a Web page. You can define if the Web page will be in the same window (_self), in a parent frame (_parent), or in a new window (_blank), or if you want it to override all current frames (_top).

Custom Behaviors

A big advantage of adding the capabilities of behaviors to Flash MX 2004 is that now developers have the ability to create their own behaviors. Over time, more and more behaviors will be found on Macromedia Exchange and third-party sites.

The ability to develop custom behaviors is useful in two ways. First, developers can create behaviors for those in their shop who are uncomfortable with Action-Script. They also can create behaviors for themselves if they have commonly used segments of code.

Behaviors in Macromedia Flash MX 2004 can be found in *C:\Documents and Settings\%username%\Local Settings\Application Data\Macromedia\Flash MX 2004\en\Configuration\Behaviors* with Window 2000/XP. You may have to show hidden files to see them by clicking Tools > Folder Options, clicking the View tab, and then under Hidden files and folders click Show hidden files and folders.

On a Macintosh, the Behaviors folder is located at *Users:%username%:Library:Application Support:Macromedia:Flash MX 2004:en:Configuration:Behaviors.*

The en folder exists only in the English version of the program. If you are using a localized version (another language), it appears with the appropriate two-letter language code (such as es = Spanish).

All of the behavior files are written in the Extensible Markup Language (XML). XML is a language that allows developers to create self-describing data. XML is discussed more in Chapter 13, "An HTML Primer."

Let's crack open a behavior that was used previously—Goto and Stop—to analyze the structure. It is located in the XML file *Movieclip_GotoAndStop.xml.* You will look at it in sections:

```
<?xml version="1.0"?>
```

The first part of any XML document is the declaration. It says that it is written in XML version 1.0.

```
<!-- ********************************************************
********************** -->
<!-- Copyright 2003 Macromedia, Inc. All Rights Reserved.-->
<!-- The following is Sample Code and is subject to all restrictions
on          -->
<!-- such code as contained in the End User License Agreement
accompanying        -->
<!-- this product.-->
<!-- ************************************************
*************************** -->
```

After the XML declaration, Macromedia has added a copyright statement within XML comments.

```
<flash_behavior version="1.0">
    <behavior_definition
        dialogID="Goto_and_Stop-dialog"
        category="Movieclip"
        name="Goto and Stop at frame or label">
        <properties>
            <property id="target" default="this"/>
            <property id="frame" default="1"/>
        </properties>
```

Now we have arrived at the start of the actual document (outside the declaration). Within you find `<flash_behavior version="1.0">`. This is the root element. All elements within the document must fall between the opening and closing root element, just like the `<html></html>` found in HTML.

After the root element, you find the `behavior_definition` tag. This is where the behavior in question is defined. First it is given a `dialogID` that identifies it to the program and in what category it is. If a current category of the same name does not exist, a new category appears in the + drop-down menu of the Behaviors Panel. Finishing this tag is the `name` attribute, which appears in the top of the dialog box opened when the behavior is selected.

Following the `behavior_definition` is the `properties` element, which holds individual property tags for use later in the document.

```
<!--The dialog window is tied to the controls below by its id-->
<!--This controls generate the dialog using the XML to UI
functionality-->

<dialog id="Goto_and_Stop-dialog" title="Goto and Stop at frame
or label" buttons="accept, cancel">
    <vbox>
        <label value="Choose the movie clip that you want to
        stop playing:                    " />
    </vbox>
    <grid>
        <rows>
            <row align="center">
                <targetlist id="target" tabindex="1"
                class="movieclip"/>
            </row>
        </rows>
        <label value=""/>
        <label value="Enter the frame number or frame label at
        which the movie clip"/>
        <label value="should stop playing:"/>
        <rows>
            <row align="center">
                <textbox literal="true" id="frame" tabindex="2"
                required="true"/>
            </row>
        </rows>
    </grid>
</dialog>
```

The dialog section defines everything you see inside of the dialog box when you choose the behavior.

```
        <actionscript>
<![CDATA[
    //Movieclip GotoAndStop Behavior
    $target$.gotoAndStop($frame$);
    //End Behavior
]]>
        </actionscript>
    </behavior_definition>
</flash_behavior>
```

This last section is the actual ActionScript that will be inserted into the movie when the behavior is created. The `$target$` and `$frame$` portions act as variables that will be filled with your selections in the dialog box.

After the `actionscript` element, you will see the closing `behavior_definition` tag completing the behavior. Finishing the XML document is the closing root `flash_behavior` tag.

Creating a Custom Behavior

We have explored a behavior that came with the program; now let's create a behavior using one of the most simple ActionScript commands available: `stop()`. The Stop command does just that—it stops the playhead. Let's explore both the XML document and the result shown in Flash MX 2004.

```
<?xml version="1.0"?>
<flash_behavior version="1.0">
```

To create this file, you can use any text editor, but Dreamweaver MX 2004 is a great choice for XML support. Start out the document with the mandatory XML declaration and the root tag. It is a good idea to create both the opening and closing root tags with several spaces in between immediately. It is easy to lose track and forget to close the tag after you have numerous lines of code.

```
<behavior_definition
    dialogID="Stop-dialog"
    category="Frame"
    name="stop">
```

Now we are opening the actual behavior definition. You must give it a `dialogID` so it is unique to Flash when it loads in numerous behaviors. You also state under what category this behavior will fall. Because the category Frame does not currently exist, it will be created. You should use a new category for customizations to set them apart from what is included in the program.

The last attribute we are filling is `stop`. This will be the name that appears in the + drop-down menu in the Behaviors Panel.

```
<dialog id="Stop-dialog" title="Frame Stop action"  buttons="accept,
cancel">
```

Here we are defining the actual dialog box and tying it together with the `behavior_definition` element with the use of the `id` attribute. Give it the title attribute of `Frame Stop action`. This title is what appears in the top of the dialog box when it is opened. Last, state that there will be two buttons—accept and cancel—that will show up as OK and Cancel to the user.

```
    <grid>
      <columns>
        <column>
<rows>
  <row align="center">
            <vbox>
          <label value="Press OK to add a Stop action to the
          current frame."/>
              </vbox>
  </row>
</rows>
        </column>
      </columns>
     </grid>
</dialog>
```

The next series of elements have to do with the appearance of the dialog box. Within the grid element, we format the structure.

Your first tag is columns. It can contain only the column element. Our dialog box will have only one column.

Inside of column we have rows. Like columns, rows can only contain the row element.

Within the row tag, place a vbox tag. This tag states that the information will be vertically oriented. You also have the option of hbox for horizontal arrangement.

Because this behavior is simple, you have only one label, which reads "Press OK to add a Stop action to the current frame."

After we have finished the label element, you must close all tags. Remember, they must be closed in the order of first element opened/last element closed. Also close the dialog element.

```
        <actionscript>
<![CDATA[
stop();
/*
Made by Eric Hunley
*/
]]>
        </actionscript>
     </behavior_definition>
</flash_behavior>
```

Now you can add the ActionScript that will be inserted into the Flash movie. Open with the self-explanatory `actionscript` tag. Within this tag, you use the XML `<![CDATA[` tag. It stands for character data, which is data that is parsed. In this case, it is the data that will be submitted to Flash.

Within the XML `<![CDATA[` tag you have inserted `stop();`. This is the actual ActionScript command. On the next line, we have `/*`. These characters start an ActionScript multiline comment, allowing you to take credit for your creation. You can type as many lines as needed without trying to evaluate it as code. It is closed with the `*/` tag

After you add the ActionScript, you must close the `actionscript`, `behavior_definition`, and `flash_behavior` elements, completing the new behavior.

Let's see the results of your efforts. First, you must save the new behavior document as *Stop.xml* in one of the marathon file paths of *C:\Documents and Settings\%username%\Local Settings\Application Data\Macromedia\Flash MX 2004\en\Configuration\Behaviors* for Windows, or *Users:%username%:Library:Application Support:Macromedia:Flash MX 2004:en:Configuration:Behaviors* for Macintosh. Remember to show hidden files in Windows, if needed.

Now let's see what happens in Flash itself. First, close the program, then reopen it. Next, follow Figure 7.17.

1. Create a new Flash document, and select the empty keyframe on Frame 1. Click the + in the Behaviors Panel. You see there is a new category called Frame. Select stop from the category.
2. The new Frame Stop action dialog box opens. Looking good so far. Click OK, and you see that the behavior was added in the panel.
3. Now look inside of the Actions Panel. You can open it by clicking Window > Development Panels > Actions, or by pressing the F9 key on your keyboard. If you look inside of the panel, you will see that, yes, a stop action has been added. The behavior is now ready for prime time.

Behaviors are destined to become an important part of the future for Flash. Along with timeline effects, they really contribute to the extensibility of the program and are helping move the interface similarities of Flash, Fireworks, and Dreamweaver closer all the time.

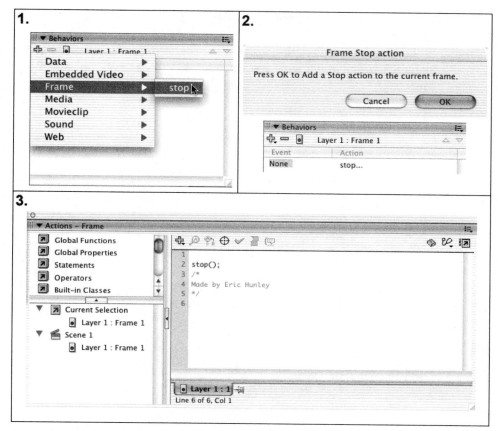

FIGURE 7.17 Results of creating a custom behavior

SUMMARY

This chapter concludes your look at using symbols and timeline effects and adding basic interactivity using behaviors. It is a lot of information, but it's invaluable.

As you can see, symbols are integral to creating Flash movies. They are extremely important and should be used liberally to keep the file size down in your movies.

Behaviors and timeline effects are moving the program into the future by adding more capacity for developers and third-party companies to add features. When programs are opened up to development, not only do the features grow, with add-ons, but their future grows even more secure as shops build customized solutions.

Let's now look at ActionScript, the programming language built into Macromedia Flash MX 2004, with an "Introduction to ActionScript and Programming Concepts."

8 Introduction to ActionScript and Programming Concepts

Within Macromedia Flash MX 2004, ultimate interactivity is achieved with a built-in language called ActionScript. ActionScript, now on version 2.0, was created exclusively for Flash and is based on the ECMA-262 standard. ECMA-262 is the standard related to JavaScript, so if you are familiar with JavaScript, the similarities between the two languages will be apparent to you.

Over time, ActionScript has grown from being a way to put basic interactivity on buttons to becoming a full-blown programming language that has Macromedia Flash MX 2004 development quickly approaching the scale of Java and .NET. As a language, ActionScript is now such a large subject that it takes books much larger than this volume to encompass it.

This chapter covers some basics of the language and how programming concepts apply. If you want to delve deeper into the capabilities of the language, a plethora of books is available. Among the well-regarded texts are any of *The Definitive Guides* by Colin Moock.

After looking at the language, we will modify the *dice.fla* file and turn it into an interactive game using ActionScript. If you want to get straight to the game, you can skip the first sections of this chapter, start with Events, and revisit the principles later. Much of this chapter can also be used as reference.

THE ACTIONS PANEL

Before we actually start looking at the language itself, let's explore the tool used for creating scripts, the Actions Panel. This panel, shown in Figure 8.1, can be accessed by clicking Window > Actions or by pressing the F9 key on your keyboard.

In previous versions of Flash, the Actions Panel had two modes: Normal and Expert. With Normal mode, all of the parameters of any command you chose were available in the window. As of Flash MX 2004, Normal mode has been removed and your only option is Expert mode.

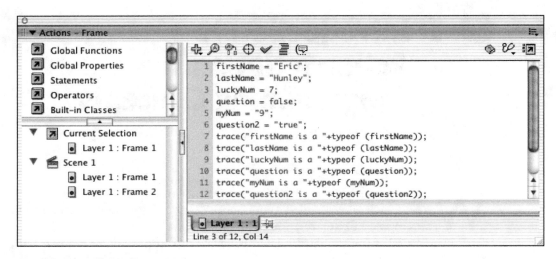

FIGURE 8.1 The Actions Panel.

With Expert mode, you don't have quite as much help. You must type or choose your commands. However, you do have code hinting available.

Code hinting is a process in which a drop-down menu or tool tip appears as you type a command, as long as the command is correct. You can then select your parameter from the drop-down menu.

Let's explore the options in the Actions Panel, shown in Figure 8.2.

When you click the + above the script window, the Add a new item to the script pop-up menu appears and offers all commands available within ActionScript.

You can also pick script commands from the left side of the Actions Panel in the Actions Toolbox. In the top-right corner of the Actions Panel is the View Options pop-up menu. This menu contains the option View Esc Shortcut Keys, which displays keyboard shortcuts available within the Actions Toolbox. You can also select View Line Numbers, to help you navigate your code, and Word Wrap. Word Wrap is a new addition to the Actions Panel as of Flash MX 2004. It is a well-received addition because lines of code can be very long. Word Wrap makes it easier to see an entire line within your script window.

When you insert a command from the Actions toolbox or the pop-up menu or just type it, you invoke what are known as code hints. Code hints are an invaluable tool to assist you when writing code. When you start a command, parameters appear on a drop-down menu. Here, you can select whatever parameter you need.

The Script navigator is new to Flash MX 2004. It enables you to navigate to all items within your movie that have script on them. Sometimes it is difficult to see what objects have scripts attached, so this element is a real time-saver.

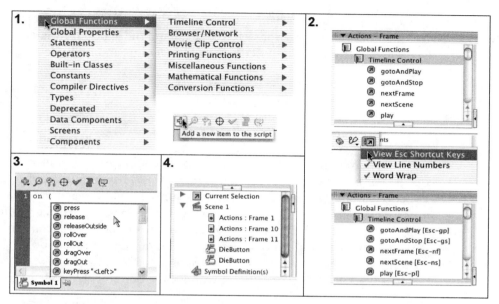

FIGURE 8.2 Options within the Actions Panel.

It is important to point out that when you add an action using either the Add a new item pop-up menu or the Actions Toolbox, you must pay close attention to where the pointer is placed. For example, when you click Global Functions > Movie Clip Control > on, a drop-down menu appears. This is fine; it's expected behavior. However, when you choose an item off the list, like press, your pointer is placed between the last s and the ending parentheses, not within the curly braces. A proper on(press){} *should have all actions within the curly braces, not the parentheses, so you must manually place the pointer in its proper location by moving it to the right of the opening curly brace ({) and pressing your Enter or Return key. You can then safely add your actions.*

CODE COMMENTS

Whenever you write code, you may wish to leave information about the code without the Flash Player interpreting it. Although it seems odd to first learn how to hide the code you are writing before addressing the code that is read, comments are an often-neglected but vital part of programming.

Comments describe what is happening in the process of the program. They enable other developers and yourself to understand the logical flow later. Two types of comments are available in ActionScript: single-line and multiple-line.

```
// This is a single line comment
/* This is a multiple line comment.
   Nothing will be read until we
   reach the final asterisk slash  */
```

Good comments should describe what is taking place overall, not what the code is. For example, //this is a function would be an unnecessary comment. (Functions will be covered later.) Any developer should understand what a function is. The comment //we are collecting the user's stats here would be appropriate because it describes what process is happening at the current time.

Comments are also invaluable to troubleshooting. They can be used to hide portions of code that don't seem to be responding correctly. This way, you can see if code is working to a certain point without the questionable code getting in the way.

VARIABLES

Literals and Variables

Variables could easily be considered the foundation of programming. If you have no means to have data that changes, what is the purpose of a programming language? Before exploring variables, let's address literals, which are a way of creating specific statements.

Let's start off with a basic example, the bane of every programmer's existence: "Hello World." The reason for this is built into tradition; "Hello World" has been used for learning nearly every program out there since at least the 1970s.

We are going to create your first script with "Hello World" and look at one of the most valuable built-in Flash commands available, – trace(), and explore literals.

First, open a new Flash document. After the document opens, select the empty keyframe on Frame 1 and open the Actions Panel by clicking Window > Development Panels > Actions or by pressing the F9 key on your keyboard. In the Actions Panel, type *trace ("Hello World!");*. Now test your movie, keeping in mind that if you are working on a Macintosh you must save your document first. The results are shown in Figure 8.3.

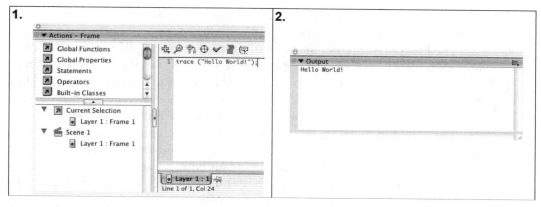

FIGURE 8.3 The Hello World program.

You may notice that your Output window does not appear or is extremely small. Drag the bottom-right corner of the window to expand it. If you are on a Windows machine, place your cursor along an edge and wait for the double-arrowed cursor to appear, then expand the window by dragging it to the desired size.

Now that we have created the Hello World program, let's look at its parts, starting with the `trace` command. `trace` is an invaluable command that you will use frequently when programming in ActionScript. It simply opens an Output window and returns a result, which is useful when you are troubleshooting your scripts. Place `trace` statements in strategic locations to determine if the program is doing what it is supposed to do.

The second thing to look at is the argument used with the trace function. We typed *Hello World!*, which is known as a string literal (also called a constant). It is a string because it is just a set of text, not a number or a Boolean (true or false). It is a literal because we are telling the program to type *Hello World!* directly. There is no interpretation, and no value must be swapped out.

This is where variables come in. Variables can be thought of as placeholders in a program. They are made up of two parts: *name* and *value*. For example, let's take the Hello World! example and modify it to the following:

```
firstname="Eric";
trace ("Hello " + firstname + "!");
```

This code gives us the result of `Hello Eric!` The reason why this code works is because `firstname` is a variable with the value of `Eric`. When `trace` is invoked in the Flash Player, it looks within the quotation marks and finds `Hello` and a space and prepares this. As it continues, it sees a + and then `firstname` without quotes. If there are no quotes, it's not a literal and must be a variable or a number.

The Flash Player (compiler) looks in memory, and, voilà, `firstname` is a variable with the value of `Eric`. It appends `Eric` to the end of the line and continues. Now the compiler sees the second + followed by quotation marks with an exclamation point inside. It appends this literal to the end of the statement. Then the compiler sees the right parenthesis with the semicolon following and knows it's done.

The + used in the example is known as the concatenation operator. Concatenation is the process of appending new content to current content. This process works especially well when combining literals with variables. In the example, we start off with `Hello` as the first part; this is a literal. Because we want to add the variable of `firstname` to the statement, we must concatenate it.

Let's break down the statement. Whenever text is typed within quotation marks, it is to be interpreted as a string literal. Add a concatenation operator and then a variable. After the variable has been added, we must complete the sentence, so we concatenate another literal.

Literals work well and are an important building block in programming, but what if we want to have the value change? This is where variables come into play.

A variable can be thought of as a container with a value, or a placeholder. When a variable is discovered, the program inserts its value in its place, which allows for the value to change.

Variables should be declared before any other actions are written. Doing so enables them to be loaded first and wait in memory for when actions call them.

When naming your variables, the first character must be a letter, underscore (_), or dollar sign ($). You cannot start a variable identifier (name) with a number. All other characters can be any combination of numbers, underscores, and dollar signs. Also, variables cannot be named any keyword that is used by the language (`for`, `while`, `function`, `object`, `true`, `false`, and so on).

A variable is assigned its value by placing an equals sign (=) between the name and desired value of the variable. The equals sign is known as the assignment operator. It assigns the value on the right to the variable on the left of the statement.

Let's look at some examples. You will declare some variables and then use the `typeof()` function to see what datatype each is. This procedure is shown in Figure 8.4.

1. Delete everything you have in the Actions Panel for the empty keyframe on Frame 1. Type the following lines:

```
firstName="Eric";
lastName="Hunley";
```

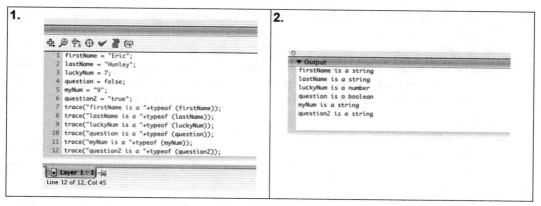

FIGURE 8.4   Using the typeof() function to view variable datatypes.

```
luckyNum=7;
question = false;
myNum="9";
question2="true";
trace ("firstName is a " + typeof(firstName));
trace ("lastName is a " + typeof(lastName));
trace ("luckyNum is a " + typeof(luckyNum));
trace ("question is a " + typeof(question));
trace ("myNum is a " + typeof(myNum));
trace ("question2 is a " + typeof(question2));
```

2. Now test your movie. Let's look in the output window and view the results. Notice that the first four variables are listed with the intended types: string, string, number, and Boolean. The last two are not—they are both listed as strings.

Let's look at what we entered when we declared and assigned values to the variables. In the first two, we surrounded the values with quotation marks, but in the third and fourth variables, the values were bare, which reflects their datatypes. Numbers and Boolean values must always be entered without quotation marks for the program to interpret them correctly.

Variable Types

Historically, Flash has been a loose-typed language. Loose-typed means a variable type need not be declared when a variable is created. You can also assign a value to a variable upon declaration. Flash also allows the type of a variable to be changed at will. This way, a variable can be declared as a string, then have a number assigned to it, and later be a Boolean value.

This behavior is different for strong-typed languages. In a strong-typed language, a variable must be declared before it is assigned a value, and it must be typed. Strong-typed languages must act in this manner because they are creating self-contained applications, whereas most Flash Movies are played in the Flash Player.

A self-contained application must reserve resources from the operating system when it is run. To have an accurate estimate of how much memory is needed at a given time, the application must know with what datatypes it is working. Some datatypes take up much less memory than others.

To explain this principle, the number 65535 requires the same amount of memory as aa in a string—16 bits. These requirements are due to ASCII translation. 256 possibilities are available with ASCII text, making each character require 8 bits of memory. Therefore, the example of aa, converted to binary is 01100001 01100001. This is a 16-bit number. If we convert 65535 into binary, the result is 1111111111111111. This is also 16 bits. To stress this point even further, if you convert the string of false to binary, you come up with a 40-bit number, whereas the Boolean of false is 1 bit—a zero.

If strong-typing did not occur, applications would have to reserve the maximum amount of memory available, causing each program to eat up all available memory on the computer. An interpreted language such as ActionScript is run through the Flash Player, which controls the memory usage as it goes through the code. Three principle values are available to variables: strings, numbers, and Boolean. Strings are, as we discovered, a combination of text including letters and numbers. Numbers cover any integer or floating-point integer (such as 10.5), either positive or negative. Boolean can contain only one of two values: true or false.

Variable Scope

If you look at all the variables we have written to this point, you see that we used the method of *variablename=value*. This method is the simplest for assigning and declaring variables.

When you create a variable using the syntax of variablename=value, you are creating what is known as a timeline variable. This variable is available to all scripts within that timeline. In other languages such as JavaScript, this variable would be a global variable, available to all parts of the script, but Flash is a bit different.

Because everything in the program is tied to timelines, and you have movie clips with independent timelines, you can't directly access one movie clip variable from another movie clip by name alone. You must type the full path to the variable, including the movie clip name, using dot syntax. A dot (.) separates the object from its method or property, as in `myMovieClip.myVar`. Any variable inside of a movie clip becomes a property of that movie clip.

You can run into issues with timeline variables if you are using a variable with the same name inside of a function or other type of block. For example, consider the following code:

```
myName = "Eric";
function hello() {
myName="Billy Bob";
trace("Hello "+ myName + "!");
}
hello();
trace( "Hello " + myName + "!");
```

When you run this code, you get the following result:

```
Hello Billy Bob!
Hello Billy Bob!
```

If you wanted the result of `Hello Eric!` on the second line, this would be a problem. We are looking at a scope issue. Because you declared `myName` as a timeline variable, it is accessible to any part of a script on the same timeline. You must have the variable `myName` inside of the function constrained to work only inside of the function.

This is where the `var` keyword comes in. If you precede a variable name with `var`, it will be a local variable. In other words, it will be available only within the function. Let's revise the code:

```
myName = "Eric";
function hello() {
var myName="Billy Bob";
trace("Hello "+ myName + "!");
}
hello();
trace( "Hello " + myName + "!");
```

Now when we test the movie, the result is:

```
Hello Billy Bob!
Hello Eric!
```

This result is because the variable myName inside of the function hello is a local variable. It is available only when the function is running. Once the function is complete, the variable is removed from memory. It is often a good idea to use local variables within functions to protect your data. We will be creating more functions later.

Global Variables

When writing ActionScript, you may want to create a variable that is accessible to every part of the program, no matter what timeline you are currently in. As of Flash MX, the _global keyword was added to make global variables available. Before then, they were not an option.

To make a variable global, type the _global keyword followed by a dot and the variable name, as in _global.myName. Now the value of myName can be retrieved by calling the variable anywhere in the entire Flash movie.

Strict Data Typing

With Flash creating programs for more and more devices, the program needed a way to allow strong-typing. It is now available with Flash MX 2004. Strict data typing is achieved in the following manner: var variablename:variabletype = value. An example would be var myNum:Number=10;. When you use strict data typing and have a data type mismatch, an error occurs when you publish your movie.

Global variables are not available with strict data typing because you must use the var *keyword when declaring a variable with a type. With global variables, the* var *keyword is forbidden.*

NOTE

Variable Conversion

Several methods and functions are available for converting data from one type to another. Some of the most commonly used include:

parseInt(*value,radix*) function: Extracts a number from a string. If the string contains a binary or hexadecimal number, the number can be converted by setting the optional radix argument to 2 or 16, as in parseInt(value,radix). A string that begins with a number returns just the number.

Convert string to number:

```
myString = "21 Days";
trace(parseInt(myString));          //returns 21
```

Convert hex string to number:

```
myString = "ff";
trace(parseInt(myString, 16));      //returns 255
```

Convert binary string to number:

```
myString= "10111011";
trace(parseInt(myString,2));        //returns 187
```

parseFloat(*value*) function: Extracts numbers from strings. It extracts one decimal point and the numbers following. Like with parseInt(), the first digits must be numeric.

int(*value*) function: Returns a whole number from a string. It does not resolve decimal points. Also, if anything other than numbers is in the string, it returns unexpected results.

Boolean() function: Returns the Boolean result of any tested value. It follows some basic rules—any number outside of zero, nonempty string, Object, or true Boolean returns true; any empty string, 0, NaN, null, or undefined variable returns false.

toString(*value*,*radix*) method: Converts any value to a string. This method is the opposite of the parseInt() function.

Number(*value*) function: Extracts a numeric value from a string. Its functionality has been changed with Flash MX 2004. Previously, you could convert a value using a radix, but you can no longer do so.

Arrays

Arrays are an important part of programming. They are technically not variables but objects. An array is an indexed list of variables. Several types of array are available, but the most basic version is created in this manner:

```
my_array = new Array();
my_array[0] = "Item1";
my_array[1] = "Item2";
my_array[3] = "Item3";
```

Arrays can be declared and have their values assigned automatically in two ways:

```
my_array = new Array("Item 1","Item 2","Item 3");
my_array = ["Item 1","Item 2","Item 3"];
```

To refer to an item in an array, you must start with the index value. Index values start with 0, which can be confusing because you are used to counting from 1. To create a trace statement accessing the value of item 3 in the array, you would type:

```
trace(my_array[2]);
```

Arrays are commonly used for moving multiple items in a single package. They are especially useful when dealing with database queries where an entire field can be dropped into one array rather than having multiple variables floating about the page.

Associative and Multidimensional Arrays

Arrays are robust objects. They can contain any value, including other arrays. The options available with arrays make working with them easier. The first of these that you examine is the associative array.

An associative array uses names (sometimes called keys) for index values instead of numbers. This way, you can access values by name as opposed to remembering index numbers. An associative array is created in the following manner:

```
person_array = new Array();
person_array.firstname="Eric";
person_array.lastname = "Hunley";
```

Values can be accessed in one of two ways:

```
trace(person_array["firstname"]);
trace(person_array.firstname);
```

Multidimensional arrays are simply arrays within arrays. To make a multidimensional array, create the array and then assign other arrays to its values:

```
people_array = new Array();
people_array[0] = new Array ("Eric","Hunley","Tucson","AZ");
people_array[1] = ["James","Bond","London","England"];
```

You can also assign other arrays that are created to the multidimensional array, as in myArray = [array1,array2]. To access the values within a multidimensional array, think about it like a spreadsheet. You must reference the parent index within the current array and then follow it with the child index:

```
trace(people_array[0][1]); //returns Hunley
trace(people_array[1][2]); //returns London
```

Array Methods

Arrays have several methods available to manipulate their data. Let's look at some of the most popular:

Array.toString(): Converts all values in an array into a comma-separated string. This method can be useful when you want to push a single-string variable with multiple values. An example would be for a database query. You may recognize this method from earlier when you converted number variables to string variables.

Array.join('*separator*'): Similar to Array.toString(); however, you can choose what character you are using to separate the values in the output. Let's look at an example:

```
my_array = new Array("Item 1","Item 2","Item 3");
trace(my_array.join('*'));
//returns Item 1*Item 2*Item 3
```

Array.concat(): Adds multiple arrays together into a new array.

Array.sort(function): Sorts arrays according to a comparison function you create. If no comparison function is used, the default is an alphabetical sort. An alphabetical sort works in this manner:

:A,B,C,1,10,2,3,4,5,6,7,8,9

Notice that in the number 10 is immediately following 1. This is due to the alphabetical sorting.

OPERATORS

If you miss attending math classes, this is the section for you. Because computers are ultimately nothing more than very fast number-crunchers, math is very important to them.

Whenever you process a mathematical equation, the equation itself is often termed an expression. An expression can be used to not only have the computer perform math but to actually assign values. With Flash being used to creating more complex applications all the time, mathematics keeps creeping in. It relates not only to an application you might create performing mortgage calculations but to overall placement and frames within a movie.

Basic Arithmetical Operators

With ActionScript being a programming language, it should come as no surprise that many mathematical options are available. Let's explore some of the most common, starting with the primary arithmetical operators: * multiply, / divide, + add (and concatenate), and − subtract.

For the most part, these operators work as expected:

```
var x=10;
var y=10;

var result= x*y;
trace(result);      // Outputs 100
result=x/y;
trace(result);      // Outputs 1
result=x+y;
trace(result);      // Outputs 20
result=x-y;
trace(result);      // Outputs 0
```

Whenever you use variables that have been created as numbers, things work as anticipated, but when you combine calculations, you must pay attention to operator precedence. Let's look at an example:

```
Result=10-3*3;
```

You may wish this calculation to result in 21, but it actually returns 1 because of operator precedence. When a calculation is performed, multiplication and division have a higher precedence than addition or subtraction. An easy way to remember this order is the saying, "My Dear Aunt Sally." The way to overcome precedence rules is by surrounding the operation you wish performed first in parentheses:

```
Result=(10-3)*3;
```

The result is now 21 because parentheses have the highest level of precedence available, and the actions within are performed first. A general overview of the rules is precedence first, and then, if there is a tie, left to right. If there is any question or doubt, use parentheses. Parentheses are also useful for clarity in reading the expression.

Another area in which you may run into issues is when you try to add a string and a number:

```
var x="10";
var y=10;

trace(x+y);
```

Although you may intend for the result to be 20, it actually returns 1010 because one of the operands is a string. The concatenation operator has a higher precedence than the addition operator. You can overcome this by using the parseInt(), parseFloat(), or Number() function:

```
var x="10";
var y=10;

trace(parseInt(x)+y);
```

Now, we have achieved the expected result. By using parseInt(), we have extracted a numeric value from x and the numbers add instead of concatenate. The parseInt() function extracts any number or series of whole numbers that lead a variable's value. If the value starts off with any character other than a number, it returns NaN (Not a Number).

```
var x= parseInt("3rd place");
trace(x);          //returns 3

var x= parseInt("Placed 3rd");
trace(x);          //returns NaN

var x= parseInt("3.14");
trace(x);          //returns 3
```

As you can see from the examples, if a number is the first digit in a string variable, its value is returned and the variable type is a number. However, if a number is not in the beginning of the value, NaN is the result.

Also of note, if the number has a decimal point, only the whole number is returned because parseInt() returns only whole integers. If you want to also return the decimal point and numbers following, use parseFloat() instead. The parseFloat() function returns numbers with a floating point decimal.

Other Arithmetical Operators

In addition to the basic arithmetical operators described in the previous section, other popular options are available. Three are ++ incrementing, -- decrementing, and % modulus.

Incrementing and decrementing simply adds or subtracts one from the value of the current variable and reassigns the result back to the variable. These operators physically change the value of the variable. Let's look at some examples:

```
var x=10;
var y=x+1;
trace(x);       //returns 10
trace(y);       //returns 11

var x=10;
var y=++x;
trace(x);       //returns 11
trace(y);       //returns 11

var x=10;
var y=x++;
trace(x);       //returns 11
trace(y);       //returns 10
```

In the first example, you can see that when we assign a value to y, we are not changing the actual value of x; we are simply borrowing it.

In the next example, the value of x is actually changed because we have incremented it. The y variable is assigned the result.

In the third example, something strange happens. The x variable is incremented as expected, but y receives the value of 10 instead of 11. This is due to the placement of the increment operator. If you look closely, you notice that in this example, the ++ is placed after x. This is known as post-fix, as opposed to pre-fix, where the increment/decrement operator is placed before. What happened in this case is y received the value of x before x was incremented.

Now let's take a look at modulus. Modulus is closely related to division. Do you remember long division, such as10/3 results in 3 with a remainder of 1? Modulus gives you the remainder. It is handy for determining if a result is odd or even. Any number modulus 2 results in 0 when it is even. It also can put commas in numbers above 1000:

```
var total=39364;
var remain=total%1000;      //remain is now 364
var result = (total-remain)/1000 + "," + remain;
trace(result);             //result is now 39,364
```

Looking at the example, you can see that we started with total. It is a five-digit number because you cannot use commas in numbers. We knew that we were evaluating a number that was over 1000, so we ran the expression of total%1000 as the variable remain. This gives you 364, which we can concatenate with a comma later. Last, we worked the result by subtracting remain value and dividing that result by 1000. This gave you the 36 to concatenate with a comma and the value of remain. We did all of this within a new variable, so the original operand of 39264 is still available for future calculations.

Assignment Operators

The last set of operators are some assignment operators. Of these, you should be quite familiar with the first, =. The = assignment operator simply takes the value or result from the right and assigns it to the variable name on the left, as in my-Name="Eric". However, some other options are available with assignment operators that perform an operation and assign a new value in one shot:

```
var x=10;
x+=10;         //equivalent of x=x+10;  result is 20
var x=10;
x-=10;         //equivalent of x=x-10;  result is 0
var x=10;
x*=10;         //equivalent of x=x*10;  result is 100
var x=10;
x/=10;         //equivalent of x=x/10;  result is 1
```

The assignment operators can be thought of as a shortcut in reassigning a new value. You see them used often in ActionScript, especially with movie clip placement as in myMovieClip_mc._x +=10;, which moves the movie clip 10 pixels along the x-plane (horizontally).

CONDITIONALS

if

The next subject is the conditional block, commonly known as if/else. This element is an important part of programming because it allows the application to make decisions and react accordingly. Let's start with if. The basic structure is:

```
if (condition){
    Actions to be taken;
}
```

Whenever you write an if statement, we are seeking truth. If this is true, do this. The most basic of truths is if a variable exists and has a value, as in:

```
var name="Eric";
if(name){
    trace("Hello " + name + "!");
}
```

This example results in Hello Eric! It works because name has a value and evaluates to true. If the variable name were undefined (not assigned a value), null, NaN, or 0, it would evaluate to false. As long as it has a string value, a positive or negative number (not 0), or the Boolean value of true, the if condition evaluates to true, and any actions are taken.

In versions of ActionScript prior to version 2.0, a variable containing a non-empty string that does not begin with a number evaluates to false. This behavior was changed in the new version to be more compliant with the ECMA standard.

NOTE

Comparison Operators

Now that we have looked at what initiates an if statement, let's look at comparison operators. Comparison operators are used to check if one item matches a particular value. For example, let's say we want to check if name is set to the value of Eric. We could use this code:

```
var name="Eric";
if(name == "Eric"){
    trace("Hello Eric!");
}
```

This code results in `Hello Eric!` However, if the variable name is set to anything else, nothing would be returned. Several comparison operators are available:

```
==     Checks for equality
===    Checks for strict equality (such as, while "10" == 10 will
       evaluate to true, "10" === 10 will be false. This is because
       they are of two different data types.
<      Less than.
>      Greater than.
<=     Less than or equal to.
>=     Greater than or equal to.
!=     Not equal. The ! means not. It flips the Boolean value of
       anything to which it is attached.
```

In addition to comparison operators, ActionScript uses what are known as logical operators. These operators evaluate more than one condition in a single conditional. The primary logical operators are:

```
&&     AND
||     OR
!      NOT
```

These operators allow you to mix and match for what you seek. For example, if you want a single result if the name variable is equal to `"Eric"` or `"Bob"`, type the following:

```
var name="Eric";
if (name == "Eric" || name="Bob"){
    trace ("Welcome back " + name + "!");
}
```

This example results in `Welcome back Eric!` If it were Bob, it would welcome Bob back.

Truth Tables

A common tool used to understand both logical and comparison operators is the truth table. It lists a series of comparisons and states whether the result is true or false. Some examples follow:

```
var x=1;
var y=2;
var z=3;

x<y                              true
y>z                              false
x<y || y>z                       true
(x<y || y>z) && (y<x || z<x)    false
!(x<y || y>z) && (y<x || z<x)   true
```

In the last example, the result is true because of the not operator. The easiest way to evaluate a comparison using the not operator is to ignore it at first. Then figure out whether the expression is true or false and flip it to the opposite. This is much easier than trying to account for the not while evaluating.

if/else

Although if works well to check a single condition, what if a decision has to be made or if you want a result no matter what is entered. This is where else comes in. The else statement works directly with if and occurs when if is false. Because this statement is dependant on the if statement, no condition occurs with the statement, which looks like this:

```
var name="Bob";
if (name == "Eric"){
    trace ("Welcome back Eric!");
}else{
    trace ("Welcome to Flash "+ name + "!");
```

Because the variable name is not Eric, the result is Welcome to Flash Bob! By creating an else statement, the variable is addressed no matter what it reads.

if/else if/else

The third possibility with basic conditional blocks is using else if. This statement is for when you want to have more than one condition that can be matched:

```
var name="Bob";
if (name == "Eric"){
    trace ("Welcome back Eric!");
}else if(name=="Bob"){
    trace ("Been a long time Bob. Where've you been?");
}else if(name == "Sue"){
```

```
trace ("Hi Sue! We've missed you!");
}else{
    trace ("Welcome to Flash "+ name + "!");
```

We now are checking for three people—Eric, Bob, or Sue. Notice that `else if` was repeated twice. When you are checking for multiple conditions, you use one `if`, then as many `else if` statements as needed for other conditions. Then close it out with an `else` when you want to cover all possibilities.

switch

An alternative to the `if/else if/else` conditional block is the `switch` statement. The `switch` statement is popular because it is easy to read. However, it is not as robust as an `if/else` block because it can check only one item and you must know specific results. A basic `switch` statement follows:

```
var name="Eric";
switch(name){
    case"Eric": trace("Hello Eric!");
    break;
    case "Bob": trace("Hello Bob!");
    break;
    default: trace("Hello "+ name+"!");
}
```

Within the `switch` structure, you start out with the `switch` keyword followed by the condition you want to check; in this case, a string variable. Within the block denoted by the opening and closing curly braces, you have a case statement for every value against which you want to check. Immediately after each case, you often find a `break` statement. This statement ends the `switch` statement if a match is found. If it is omitted, when a case is found true, the Flash Player performs all actions it sees until the next break action or default statement. The default statement has the same functionality of an `else` condition. It is invoked if all cases result in false.

The Conditional Operator

The last conditional we explore is the conditional operator. It is the only operator that has three operands within. It is structured as:

```
(condition)? action when false : action when true;
```

These operators act in a similar manner to a basic if/else statement. First you set the condition. Then you state what should happen when it is true. Last, you state what should occur when it is false. These operators are popular to use in variable assignment:

```
var name = "Eric";
var reply=(name=="Eric")? "Hi Eric!": "Welcome "+name+"!";
trace (reply);
```

The example shows the result of Hi Eric! The value of reply has been set from the conditional operator.

LOOPS

Loops are an essential part of programming. In ActionScript, they can be thought of as specialized conditionals; however, they persist until a condition is false. Two basic types of loop are available: while and for.

while

A while loop is a loop that simply loops until it is proven false. It is robust and open-ended, which can make it dangerous. The basic structure follows:

```
While (condition){
    actions;
}
```

A while loop works with numbers and strings and has the broadest range of all loops. Let's see an example that uses a number as an argument:

```
trace("Counting...");
var x=1;
while (x<=100){
trace("This is number " + x + ".");
x++
}
```

This basic loop counts from 1 to 100 and prints the current value of x in each iteration. It is structured with the variable x being declared and assigned before the loop is entered. Then as we enter the loop, we have your condition that is being matched. If x is less than or equal to 100, we perform the action. We are then performing a basic `trace()` and using x to output the current number. Finish off the statement with an incrementing x so we can eventually complete the `while`. If we don't include it, we would have an infinite loop, which is extremely dangerous. It can crash a computer as all resources are used up performing the loop.

for

The next loop is the `for` loop. The `for` loop is a specialized loop, often referred to as the counting loop. It is optimized to work with a defined count and is structured as follows:

```
for (initialization;condition;count){
actions;
}
```

It has all of the counting mechanisms built into the arguments of the loop. Let's look at the `while` loop structured as a `for` loop:

```
trace("Counting...");
for (var i=1;i<=100;i++){
    trace ("This is number " + i + ".");
}
```

The same code with a `while` loop takes more lines to express. Although a `for` loop is optimized, it is not obvious what is happening. Let's look at what happens by using the example:

1. Start with the initialization, which in your case is `i=1`. This initialization is used only when the loop is first entered.
2. Next, let's look at the condition. We are saying that it must be less than or equal to 100.
3. The `for` loop performs the actions inside.
4. Now, the `for` loop looks at the increment/decrement. It may seem odd that it doesn't look at the counter before the actions, but this is the structure of the loop. It is created so you can define all of this information in one shot.
5. We are now on the next iteration. It immediately looks at the condition and ignores the initialization, as that is read only when the loop is first entered.
6. If the comparison proves true, all actions are performed.
7. The incrementer is read.

As you can see, this loop has all of the information placed inside of the parentheses, but it reacts in a slightly different manner than a `while` loop. Remember, it is optimized for counting.

for . . . in

Whereas a `for` loop is a specialized loop for counting, the `for...` `in` loop is a specialized loop for counting items in an array or object. The basic syntax for using a `for...` `in` loop follows:

```
for (properties in Array/Object){
Actions;
}
```

An example using an object follows:

```
Person = new Object();
Person.firstname = "Eric";
Person.lastname = "Hunley";
Person.city = "Tucson";
Person.state = "AZ";

for(prop in Person){
trace (prop + " has the value of " + Person[prop]);}
```

Notice in the example that `prop` is used in two ways. The first instance of `prop` returns the property name, whereas the second use is combined with the object name and placed within square brackets to return the value. If an array is used, the first use of `prop` returns the index number.

break/continue

Within loops, you sometimes need to leave a loop if a condition is met. This is where a `break` statement comes in. For example, if you have an array with names and wanted to output information if `"Eric"` is found, then leave the loop, you might have a statement like this:

```
trace("Searching names...");
names = new Array("Sally", "Joe", "Betsy", "Eric", "Billy");
for (i=0; i<names.length; i++) {
    if (names[i] != "Eric") {
        trace(names[i]+" is the current name.");
    } else {
```

```
        trace("Found him! Eric is at index "+i+" in names.");
        break;
    }
}
```

This code runs until `Eric` is found. At this point, it breaks out of the loop because there is no purpose in continuing the search.

The `continue` statement is similar to the `break` statement in the sense that no statements are performed after it is used. However, unlike the `break`, it re-enters the loop. Let's look at a loop that uses the `continue` statement:

```
trace("Searching names...");
names = new Array("Sally", "Joe", "Betsy", "Eric", "Billy");
for (i=0; i<names.length; i++) {
    if (names[i] != "Eric") {
        continue;
    }
    trace("Found him! Eric is at index "+i+" in names.");
    break;
}
```

In this example, we have used both the `continue` and `break` statements. If you look at it, you will see that within the loop, there is an `if` statement checking if the current index value is not equal to `Eric`. If it is not equal, the `continue` statement prevents it from finishing the statements in the loop. It will reenter the loop at the top.

Once `Eric` is found, the `trace` action will take place. The `break` statement will end the loop.

do

The `do` statement is used in combination with a `while` loop. It was created to force one iteration of a loop whether or not the loop condition returns false. Its basic structure is:

```
do {
actions;
} while(condition)
```

FUNCTIONS

When you are programming, you sometimes have a series of actions that you want to apply more than once or in different places. This is where functions come in. They can be thought of as mini-programs. As a rule, if you are going to perform actions more than once, write a function.

Basic Functions

When writing a function, first declare it using the `function` keyword. The syntax for a function can be written in two ways:

```
function functionname (arguments){
actions;
}

functionname= function(arguments){
actions;
};
```

The second version of creating functions is usually used to create methods on objects. Notice the ending semicolon. In earlier versions of Flash, you had to type the semicolon. As of Flash MX 2004, the semicolon is added automatically. After functions are created, they are invoked by using a function call. Some examples of function creation and calls follow:

```
function hello() {
    trace("Hello world!");
}
hello();
speak = function () {
    trace("Arf! Arf!");
};
speak();
```

Notice that both examples generate results when the `function` call is used. Both of these examples did not have parameters or arguments.

Arguments and Parameters

Although you can create functions that don't accept any arguments, they are not usually useful. Let's modify one of the functions to accept an argument:

```
function hello(name){
trace("Hello " + name + "!");
}
hello("Eric");
```

Notice in this version, we sent the string value of Eric, which caused the function to create a more personalized trace statement.

Functions that Return a Value

Often, you want a function to return a value, such as when you want to assign results to a variable. Let's look at a function:

```
function square (x){
x*=x;
}
myNum = square (10);
trace(myNum);
```

When you run this example, you find that it results in undefined because the square has not returned a value, causing myNum to be undefined. A variable is undefined if it has never been assigned a value. There is no way of knowing what type it is. To correct the situation, you must add a return statement to the function as follows:

```
function square (x){
x*=x;
return x;
}
myNum = square (10);
trace(myNum);
```

This time, the results are as expected. The value of 100 was assigned to the variable, so the trace statement reflects its value. The return statement if followed by a value returns that value; otherwise, it just ends the function (like a break statement in a loop).

OBJECTS

Objects are an intrinsic part of modern programming. Most powerful computer languages have an aspect of what is called object-oriented programming. Objects are useful because they are self-contained components in programming.

Objects contain both properties (built-in variables) and methods (internal functions). You can create an object using the built-in object constructor. Let's create an object, then add properties and a method:

```
Person = new Object();
Person.firstname = "Eric";
Person.lastname = "Hunley";
Person.city = "Tucson";
Person.state = "AZ";

Person.output = function (){
    trace (this.firstname + " " + this.lastname + " lives in " +
this.city + ", " + this.state + ".");
};
Person.output();
```

First, we created an object called `Person`. Then, we set `firstname`, `lastname`, `city`, and `state` properties of the new object by using dot syntax (`Objectname.prop-ertyname = value;`). Last, we created a method called `output`. We used the function constructor to create an anonymous function. If we had created a function with a name, it would be accessible outside of the object. By having it anonymous, it is set as a method of `Person` and can be referenced only using `Person` in the path.

In addition to being able to create your own objects in Flash, several objects are built in for added functionality. Two prime examples are the `Math` and `Date` objects.

The `Math` object has methods and properties that assist in mathematical calculations. We will use some methods from the `Math` object in the upcoming dice game.

The `Date` object is useful for returning date and time information. The primary method of using the `Date` object is to create a new object as a date.

```
my_date = new Date();
```

Once you have created the new object, you can retrieve multiple values using its built-in methods, including:

getDate(): Returns the day of the month.

getDay(): Returns the day of the week based on an array. Sunday is returned as 0 and Saturday as 6. You must convert its output when used.

getFullYear(): Returns the entire year, as in 2004.

getHours(): Returns the current hour based on a 24-hour clock (for example, 1 p.m. will be 13).

getMinutes(): Returns minutes.

getMonth(): Returns the current month based on an array. January is returned as 0, and December as 11. You must covert this output as you do with getDay() results.

getSeconds(): Returns current second.

getYear(): Returns current year minus 1900, for example, 2004 results in 104.

toString(): Outputs the date and time in a string format. It returns a date formatted like Sat Oct 11 14:35:29 GMT-0700 2004.

As you can see you have several options from which to choose. And these options are just a few of those available. Let's now look at how you can create some functions to output the date and time in a more readable format for many users. Let's start with the time. Because the time outputted by Flash is based on a 24-hour clock, you must create a function to convert it to reflect a.m. and p.m. Underneath the newly created Date object my_date, type the following code:

```
function myTime(){
    var currentTime;
    if(my_date.getHours() > 12){
        currentTime = my_date.getHours() - 12 + ":" +
        my_date.getMinutes() + "PM";
    }else if((my_date.getHours() < 12) && (my_date.getHours() !=
    0)){
        currentTime = my_date.getHours() + ":" +
        my_date.getMinutes() + "AM";
    }else if(my_date.getHours() == 12){
        currentTime = my_date.getHours() + ":" +
        my_date.getMinutes() + "PM";
    }else{
        currentTime = "12:" + my_date.getMinutes() + "AM";
    }
    return currentTime;
}
trace(myTime());
```

Notice that when you test your movie, the time is reflected in a 12-hour format.

Now let's look at the day and month. Because both of these values are based on an array, let's create functions for both. We will be creating your own arrays with a more verbose description of each value and then returning the value from the array.

```
function weekday() {
    myDay = Array("Sunday", "Monday", "Tuesday", "Wednesday",
    "Thursday", "Friday", "Saturday");
    return myDay[my_date.getDay()];
}
function myMonth(){
    var month = new Array("January","February","March","April",
    "May","June","July","August","September","October","November",
    "December");
    return month[my_date.getMonth()];
}
```

Now that we have created functions that resolve the issues with the date format, let's test them. Create a `trace()` statement reflecting your formatting choices:

```
trace("It is now " + myTime() + " on " + weekday() + ", " +
myMonth() + " " + my_date.getDate() + ", " + my_date.getFullYear() +
".");
```

You should see a much easier-to-read result, formatted as: It is now 2:57PM on Saturday, October 11, 2004. By using a little creativity, you can format the date in any manner you wish.

EXTERNAL VARIABLES

Often, when you are creating within Flash, you need to communicate outside of the program. For example, if you want to have connectivity to a database, you must have an intermediary language, like ColdFusion or PHP.

Flash supports the ability to send, load, or send and load external variables for use in your application. This is good, because instead of updating an .fla file, which can be very time-consuming, you can simply update a text file or script that the movie is using. Let's look at the most basic tool available, the `LoadVars()` object.

1. First, you must create a text file using any text editor. You can save this file as *variables.txt*.
2. Within the text file, add some variables for the Flash Player to read:

```
firstname=John&lastname=Doe&address=123+Main+St&city=
New+York&state=New+York&zip=55304
```

Notice in the text file some + (plus signs) have been added. If more than one word is in a variable, it must be URL encoded. Put simply, spaces must be replaced with the + (plus sign).

3. Now that we have created tour variables, let's build a new `LoadVars()` object using the following code:

```
Contacts = new LoadVars();
```

4. When we have created the new `LoadVars()` object, you must define what happens when the object is loaded. To do this, use the built-in event handler of `onLoad` with the following code:

```
Contacts.onLoad = function(success) {
        if (success) {
trace(this.firstname+" " +
this.lastname+"\$$\n"+this.address+"\$$\n"+this.city+",
"+this.state+"
"+this.zip);
        } else {
trace("The external variables failed to load");
        }
};
/*The semi-colon denotes an anonymous function (function without a
name).*/
```

5. In the event handler, precede each of the variable names with the keyword `this`. When external variables are loaded, they become properties of the `LoadVars` object you created; in this case, `Contacts`. You use `this.variable-name` as a shortcut for `Contacts.variablename` because we are inside `Contacts`. Elsewhere in applications, refer to each variable as a property of the `LoadVars` object.
6. After you create your function to react to the `onLoad` event, we can load your variables using the `LoadVars.load(url)` method.

```
Contacts.load("variables.txt");
```

7. We had to put the load method after we created the event handler for onLoad because we can't call a function that hasn't been created.

EVENTS

ActionScript works with content in a Flash movie and is event-driven, meaning that it reacts according to what the user does. Will the user push a button, drag the mouse, or enter text? By building responses to events, you create truly dynamic movies and allow interactivity.

Events are broken down into timeline events, button events, and movie clip events. Other events are available, but let's focus on these general areas.

Timeline Events

Whenever the playhead enters a frame, a timeline event occurs. All of the actions we have created so far have been reacting to this basic event. You need only to list your actions on a frame in the main timeline or on a keyframe inside of a movie clip, and they are performed. Some basic timeline actions include:

gotoAndPlay(): Takes the playhead to a specified frame number or label and plays from there.

gotoAndStop(): Stops the playhead on a targeted frame.

nextFrame(): Advances the playhead one frame forward and stops. This action is useful for creating slide navigation.

play(): Starts playing the movie.

prevFrame(): Moves the playhead to the previous frame and stops.

stop(): Stops the playhead.

stopAllSounds(): Stops all sounds playing in the movie. This action works well when assigned to a mute button.

Most timeline control actions are attached to buttons because buttons have no timeline independence. If you put an action on a button, it influences its parent object. If a button is placed on the main timeline (_root), the whole stage is affected, whereas a button inside a movie clip affects only the movie clip.

on **Handler**

Initially, the on handler was used for buttons, but as of Flash MX, its functionality was added to movie clips.

Several options are available as arguments:

on(press){*actions*}: Initiates all actions when the mouse button is pressed while over a button or movie clip.

on(release){*actions*}: Requires the mouse button to be pressed and released while directly over a button or movie clip.

on(releaseOutside){*actions*}: Occurs if the mouse button was pressed while directly over a button or movie clip but released after moving away from the button or movie clip.

on(rollOver){*actions*}: Initiates actions when the mouse pointer passes over a movie clip or button.

on(rollOut){*actions*}: Occurs after the mouse pointer has passed over a button or movie clip and has moved away.

on(dragOver){*actions*}: Initiates actions when the mouse button is pressed and held down while the pointer is dragged off of the object and then back over it.

on(dragOut){*actions*}: Occurs when the mouse button is pressed while over an object and then dragged away from the object while it remains pressed.

on(keyPress "*<key>*"){*actions*}: Initiates actions according to what button is pressed on the keyboard. Several predefined keys show up in code hinting between <>, such as on(keyPress "<Space>"). You can also type a number or letter key within quotation marks, such as on(keyPress "9").

When using the on handler, if you want the actions to be initiated by more than one event, place multiple events in the argument, separated by commas, such as on(press,keyPress "<space>").

Let's perform a quick exercise to see how to apply an on handler to a button, as shown in Figure 8.5.

1. Create a circle on the stage using any color of stroke and fill you like. Convert it into a symbol with the name of *circle* and Behavior of Button.
2. While your circle button is still selected on the stage, give the instance the name of *circle_btn* in the Property Inspector.
3. Now, while *circle_btn* is still selected, open the Actions Panel and type the following lines:

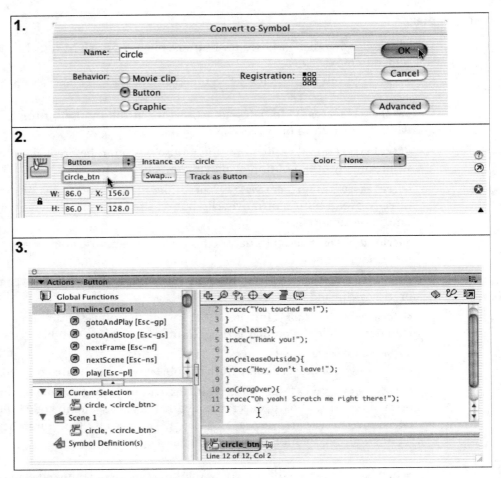

FIGURE 8.5 Applying the on handler.

```
on(press){
trace("You touched me!");
}
on(release){
trace("Thank you!");
}
on(releaseOutside){
trace("Hey, don't leave!");
}
```

```
on(dragOver){
trace("Oh yeah! Scratch me right there!");
}
```

4. Test your movie.

When you test your movie, you should see how the button reacts to different types of mouse input. Remember that you must click on a button and drag the cursor off and on the button to invoke the on(dragOver) event handler. The on(press) handler also initiates when you attempt the drag-over, because the press is part of the overall action.

onClipEvent **Handler**

When you want to have a clip event kick off actions, use the onClipEvent (event){actions} handler. The onClipEvent handler is directly tied to movie clips, including _root. Choose from several options:

onClipEvent (load) {*actions*}: Takes action when a movie clip enters the movie.

onClipEvent (unload) {*actions*}: Takes action when a movie clip exits the stage.

onClipEvent (enterFrame) {*actions*}: Takes action every time a movie clip enters a frame. This handler is a wonderful way of looping a continuous action because it occurs at the movie frame rate.

onClipEvent (mouseDown) {*actions*}: Initiates actions every time the mouse button is pressed. It does not matter where the mouse pointer is on the stage.

onClipEvent (mouseMove) {*actions*}: Initiates action whenever the mouse is move. This handler is location independent.

onClipEvent (mouseUp) {*actions*}: Requires the mouse button to be pressed and released before the action occurs.

onClipEvent (keyDown) {*actions*}: Initiates actions when any key on the keyboard is pressed.

onClipEvent (keyUp) {*actions*}: Initiates actions when any key on the keyboard is pressed and released.

onClipEvent (data) {*actions*}: Takes action when a stream of data being loaded into a movie clip completes.

Let's now look at creating a basic movie clip with an onClipEvent(), as shown in Figure 8.6:

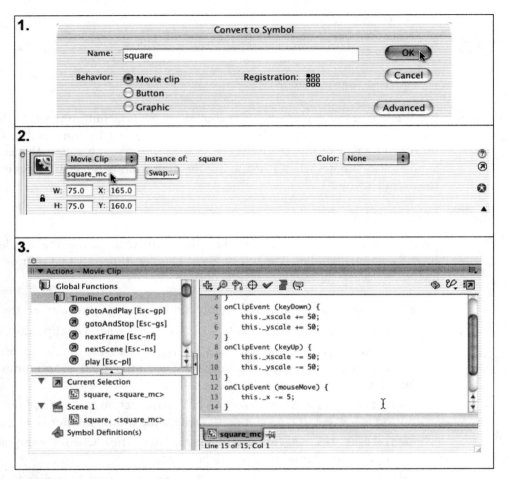

FIGURE 8.6 Using onClipEvent().

1. Create a new Flash document and draw a square on the stage. You can choose any fill and stroke color you wish. Convert the shape into a symbol with the name of *square* and the Behavior of Movie Clip.
2. While the movie clip instance is selected on the stage, give it the name of *square_mc* in the Properties inspector.
3. With *square_mc* still selected, open the Actions Panel and enter the following code:

```
onClipEvent(enterFrame){
        this._x += 5;
}
```

```
onClipEvent(keyDown){
        this._xscale +=50;
        this._yscale +=50;
}
onClipEvent(keyUp){
        this._xscale -=50;
        this._yscale -=50;
}
onClipEvent(mouseMove){
        this._x -= 5;
}
```

You must select the keyframe on Frame 1 and enter the following code into the Actions Panel to set your square to the left when the movie begins:

```
square_mc._x=0;
```

4. Test your movie.

When you test your movie, the square should travel constantly to the right. If you move your mouse, the square should move to the left. When you press a key (any key) on your keyboard, the square will increase in size and then shrink down again when the key is released. Note that the square will continue growing if you press and hold key on the keyboard.

Event Handler Properties

As we move into the future with Flash, we must focus on alternate methods of attaching event handlers. One of the biggest challenges in ActionScript programming, historically, has been that scripts tend to be spread out all over a movie. This issue was addressed in Flash MX.

What we have seen so far is attaching a handler directly to a button or movie clip, which requires scripts to be at different locations throughout the movie.

Let's look at a different approach. We now can attach event handlers directly using dot syntax. Movie clips, buttons, and other objects in Flash MX 2004 have event handler properties built in.

Instead of selecting your button or movie clip and typing either "on" or "onClipEvent" within the Actions window for the object, you can place the script right on the main timeline. You add the actual actions that will be invoked by creating an anonymous function within the event handler property on the object. The process is shown in Figure 8.7:

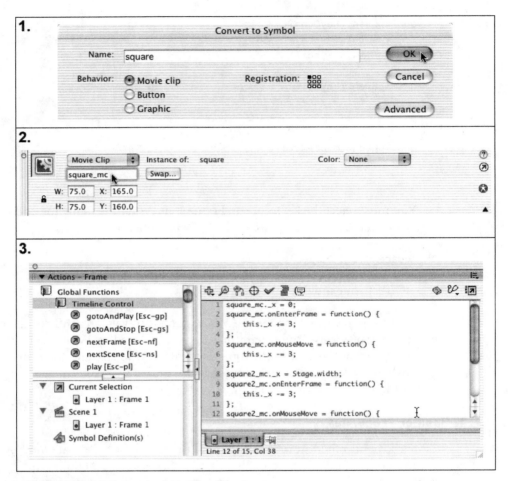

FIGURE 8.7 Adding event handlers directly.

1. Create a new Flash movie. On the stage, draw a square using the Rectangle Tool, choosing any fill and stroke color you wish. Select the newly drawn rectangle and convert it to a symbol by either right-clicking (Control + click on a Macintosh), or by clicking Modify > Convert to Symbol. Give the new symbol the name of *square* and a Behavior of Movie Clip.
2. Now, with the newly created movie clip is selected within the Properties inspector, name the instance *square_mc*.
3. Select the keyframe on Frame 1, open the Actions panel, and type the following code:

```
square_mc._x = 0;
square_mc.onEnterFrame= function(){
this._x+=3;
};
square_mc.onMouseMove = function() {
    this._x-=3;
};
```

4. Now test your movie.

You should notice when you test your movie that the rectangle moves from left to right across the screen. If you move your mouse, the rectangle moves to the left. Let's enhance the movie a bit more:

1. Copy your square_mc instance and paste it on the stage.
2. Select the copy of square_mc you just created and rename *square2_mc* in the Property Inspector.
3. Now click the keyframe of Frame 1 in the main timeline and append the following code in the Actions Panel:

```
square2_mc._x = Stage.width;
square2_mc.onEnterFrame = function() {
    this._x -= 3;
};
square2_mc.onMouseMove = function() {
    this._x += 3;
};
```

4. Test your movie.

Now, you can see that we are talking to two movie clips on the same stage without leaving the keyframe. Imagine if this were 20 clips?

By having the script centralized, we can control your actions from a single area and can even write them in a separate file with the extension .as. You can then type the script using any text editor. (Macromedia Flash MX 2004 Professional has one built in.) Once you have the script in a separate .as file, you can bring it into your Flash movie with the command `#include "filename.as"`. It is extremely important to note that you should not have a semicolon on the end of the `include` statement.

So if using event handler properties on objects is the preferred method, why cover `on()` and `onClipEvent()`? The simple answer to this is for backward compatibility. Event handler properties were not introduced until Flash MX, and many users still have Flash 5. You may also have to update scripts that were written in Flash 5. If you are developing for the use of the Flash Player version 7, however, you should focus on using event handler properties.

BUTTON, MOVIE CLIP, AND TEXT FIELD PROPERTIES

When you use actions to interact with objects in a Flash movie, you usually are interacting with their properties. ActionScript can interact with essentially any object with a name (which excludes graphic symbols and groups).

Three items you frequently interact with are buttons, movie clips, and text fields. By interacting with their properties, you can modify numerous elements, including their shape, size, color, placement, and even content. Let's look at some properties we frequently interact with in each of these three items.

Common Properties of Buttons, Movie Clips, and Text Fields

_accProps: Lets you control screen reader accessibility options for SWF files, movie clips, buttons, dynamic text fields, and input text fields at runtime.

_alpha: Sets the transparency of objects. Values are from 0 (full transparency) to 100 (none).

_height: Sets the height of objects, determined by pixels.

_name: Defines the instance name.

_rotation: Sets the rotation of an object, based on original position. Values include from 1–180 or the inverse.

_visible: Determines if an object is visible. Values are true or false.

_width: Sets the width of an object, determined by pixels.

_x: Defines the x (horizontal) placement of an object inside of its parent. It is based on the object's registration point, which is the top-left corner by default. This is a change from previous versions of Flash, which defaulted to the center of an object upon creation.

_xscale: Scales the width of the object. Value is applied as a percentage but entered as an integer (200 = 200%). You cannot use the percent sign (%) because ActionScript would treat it as a modulus.

_y: Defines the y (vertical) placement of an object inside of its parent. It is based on the object's registration point, which is the top-left corner by default. This is a change from previous versions of Flash, which defaulted to the center of an object upon creation.

_yscale: Scales the height of the object. Value is applied as a percentage but entered as an integer (200 = 200%). You cannot use the percent sign (%) because ActionScript would treat it as a modulus.

tabEnabled: Determines if an object is included in tab ordering. If set to false, it will not be listed in the tab order.

tabIndex: Allows you to customize the tab order of objects.

Common Properties of Buttons and Movie Clips

enabled: Determines if the on() handler capabilities are enabled. Values are true (default) and false.

useHandCursor: Displays a hand cursor with the mouse if a on() handler is set.

Movie Clip Properties

_currentframe: Refers to the frame where the playhead currently is in the movie clip.

_framesloaded: Displays the number of frames that have been loaded from an embedded .swf.

totalframes: Returns the total number of frames within a movie clip.

Text Field Properties

autoSize: Allows text fields to be automatically sized to accommodate text. It also controls alignment. Values include none or false, left or true, right, and center.

background: Determines if a background fill is in a text field.

backgroundColor: Defines the color of the background in a text field. Default is white (0xFFFFFF). If a border and background are not set, background color is not visible.

border: Applies a border around a text field.

borderColor: Returns the color of the border.

embedFonts: Embed font outlines in the published movie. If set to false, device fonts are used.

length: Displays the number of characters within a text field.

maxChars: Constrains the number of characters a user can enter.

multiline: Determines through use of Boolean values if a text field is multiline.

password: Displays asterisks instead of characters in a text field when set to true.

`selectable:` Allows or disallows selection of text.

`text:` Sets and returns the actual text within a text field.

`textColor:` Defines the color of the text in the field.

`textHeight:` Defines the height of the text.

`textWidth:` Defines the width of the text.

`type:` Sets the text field type to either input or dynamic.

`wordWrap:` Allows word wrap in a text field.

MOVIE CLIP METHODS

When you communicate with movie clips, we often want them to do something. Frequently, you want to move the playhead. Several methods are available in movie clips to facilitate such activities. We looked at some of these previously with behaviors, but now let's see how they relate to movie clips using the name *my_mc* to represent a movie clip.

`my_mc.gotoAndPlay(target):` Moves the playhead to a frame and initiates playback from there. It can point to either a frame number or label.

`my_mc.gotoAndStop(target):` Moves the playhead to the specified frame number or label and stops.

`my_mc.nextFrame():` Advances the playhead one frame forward and stops.

`my_mc.prevFrame():` Moves the playhead to the previous frame and stops.

`my_mc.play():` Initiates playback.

`my_mc.stop():` Stops the playhead on the current frame.

CODE HINTING WITH OBJECT NAMES

You may have noticed in many of the samples that objects are created with an underscore (_) followed by a suffix, such as `myDate_date`. This was intentional and not just a naming convention. It is a built-in feature of Flash MX 2004.

When you name certain objects with an underscore suffix, the Actions Panel generates code hints as soon as you type a period. These hints are extremely helpful because all properties, methods, and event handlers appear on a list. And as you have seen, you have a lot of choices.

Not only is the quantity overwhelming, there is a distinct lack of consistency in naming. Take for example `my_mc`. Let's say you want to refer to some properties. There is `my_mc._accProps`, which uses the naming convention of an underscore with two concatenated words. The second word is capitalized. If you want `my_mc._currentframe`, the underscore remains, but both words are lowercase. What if you choose `my_mc.enabled`? Now the underscore is gone.

With ActionScript being case sensitive, this is a real issue. Code hinting is good to use, as shown in Table 8.1, wherever possible to overcome these hurdles.

TABLE 8.1   Objects and Suffixes that Generate Code Hints

Objects	Suffixes
Array	_array
Button	_btn
Date	_date
LoadVars	_lv
MovieClip	_mc
Sound	_sound
String	_str
TextField	_txt
TextFormat	_fmt
Video	_video
XML	_xml

APPLYING ACTIONSCRIPT

Now, let's look at creating some interactivity using ActionScript. We will be using *dice.fla*, which we created earlier.

What we are trying to achieve in the dice game is a way for the user to roll the dice, have the dice roll a random number, and display the results to the user. We will then enhance the game from there. Let's start with controlling the roll of the dice, as shown in Figure 8.8.

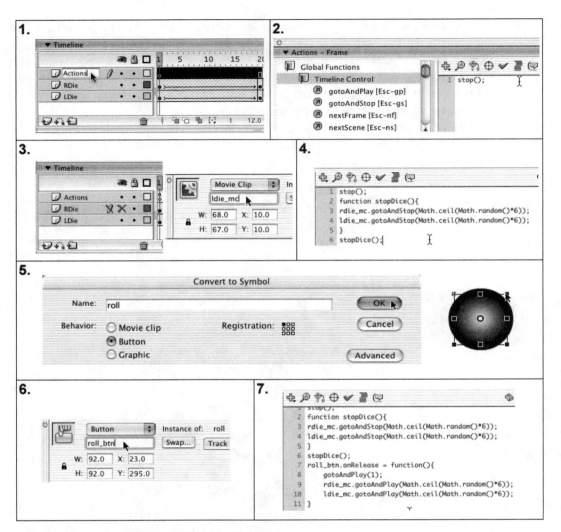

FIGURE 8.8 Controlling the roll of the dice.

1. The first thing we want to do is stop the dice from continuously rolling. We want to have the user control this, so let's create a new layer named Actions above the RDie layer. Create this layer to have a centralized location for your scripts.

2. After you create the new layer, select the empty keyframe on Frame 1 and open the Actions Panel. Insert the following code:

```
stop();
```

3. We want the dice to be still at the start of the movie. Select the visible die on the stage and name the instance *rdie_mc*. Hide the RDie layer and select the other die instance on the stage. Name this one *ldie_mc*.
4. Click the empty keyframe on Frame 1 in the Actions layer and add the following code underneath your `stop()` action:

```
function stopDice(){
rdie_mc.gotoAndStop(Math.ceil(Math.random()*6));
ldie_mc.gotoAndStop(Math.ceil(Math.random()*6));
}
stopDice();
```

Remember, if you are going to perform an action more than once, you should create a function. We will be using actions in `stopDice()` again and so have created it as a function and called it after creation. We are also using math object methods twice. First, we generate a random number and multiply it by six. This method can give you a floating-point number, which would not match a frame. Frames are all integers. Surrounding `Math.random` with `Math.ceil` causes the number to be rounded up. We cannot use the `Math.round` function, because it rounds both up and down. We can get a result of 0, which does not match any frame number.

5. Now, add a button where the user initiates the action. Select the RDie layer, insert a new layer, and name it *Button*. Open the Library by clicking Window > Library, and drag an instance of dot onto the stage. Resize dot to make it proportionate, and place it in the bottom-left corner of the stage. After placing it, convert it into a symbol with the Name of roll and Behavior of Button. You can achieve a nice rollover effect with minimal size increase by performing manipulations on the graphic symbol inside your button:
   a. Double-click to open your button. Copy your graphic symbol, and then click Edit > Paste in Place. This command places another instance of the graphic symbol on top of the first. Resize your new copy to make it smaller.
   b. After you have your desired size, click Tint in the Color drop-down menu of the Property Inspector. Pick whatever shade you want. Do the same with the graphic symbol in the back.
   c. Insert a new keyframe on Frame 2, and change the tint of your graphic symbol in the back for a rollover state. Now you have a new rollover button with barely any size increase in the movie.
6. When you have finished your button, return to the main timeline by clicking Scene 1 above the timeline. Name your button instance *roll_btn* in the Property Inspector.

7. After you have named your button, select the empty keyframe on Frame 1 in the Actions layer. Type the following code in the Actions Panel to drive the movie:

```
roll_btn.onRelease = function(){
        gotoAndPlay(1);
        rdie_mc.gotoAndPlay(Math.ceil(Math.random()*6));
        ldie_mc.gotoAndPlay(Math.ceil(Math.random()*6));
}
```

In this snippet of code, you add a function to the onRelease event handler of *roll_btn*. Within the function, you add gotoAndPlay(1). Because the button is dependent on its parent, the main timeline will start playing. We also used gotoAndPlay() with math object methods to start the movie clips on a random frame. This time, we used gotoAndPlay() instead of gotoAndStop() because you want the clips to appear as if they are rolling.

When you test your movie, you see that the dice are stopped when the movie starts. You also see that when the button is pressed, the dice roll across the stage with their faces changing as they move. We are off to a great start.

Now, add some more actions to flesh out the movement. Currently, the game is not stopping at the end, so that is one of the items addressed in Figure 8.9. We also want to have a label on the button and the results of the dice roll displayed to the user in a textual format. Let's get started.

1. First, we need a label for the button. Select the Button layer, and create a Dynamic Text field with a font size of 18 and a color that contrasts with the button for visibility. Center-align the text. Drag a text field large enough to fit the word *reset*. Name the field *roll_txt*. You may want to select both your new TextField and roll_btn, and use the Align Panel to center them on each other. (Make sure that To stage is not selected.)
2. Now that we have created a label, let's add some script to give it an initial value. We also want it to change color along with the button when the mouse passes over the button. To do this, add some more code. Right after the stopDice() function call in the keyframe on Frame 1 of the Actions layer, insert the following lines:

```
roll_txt.selectable = false;
roll_txt.text = "Roll";
roll_btn.onRollOver = function(){
        roll_txt.textColor="0xff0000";
}
```

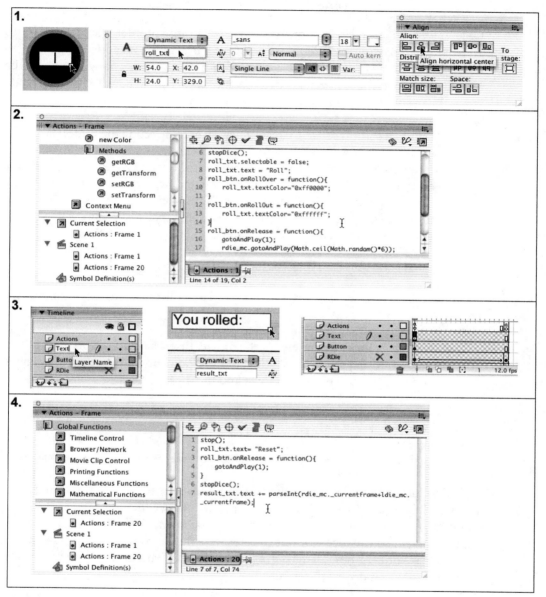

FIGURE 8.9 Adding more content to the dice game.

```
roll_btn.onRollOut = function(){
        roll_txt.textColor="0xffffff";
}
```

What we have done with this code is to first make `roll_txt` no longer selectable. If we left it at the default or true, the user's mouse pointer would change into an I-bar when passing over that portion of `roll_btn`. Next, we added a function to the `onRollOver` event handler of `roll_btn` to have the text change color as the mouse passes over it. We then needed to get `roll_txt` to go back to its initial state when the mouse leaves, so we added a function to the `onRollOut` event handler.

3. Let's add some feedback. Create a new layer by selecting the Button layer and pressing the New Layer button. Name this layer *Text*. Within the Text layer create a new Dynamic TextField with the font size of 24. Place it toward the bottom in the center of the stage. In the text field, type *You rolled:*, leaving enough space for a two-digit number. Name the text field `result_txt`. Your timeline should resemble what is shown in panel 3 of Figure 8.9. Now, in keyframe 1 of the Actions layer, add the following code to the end:

```
result_txt.text = "You rolled: ";
```

This code causes `result_txt` to reset to "You rolled:" at the beginning of the movie.

4. Now, let's focus on the end of the movie. Insert a keyframe on Frame 20 in the Actions layer and have your Actions Panel open. In the Actions Panel, add code to stop both the movie and the dice:

```
stop();
roll_txt.text= "Reset";
stopDice();
result_txt.text += (rdie_mc._currentframe + ldie_mc._currentframe);
```

With this code, we have completed the rolling sequence. When this frame is entered, the playhead is stopped with the `stop()` action. We then set `roll_text` to read Reset as `roll_btn` takes you back to Frame 1 in the movie. We called the `stopDice()` function again so the dice can return a result. And we concatenated the result of `currentframe` of `ldie_mc` added to `rdie_mc` to your text. This gives the user feedback. Test your movie and view the results.

We used parentheses () around `rdie_mc._currentframe + ldie_mc._currentframe`. *Normally these are not necessary because frame numbers are evaluated as numbers. We placed the parentheses here only because we are concatenating the result with a string, so we want to concatenate the result, not each individual number. Having the addition take place within the parentheses causes the frame numbers to be added together first.*

Now that we have created a functional application, let's improve on it a little to make it more exciting for the user to play. You can add to the interactivity by giving the user an option to pick what he wants the result to be and display whether he won or lost. This process is shown in Figure 8.10.

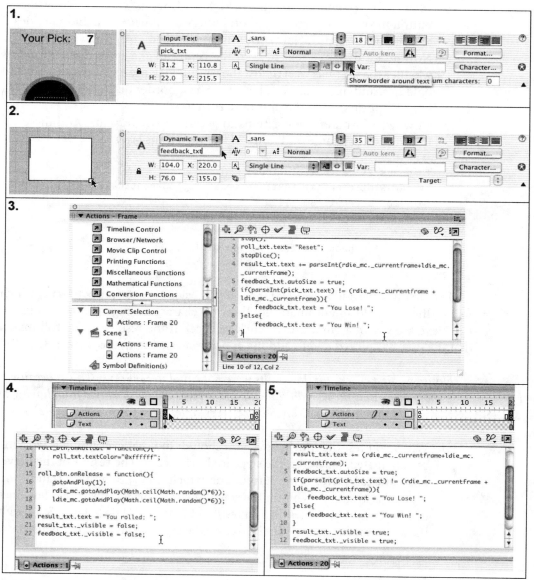

FIGURE 8.10   Displaying results for the user.

1. The first thing you do is add some text fields, which serve for results and input for the user. First, add a static text field with the text "Your Pick:". Use a font size of 18. To the right of the static text, create an input text field with enough room to have two digits at the font size of 18 and boldface. You may wish to insert a number as a demonstration that shows the user what should be entered into the field. You also must click the Show border button in your Property Inspector. Otherwise, the user will have no idea if data should be typed. Name your input text field *pick_txt*.

2. Now add a dynamic text field in the center of the stage that announces whether the user has won or lost the round. Pick a large font size of 40 and boldface, and make sure you have the Show border button depressed. (If a border appears, press the button to turn it off.)

3. Now, we must add some actions to get the desired results. Add these actions to the keyframe on Frame 20 in the Actions layer:

```
feedback_txt.autoSize = true;
if(parseInt(pick_txt.text) != (rdie_mc._currentframe +
ldie_mc._currentframe)){
        feedback_txt.text = "You Lose! ";
}else{
        feedback_txt.text = "You Win! ";
}
```

The first line we added set the `feedback_txt` `autoSize` property to true, which enables the text field to automatically show all characters, regardless of its initial size. Next, we put in a conditional block to check if the results of the roll match what the user has picked and to add the appropriate string to `feedback_txt`.

Notice we first checked if the results were not equal to `pick_txt`. This is because it is more likely that the user didn't win, and it saves the Flash Player from having to go through the entire conditional block every time.

4. When you test the movie now, you should find that everything is working as anticipated. However, the stage looks cluttered. The results of the previous game carry over to the current one, which could be confusing, and "You rolled:" is always present on the stage. We can correct this with a few lines of code in the keyframes on Frames 1 and 20 of the Actions layer. Start with the keyframe on Frame 1 in the Actions layer by adding the following code:

```
result_txt._visible = false;
feedback_txt._visible = false;
```

This code hides the text fields when you enter 1. Because the dice haven't been rolled at this point, their visibility is not necessary.

5. Now add the following code in the keyframe on Frame 20:

```
result_txt._visible = true;
feedback_txt._visible = true;
```

Because we have results you want to display now, turn the visibility back on after we generate the content for the fields. Test your movie.

Now that we have all the mechanics worked out with the user having the opportunity to win or lose, let's raise the stakes a bit. Add functionality that allows a user to make a bet and either win or lose money, depending on the roll. We must give the user funds to start with, so create a field for that also. This procedure is shown in Figure 8.11.

1. Create a static text area below pick_txt that contain the text of "Your Bet: $". Next to it, create an input text field with the name of bet_txt. Copy your current Your pick: static text field and pick_txt, and paste them

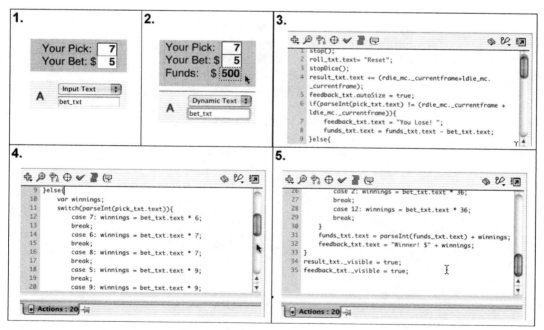

FIGURE 8.11   Raising the stakes of the dice game.

below. (Be sure to rename the *pick_txt* copy to *bet_txt*.) Also put an initial value of 5 in bet_txt.

2. Now, create a new static text field directly underneath your bet section that reads "Funds: $". To the right of this field, create a new dynamic text field with a font size of 18 and boldface. Make sure the Show border button is not selected. Name this field *funds_txt* in the Properties inspector.

3. Now it's time for some code. The game must react according to the bet, and either add or subtract from funds_txt appropriately. Start by adjusting the conditional in the keyframe at Frame 20 in the Actions Panel. Within your if statement, at the end of your line that states "feedback_txt.text = "You Lose! ", press your Enter/Return key and add the following code:

```
funds_txt.text = funds_txt.text - bet_txt.text;
```

4. Let's tackle the else statement. This is where the program reacts if the user wins. We could make it really simple and just have them win their bet amount, but that wouldn't be fair. We should address the odds and give the user a real incentive. A switch conditional serves this purpose well. Go into the else statement now and, after the opening curly brace, press Enter/Return, and enter the following code:

```
var winnings;
switch(parseInt(pick_txt.text)){
    case 7: winnings = bet_txt.text * 6;
    break;
    case 6: winnings = bet_txt.text * 7;
    break;
    case 8: winnings = bet_txt.text * 7;
    break;
    case 5: winnings = bet_txt.text * 9;
    break;
    case 9: winnings = bet_txt.text * 9;
    break;
    case 4: winnings = bet_txt.text * 12;
    break;
    case 10: winnings = bet_txt.text * 12;
    break;
    case 3: winnings= bet_txt.text * 18;
    break;
    case 11: winnings = bet_txt.text * 18;
    break;
    case 2: winnings = bet_txt.text * 36;
```

```
        break;
        case 12: winnings = bet_txt.text * 36;
        break;
    }
```

Notice the order of the switch block. *It is written in the manner of the most likely matches being listed first. It is especially important here with so many possible results.*

5. Now that we have a switch block built that feeds a local variable called winnings, we need to apply the winnings. We want the winnings to be reflected in *funds_txt*, and it would be nice to tell the user that he is a winner and what was won. Let's start with the code needed to recalculate *funds_txt*:

```
funds_txt.text = parseInt(funds_txt.text) + winnings;
```

Next, revise the line saying:

```
feedback_txt.text = "You Win! ";
```

To read:

```
feedback_txt.text = "Winner! $" + winnings;
```

Now test the movie.

We have now completed all the elements to create an interactive game. In making this game, you can see how ActionScript can be used to tie multiple facets together. Without ActionScript, we couldn't enhance the user experience by adding full interactivity.

All that is left is to finish the game. Feel free to be creative and build a nice logo. Figure 8.12 shows a completed version of *dice.swf* when run.

The completed version of the game shown in Figure 8.12 has a logo created in a similar manner to the button. It is two copies of a dot instance, sized and tinted different colors. The text is three static text fields created with a different font (Papyrus). Then, they were broken apart twice and the vector shapes grouped. This knocked the file size down one Kilobyte.

Because we focused on using symbols, the entire application shown is under 5K. It is a fully interactive game, yet is the size of a thumbnail picture. This is the power of Flash.

FIGURE 8.12   A completed version of the dice game.

Possible Improvements

Although we have a complete, functional game, there is always room for improvement. If we wanted to get this game ready for prime-time viewing, you should refine it further. Some possibilities that you could consider follow:

Require the user to enter both a number and a bet amount. A possible resolution to this is to revise the code within your roll_btn.onRelease event handler within the keyframe on Frame 1 in the Actions layer as follows:

```
roll_btn.onRelease = function() {
    if (pick_txt.text && bet_txt.text) {
        feedback_txt._visible = false;
        gotoAndPlay(1);
        rdie_mc.gotoAndPlay(Math.ceil(Math.random()*6));
        ldie_mc.gotoAndPlay(Math.ceil(Math.random()*6));
    } else {
        feedback_txt._visible = true;
        feedback_txt.autoSize = true;
        feedback_txt.text = "Complete All Fields";
    }
};
```

The user can currently go in the hole. You don't want the user to keep playing into negative digits. A possible solution is to add another keyframe that states the game is over with the option of allowing the user to restart the game. You can insert a frame on the following layers—Logo (if you created one with a logo for the game), Text, and Button. Insert a keyframe on the Actions layer and type the following script:

```
roll_txt.text = "Restart?";
feedback_txt.text = "Game Over";
roll_btn.onRelease = function(){
    gotoAndPlay(1);
    funds_txt.text = 500;
}
```

Make sure the `funds_txt` text field can expand should the user make a good run of it and win copious amounts of cash. You can accomplish this by adding the following line of code at the end in keyframe 1 of the Actions layer:

```
funds_txt.autoSize = true;
```

The user must choose a number only between 2 and 12. As the game stands, he can choose anything he wishes.

Make sure the user does not try to bet any more than $500 because that is all you have given for funds.

The user should enter numbers only for `pick_txt` **and** `bet_txt`.

If a user enters a number followed by letters, Flash still evaluates it as a number using the `parseInt()` **function.** How can that be addressed?

ON THE CD The last four examples do not have solutions here; they are for you to ponder. After you feel you may have come up with some methods, look on the CD-ROM in Flash > Chapter 08 for *DiceRevised.fla*. This file has code that addresses all of the previously mentioned considerations.

SUMMARY

ActionScript is a robust language, and in-depth coverage of all its features is beyond the scope of this book. With the popularity of Flash MX 2004, legions of books on ActionScript are on the market in addition to countless Web resources. If you want to take your Flash movies to the next level, you really need to start learning ActionScript.

Now that we have completed some content using ActionScript, you need to consider publishing your movies. Let's move on and start "Saving Flash Movies and Creating Flash Web Sites."

9 Saving Flash Movies and Creating Flash Web Sites

Now that we have learned to create some content within Macromedia Flash MX 2004, let's look at publishing your content. A .fla file is your working copy of the file and is not intended for distribution to others. To share your content with the masses, you must publish it. Fortunately, Flash offers several ways to publish your material. All of your options for publishing are shown in Figure 9.1 and are accessed by clicking File > Publish Settings or by clicking the Settings button next to Publish: in the Property Inspector. Each of these methods is covered in this chapter, as well as methods to optimize your Flash movies.

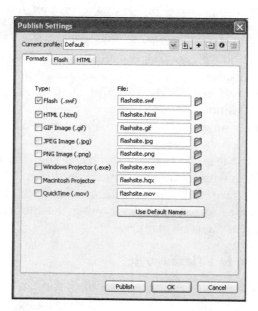

FIGURE 9.1 Publish settings available in Flash MX 2004.

MAKING A FLASH WEB SITE

You start this chapter by making a Flash Web site. Two forms of Flash Web sites are available. The first popular form is to have one Web page with an embedded .swf file. All content for the site is inside either one .swf or several .swfs used in conjunction with each other. The other form is to have a normal Web site with a great deal of the content created with Flash on each page. A good example of the second type of Web site is *www.macromedia.com*.

Some major issues that you should consider when creating a Flash site follow. First, too much of anything is not good. Flash sites often have so much animation that, instead of enhancing the site, proves distracting. Navigational issues are also a consideration. Flash content used for navigation is not typical because it is created by the designer. If more attention is paid to appearance than design, users can become confused. An example of something users are used to is a visited link. If a user has selected a link previously, the link turns another color. This behavior has to be added to a Flash Web site. Often, search engines have a difficult time with Flash movies and cannot index the contents of your page. You must add tags within your actual HTML page to reflect the content and get the page rated higher by search engines.

When using Flash to create a site, consider your audience. Will they have the latest version of the Flash Player? It is likely they do have a Flash Player, but if they don't have the latest version, they can't play features you have put in that are strictly for the version 7 player. You can create content and publish it for older versions of Flash Players, but you may lose features that are only available in Macromedia Flash MX 2004, such as ActionScript 2.0, Cascading Style Sheet support, and improved accessibility. If you want to use only Flash when creating content, consider using it only on a section of your site, such as online quiz or interactive product demonstration.

Usually the best way to approach creating Flash sites is the second method, of mixing Flash with traditional content. In this method, your pages are still built in HTML but have Flash peppered throughout, such as images to enhance your pages. Instead of the .swf containing everything, the internal links connect to other HTML pages built in the same manner.

Adding Navigation to a Flash Movie

As you have seen, by adding some scripts, you can really enhance your Flash movie. Let's take this principle and look at making a self-contained Web site within one Flash movie. You will create a very simple movie with internal navigation. Start this project by following the steps shown in Figure 9.2.

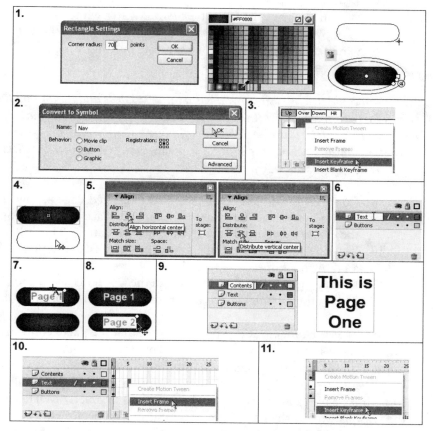

FIGURE 9.2 Creating the initial content for the Flash Web site.

1. Name the first layer *Buttons*. Create a new rounded rectangle with a corner radius of 70 with a blue radial gradient fill. You can use the Fill Transform Tool to further modify the shape.
2. Next, convert the rectangle into a button and name it *Nav*.
3. Double-click the button to enter Symbol-Editing mode, insert a keyframe in Up, and change the fill color.
4. Exit Symbol-Editing mode and return to the main timeline. Create three more copies of the button on the stage.
5. When you have four buttons, select all of them and align them to the horizontal center (make sure the To stage button is not selected) and distribute them to vertical center. This action neatens their appearance on the stage.
6. Now create a new layer named *Text*, then lock the Button layer.

7. Within the new Text layer, type *Page 1* with a white font sized small enough to fit over the button. You didn't put the text inside the button because we would then need to have four separate buttons, which is not the most efficient use of symbols for file size.

You could just as easily, if you wish, put text labels and buttons on the same layer. This arrangement works because the text is a group and the buttons are symbols. You can place text over a button without having the cookie-cutter effect. If your text appears behind the button, you can change the order by clicking Modify > Arrange and choosing from your available options.

8. Continue creating text for each button labeled Page 2, Page 3, and Page 4.
9. Create a new layer and name it *Contents*. Place a text field on the stage in the empty keyframe of the Contents layer stating "This is Page One".
10. You now have to extend the frames on your Text and Button layers. Insert a Frame on 4 in each of these layers.
11. Insert a new keyframe at Frame 2 in the Contents layer, and change *One* to *Two* in the Text field. Repeat this procedure for Frames 3 and 4.

If you test the movie at this point, you see that the pages continuously change. This behavior is not what we want, but, as you have seen, it is natural with Flash because it is built into the design.

Flash was originally created to make animations, and you will find that you sometimes have to fight against it when you add interactivity. This quirk is one of the reasons why Flash is a unique programming environment. This next phase of the project, shown in Figure 9.3, corrects this issue and gets the buttons working.

1. You are now going to create two new layers to keep the content organized. Click the Contents layer to selected it, and press the Insert Layer button. By having the Contents Layer selected, the new layer is located on the top of it. Name the new layer *Actions*. Press the Insert Layer button again to create another layer. Name this layer *Labels*.
2. In the empty keyframe on Frame 1 in the Actions layer, add a stop(); action. (If your Actions Panel is not open, click Window > Actions or press the F9 key.) A lowercase *a* appears in the frame when you have added an action.
3. Insert keyframes on Frames 2, 3, and 4. Within each keyframe add stop();. You now see four empty keyframes with a lowercase *a* indicating a script is attached to each.

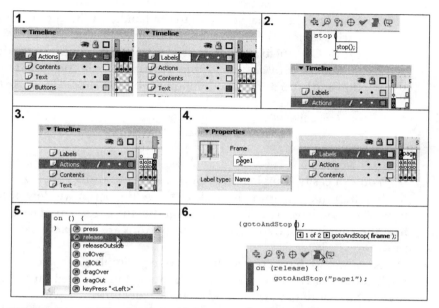

FIGURE 9.3   Adding frame and button actions to the project.

4. Now we must add labels to our movie. We have two methods of referring to a frame: by number or using frame labels. Frame labels are an excellent means of navigation within a movie because if you move the frame to another location, you don't have to change every ActionScript referring to it. The labels remain the same. To add labels, select the empty keyframe on Frame 1 in the Labels layer and type *page1* (no spaces) in the Frame Label field of the Property Inspector. Insert an empty keyframe in each of the remaining frames and label them *page2*, *page 3*, and *page4*.

5. Unlock the Buttons layer so you can select the buttons. Select the button for Page 1 and double-click on under Movie Control in the Actions Panel. This action opens the code hints, showing multiple options. Select `release`.

After choosing an option in the code hints window, the cursor ends up inside the parentheses next to the argument keyword. Make certain you move the cursor between the curly braces before selecting your new command. Otherwise, your next command will appear inside of the parentheses and your script will not function.

6. Now add the actual action to the on handler. With the cursor between the curly braces of the on (release){} handler, double-click gotoAndStop under Movie Control to add it to your script. Flash prompts you to add a frame argument to gotoAndStop. Within the parentheses, add "page1" (with quotation marks). Your final output on the button should look like this:

```
on (release) {
            gotoAndStop("page1");
}
```

You can easily complete the rest of your buttons by copying the script from the first button and pasting it inside of the ActionScript window of the next button. When you have pasted the script, modify the argument of gotoAndStop to reflect the appropriate frame. When your buttons are complete, save and test your movie.

Now that we have created the core of our simple Flash site, we must actually publish our material. To create a Flash movie to be viewed on the Internet, you need to have both the .swf file and an HTML document. These files are the default options for publishing Flash movies. You can preview the movie by clicking File > Publish Preview > Default (html) or by pressing Ctrl/Command + F12, which opens your movie in a browser window, as shown in Figure 9.4.

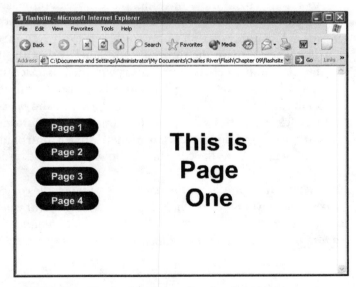

FIGURE 9.4 Previewing the project in a browser.

The Flash movie is in your browser and looking pretty good. Some issues, however, will arise. To demonstrate one of these issues, use the following steps:

1. With your mouse, select the URL in the address bar of your browser and copy it.
2. Now press your Home Page button to take you to another site.
3. When your home page has loaded, highlight and delete the URL in the address field, paste the URL you copied in step 2, and press Enter/Return. This action takes you back to your Flash site.
4. Press different buttons on the page to take you through the movie.
5. Now press the Back button on your browser. Notice that you don't go back your previous page in the Flash movie; you completely leave your Flash site and are looking at your home page.

This behavior was criticized in earlier versions of Flash and presented a serious problem because users could be confused. This issue was addressed in the release of Flash MX. Now let's adjust the movie and publishing settings to resolve this issue in your movie, as shown in Figure 9.5. Because we have already labeled our movie, the process is relatively easy.

1. Select the keyframe at Frame 1 in the Labels layer. In the Property Inspector, use the drop-down menu next to Type to change the label into an Anchor. Repeat this process for all four keyframes in the Labels layer.
2. Now go into Publish Settings by clicking File > Publish Settings. (You can also reach this dialog box by deselecting everything on the stage and clicking Settings in the Property Inspector.) In the Publish Settings dialog box,

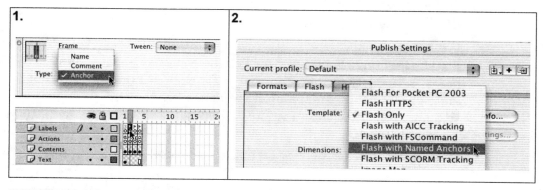

FIGURE 9.5 Using named anchors in the Flash project.

click the HTML tab and select Flash with Named Anchors in the Template drop-down menu. This option inserts the code that enables communication between the .swf and the HTML page.

Anchor labels revert to normal frame labels if the Flash movie is published in a format earlier than version 6 of the Flash Player.

Now when you test your movie, you see that your browser's Back and Forward buttons work with your .swf file. Your Flash site is now complete and working. When publishing the movie to the Internet, remember that both the HTML and .swf files of the same name must be uploaded. Your visitors will load the HTML page, which will in turn instruct the browser to start the Flash plug-in or direct the user to download it. You have started to look at the Publish Settings, but several other options are available within your Publish Settings dialog box. Let's take a look at these.

PUBLISH SETTINGS

Flash can publish content in several formats. These formats are shown in the initial Publish Settings dialog box. When you select an option, your content is published in that format in addition to all other currently selected formats. A tab also appears to refine the settings for a selected format. The initial Publish Settings are shown in Figure 9.6 and are described as follows:

Flash (.swf): Creates the actual Flash movie for viewing in the Flash Player.

HTML (.html): Represents the Web page created in conjunction with the .swf file for Internet publication.

GIF Image (.gif): Saves content in the Graphics Interchange Format.

JPEG Image (.jpg): Publishes to the Joint Photographers Expert Group format.

PNG Image (.png): Publishes to the Portable Network Graphics format, a proposed replacement for the proprietary GIF. Note that this format is not the same .png format used for Fireworks working files.

Windows Projector (.exe): Creates a standalone application for use in Windows systems.

Macintosh Projector: Creates a standalone application for use in Macintosh systems.

QuickTime (.mov): Publishes the movie in the QuickTime video format created by Apple.

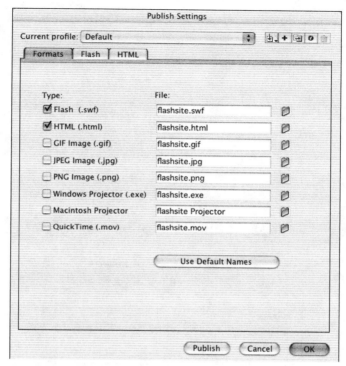

FIGURE 9.6   Flash publishing options.

 You can also open your Publish Settings dialog box by selecting an area off the stage and then pressing the Publish button in the Property Inspector that reflects your current Flash Player settings.

Flash (.swf) Format Publishing Settings

Figure 9.7 shows the Flash format publishing options. You have the following choices when publishing in the Flash native format:

Version: Allows you to publish your Flash movie for use in previous versions of the Flash Player for backward compatibility. You can publish to versions back to Flash Player 1. This setting is helpful if you want to publish to the widest possible audience.

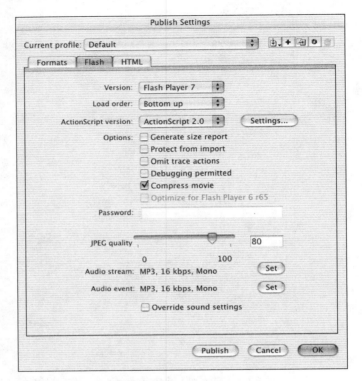

FIGURE 9.7 The Flash (.swf) format.

Load order: Determines in what order the layers in the Flash movie load. You have two choices here—Bottom Up (default) or Top Down. The default is to load the bottom layer first and everything above it after. If you have something large on one of the upper layers, such as a photograph, you may want to change the order of loading.

ActionScript version: Allows you to choose between ActionScript Version 1.0 and 2.0. If you are publishing content to be read in earlier versions of Flash, you must select Version 1.0. If you have created ActionScript classes (templates for objects) in separate files, you can specify their path by clicking the Settings button.

Options: Provides general options for publication:

Generate size report: Creates a text file reflecting information about your file, as shown in Figure 9.8. This option breaks down the movie to show how much file space each piece of content takes up in the final movie. This

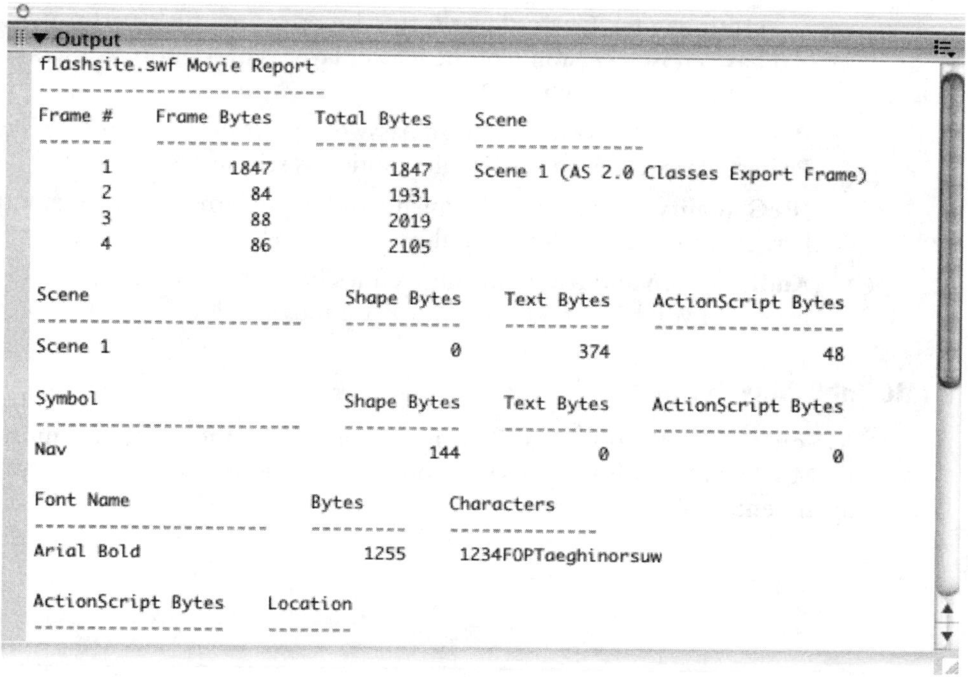

```
Output
flashsite.swf Movie Report
----------------------------
Frame #    Frame Bytes    Total Bytes    Scene
-------    -----------    -----------    ----------------
      1           1847           1847    Scene 1 (AS 2.0 Classes Export Frame)
      2             84           1931
      3             88           2019
      4             86           2105

Scene                        Shape Bytes    Text Bytes    ActionScript Bytes
-------------------------    -----------    ----------    ------------------
Scene 1                                0           374                    48

Symbol                       Shape Bytes    Text Bytes    ActionScript Bytes
-------------------------    -----------    ----------    ------------------
Nav                                  144             0                     0

Font Name                    Bytes        Characters
----------------------       ---------    --------------
Arial Bold                        1255    1234FOPTaeghinorsuw

ActionScript Bytes    Location
------------------    --------
```

FIGURE 9.8 A size report created upon publication of a Flash movie.

process can alert you to problem areas, such as a frame being excessively large and thus causing your movie to stall when streaming.

Protect from import: Protects your content from other designers importing your .swf into their Flash movies. When you choose this option, you can select a password for your file.

Omit trace actions: Prevents `trace` commands from displaying when the movie is played. Often when developers are working on their ActionScript, they may use the `trace` command, which causes text results to appear in the Output window. This command can be useful for troubleshooting, but often, a few may be left in the document.

Debugging permitted: Allows for the Flash Debugger to be used remotely on the published movie. It also allows you to enter a password to protect your content.

Compress movie: Allows the published movie to be compressed to be even smaller than previous versions. This option was introduced in Flash MX.

Optimize for Flash Player 6 r65: Increases the file's performance, if you have chosen version 6 of the Flash Player. This option requires your users to have r65 or higher.

Password: Allows you to create a password to protect your movie if either the Protect from import or Debugging option is selected.

JPEG quality: Determines the quality of the final image. The higher the number, the better the picture (but the file is larger).

Audio stream and **Audio event:** Defines how you want the audio to be compressed if you have sounds in your Flash movie.

HTML Publishing Settings

As you have seen, to have a Flash movie played on the Web, you must have an HTML document with it. Let's now look at the options available when creating this document, as shown in Figure 9.9.

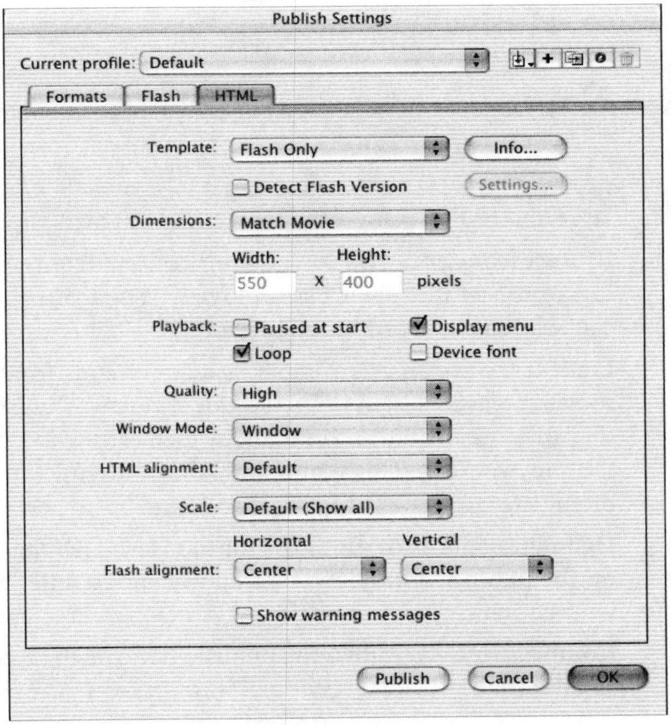

FIGURE 9.9 HTML Publish Settings.

Template: Contains the format settings for publishing the HTML page.

> **Flash Only (for Pocket PC 2003):** Optimizes the Web page for viewing on the Pocket PC operating system.
>
> **Flash HTTPS:** Allows you to work with Flash movies and HTTPS (Hyper-Text Transfer Protocol over Secure Sockets Layer). This option is new to Flash MX 2004.
>
> **Flash Only:** Displays the Flash movie in a Web page.
>
> **Flash w/AICC Tracking:** Allows you to create content for e-learning. This option is for working with Aviation Industry Computer-Based Training Committee standards.
>
> **Flash with FSCommand:** Shows the Flash movie inside of a Web page and communicates with scripts like JavaScript outside of the Flash movie.
>
> **Flash with Named Anchors:** Facilitates communication with the browser for navigation.
>
> **Flash w/SCORM Tracking:** Allows you to work with e-learning content created to work with the Sharable Content Object Reference Model (SCORM).
>
> **Image Map:** Allows you to create an HTML page with an exported .gif. .png, or .jpg file as an image map.
>
> **QuickTime:** Publishes an HTML page set up to play a QuickTime file, if you have chosen this as a publishing option.

Dimensions: Determines how large visually you want your movie to appear in the browser.

> **Match Movie:** Displays the movie at its actual size. This is the default setting.
>
> **Pixels:** Defines the movie size to a specific pixel count. This option is useful when you are publishing to a particular target device, such as a Pocket PC.

Percent: Allows you to define what percentage of the browser window the movie fills. You can use this option when making a Flash site for scaling the movie to 100 percent. The movie is scaled up and down to match the browser window. Because Flash is a vector-based application, you can scale the movie to any size without losing resolution (unless you have a .jpg or .gif image embedded in the movie).

Playback: Controls how the .swf file interacts with the player and browser.

> **Paused at start:** Allows you to have the movie not play immediately. This option is useful if you want the user to initiate the movie.

Display menu: Determines if the shortcut menu will be available when the user right-clicks (Control + click on a Macintosh) the movie during playback.

Loop: Determines if the movie automatically loops when it is played. It is better to use a stop action within the movie if you want more control.

Device font: Causes the browser to look for fonts on the user's system. This feature can keep the file size down because, by default, your movie has the entire font embedded.

Quality: Defines the video playback quality. Playing complicated Flash movies can be difficult for computer processors. You can adjust settings to accommodate for issues.

Low: Sets the image quality to low to play the movie faster.

Auto Low: Starts the image quality at low but improves if the frame rate allows.

Auto High: Starts the image quality at high but degrades to improve performance if frame rates drop.

Medium: Sets the image quality at medium.

High: Sets image quality to high.

Best: Sets the image quality to best. This setting should be used only for CD-ROMs or strong bandwidth links.

Window Mode: Reflects how the Flash movie will be seen on the page. When a Flash movie is on a page, it appears inside its own window.

Window: Reserves the window on the page for the .swf file. This is the default setting.

Opaque windowless: Enables you to have objects move behind the Flash movie on the Web page and not be seen.

Transparent windowless: Causes all blank areas in the Flash movie to be transparent. Any content underneath these areas is seen. This setting can be taxing on processors.

HTML alignment: Positions the Flash movie window on the page. Your choices are Default, Left, Right, Top, and Bottom.

Scale: Places the Flash movie within a specified area on the stage.

Default (Show all): Causes the Flash Movie to display within the defined area with no distortion, but borders may appear.

No border: Prevents borders and does not allow distortion, but crops if needed.

Exact fit: Causes the movie to be resized to match the area exactly without regard to distortion.

No scale: Causes the movie to not be scaleable. If it is larger than the area you defined, it appears as if you are viewing it through a small window.

Flash alignment: Sets how a Flash movie is aligned within its window. This setting can be important if cropping is involved. You can align both horizontally and vertically.

Horizontal: Left, Right, and Center.

Vertical: Top, Bottom, and Center.

Show warning messages: Warns you if you have picked a setting with a conflict. For example, if you pick an image map setting without an image format in your Publish Settings, it generates an error.

GIF Format Settings

With the GIF publishing options, you can define whether or not you want the output to be a still image or animated, the size of the image, whether it is transparent, and other settings. You can use Flash to export static or animated .gifs for non-Flash areas on your site. By default, it publishes the first frame of the movie as a .gif file, unless you explicitly change this by marking a frame with the #static label.

JPEG Image Settings

Your JPEG export options are width, height, amount of compression (quality), and whether you want the image to be progressive. JPEG is the preferred format for photographic style or if you have many gradients. By default, the first frame of the movie is the .jpg file, unless you explicitly change this by marking a frame with the #static label.

PNG Image Settings

You can refine your color choices and sizes when publishing. By default, Flash publishes the first frame of the movie as the .png file, unless you explicitly change this by marking a frame with the #static label.

Windows Projector

No options are available when you publish to the Windows Projector format. What Flash actually does is export a copy of your file with all Flash Player components needed to play it. This format is a great way to create content for CD-ROMs. You can even execute other programs from within the standalone application. An example of this format is on the Macromedia Studio MX 2004 CD-ROMs.

Macintosh Projector

This format is the same as the Windows Projector but for Macintosh systems.

QuickTime Settings

In these settings, you can change the width, height, alpha (transparency), and sound and playback settings, as well as others. When publishing to QuickTime, your movie is animated but not interactive.

OPTIMIZATION WITH THE BANDWIDTH PROFILER

An extremely useful tool in Macromedia Flash MX 2004 is the Bandwidth Profiler. You can open this tool when you test your movie by pressing Ctrl + Enter (Command + Return on a Macintosh) and clicking View > Bandwidth profiler (or pressing Ctrl/Command + B). In the Bandwidth Profiler, you can view file size, check bandwidth utilization in a graph, and simulate streaming over a modem connection. The Bandwidth Profiler is shown in Figure 9.10.

Panel 1 in Figure 9.10 shows the default view of the Bandwidth Profiler, the streaming graph. This graph shows you how the movie will play as it is streamed over time at the bandwidth rate you have selected.

Panel 2 shows the Frame By Frame Graph, which breaks down how much data is used on each actual frame. This graph is especially useful because you can see if one frame, somewhere in your movie, has an excessive amount of content. When a frame is very large, the movie pauses during playback while waiting for the content to download.

Panel 3 shows the Simulate Download option. This option causes the Flash Player to mimic a modem at a selected bandwidth rate, which allows you to experience firsthand what occurs at the connection speed without having to actually upload the file. You can choose your modem settings under the Debug menu. You can also customize your bandwidth settings by clicking View > Download Settings > Customize. This capability can be helpful if you are publishing for a high-bandwidth connection or a CD-ROM.

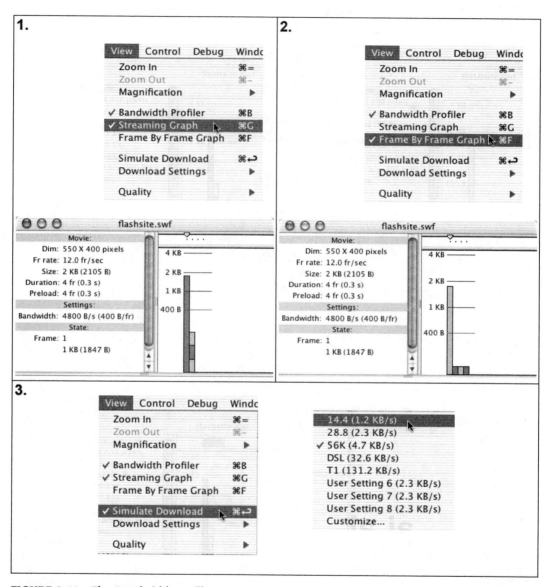

FIGURE 9.10   The Bandwidth Profiler.

SUMMARY

You have now seen how to create content with Macromedia Flash MX 2004 and, in this chapter, how to publish it for the world to see. Flash is a very robust program with much more than meets the eye. To cover everything available in the program would take more than one book.

Now let's move on and look at editing images and graphics for your Web site by "Exploring Macrocmedia Fireworks MX 2004."

10 Exploring Macromedia Fireworks MX 2004

Fireworks MX 2004 is a powerful but often misunderstood tool. Much of what you see covered in Fireworks shows ways that you can edit photos and create vector images. The fact that it has dual capabilities is a wonderful thing, but it really doesn't begin to demonstrate the power of the tool. If you just want to edit photos or draw vector images, hundreds of programs are out there that serve this need. Why bother investing in a solution like Fireworks when you have so many choices? The answer is simple: Fireworks is not just a photo and vector graphic editor, but rather a page design tool.

CREATING A NEW DOCUMENT

Fireworks works with both vector and raster images. Any drawing you create in Fireworks is created as vectors, so you can size and format the images with no resolution loss before exporting. Any picture you import or open in Fireworks is in a raster format.

A great feature of Fireworks is that you can work with both vector and raster images within the same document. When you open Fireworks, a Start page is displayed, as shown in Figure 10.1.

The Start page is new to the MX 2004 family and is shared in Macromedia Flash MX 2004, Fireworks MX 2004, and Dreamweaver MX 2004. It is a convenient, centralized starting point to pick from your most recently opened files, create a new file, visit the Macromedia Exchange, and get help. It is yet another common feature among the main Macromedia Web family of products to give users a common interface.

Let's now create a new Fireworks document. To create a new document, click the Create New Fireworks File link on the Start page, click File > New, or press Ctrl/Command + N on the keyboard. All these actions open the window shown in Figure 10.2.

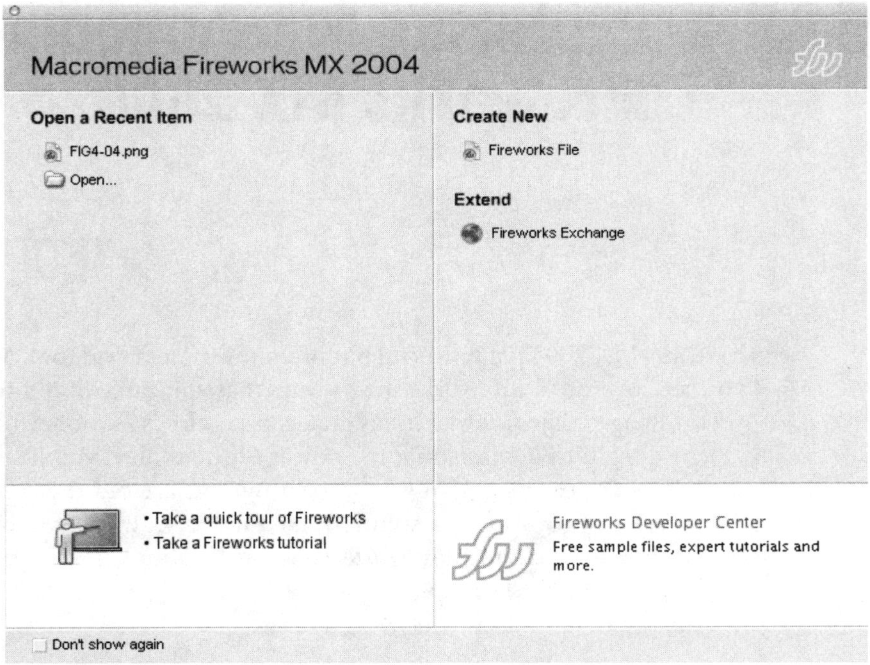

FIGURE 10.1 Fireworks Start page.

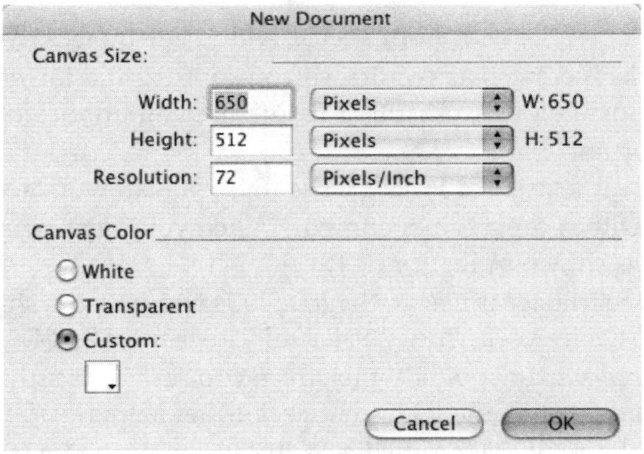

FIGURE 10.2 New Document window.

Within this window are the options for setting the width and height of the document in pixels, inches, or centimeters; the resolution; and the canvas (background) color.

We must first address the size of the document. We are using Fireworks to design a Web page, so look at the screen resolutions shown in Figure 10.3.

This diagram is based on one of the most common design formats, with the company name across the top and the navigation panel on the left. On sites like this every page usually shares this design. It is not the most original, but it has merit because it's so common so users feel comfortable navigating through it.

User monitor settings are one of the most important considerations. You must create the best design that reaches the most people.

Over the last several years, nearly all monitors sold support at least an 800x600 resolution, making it the most popular size to target in design. It covers approximately 95 percent of your audience or more and is a fairly safe bet. Even though monitors that support higher resolutions are coming out all the time, with the rapid aging of Baby Boomers in the United States, expect 800x600 to be the prevalent resolution for a while. It is easier for those with poor eyesight to read, plus it has the added advantage of more screen real estate, so both content and white space can be used.

When considering the resolution, however, think of your target audience. If it is likely that a great number of them have older equipment, designing for a resolution of 640x480 is a safe approach. If you are aiming for a general audience,

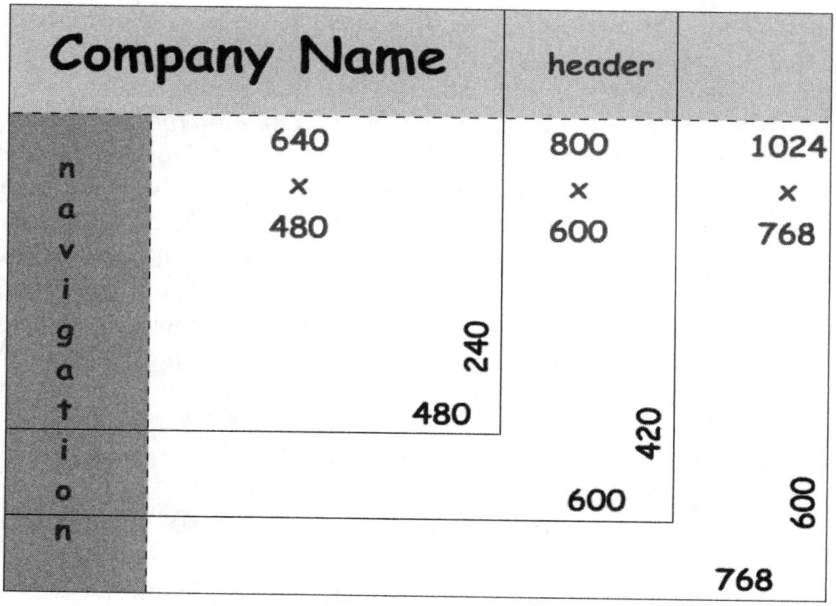

FIGURE 10.3   Three main monitor resolution settings and page sizes.

800x600 is the best choice. But if you are designing for a specialized audience, such as graphic designers and professional photographers, they usually have their monitor settings set very high and may not respect a site created in a lower resolution. For this type of audience, 1024x768 is the best solution.

But let's throw more considerations into the mix. What platform are your users using? By default, Macintoshes are set with a narrower browser display. Will users be using their browsers at full screen and not have their History or Search windows open? Let's look at this decision systematically.

Most Latin-based languages read from left to right and top to bottom, so let's use this information. Most monitors are capable of displaying at least 800x600, and we want to have space to place your content. You must account for at least a 300-pixel loss in usable screen space due to the menu bar, navigational buttons, address bar, links bar, status bar, and scroll bars. We really have to fight to get anything out of the window. Also, expect the possibility that your audience may have their browsers set to a lower width or may have extraneous items, such as a search window, open.

With these considerations in mind, set up our document to be 600x420, which accounts for some loss of real estate with the toolbars and status bar open. Also try to put your company name toward the top and set up your page with the most important information and navigational elements to the left. This layout isn't the only way a page can be designed to overcome these hurdles, but it's a good first compromise. This way, no matter how much the users have open, we can convey the context of our site at a glance.

The next thing to worry about is resolution. When dealing with a print medium like magazines and books, the higher the resolution the better, with a 300-dpi resolution or more being desired to get decent output. However, we are not designing for print; we are designing for the Web. Web content is viewed primarily on monitors, and they only have the capability of displaying 72 dots per inch. Have you ever scanned something that displayed huge on the monitor? Or maybe received a photograph from a friend and thought "Boy, what an ego. I could wallpaper a room with this photo?" This large display occurs because most scanners and digital cameras default to a quality of 300 dpi or better. Because monitors are incapable of displaying a higher resolution than 72 dpi, they display the photo at a much larger size. A 4x6 photo scanned at a 300-dpi resolution displays on screen at the size of 16.7x28. This is larger than the actual visible size of the monitor, so some serious scrolling is necessary.

Set your resolution to 72 dpi with the knowledge that we are developing for monitors and not print.

Lastly, you must consider the following three options for canvas color:

White: The most popular background color for Web pages. Because most users are comfortable with books and newspapers, white works well for them. Also, it has the advantage of allowing everything to be easily seen on it and is easiest to read if dark-colored text is used.

Transparent: This setting is a good choice if you are making not a Web page but a drawing to export as a .gif file. With a transparent background on a .gif file, your illustration appears to be free-floating.

Custom: This setting is for all other colors. Be careful when considering other colors. Make sure the text you use can be offset from the background and easily legible. Take special care that you don't pick colors such as red and green for a background and text, because someone who is color blind cannot see anything but a gray page.

For your first document, play it safe and choose the following settings:

- Page size—Make sure Pixels is selected in each drop-down menu, and type 600 and 420 for the width and height.
- Resolution—Select Pixels/Inch and type 72.
- Canvas—Select white, then press OK.

We have now made your overall page. All of your graphics appear in here, and the contents will later be imported into Dreamweaver during the site design. Let's look at the screens. One of the great features of Macromedia products is that their interfaces look nearly identical on both Macintosh and PC. Let's take a peek now, in Figures 10.4 and 10.5:

At a first glance, both interfaces appear identical, and, for the most part, they are. The primary differences between the two interfaces are the menu bar and the panels on the right. The menu bar in a Macintosh is at the uppermost portion of the screen and is identical in applications. By not having the application title bar, as seen in Windows, Macintosh offers more pixels of screen real estate. This appearance is a component of the operating system and has nothing to do with the Macromedia design. The second difference between the two is in the panels. The Windows version of the application has the panels "snapped in" on the interface, whereas the Macintosh has the panel set as free-floating.

With such an overall consistency, a Web designer can go from Windows to Macintosh and back with ease. Let's go ahead and break down the components of the interface:

Menu Bar: Contains nearly every operation of the program through all of the options. It is the application's overall command control center, providing

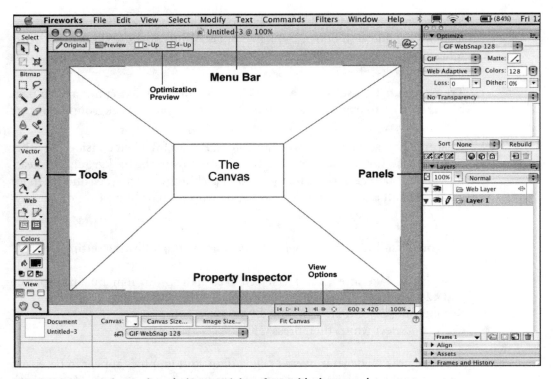

FIGURE 10.4 Main Macintosh (OS 10.3) interface with the new document.

options for creating files, editing features, saving, and modifying. It also controls what tools and panels are seen or hidden and advanced features within the program. Many of the selections can be found in other locations.

Tools Panel: Represents the bread and butter of the application. This area contains the tools you select to draw and edit both vector graphics and images. It has been updated since Fireworks 4 and offers both the bitmap tools (Marquee, Lasso, Magic Wand, and so on) and vector tools (Line Tool, Pen Tool, Shape Tool, and so on). This layout is a distinct improvement over Fireworks 4 because it enables you to work on both your vector and raster components at the same time, in the same document, with greater ease. In Fireworks 4, you had to change back and forth between Bitmap mode and Vector mode.

Property Inspector: Contains the majority of your editing features. This element was introduced in Fireworks MX. It first appeared in Dreamweaver 4, and apparently proved so popular that it is now shared in Dreamweaver MX 2004, Fireworks MX 2004, and Flash MX 2004. This functionality is worth the price of admission alone. It really improves your workflow. As you jump be-

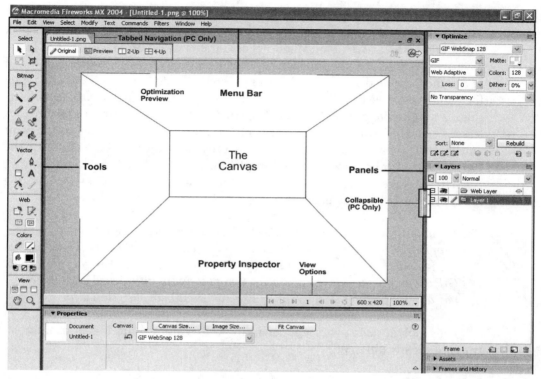

FIGURE 10.5   Main Windows (Windows XP Professional) interface with the new document.

tween the three core applications in Studio MX 2004, you will find you spend most of your time between the Tools Panel and Property Inspector. In Fireworks 4 you had to dig through numerous panels to edit documents.

Panels: Provide addition options to complement the Property Inspector. These panels are on the right of the screen. In the Windows version of Fireworks MX 2004, you can press the arrow in the center of the left edge in the panel set to collapse the panels, affording more real estate for the canvas.

Although collapsible panels are available only in Windows, Mac users shouldn't feel left out. By pressing either the Tab or F4 key, all panels are hidden, giving more room to work on your document. This shortcut works in both versions of the program.

Tabbed Navigation (PC only): Enables you to quickly change between what document is in focus, instead of having to click Window > <document name>. This feature is new feature to Fireworks MX 2004.

One of the first things we need to do with your new document is to save it. You can never save a document too many times. To initially save your document, click either File > Save (Ctrl + S on Windows or Command + S on Macintosh) or File > Save As. Because the document has never been saved before, either command opens the Save As dialog box. The overall Fireworks document is saved as a .png file. Users don't see this file, but it is your working file that includes all layers, settings, and other items and is modifiable. Anything output for users or for final release is exported from Fireworks. This method of creation goes back to the print world. When a page is created for the press, often all of the pieces are pasted on the page so they can be moved around in placement. The pasted-up original wasn't given to the readers, but a visual copy was sent to the press for publication. The .png file is your pasted-up original.

An image file type created for the Web is also named .png (Portable Network Graphics). This format is not the same as the Fireworks .png format. It is a proposed open-standard replacement for the .gif (Graphics Interchange Format) file format. GIF is a proprietary file type owned by Compuserve (in turn owned by AOL), as opposed to JPEG (Joint Photographers Experts Group), an open standard.

Let's look at saving your document in both Windows and Macintosh; the setups are slightly different.

Saving in Macintosh

First you see the general Save dialog box, shown in Figure 10.6.

By default, Fireworks tries to save your document in the Pictures folder. This default setting is good because most documents are in this central location, making it easier for you to back up your information. Take this organization a step further and create a new folder to define documents as Fireworks. Click the drop-down arrow to the right of Documents to open the dialog box shown in Figure 10.7.

```
                              Save

        Save As:  Untitled-1.png               ▼

         Where:   📁 Pictures              ↕

    ☑ Add Filename Extension

                                    Cancel    Save
```

FIGURE 10.6 The Macintosh (OS 10.3) Save dialog box.

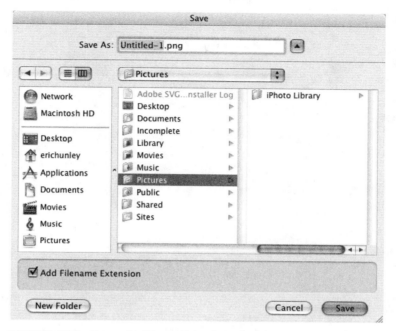

FIGURE 10.7 Expanded Save dialog box (Macintosh).

In the expanded view of the Save dialog box, you have more options. You can see the folder structure and navigate up and down through it.

Now click the New Folder button. After clicking the New Folder button, you see the New Folder dialog box, shown in Figure 10.8. Name the folder Fireworks-Web, so we can keep track of our Fireworks content.

Now that the folder has been created you are returned to the main Save dialog box, with the newly created folder highlighted, as shown in Figure 10.9.

You may also want to create folders underneath your main Fireworks folder for each Web site you are building to help you keep everything organized.

FIGURE 10.8 The New Folder dialog box.

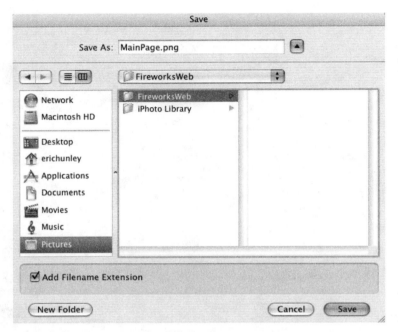

FIGURE 10.9 The newly created folder is highlighted, and the document automatically is placed in it. Notice the Add Filename Extension option is selected.

Make sure the Add Filename Extension option is selected. If it is not, when you transfer the file to a Windows system, or even share it with a Windows user, the folder will not open. This problem represents an operating system difference between Macintosh and Windows. Macintosh automatically knows what a file type is, but Windows must be told.

Name your file *MainPage*, and save it.

SAVING IN WINDOWS

First you see the general Save As dialog box, shown in Figure 10.10.

By default, Fireworks tries to save your file in the My Pictures folder under My Documents. This behavior is an improvement over Fireworks 4, which defaulted to C:\Program Files\Macromedia\Fireworks. But we still want to give our Fireworks content its own folder. Click the New Folder button, as shown in Figure 10.11.

This action open a New Folder, also highlighted in Figure 10.11.

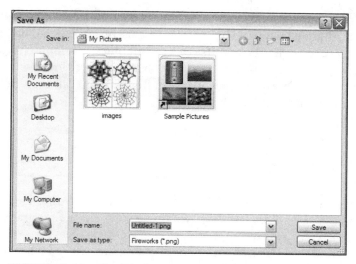

FIGURE 10.10   The Windows Save As dialog box.

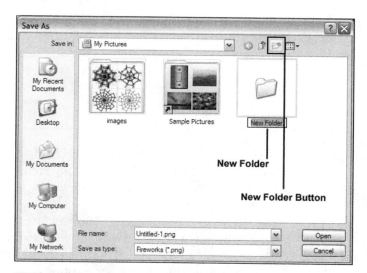

FIGURE 10.11   The New Folder button.

Name the folder *FireworksWeb*. This folder help you keep your content sorted clearly. If you accidentally click anywhere else on the screen and the folder is no longer highlighted, just right-click, select Rename, and type the correct name.

After you have the new folder created and named, double-click it to save your document inside the folder.

Now name the file *MainPage.png*.

We have now created your basic layout page that we will use for the rest of this chapter. Although we could have created a page of any size and had it work, it is important to realize that Fireworks is a Web graphics development tool. As such, we will view your results in a browser by clicking File > Preview in Browser or by pressing the F12 key on the keyboard. In this way you can get a fair representation of what your users will see on the Web.

EXPLORING THE TOOLS

Throughout the rest of this chapter we will explore the different tools available in Fireworks. You will find that Fireworks is a truly unique program in that it works with both vector and raster graphics. This ability is ideal for Web design because you can comfortably create the majority of graphics needed for your Web site without having to change tools.

A great deal of overlap is present between Fireworks and FreeHand, so some of the tools are identical or extremely similar and, therefore, are not explored as deeply in this chapter. Because you have already studied their functionality in Free-Hand, you should feel comfortable jumping right in here.

STROKES

As you learned in the chapters covering Flash and FreeHand, all vector graphics comprise two parts: paths and fills. If a path has a color, it is referred to as a stroke or line. Here we explore what strokes are available in Fireworks, as shown in Figure 10.12.

To select your stroke color, size, type, edge, and texture, use the stroke properties area in the Property Inspector. You can also modify your stroke color within the Tools Panel. When you select an object with both a fill and a stroke, you find within the Property Inspector that you now have the options to choose Stroke Inside, Stroke Centered, and Stroke Outside. Stroke Inside applies the stroke width inside of the shape, causing less fill. Stroke Centered (the default) causes the width of the stroke to be evenly dispersed inside and outside of the shape. Stroke Outside places the stroke completely outside of the object.

When you select the Texture drop-down menu, you find an assortment of options available, complete with a preview. When you pick an option, you can set the Amount of Texture to the right of the Texture drop-down.

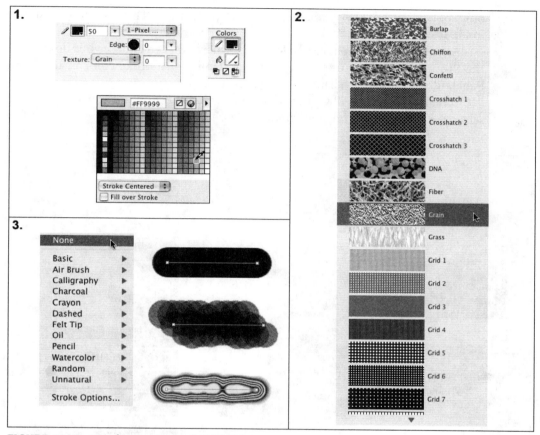

FIGURE 10.12 Strokes in Fireworks MX 2004.

The Stroke category drop-down menu provides numerous options, everything from elegant to bizarre. The examples shown are Basic > Soft Rounded, Unnatural > Viscous Alien Paint, and Unnatural > Toxic Waste. New to Fireworks MX 2004, you also now have the option of using the Dashed category. This category is a long awaited and welcomed addition to Fireworks.

FILLS

Not only do you have strokes available, like in any vector program, Fireworks MX 2004 also offers numerous fills. With the assorted fills, you have the option of not only solid colors but also gradients, patterns, and textures. These options are shown in Figure 10.13.

As with strokes, you have two locations where you can choose your desired fill: the Property Inspector or the Tools Panel. Unlike the stroke color in the Tools Panel, fill options are available in both locations.

When you choose Fill Options, the Fill Options pop-up window opens. If you select the Fill Category pop-up window in either the Fill Options pop-up window

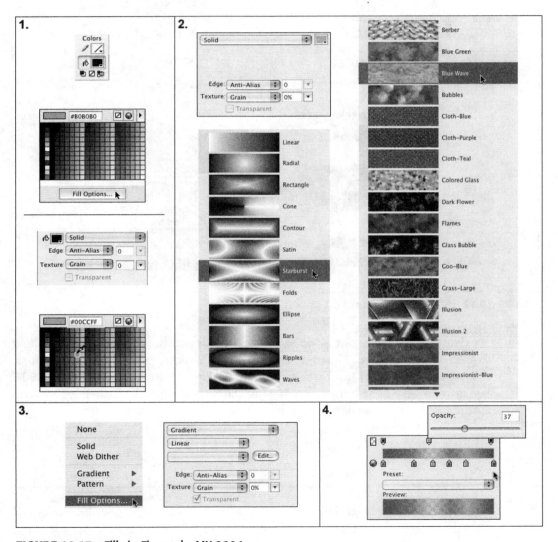

FIGURE 10.13 Fills in Fireworks MX 2004.

or the Property Inspector, you can select from Solid, Web Dither, Gradient, or Pattern. This action opens a preview screen showing which options are available. Gradients and Patterns are shown in Figure 10.13.

If you want to adjust gradient fill settings further, open the Fill Options pop-up window. Here you can select what type of gradient to use.

You can then press the Edit button to open the Edit Gradient pop-up window. On the bottom half of the color ramp (the upper preview in the window), choose what colors you want in your gradient. If you want to add a color, click along the ramp where you would like the new color placed. This action adds a new swatch. You can modify the color of the new swatch by clicking it and choosing a new color. If you want to remove a swatch, drag the swatch out of the window. On the upper part of the color ramp are the opacity swatches. These swatches allow you to add transparency along the ramp. Click one of these swatches to open an opacity slider; you can then adjust the transparency. If you want to add or take away any of the opacity swatches, follow the same technique as for the color swatches.

SELECT TOOLS

The first tools available in the Tools Panel are the Select Tools. The first of these tools is the Pointer Tool (black arrow). Of all the Pointer tools in Macromedia Studio MX 2004, the Fireworks MX 2004 Pointer Tool has the least functionality. It is primarily used to select and move objects on the canvas. You can also resize objects by pulling on the corner points, but that is really about all there is to this tool.

Nested underneath the Select tool is the Select Behind Tool. This tool allows you to select objects underneath the current object. You can adjust which object in the hierarchy is selected by clicking multiple times. Each click brings you to a lower item. Keep clicking until you have chosen the object you want.

You use the Subselection (white arrow) Tool to manipulate actual vector points and handles or objects within groups. This tool offers more functionality than the Pointer Tool because it is the traditional vector manipulation tool within illustration programs.

The next of the Select tools are the Scale, Skew, and Distort Tools.

Scale Tool: Allows you to scale and rotate a selected object in a freeform manner.

Skew Tool: Allows you to give depth to objects by modifying their angles on edges. It can also be used to rotate.

Distort Tool: Modifies an entire edge while skewing. The Distort Tool works with individual corners.

The Scale, Skew, and Distort Tools work in a similar manner across all of the graphic creation tools found within Studio MX 2004.

The last two tools in this section are the Crop and Export Area Tools.

Crop Tool: Allows you to select an area of an image, then double-click your selection to crop all areas in the image not selected.

Export Area Tool: Allows you to select a specific area of a document. When you double-click the area, the Export Preview window opens, allowing you to choose what export settings you want. You also can right-click (Control + click on a Macintosh) the selection to export it without previewing it.

VECTOR TOOLS

In Fireworks MX 2004, you find many vector tools available that are nearly identical to those in FreeHand MX.

Line Tool

The Line Tool in Fireworks MX 2004 works in an identical fashion to that in Flash MX 2004 and FreeHand MX. It creates a path by drawing two points. If you want to constrain it to 45 degree angles, press the Shift key as you draw.

Pen Tool

The Pen Tool works with the same functionality as in FreeHand MX. Use a combination of clicking and dragging to drag out curves, hold the Shift key to constrain the line to the nearest 45 degree angle, and press and hold the Alt/Option key to change the direction of the curve while drawing. Chapter Two contains some Pen Tool examples.

Vector Path and Redraw Path Tools

The Vector Path and Redraw Path Tools give you a more freeform ability to create and manipulate strokes if you don't want to use the Pen Tool. These tools are shown in Figure 10.14.

The Vector Path Tool simply plots points, where needed, to create the stroke you want. You must be careful with the complexity of your vector graphics when using this tool. Notice in the figure how many vector points were required to mimic the relatively simple path input? Consider clicking Modify > Alter Path > Simplify when you use the Vector Path Tool.

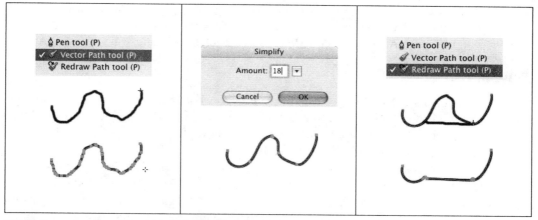

FIGURE 10.14   The Vector Path and Redraw Path Tools.

The Simplify option subtracts from the total number of vector points, using the number you specify, while trying to maintain the original shape. In Figure 10.14. Simplify is applied with an amount of 18. This action really cleaned up the total number of points and even smoothed out the final shape. Experiment to find the right number of points, pick a number, and apply it. If the number is too much or too little, click Edit > Undo or press Ctrl/Command + Z and try again.

The Redraw Path Tool allows you to select an item on the stage using your Pointer (black arrow) or Subselection (white arrow) Tool. After you have selected an object, use the Redraw Path Tool to create a new course for the path to travel. This tool is shown in the third pane of Figure 10.14.

Rectangle Tool

The Rectangle Tool is similar to that in FreeHand MX, but it is not as strong. You have the ability to have rounded corners, which you can specify in the Property Inspector under Rectangle Roundness. You can also change the roundness at any point after creation. However, you don't have as much control on the corners.

You cannot individually pick which corners are rounded, as you can in FreeHand MX, and you cannot create chamfer corners with this tool. Fortunately, you have an Auto Shape Tool, which will be covered later, that can create chamfer rectangles.

Ellipse Tool

Found underneath the Rectangle Tool, the Ellipse Tool works in an identical manner to the Rectangle Tool in FreeHand MX. If you want to create a perfect circle, press the Shift key while drawing it. If you want the circle created from the center

out, press the Alt/Option key while drawing it. Also, you can move the shape to another location on the canvas by pressing the space bar and moving the shape. When
you release the space bar, control is passed back to the Ellipse Tool.

Polygon Tool

In Fireworks MX 2004, you will find a Polygon Tool that allows you to create poly-
gon and star shapes. This tool is similar to that in Flash MX 2004 and FreeHand
MX, but like the Rectangle Tool, it does not have the power available in FreeHand
MX. Let's look at this tool in Figure 10.15.

To create a polygon or star shape, you must first specify what it is and what the
parameters are within the Property Inspector. Here you can choose sides, which is
applicable to both polygon and star shapes, and Angle, which applies only to the
star shape. When you use angle, the higher the number, the shallower your angle is.
One major difference between Fireworks MX 2004 and FreeHand MX when using
this tool is that in Fireworks you must pick all of your parameters prior to creation
and cannot adjust them after the object is created.

In panel 2 of Figure 10.15 is a standard five-sided polygon. It takes on the properties of the fill and stroke you choose in the Property Inspector or in the Colors
section of the Tools Panel.

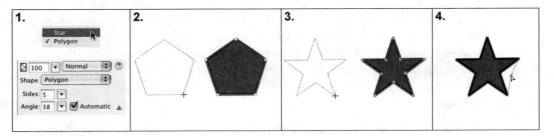

FIGURE 10.15   Using the Polygon Tool.

Panel 3 shows a five-pointed star shape. Again, it takes on the fill and color you
specify.

After the star shape is created, if you try to adjust it using the Subselection
Tool, only the single point will move, as shown in panel 4.

Although the basic Polygon Tool is very limited, this limitation has been addressed in the current version of Fireworks. Fireworks MX 2004 now has the Auto
Shapes Tool, which is described in the next section. One of the Auto Shapes available is Star, which gives you much more control.

Auto Shapes Tool

The Auto Shapes Tool is a new addition to Fireworks MX 2004. These tools greatly enhance the ease of use of the application. It is essentially a repository of commonly used vector shapes that can prove tedious to create manually.

Not only are the shapes precreated for your use, but each has diamond-shaped control points available for changing the parameters. With these points you can change the size, number of points/sides, style, rotation, and more, depending on the object. These control points remain available after you have created the objects, so you can freely adjust them in the future.

Perhaps the best part of the Auto Shapes Tool is that new shapes are created all the time. Third parties or individual developers using documentation available at *www.macromedia.com* can create them. Expect to see more and more in the future. Let's looking at the Auto Shapes Tool in Figure 10.16.

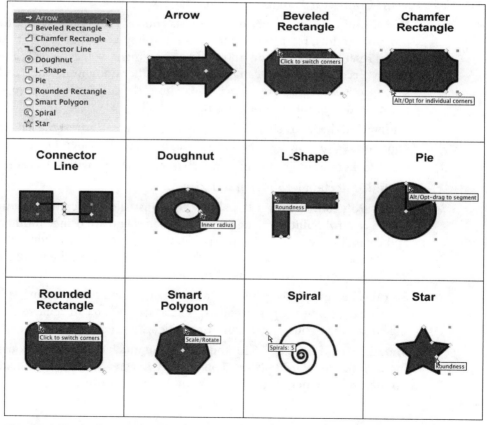

FIGURE 10.16   The Auto Shapes Tool.

Arrow: Creates an arrow that contains both a fill and a stroke. With the control points you can adjust the arrowhead size, its tip, arrow length, thickness, whether it has a bend, and the roundness of the bend.

The Beveled, Chamfer, and Rounded Rectangles are essentially the same shape; they just start with their own styles. They all have options to click the control points in the corners to change them to one of the other corner styles. If you press the Alt/Option key when clicking a corner, your action affects only the individual corner. The other control point available is for resizing the rectangle.

Beveled Rectangle: Starts in beveled form.

Chamfer Rectangle: Starts in chamfered form.

Connector Line: Connects shapes on the stage with a line. Its control points allow you to rotate, change direction, and curve the corners. It is not as robust as the Connector Tool found in FreeHand MX.

Doughnut: Creates doughnut shapes. Its control points enable you to change the inner radius, reset the center (make it disappear), and segment the shape. If you reset the inner radius and pull out a segment, you can create a pie shape with a piece cut out. You can then create another doughnut shape and use the same process to create your piece. If you press the Alt/Option key, you can segment the doughnut, leaving the stroke and fill.

L-Shape: Makes an L-shape. Use the control points to adjust the length of each segment, the thickness of the L, and whether or not the bend is rounded.

Pie: Works in a similar manner to the Doughnut, only without a center radius.

Rounded Rectangle: Starts in rounded form.

Smart Polygon: Provides the ability to adjust the shape after creation. You have a control point to change how many sides you are using, another to scale and rotate it, one to add a center polygon to make it like a doughnut, and another to segment it. This shape has far better control than the regular Polygon Tool, and you may want to use it instead.

Spiral: Creates spirals. This tool allows you to select how many spirals and whether the shape is open or closed (like a snail). You can achieve an interesting effect when you apply a contour gradient to this shape.

Star: Creates a star shape. This tool offers you much of the power you are missing with the standard Polygon Tool. Here you can adjust the size, acuteness of points, and whether or not the peaks or valleys are rounded.

Assets Panel Shapes Tab

If the Auto Shapes Tool options are not enough for you, another tab is available. Access this tool by clicking Window > Auto Shapes.

Within the Assets Panel Shapes tab, you can find additional shapes. You can also get more. These shapes tend to be more complex than what you find in the Tools Panel, so you should keep them separate. Let's explore this panel, shown in Figure 10.17.

Clock: Provides a clock image. You can change the time by either dragging the minutes or hours control points or by clicking the center point to open a dialog box. Because the shape is a group, you can select individual components with the Subselection Tool to change colors. Keep in mind that if you go too far with your changes, Fireworks MX 2004 will warn you that you may break the functionality of the Auto Shape.

Cog: Makes a gear type of shape. You can use the control points to modify the center radius and the gear shapes.

Cube: Creates a cube shape for a 3D effect. You can change its offset and perspective using control points.

Cylinder: Creates a 3D cylindrical shape. You can change its offset and perspective.

Frame: Creates a frame that automatically fits around an imported bitmap or any content on the canvas. When using it, select a raster image or shape on the stage and drag the Frame shape onto the item you have selected. You can control the thickness, pattern, and corner type of the frame using control points. Fill control handles allow you to position the grain within the frame.

Perspective: Drops a perspective grid onto the stage to guide you when you are skewing objects to show depth. You can adjust its angles and size using control points.

Tabs: Adds tabbed navigation to a Web page created in Fireworks. You can add and delete from the row and change the hue (tint) using control points. To make them clickable, hotspots must be created over the objects. We will learn about these later.

Talking: Creates a comic-book-style conversation bubble shape. You can adjust its shape using control points.

Tube: Adds an inner radius front and rear to the Cylinder shape.

Auto Shapes should prove very important to the growth of Fireworks MX 2004. By offering this kind of flexibility, Macromedia is closing the gap between Fire-

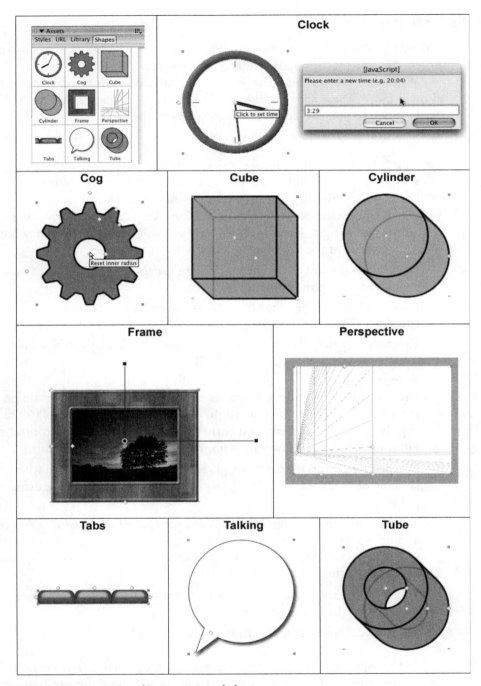

FIGURE 10.17 Using the Assets Panel shapes.

works and FreeHand very rapidly. You can find more Auto Shapes on Macromedia Exchange by clicking Get More Auto Shapes on the Assets Options menu while the Shapes tab is selected.

Text Tool

As in FreeHand and Flash, the Text Tool is an important part of design in Fireworks. It is especially important in Fireworks because you often want to use a customized font that will not be available on your users' computers. The only way to guarantee proper rendering of customized text is to convert it into an image. This task is a Fireworks specialty.

Most text options can be found in the Property Inspector. Let's look at the basics of using the Text Tool in Fireworks, as shown in Figure 10.18.

As you learned in the Flash chapters, most text properties can be controlled in the Property Inspector. Here you find many familiar aspects to control the text input, like the size, font, color, bold, italic, underline, and paragraph placement (left, center, right, justify, and stretched alignment, which causes the text to fit an area). Notice the other options, including Effects, which are covered later.

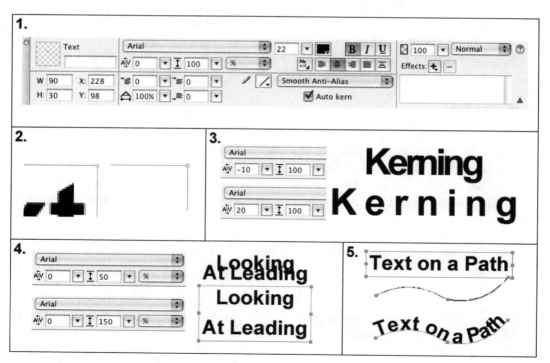

FIGURE 10.18 Using the Text Tool.

Whenever you are going to place text on the canvas, you are creating a text block. Two types of text block are available: auto-sizing and fixed width. An auto-sizing text block is created when you click the canvas with the Text Tool and just start typing. The block grows to fit text as you type. An auto-sizing text block is depicted with an open circle in the top-right corner. On the other hand, a fixed-width text block is created when you drag a text block in the same manner that you create a rectangle, or if you resize an auto-sizing text block. It does not expand as you type, and new text appears on the line below. A fixed-width text block is indicated by an open square on the top-right corner. You can convert a fixed-width text block to an auto-size text box by double-clicking the open square.

One of the common text-editing features you will use is kerning. Kerning is the process of adjusting the space between individual characters to make the text flow better visibly. Most computer fonts have built-in kerning. You can adjust the setting to make the kerning narrower or wider, as shown in panel 3 of Figure 10.18. Kerning is available in all programs in Studio MX 2004.

Another popular editing function is leading. *Leading* is a term that carries over from typesetting. Originally, typesetters used actual strips of lead to space lines of text.

As in FreeHand MX, you can attach text to a path. Just create text and a path, press Shift + click to select both, then click Text > Attach to Path. Your result should resemble what is shown in panel 5 of Figure 10.18. Where Fireworks MX 2004 departs from FreeHand MX is that you cannot place text on the top and bottom of an ellipse in one step as you can with FreeHand MX.

Freeform Tool

The Freeform Tool works in an identical manner as that in FreeHand MX. It modifies a shape that is created on the stage as if it were a lump of clay. You can adjust the width of the shape either in the Property Inspector or dynamically by pressing the right or left arrow keys while you are using the tool. If you have a digitizing tablet, this tool responds to the pressure on your pen if the Pressure option is selected.

Remember, you must ungroup rectangles before you can use this tool on them. Do this by clicking Modify > Ungroup (or right-clicking/Control + click > Ungroup).

If you click a corner point using your Subselection Tool (white arrow), a dialog box opens, prompting you that a rectangle must first be ungrouped. If you click OK, the rectangle is ungrouped automatically.

Reshape Area Tool

The Reshape Area Tool works in a similar manner to the Freeform Tool, only it tapers to become thinner as it progresses. You can control the size and strength of the tool in the Property Inspector. You can also dynamically resize the path as it is being created with a pressure-sensitive tablet or your arrow keys.

Path Scrubber Tools—Additive and Subtractive

The Path Scrubber Tools are for further modifying paths created with a pressure-sensitive tablet. The Additive Tool widens the stroke and the Subtractive Tool makes the path narrower. If you don't have a pressure-sensitive tablet, you most likely will use this tool.

Knife Tool

The Knife Tool also has the same functionality as that in FreeHand MX. When you have a path selected, the Knife Tool dissects the path into two. You must use the Knife Tool if you want to separate paths in Fireworks MX 2004 and FreeHand MX, unlike in Macromedia Flash MX 2004, because the two programs create paths as objects.

BITMAP TOOLS

In Fireworks MX 2004, the Bitmap Tools are available for editing both raster and vector graphics. This capability is what starts to give the program an edge over FreeHand MX for Web design. These are not lightweight but full-fledged photo manipulation tools found in top-of-the-line applications. With its combination of vector creation and photo manipulation, Fireworks MX 2004 is an industry standout.

Marquee and Oval Marquee Tools

The first tools covered are the Marquee and Oval Tools. Although these tools can be used for both vector and raster graphics, they are traditionally found in photo-editing programs. Let's explore these tools, shown in Figure 10.19.

To select with the Marquee Tool, drag a rectangle around the area you want use for editing. If you want the selection to be a perfect square, press the Shift key while you drag. You can also create the rectangle from the center out. To do this, press the Alt/Option key while creating the rectangle.

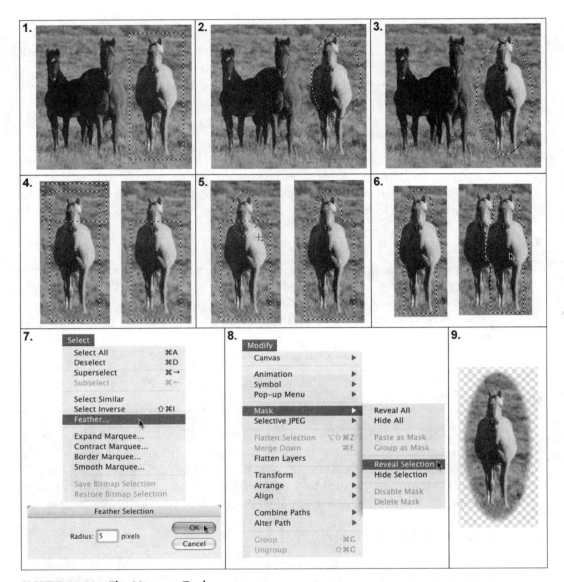

FIGURE 10.19 The Marquee Tools.

To use an Oval Marquee Tool, drag your oval around the area you want to select. Like the Marquee Tool, the Oval Marquee Tool can be created from the center out by pressing the Alt/Option key while dragging the oval. Pressing Shift creates a perfect circle.

If you want to add to your current Marquee Tool, press the Shift key, then create another Marquee or Oval Marquee. The new area chosen is added to your current selection.

When you want to subtract from a current selection, press the Alt/Option key when creating a new Marquee/Oval Marquee. The new Marquee, along with the overlap into the original marquee, is removed.

After you have used the Marquee Tools to make your selection, you can switch to the Pointer Tool. If you drag the shape with the Pointer Tool, the contents of the shape are cut out of the image. You can also create a clone of the selected area by pressing the Alt/Option key and dragging the selection with the Pointer Tool. The selected area is duplicated, as shown in panel 6 of Figure 10.19.

Another fun effect you can create using the Marquee or Oval Marquee Tool is to feather the edges an area of an image. First select an area of an image. After it is selected, click Select > Feather to open the Feather dialog box, as shown in panel 7. Feathering is the process of making the edges of an object more transparent in a series of steps using different levels of opacity, until the shape ends.

After applying your feather, click Modify > Mask > Reveal Selection as a quick way to have the rest of the image disappear. If you don't want to retain any of the rest of the image, click Select > Select Inverse (this command changes the selected area to be the rest of the image), then press the Delete key.

Now you see your selection by itself on the canvas with feathered edges.

When you want to show only part of an image, it is often a good idea to use masking. You achieve the effect of the rest of the image disappearing, but you have not physically altered it. If you need to modify your selection, you still have pixels to play with.

Lasso and Polygon Lasso Tools

The Lasso Tools come in where the Marquee Tools leave off. Although the Marquee Tools allow you to select areas as a rectangle or oval, the Lasso Tools allow you to create freeform shapes. Let's explore these tools in Figure 10.20.

Selecting an area with the Lasso Tool is much like using the Pencil Tool. Simply click and draw a line with your mouse until you have surrounded the area you want to select. If you release your mouse button prior to meeting up with your start point, Fireworks automatically completes the path to create a shape, as shown in Figure 10.20.

It is a good idea to select a wider area around an object, then continue using the Lasso Tool to trim the selection. You can accomplish this by pressing the Alt/Op-

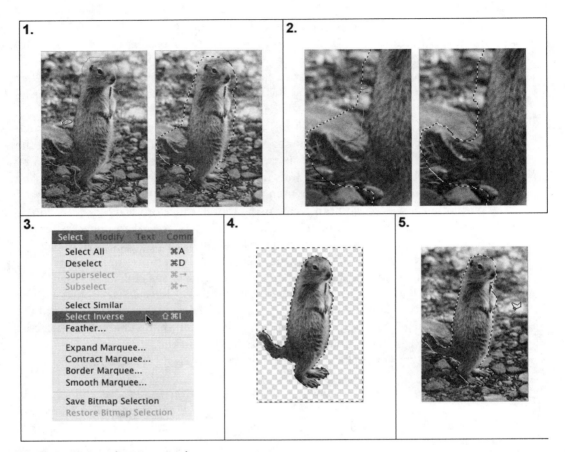

FIGURE 10.20   The Lasso Tools.

tion keys and drawing a new area to subtract from the selection. (The Shift key adds to the selection. By modifying your selection in stages, you can zoom in to be more accurate and click Edit > Undo (or Control/Command + Z) to go back a step if you make a mistake.

After you have made your selection, click Select > Select Inverse and press the Delete key.

After deleting the background, your selection stands alone on the canvas. You can choose many other modifications on a selected object, such as sharpen, blur, or any of the Live Effects.

The Polygon Lasso Tool creates a straight path between points where you click. The process is to click and release to create a starting point. Then move your mouse and click and release again where you want your next point. Continue until you have made your complete selection, then double-click to release the tool.

It is extremely important that you remember to double-click to release the Polygon Lasso Tool. If you do not double-click, you find that it follows you everywhere—like being caught in a spider's web.

NOTE

Magic Wand Tool

The Magic Wand Tool is used in Studio MX 2004 to select similar adjacent colors from an image. It can be a useful tool to use with your Marquee and Lasso Tools for selecting portions of images.

By adjusting its tolerance, the range of colors selected increases or shrinks. Let's explore this tool, shown in Figure 10.21.

When you have the Tolerance setting in the Property Inspector set to a low number, less is selected because the tool selects a smaller range of colors based on the pixel you initially click.

Notice when the Tolerance is set to 50, more is being selected from the image.

When the tolerance is set to 100, nearly all of the flower petals are selected. The stems were added to the selection by pressing the Shift key and clicking them.

If you want to select all areas in a document that have a similar color that you have chosen with the Magic Wand Tool, click Select > Select Similar. This option is a handy alternative to pressing Shift + clicking similar colors that are not physically connected.

TIP

FIGURE 10.21 The Magic Wand Tool.

Brush Tool

The Brush Tool is fairly straightforward. You can brush strokes onto bitmaps. You have the same options available to you as for normal strokes. The only difference is that you cannot adjust the stroke after it has been applied because the new stroke becomes part of the bitmap. If you select Preserve Transparency in the Property Inspector, the tool is only effective on visible pixels in the image.

Pencil Tool

The Pencil Tool is similar to the Brush Tool except you are limited to a one-pixel stroke. Preserve Transparency can also be used. Auto Erase, when checked, causes all pixels passed over to change to the fill color when you drag your mouse over them.

Eraser Tool

As we have seen previously, the Eraser Tool can almost be thought of as a Brush Tool in reverse. When used, the areas to which you apply the tool change to match the canvas color. One interesting option of this tool is the Opacity setting in the Property Inspector.

When you choose a lower value for the opacity, the erased areas become more transparent as you erase them. You can use this option to give a bitmap a faded effect.

Blur Tool

When you use this tool, areas in an image that you pass over with the mouse button pressed blur. This tool can be used when you want to blur specific areas of the bitmap but not the whole image.

Settings for this tool include the size and shape (square or circle) of the tool. You can also adjust the edge, which determines how much of a buffer you have as the tool is applied. In addition, you can modify the intensity and determine how much of a blur is applied.

Sharpen Tool

The Sharpen Tool works in the exact opposite manner as the Blur Tool. It also offers the same options. When you apply the Sharpen Tool, Fireworks increases the contrast between adjacent pixels.

Dodge and Burn Tools

The Dodge and Burn Tools work with one another to either lighten an image by emulating increased exposure (Dodge) or darkening the image (Burn). You can toggle between the tools by pressing the Alt/Option key while one of the two tools is selected.

Settings for these tools include the size, shape, and edge of the brush. Other settings offered include Range, which specifies what is modified more (Highlights, Midtones, or Shadows), and Exposure, which determines the intensity of the effect.

Smudge Tool

The Smudge Tool, when applied, gives the effect that an image was rubbed, causing colors to run into one another. You can choose the usual brush head settings along with what color the smudge is as it starts and how much pressure is applied.

If you don't select a smudge color, Fireworks uses the pixel colors underneath the tool when applied.

You can also choose the option of Whole Document. When selected, Fireworks uses the whole document, which pulls color from all objects. When it is not selected, only the active (selected) object is smudged.

Rubber Stamp Tool

The Rubber Stamp Tool is an interesting tool. It allows you to selectively clone and paint portions of an image from one part of the image to another part of the image or document. Let's look at this tool applied, as shown in Figure 10.22.

To use this tool, start with an image that has elements you would like to copy. With the tool selected, you see a target cursor. Click and release the target cursor to select the area you want to clone.

After you have placed your target, as you move your mouse, you see a + (plus sign) that shows the area being cloned. You also see an open circle indicating where the clone will be painted.

When you click and drag the mouse, you begin to copy the area around your target.

FIGURE 10.22   Using the Rubber Stamp Tool.

When using the Rubber Stamp Tool, you may find it a little odd having two cursors moving around. You can control the output of the clone by first visually tracking the plus sign after you click the mouse button. Use the plus sign to select the outer edges of your original area. When you have covered all of the outer edges, you can then focus your attention on where you are painting the clone. This method is helpful because you may accidentally clone too large of an area unintentionally when you are focused on the clone instead of on the original.

Replace Color Tool

The Replace Color Tool is a new addition to Fireworks MX 2004. It allows you to select a color and then replace only that color with an alternate. This tool can be useful for freeform color replacement in an image. Let's explore this tool, shown in Figure 10.23.

With this tool, you must select two colors: the color you want to replace and the color with which you want to replace it. Perhaps the best method for sampling the color you want to replace is to click the Change swatch. When the pop-up window with colors appears, instead of choosing a standard color, move your eyedropper all the way to the image itself. In the image, click the color you want to replace.

After you choose the To color in the Property Inspector, start painting over the image. Notice how the petal in panel 2 of Figure 10.23 was spared as the brush passed over it.

When you are painting over an object, you can set the Tolerance and Strength options to determine how wide a range of colors is replaced and how strong the replacement color is. Panel 3 shows a Strength of 200 (max) and a Tolerance of 100 (Half).

When the Tolerance is set to a high level (in this case, 200 out of 255), it replaces a wide range of colors. Notice how even the stem was replaced. Only the petals survived because they are extremely different from the blue color that was selected for the Change swatch.

FIGURE 10.23   The Replace Color Tool.

Red Eye Removal Tool

The Red Eye Removal Tool is new to Fireworks MX 2004. It allows you to select areas of red and replace them with gray and black tones. You can adjust the Tolerance and Strength to determine the level of the effect.

Eyedropper Tool

If you want to select a color from an object or image on the stage, the Eyedropper Tool can be of great assistance. On your Tools Panel, you see that the Fill and Stroke swatch areas can be selected. Whichever you have selected inherits the color sampled with the Eyedropper Tool.

Within the Property Inspector is the Sample drop-down menu. Here you can adjust the Eyedropper Tool to sample one pixel for its base color or multiple pixels and average the result. Your options are 1 Pixel, 3x3 Average, and 5x5 Average.

Paint Bucket Tool

The Paint Bucket Tool works in a similar manner to the Replace Color Tool, only it is applied to all connected pixels within the range of colors you have selected. It is useful if you want to change large areas of color. Figure 10.24 shows this tool applied.

In Figure 10.24, the Paint Bucket Tool has been applied to the background of the image with a Tolerance of 50, chosen in the Property Inspector. Other options that can be chosen with this tool are Fill Selection, Opacity, Blend Mode, and Preserve Transparency.

When Fill Selection is chosen, the entire selected object is filled and Tolerance is ignored. Opacity adjusts the transparency of the fill color, allowing the original fill to show through and blending the two colors.

FIGURE 10.24   Using the Paint Bucket Tool.

Blend Mode adds several options to the mix. Here you can adjust multiple settings including Darken, Lighten, Difference, Hue, Color, Luminosity, Invert, Tint, and Erase. Let's look at what these effects do:

Darken: Causes the range of colors to be darkened and tinted with the chosen fill color.

Lighten: Causes the reverse effect of Darken.

Difference: Takes the difference in the colors and applies it.

Hue: Blends the selected fill color with the object.

Color: Modifies the range of colors in the object to the fill color.

Luminosity: Adds a glow to the selected colors.

Invert: Reverses the selected color and then applies the modified color to the image.

Tint: Adds the color to the selection.

Erase: Completely removes matching colors within the tolerance. This option is useful when you want to quickly eliminate an area of color.

Gradient Tool

The Gradient Tool works in a similar manner to the Paint Bucket Tool, only it is limited to applying gradients. You can achieve the exact same results with the Paint Bucket Tool and a gradient selected. This tool conveniently starts with a gradient. Figure 10.25 shows the tool used with a black-and-white contour gradient as the fill and a Tolerance of 50.

FIGURE 10.25   The Gradient Tool.

LIVE EFFECTS

Like FreeHand MX, Fireworks MX 2004 has Live Effects. As a matter of fact, Live Effects was first available in Fireworks. Live Effects is an extremely useful tool for applying effects to shapes and images.

As was discussed earlier, the advantage to using Live Effects is that an effect is visible in the output, but the integrity of the original object is not compromised. This way, you can adjust or remove the Live Effects easily. They are found in the Property Inspector, as shown in Figure 10.26.

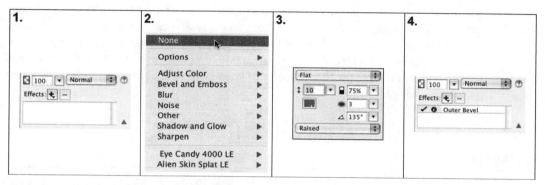

FIGURE 10.26   Live Effects in the Property Inspector.

You can see the area for Live Effects on the right side of the Property Inspector whenever an object is selected on stage.

To add an effect, click the Add Effects button (plus sign) to open the Effects pop-up menu, shown in panel 2 of Figure 10.26.

Some effects offer a pop-up window in which you can adjust settings.

When a Live Effect has been applied to an object, it is listed in the Property Inspector, as shown in panel 4. If you need to adjust the settings of an effect, click the i on the blue disc next to the effect's name. If you want to remove an existing effect, select the effect and press the minus symbol next to the Add Effects button.

If the Property Inspector is at half-height, you cannot see the effects in the window. Press the Edit Effects button to edit your effects. You can also expand the Property Inspector by clicking the triangle in the bottom-right corner.

NOTE

FIREWORKS MX 2004 OR FREEHAND MX?

You may be asking yourself: "With so much crossover between Fireworks MX 2004 and FreeHand MX, which should I use?" This is a very reasonable question.

The most likely answer in Web development is that you will use Fireworks MX 2004 the majority of the time. You only delve into FreeHand MX if you are planning materials that you will be using for print in addition to the Web, or if you are in need of advanced vector graphic capability, especially for use in Flash MX 2004.

Fireworks MX 2004 does not have all of the vector graphic strength of FreeHand MX, but it contains a sizeable portion of features that are available in the second program. When you add in the capacity to work with raster graphics, which are a major part of Web design, you find that you can get more accomplished using a single tool.

The ability to work with both types of graphics is powerful. Also, with its superb integration with Dreamweaver MX 2004, Fireworks MX 2004 will prove itself to be a real workhorse for the majority of your graphical content on the Web, when used to its full potential.

SUMMARY

In this chapter, we created our basic Web page template and explored some tools available in Fireworks MX 2004. We have seen the variety of tools and types of graphics Fireworks can work with, proving it to be a versatile application.

Although we have explored many of the tools, there is still much to cover in the program. We need to learn how it can be used for the Web. Let's move on and start to build our Web page design and add interactivity by "Creating Content with Fireworks MX 2004."

11 Creating Content with Fireworks MX 2004

This is the chapter where we begin to have some fun with Fireworks MX 2004. We have explored enough features to get started in putting them together to create Web page designs.

We will work with placing content on the page, in addition to adding interactivity, all while looking at more features available in the program. Our first design involves images and buttons. We will build the complete page in Fireworks MX 2004 and later import it into Dreamweaver MX 2004. Our result is shown in Figure 11.1.

Within this page, the text and all vector graphics are created with the Pen, Text, and Rectangle Tools. The areas around all text are hotspots that link to other pages.

FIGURE 11.1 Our first Web page.

All of the images have been imported and are buttons. When the user's mouse passes over any image, the image slides out from underneath the block and displays more information.

Now you have an idea of what will be happening in the finished page. It's time to start building.

CREATING THE LAYOUT

First you need to create content to make up the page background. This process is shown in Figure 11.2.

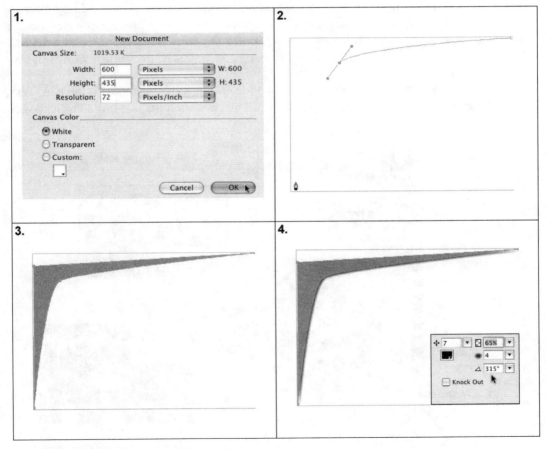

FIGURE 11.2 Starting the page background.

1. The first thing we do is create a new canvas for the page. Create it with a width of 600, height of 435, resolution of 72 dpi, and a canvas color of White. A height of 420 is ideal, but we should be able to get away with 435. The main concern is having a page that is too wide. When you design a page that is wider than the browser can display, the dreaded horizontal scroll bar appears in the browser. We have more flexibility with height because most users are used to scrolling up and down to read longer documents.

2. Next, use the Pen Tool to create the outline. First, select the Pen Tool and set the fill to #3B94D9 and the stroke to none. (In the top-right corner of the colors area is a box with a slash through it.) To create the shape, click the top-right corner with the Pen Tool and immediately release. Then click and drag a vector handle, and pull out a curve for the bend in the swoosh we are creating. Next, click and release in the bottom-left corner of the stage. Click and immediately release on the left edge of the stage, about 90 percent of the way to the upper-left corner. Last, complete the shape by clicking the first point you placed.

3. Use the Subselection Tool (white arrow) to adjust your points until your swoosh resembles the figure.

4. Add the Live Effect of Drop Shadow with the default settings of an offset of 7, a color well (fill) of 7, opacity at 65, softness of 4, and an angle of 315 degrees. Your result should resemble what is shown in panel 4 of Figure 11.2.

Now that we have created our basic swoosh for the page layout, it is time to create your multicolored blocks for the top-left corner of the canvas. We will be continuing our layout in Figure 11.3.

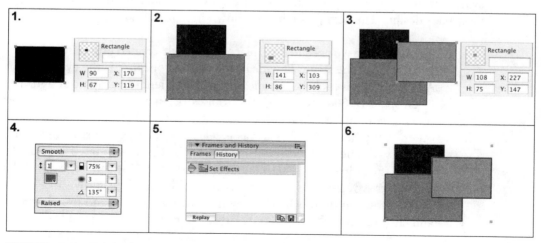

FIGURE 11.3 Continuing to create the background.

1. Create a rectangle with a black stroke and fill. Set its width to 90 and height to 67.
2. Now create a new rectangle on top of the black rectangle. Set the stroke to 1 and black. The fill color should be set to #996699. The width must be 141 and the height 86.
3. Our last rectangle should have a fill of #3C94D8, stroke of 1 pixel and black, width of 108, and height of 75. Place the third rectangle as shown.
4. Now, add an Outer Bevel Live Effect to make the rectangles pop a bit more. Pick any of the rectangles and add an Outer Bevel effect with a Bevel Edge shape of Smooth, a width of 1, and a bevel color of gray (#666666).
5. Now, rather than redo the same steps manually, use a tool that Fireworks offers—the History Panel. The History Panel is a visual representation of undo steps in memory. With this tool, you can select multiple steps and then replay these steps. Click Window > History. This action opens the Frames and History Panel with the History tab in focus. The actions from the previous step should be shown as Set Effects. Select the next rectangle you need to apply beveling to with your Pointer Tool. Now select Set Effects and press the Replay button. Repeat this process with the last rectangle.
6. You should now have all three rectangles complete with a small outer bevel. Select all three and group them by clicking Modify > Group. (You can also right-click (Control + click on a Macintosh) the group, or press Ctrl/Command + G.) This action keeps the rectangles together.

Now it's time to wrap up the background. We have your rectangles and swoosh, but we need to place them on the canvas to make up the logo section of your page design. The next procedure is shown in Figure 11.4.

1. The first thing we need to do is place your newly created group into the top-left corner of the stage. The ideal tool for this purpose is the ever-familiar Align Tool. This tool is truly one of your best friends in graphic design. The Fireworks MX 2004 version of this tool works in a nearly identical manner to what you find in Flash MX 2004. The top row aligns objects to one another or the canvas (if To Canvas is selected). The second row distributes objects with one another or to the canvas. The third row match sizes of objects to the largest object selected or space shapes. One difference with the Fireworks MX 2004 Align Panel is the ability to align individual vector points. You can do this by clicking the Anchors button and pressing Shift and clicking on multiple vector points with the Subselection Tool. You then can align these points with one another. Select To Canvas (make sure An-

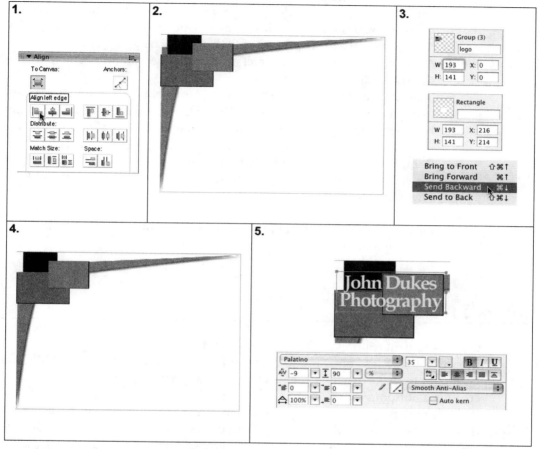

FIGURE 11.4 Completing the background.

chors is not selected), then select your new group of rectangles. When we have selected them, press the Align left edge and Align top edge buttons.

2. Now, your rectangle group is aligned with the top-left corner of the stage. However, notice that some of the swoosh is showing on the left side of the group. This is not what we want, so you must adjust the drawing.

3. Look at the width and height of the group of rectangles. The settings should read W 192 and H 141. Take note of this. Now create a new rectangle with a white fill and no stroke. After you have created it, set its width and height to 192x141 to match the group. Using the Align Panel, align the new rectangle to the top-left corner of the canvas. You will find that it is on top of your rectangle group. No worries; simply click Modify > Arrange > Send

Backward (or press Ctrl/Command + down arrow key) to send it back one layer. Doing so should place it above the swoosh and below your rectangles. If not, repeat the process again until the new rectangle is placed correctly.

4. After adding your new white rectangle, your page should resemble what is shown in panel 4 of Figure 11.4.

5. Now it's time to add some text with the Text Tool. Type John Dukes Photography in a yellow shade (#F3F710). The font in the figure is 35-point bold Palatino, and center alignment is applied. If you don't have the Palatino font, choose an appropriate serif font. (Times or Times New Roman works.) The kerning and leading have also been set. The leading for the entire font block is 90, and the kerning for John Dukes is 9 and Photography is set to 8.

Now that you have completed the basic layout, save your file as *background.png*. We will be using it in two ways later.

ADDING HOTSPOTS

One of the great features of Fireworks MX 2004 is the ability to add HTML attributes to your design, not only to create images but also to support HTML and JavaScript to make dynamic pages. The HTML element we are going to look at is creating a hotspot.

A *hotspot* is a nickname for an image map. An image map is simply an image that has coordinates qualified in HTML for use as a hyperlink. Fireworks MX 2004 and Dreamweaver MX 2004 make creating image maps a pleasure compared to creating them by hand-coding.

An image map consists of two parts: the attribute within an image that points to the map and the map itself. The map contains coordinates that create one of three shapes: a rectangle, a circle, or a polygon. When creating by hand, you must manually enter each coordinate to create the map—a tedious exercise. However, with Fireworks MX 2004 (and Dreamweaver MX 2004), creating image maps is a breeze. All you need to do is select the Hotspot Tool (found under Web in the Tools Panel), and draw your shape on the image. Fireworks does the rest of the work for you. When you export your page, Fireworks creates all of the HTML required to acknowledge your hotspot.

Because you are going to keep using this layout, let's add a hotspot to the logo on the top-left corner of the page. Figure 11.5 shows a hotspot being added to your document.

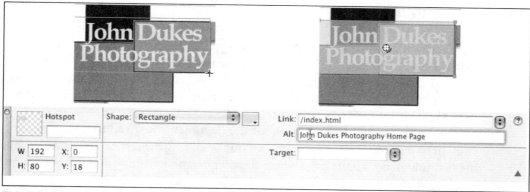

FIGURE 11.5   Adding a hotspot to an image.

The first thing we need to do is activate the Hotspot Tool. It is the top-left tool in the Web section of the Tools Panel. When you have selected it, you see in the Property Inspector that you can choose from three shapes: Rectangle, Circle, and Polygon. For the widest level of browser compatibility, consider using the Rectangle. Not all browsers support the other two shapes.

To create the actual hotspot, draw a rectangle shape, as shown in Figure 11.5. When you have completed the rectangle, it should resemble what is shown in the figure.

Now that the hotspot is complete, add the link for it. Because this image is the main logo for the site, make it point to the home page, which is *index.html*. Notice the preceding slash (/) before index. This character indicates that we are making this link document root-relative, meaning that when the link is hit, the browser will go all the way to the start of the site, then look for the document from there. Because you are going to be using this document as a shell for all of your Web pages, we have no idea where the page might be in terms of site hierarchy.

Next, fill out the Alt field to complete the Alt attribute in an HTML image tag. The Alt attribute offers text as a substitute for images. This attribute is especially important for visually impaired users who may be using a screen reader. They can't see the image, so the reader reads the text to them. With this logo being a part of the navigation scheme, it is critical that this type of accessibility is addressed.

Keep in mind that not only the visually impaired need the Alt tag. Some users turn off images to speed up the loading of pages. This practice is especially common for users of embedded devices like PDAs and cell phones. You should use the Alt tag to accommodate the widest possible audience.

After you have added your hotspot, save the document again. We will continue using it throughout this chapter.

ADDING MORE CONTENT

Now that we have the basic layout for *background.png*, save a copy under another name. Click File > Save As and save the document as *categories.png*. We will continue with the document as *categories.png*. You save the document under another name so we can add to it without losing the original design. *Background.png* will be used for multiple pages in the future.

Now that we have a new name for the document, we need to add some more content to this version of the page. Start out by adding the rest of the rectangles and the text that make up the page where the user can pick from some of the main categories for photos to view. This procedure is shown in Figure 11.6.

1. Create your first rectangle with the properties of a 2-point black stroke, a fill color of #3C94D8, a width of 131, and a height of 69. Place it on the stage at the x- and y-coordinates of 385 and 55, respectively.
2. Now create the second rectangle with a 2-point black stroke. Add a fill color of #996699, and a width and height of 161 and 69. Place the rectangle at the x- and y-coordinate of 65 and 235.
3. The final rectangle is all black with a 2-point stroke. Its width and height are 140 and 105, and it should be placed at the x- and y-coordinates of 437 and 318.
4. The first text field should read *Foliage*, with the font of Arial, the size of 30, and the color of #FFFF00. Center it on the box using the Align Tool, and add a drop shadow with the default settings.

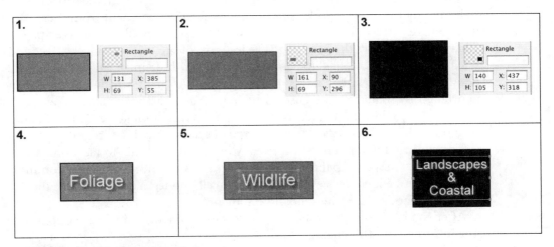

FIGURE 11.6 Starting *categories.png*.

5. The next text field reads *Wildlife* and has the same settings as the Foliage text field.

6. Our last text field reads *Landscapes & Coastal* on three lines. It will be Arial, with a font size of 24, and a color of #FFFF00, and have a drop shadow with an offset of 3 and color well of #ADADB5 applied. It should be centered over its rectangle, like your other two text fields.

We have now completed the basic rectangles we are using in *categories.png*. Now add hotspots with the appropriate links of *foliage.html*, *wildlife.html*, and *landscapescoastal.html*. The Alt field should be completed for each hotspot as well. Now let's look at creating buttons in Fireworks.

CREATING BUTTONS, POP-UP MENUS, AND OTHER BEHAVIORS

Fireworks enables you to create buttons, pop-up menus, and more by writing the JavaScript involved to make each of these behaviors work. Any added JavaScript functionality is referred to as a behavior.

Creating a Button

The first behavior we will learn is making a button. These components are commonly used on Web pages. They offer an alternative to having plain text links. Let's create a basic rollover button, as shown in Figure 11.7.

You have two methods of creating a button in Fireworks. The first of these is to use the Edit menu to create a new symbol.

Click Edit > Insert > New Button; right-click (Control + click on a Macintosh) and click Insert New Button; press Shift + Ctrl/Command + F8; or click Edit > Insert > New Symbol and choose Button from your options. Any of these options opens the Button Editor in which you can draw your content. The second method is to create an object on the stage and then click Modify > Symbol > Convert to Symbol (or right-click [Control + click on a Macintosh] and click Convert to Symbol).

If you create a new symbol it does not appear on the canvas. You must drag an instance of the symbol from the Library. If the Library is not open, click Window > Library.

Choose the second of these methods. This method is preferable because it enables you to place the content relative to the rest of the canvas before creation. The first method forces you to guess how the button will appear. The steps we will take correspond to the panels in Figure 11.7.

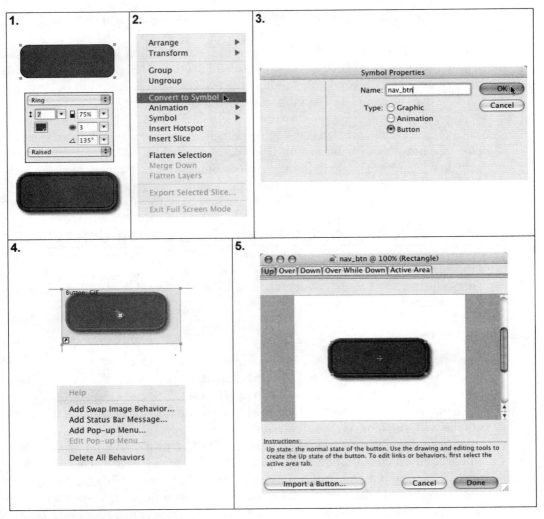

FIGURE 11.7 Creating a rollover button.

1. Create a rectangle on the stage. Choose any fill and stroke color you want. (Figure 11.7 shows blue for the fill and black for the stroke.) Add a rectangle roundness, if you want, in the Property Inspector. (Figure 11.7 shows a roundness of 50.) Live Effects are also added in the figure to make the rectangle appear more like a button. These Live Effects are an Outer Bevel with the Bevel Edge shape of Ring and a width of 7. The Bevel color is a darker shade of blue than the surface. Next, add a drop shadow with the defaults to give the shape more depth.

2. Next, choose Convert to Symbol using one of the three methods: click Modify > Symbol > Convert to Symbol, right-click (Control + click on a Macintosh) Convert to Symbol, or press the F8 key.

3. The Symbol Properties dialog box opens. Name the button and choose the Type of Button.

4. On your canvas you see that the button appears with a partially transparent green rectangle over it. This rectangle is known as a *slice*. Slices are used to cut up your document and add HTML and behaviors to the content. Because this is a button, it will have JavaScript and HTML attached to the image, so Fireworks automatically slices it for you. We will learn about slices later. We now need to get into the button to modify its states. Notice a target shape in the middle of the button. This shape opens the pop-up menu shown in panel 4. Do not use this menu because it does not take you to the Button Editor.

5. To open the Button Editor shown in pane 5, you can click Modify > Symbol > Edit Symbol or right-click (Control + click on a Macintosh) Symbol > Edit Symbol. The easiest method, however, is to double-click the surface of the button itself. Make certain that when you double-click you do not hit the target in the middle. You then see the Button Editor, where we will add states for the button.

Adding an Over State to Buttons

Now that we have created a basic button, it is time to modify its states. Button states react to what the user does with his mouse. Let's start with an Over State, shown in Figure 11.8.

1. To start out, we need to have the Button Editor open. If you don't have it open at this point, open it using one of the three methods mentioned earlier. As you look at the Button Editor you can see several tabs running across the top and three buttons on the bottom. The tabs across the top are for setting the different states for a button; the buttons across the bottom allow you to import a button, cancel the operation, or finish your editing. We are currently in the Up state. The Up state is how the button appears on the stage when the page loads and is not in focus. The Up state is the normal state for the button.

2. Now you add some text to the button. Ultimately, we are creating four buttons: Home, About, Contact, and Links. These buttons are commonly used in small Web sites. First create Contact because it is the longest word. If we start with Home and then place it to fill the button, longer words will not

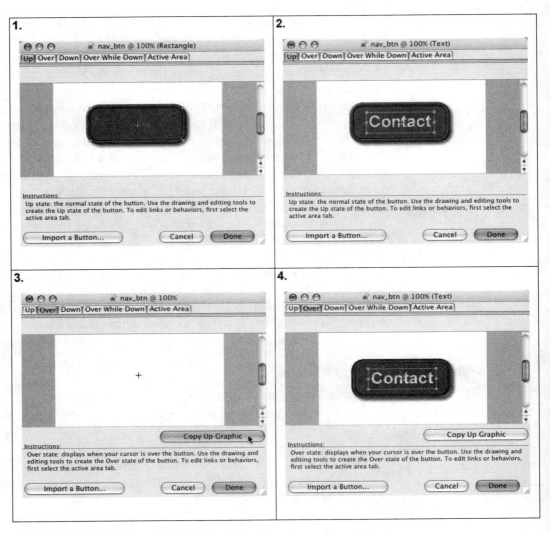

FIGURE 11.8 Adding an Over State to the button.

fit at the same font size. In panel 2 of Figure 11.8, Contact is set in white, 20-point, bold Arial. In addition, an Inner Bevel has been added to the font to make it stand out. The bevel settings are the default.

3. Now we need to modify the Over state. The Over state is how the button appears when the user's pointer passes over the graphic. The Button Editor window is empty because we must dictate what you want to use for the Over state. You can create a completely different shape if you want, but we

are going to base it on the Up state image. To pull in the Up state image, press the Copy Up Graphic button that has appeared.

4. Now that we have a graphic to work with, modify it so it appears different when the pointer passes over it. You can change any property in the button to make the effect subtle or obvious—it all depends on your preference. Apply a subtle effect by modifying only the text and rectangle bevels. The ability to modify the bevels is a useful feature of Fireworks. This feature enables you to make it appear as if a button has been physically depressed with the use of the Button Preset property in the Bevel pop-up window. The bevel for the text has been modified to have the Button preset of Inverted, whereas the rectangle has the Button preset of Inset.

Once you have finished creating your button, press Done and save your file. It's time to look at the result in a browser. Click File > Preview in Browser and choose your browser or press the F12 key. When the button is displayed in the browser, move your pointer over it. It should appear as if it has been depressed.

Finishing the Button States

Now that you have created your basic button and an Over state, let's explore the other three states and what they mean. The four button states were created in Fireworks to add the ability to create navigation bars. Essentially, in navigation bars, the states work as follows:

Up: Represents the normal state for the button.

Over: Shows how the button reacts when the pointer passes over the button.

Down: Provides two behaviors. When the user actually clicks the button, the Down state shows how the button appears. If Include Nav Bar State is selected while the graphic is created in the Down state, the button stays down. This means if a user clicks the button to go to another page and then comes back to the referring page, the button will still be in a Down state, acting like a visited link.

Over While Down: Reflects the button's appearance when the pointer passes over a button while it is in a Down state.

Now let's finish your button states, as shown in Figure 11.9.

1. First we are going to create our Down state. Notice that Include Nav Bar Down state is already selected—leave it alone. Press the Copy Over Graphic

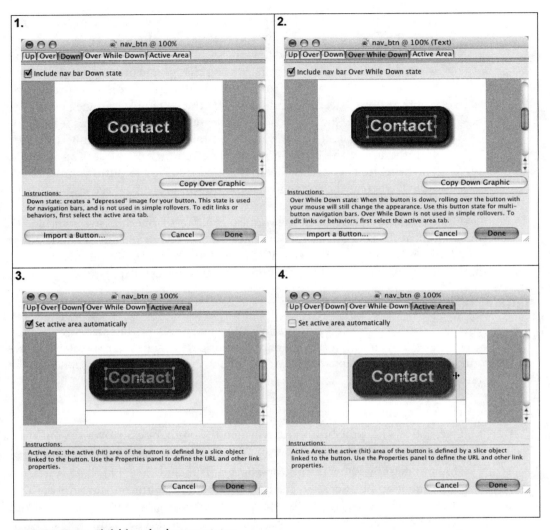

FIGURE 11.9 Finishing the button states.

button to place an image in the window. Next, change the fill of the rectangle to an even darker color. (Figure 11.9 uses #003366.)

2. The last state is Over While Down. Copy the Down Graphic into this state. Include Nav Bar Over While Down state is automatically selected when you bring in the graphic. Leave this option alone again. For this state, the fill of the rectangle shown was changed to blue (#0000FF). The button preset in the text bevel was changed to Highlighted.

3. We now need to look at the Active Area tab. The active area is the area on the page that reacts to the pointer passing over or clicking it. Notice that Set active area is checked by default. This setting usually works well, but in your button, it is creating a large area because of the beveling and drop shadow we have added. By default, Fireworks provides a small buffer around objects, but this buffer is even more extreme because the drop shadow and beveling are part of the object. Because you are going to be stacking buttons on top of one another, that buffer is too much space.

4. Uncheck Set active area automatically so we can adjust the rectangle that represents it. Once it is unchecked, pass your pointer over one of the guides until you see a double arrow with a bar between the arrows. When your cursor becomes this shape, drag the guide closer to the button, taking note of the drop shadow so you don't cut it off. Repeat this process for all four sides of the graphic.

Editing Button Instances

After you have completed all the states for the button, press Done. This action applies the changes and returns you to the canvas. It's now time to create your other three buttons. Fireworks makes this procedure incredibly easy.

Each copy of a button on the stage is known as an *instance*. Fireworks allows you to modify each instance to give it its own identity and relevant HTML. This capability is helpful because you don't have to create multiple individual buttons; you only need to modify each instance. Let's put this principle into practice. This next procedure is shown in Figure 11.10.

1. Select your button and click Edit > Clone (right-click [Control + click on a Macintosh] Edit > Clone) or Edit > Copy (Ctrl/Command + C, or right-click [Control + click on a Macintosh] Edit > Copy) and Edit > Paste (Ctrl/Command + V or right-click [Control + click on a Macintosh] Edit > Paste) to create a copy. A useful features of Fireworks is that when you copy and paste or clone, the duplicate is put in the exact same location as the original. With the duplicate is still selected, press Shift + down arrow key (moves more pixels each time you press an arrow) to move the clone down on the page. You definitely want to use your arrow keys for this type of operation because you don't want the buttons to fall out of alignment.

2. Repeat the copy/clone process twice more until you have all four instances of your button lined up as shown in panel 2 of Figure 11.10. Try to align the red guides with one another precisely so no overlap or extra space is present between buttons.

3. After you have moved your buttons into place, the set should resemble pane 3.

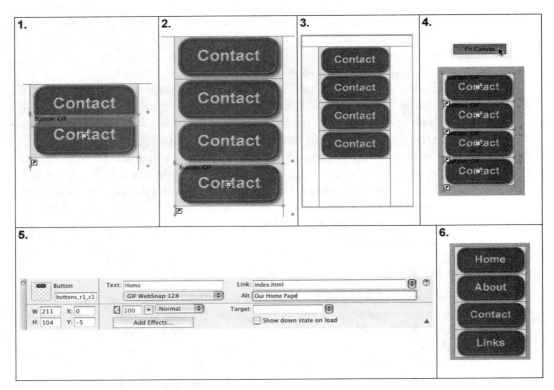

FIGURE 11.10 Finishing the buttons.

4. You may have some excess canvas around your buttons, like what is shown in panel 4. To remove this excess canvas, click in a blank area off the canvas, then press the Fit Canvas button on the Property Inspector. This command causes the canvas to fit perfectly around your buttons. The Fit Canvas button in the Property Inspector is a convenient new feature in Fireworks MX 2004. Previously, your only options were to click Modify > Canvas > Fit Canvas or press Ctrl + Alt (Command + Option + F on a Macintosh).

5. Now it is time to change the labels on your buttons and add the links. Fireworks makes this step incredibly simple. All you need to do is select an instance of a button and type in the following areas of the Property Inspector: Text, Link, and Alt. You also have the option of Target, but we will use the default of _self (loads new content into current window). Within the first button, type *Home* in the Text field, *index.html* in the Link field, and *Our Home Page* in the Alt field. It is critical that you use Alt because we are creating navigation. Repeat this process for the rest of the buttons using the values shown in Table 11.1.

TABLE 11.1   Button Values

Text	Link	Alt
About	about.html	About us
Contact	contact.html	Contact Information
Links	links.html	Some Helpful Links

6. When you have completed all of your button instances, your document should resemble what is shown in pane 6.

You must add text to a button inside the Button Editor or when you create your object before converting it to a button. If no text is present in a button instance, you cannot use the Text field in the Property Inspector when your instance is selected. The Property Inspector can only modify text that currently exists in a button, not add new text.

It's now time to save your file again. After you have saved the file, preview it in your browser by clicking File > Preview and choosing your preferred browser, or by pressing your F12 key. The resulting temporary Web page should resemble what is shown in Figure 11.11.

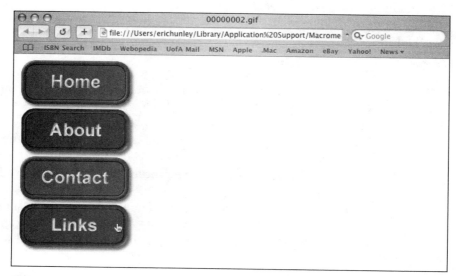

FIGURE 11.11   Previewing the buttons in a browser.

Try out your buttons. When you click on each, you wind up getting a Page Not Found error, but when you return by pressing the Back button, you see what the buttons look like in the Down state. You can also move your mouse over the Down state button to see the effect of the Over While Down state. Figure 11.11 shows the About button instance in the Down state and Links in the Over state.

Adding Buttons to the Page Layout

We know how to create buttons at this point, so it is time to add some to our page layout. The buttons we are creating for our layout are somewhat more complex, but they give you the opportunity to see how flexible Fireworks is as an application. Use the *categories.png* file.

The first thing we must do is take care of your images. Each of your buttons is going to be made up of images, so make sure they are sized correctly and add effects.

ON THE CD

First, import all of the necessary images. On the CD-ROM that accompanies this book, you can find them in *Fireworks/Chapter 11/button images*. Seven images are available: *flower.jpg, foxyawn.gif, gatorclose.gif, hawkssil.gif, lighthouse.gif, lightning.gif,* and *loneoak.gif.* Bring in each of these images by clicking File > Import and then clicking to place them on stage, or by dragging them straight into Fireworks. After you import them all, you will notice they are all different sizes and shapes, as shown in Figure 11.2.

You must scale the images and clean off the copyright statements on each. Although you should be concerned about the photographer's copyrights, this Web site is his, and the copyrights will be noted elsewhere. Also, these images are too small for anyone to bother taking them.

Start by resizing the largest of the images, the yawning fox, as shown in Figure 11.13.

1. The first thing we do is bring the image in front of all of the others so we can focus exclusively on it. Click Modify > Arrange > Bring to Front (Ctrl/Command + Shift + up arrow key) while the image is selected. This action put the image in focus.
2. The next step is to draw a rectangle the size we want to have the image displayed. In this case, make a rectangle 112x97 pixels with no fill and a black stroke of 1. Move the rectangle over the fox picture until his head is framed, as shown in panel 2 of Figure 11.13.
3. Add an outer bevel to the rectangle. The Bevel Edge shape should be flat. Give it a width of 2 and a Bevel color of #7B7342. At first you cannot see the Bevel effect displayed on the rectangle, but it will be revealed soon.

FIGURE 11.12   The images after importing.

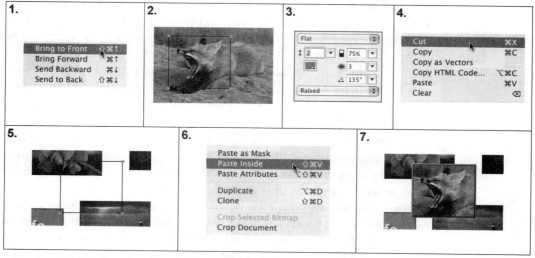

FIGURE 11.13   Modifying the Yawning Fox image.

4. Now click the photo of the fox and click Edit > Cut. This command removes the image from the canvas.
5. Click your rectangle to select it. You should be looking at a canvas that resembles pane 5.
6. Choose Edit > Paste Inside. The yawning fox appears inside the rectangle as a mask. Notice that the beveling is now visible.

Repeat this process with all of the images in the document. Figure 11.14 displays a breakdown of the rectangle sizes, beveling attributes, and final result, based on each picture.

Before we continue with the John Dukes Photography categories layout, we need to learn more about masks and pop-up menus. Let's start out by exploring other masks available in Fireworks.

More Masking Methods

In the previous steps, rather than cut up the yawning fox and other images, we created another mask. Doing this preserved the actual image and achieved the effect we wanted. This is the second type of mask we have now learned in Fireworks. There are actually multiple ways to create masks in the program. Let's look at some of them, as shown in Figure 11.15.

1. The first mask is the reverse of what we used for all of your images on the page. Instead of cutting the object that is to be masked, we cut the object that is going to be the mask. To start, use your Pen Tool and draw a line around an image you want to mask. In the case of the owl image shown, a white stroke is being used to assist visibility of the stroke. (You can always change the color later.)
2. After you finish the stroke, the object should look like what is shown in panel 2 of Figure 11.15. You then cut the newly created stroke by clicking Edit > Cut (Ctrl/Command + X or right-click [Control + click on a Macintosh] Edit > Cut).
3. Next select the image to be masked and then click Edit > Paste as Mask. Your results should resemble what is shown in panel 3.
4. The next pair of masks we create involve using two bitmap images. For the mask to work correctly, the bitmap image must have a transparent background. Choose your Magic Wand Tool and click the areas you want to be transparent. Once an area is selected, press the Delete key to remove the pixels from the image. You can speed things up a bit if you select a color and then click Select > Select Similar and press the Delete key. You may

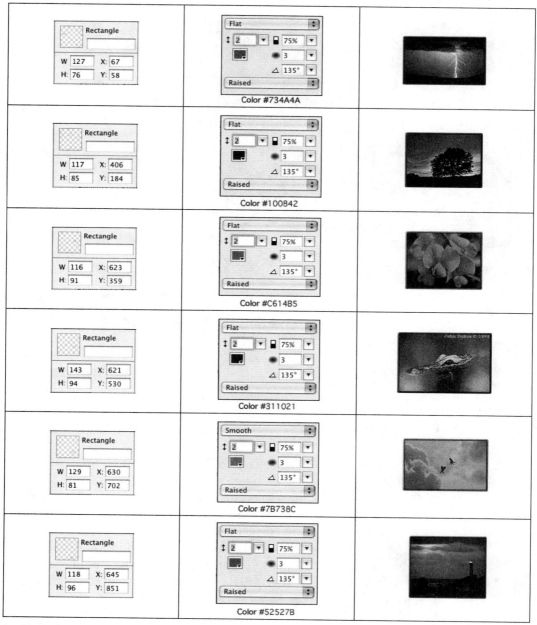

FIGURE 11.14 Preparing the images.

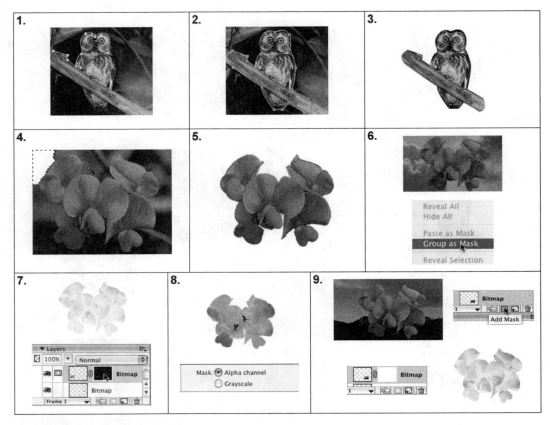

FIGURE 11.15 Exploring masks in Fireworks.

    want to also use your Eraser Tool to eliminate any stray pixels not picked up by the Magic Wand Tool.

5. After removing all of the background, your image should resemble what is shown in panel 5. You are now ready to begin working.

6. The first thing you should do is position the modified image over the object you want to mask. If the image tries to go behind the other object, click Modify > Arrange > Bring to Front (Ctrl/Command + Shift + up arrow key) to place it on top. After you have placed the image, you can use more than one method to create your mask. You can cut the top object, select the bottom, and then click Edit > Paste as Mask, like we did for the previous mask. You also can select both objects and click Modify > Mask > Group as Mask. Yet another option is to select the object underneath, cut it, and then, after selecting the top object, click Edit > Paste Inside.

7. If you performed one of the first two methods in the previous step, your image should resemble what is shown in panel 7. It's now time to look at the Layers Panel. If you don't see the panel already open in the Panel set, click Window > Layers to open it. The Layers Panel offers a visual representation of all the objects in your document. Like many image editing applications, Fireworks places any created shape or imported image onto its own layer. As you have seen in both Flash and FreeHand, you can show or hide these layers. In addition, you can always change their order by dragging them into a new location on the stack. (This method can be quicker than using Modify > Arrange.) If you scroll up and down you should see your masked object. It shows a preview of the image and then the mask to the right. Click the Mask portion of the layer (the block on the right).

8. When you have selected the Mask inside of your layer, you see that you have new options available to you in the Property Inspector: Alpha Channel and Grayscale. If you used one of the first two methods in step 6, Grayscale will be selected. Pane 7 shows a Grayscale mask. Grayscale causes the masking object to be converted to grayscale and be partially transparent, blending the two images together. Any area in the converted image that is white will be completely transparent, whereas black is not. The shades in between have different levels of transparency, depending on how dark or light they are. When you choose Alpha Channel, Fireworks finds wherever you have visible pixels (Alpha) and allows the masked object to be seen through the resulting shape. Pane 8 shows Alpha Channel applied.

If you want to get an Alpha Channel mask immediately, use the following method: Cut the object to be masked, then select the image that will act as a mask. Click Edit > Paste Inside. You now have an Alpha Channel mask.

9. Yet another method of creating a mask is to use the Layers Panel. Place the object that will act as a mask on top of the image you want masked, as shown in panel 9. Cut the image that will be the mask. Now select the picture to be masked and look in the Layers Panel. You should see your selected object highlighted in the Layers Panel. While it is highlighted, click the Add Mask button, and an empty mask box appears in the layer. With the mask box selected, click Edit > Paste to create your mask. One of the advantages of this method is the mask is already selected in the Property Inspector, should you wish to change the type.

This concludes the brief interlude with Fireworks and masks. As you can see, the program is of great assistance in creating masks, and multiple ways are available of accomplishing each type of mask. Believe it or not, Firework MX 2004 has even more methods to create masks, but what we have learned should be sufficient to get you started.

Creating Pop-Up Menus

Now that we have created some basic buttons and explored their four states, it is time to move on and add some more complexity to the page. We will create another set of buttons and then add a pop-up menu.

Pop-up menus are popular in Web design because they enable users to navigate deeper into a Web site without leaving the screen. They also help give a hierarchical representation of the navigation within a site. We will build one, starting with Figure 11.16.

1. Create a stack of buttons. What you see in Figure 11.16 is based on a button created as a rectangle with a 1-pixel black stroke and a blue (#00009F) fill. The rectangle had a bevel applied with a width of 2, and a Bevel color of black. Its size is 109x27. The text has a font yellow (#FFFF00), 22-point Arial. It also has an Inset Emboss effect applied with a width of 2. Create only an Up and Over state for the buttons with the Over State having a fill of black in the rectangle and a font color of white. Label the buttons as Home, About, Products, Support, and Press. You can add links later, if you want.
2. After you have created your button set, select the Products button to make a target appear. Click the target in the center and choose Add Pop-up Menu from the options, as shown in panel 2.
3. The Pop-up Menu Editor opens. This dialog box consists of four tabs: Content, Appearance, Advanced, and Position. Begin with the Content tab.
4. Within the Content tab is where you place all of your labels, and where they link. Let's begin by placing a label called *Electronics* in the first field. Create the label by double-clicking the field and typing a value. Add the link of *electronics.html*. We are not going to use the Target field because all of these pages should load into the current window. Next press the Add Menu (plus sign) button to insert a new field. Label the field *Televisions* with a URL of *televisions.html*. You can remove menu items by pressing the Delete Menu (minus sign) button. Because Televisions should be a subcategory of Electronics, press the Indent Menu button. This action forces Televisions to be a subset of Electronics. If you want to promote a menu item, press the Outdent Menu button, located immediately to the left.

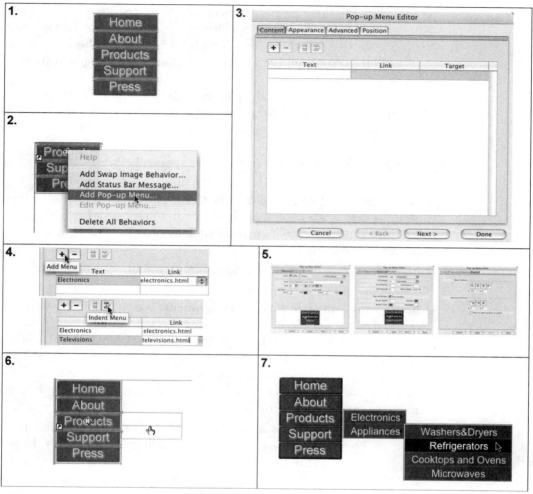

FIGURE 11.16   Creating buttons for a pop-up menu.

5. Continue creating your menu items. Televisions has three submenus: Big Screen (*tv40plusin.html*), Standard (*tvstandard.html*), and Small (*tvsmall.html*). Small in turn has two submenus: Portable (*portable.html*) and 13" and Below (*tvlessthan13.html*). You also create another category called *Appliances* (*appliances.html*). A quick shortcut to having the next category placed all the way to the left is to use the field that Fireworks automatically generates for you. (Every time you use the Add Menu button, the new field

is placed at the same level as the currently selected item.) Underneath Appliances, place Washers & Dryers (*washers.html*), Refrigerators (*refers.html*), Cooktops and Ovens (*cooktops.html*), and Microwaves (*microwaves.html*). You could add more if you want, but these give you a good view of how this tool works.

6. When you have completed the Content tab, it's time to work your way through the other three. A breakdown of what each is and what you will do with it follows:

Appearance: Controls how your menu items appear. Let's look at the choices within.

Select from HTML or Images for the Cells. The difference between these options is that Images uses included bitmaps to represent the background of the cell, which can make a menu item look nicer but does add to the file size. We will be using HTML.

Choose what type of menu: Vertical, or Horizontal. Stick with the default of Vertical.

Choose your font style, size, and alignment. We will be using Verdana, Arial, Helvetica, sans-serif. After choosing this font group, delete Verdana and the comma following it from the list. Because we have chosen Arial for your buttons, we want to match it first. Choose the size of 18, which is smaller than the size used on the buttons, but it will look better when the menu is used. (It won't cover as much of the page.) Lastly, use a center alignment to match the buttons.

Choose the Up and Over states. These states react in the same manner as they do in buttons. For the Up state, choose yellow (#FFFF00) for the text and blue (#00009F) for the cell to match the buttons. Use white for the text and black for the cell in the Over state. Notice there is a preview below where you can see the results.

Advanced: Refines your settings further. You have several areas to adjust:

Cell Width: Provides two options to choose from in the drop-down menu to the right—Automatic and Pixels. Automatic sizes the cells in each set to be wide enough to display the longest text. If you choose Pixels, all cells will be that width. Stick with Automatic for now.

Cell Height: Works the same way as Cell Width, only it adjusts for the height of your chosen font if you choose Automatic. If you select Pixels, all cells share the specified height. Again, use Automatic.

Cell Padding and Spacing: Provide buffers. Cell Padding dictates how much space is between your text and the edges of each cell. Cell Spacing determines the amount of space between each cell. Leave both of these settings at their defaults.

Text Indent: Determines if and how far the text is indented in the cells. Leave this setting at 0.

Menu Delay: Sets how long the menu remains open should a user's pointer drift off of it. It is important to have this set because a user can become very frustrated when he loses the menu. Leave it at the default setting of 1000 ms (1 second).

Pop-up Borders: Determines if you have borders between the cells. If you have Show Borders unchecked, the Cell Spacing option is not available. Leave Show Borders at the default setting (checked). You can also adjust the width, shadow, color, and highlight of the border. Leave these settings alone. The preview window at the bottom of the screen again shows you what your menu looks like.

Position: Dictates how your menus and submenus lay out on the screen here. You have visual representations of each selection. Just type an x-coordinate of 116 (the width of your button minus one) and a y-coordinate of 0 (to line up with the top of your button). Set Submenu to 0x0.

7. When you have completed the steps for creating your pop-up menu, press Done to return to the main screen. Notice that when you have the Products button selected, an outline representing your pop-up menu appears. Your pointer becomes a finger as you pass over it. If you double-click this outline, you will return to the Pop-up Menu Editor. You also can use your mouse to manually readjust the position of the menus by dragging the outline.

8. Preview your menu in the browser by clicking File > Preview in Browser (pick your browser) or by pressing the F12 key. Your results should resemble what is shown in pane 7 of Figure 11.16.

When you create pop-up menus, make sure that your main buttons point to a page that provides an alternate means to reaching the products. This is especially important for accessibility because screen readers have a difficult time navigating pop-up menus. They also do not function for users who have turned off JavaScript.

Finishing the Layout

Now we have learned enough information to enable you to finish your page layout. We will be creating buttons, but these buttons are going to be a bit trickier than what we have worked with up to this point.

If you open *categories.png*, you will be ready to work. The first thing you should do is move all the images into their locations. All animal shots should be overlapping the Wildlife rectangle. You also want to move the other shots into place. The tree and flower shots should be covering Foliage, and the lightning and lighthouse images should cover Landscapes & Coastal. Your results should resemble what is shown in Figure 11.17.

Now that we have all of your images in the general locations where they should be, the real work begins. First, we must have all of the images behind the rectangles. You can do this by pressing Shift and clicking all of the images, then clicking Modify > Arrange > Send to Back (or pressing Ctrl + Shift + down arrow key).

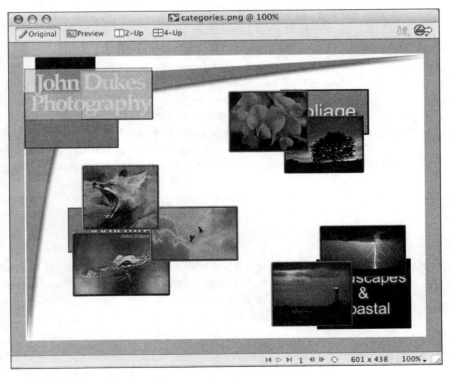

FIGURE 11.17 Pictures laid out on the design.

After you have sent all the images to the back so they appear behind the rectangles, arrange them so they are covered by either the rectangle or a combination of the rectangle and another image (if they are wider or taller than the rectangle they are under).

Because you have the images in the right area, let's start making buttons, as shown in Figure 11.18.

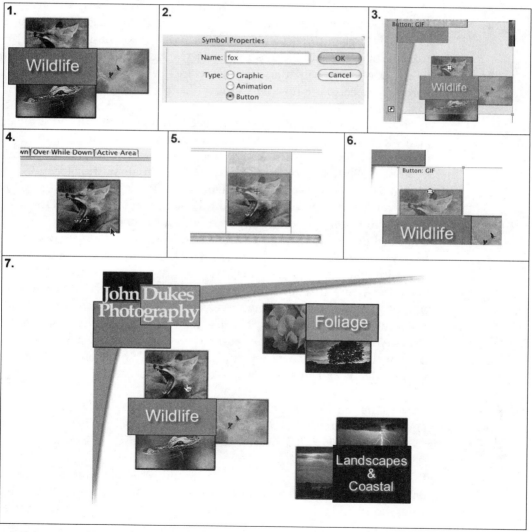

FIGURE 11.18   Creating the buttons.

1. When you look at the page, your images should be laid out as shown in Figure 1.17. If you have an issue with any of the images overlapping incorrectly, click Modify > Arrange > Send Backward as many times as necessary to place the pictures. You can also use the Layers Panel and drag the layers to the correct location.

2. Start with the image of the yawning fox. Select this image and click Modify > Convert to Symbol or press the F8 key. When the Symbol Properties dialog box opens, give the image the Name of *fox* and Type of Button.

3. When you return to the main canvas, notice that the slice is taking up an extremely large area. This is okay; it is because this is a masked image. Fireworks creates the slice based on the entire image, including what is hidden by the mask. You will adjust the active area in the button. While we are here, you need to see how far to move the fox for it to show completely. Make sure the fox is selected and press Shift + up arrow key as many times as needed to reveal the image. If you need to nudge it less, just press the up arrow key however many times as necessary. Take note of what you have chosen (four Shift + up arrow keys should be close) and reverse the process by pressing Shift + down arrow key to return it to its starting location.

4. Now it's time to edit your button. Double-click the slice (avoid the target in the center) to open the Button Editor. Go immediately to the Over state because you won't be adding any text. In the Over state, click the Copy Up Graphic button and then move the graphic four Shift + up arrows up (or however many you counted). It should look like what is shown in panel 4 of Figure 11.18.

5. Go to the Active Area tab. While in here, adjust the guides to cover the portion of the image representing the Over state. We don't want to actually cover the Up state completely because each rectangle has its own hotspot. Before you leave this tab, make sure to uncheck Set active area automatically or the active area will revert to the default. When you have adjusted your guides, click Done to return to the main canvas.

Whichever state you were on before selecting the Active Area tab is shown in the window at full resolution. Therefore, if your Over state resolution is faded, click the Over State tab, and then click back on the Active State tab to make it clearer.

6. Back on the main canvas, your slice should resemble what is shown in panel 6. If it does not, double-click it again to reenter the Button Editor and adjust your guides in the Active Area tab. It may take several tries until you get it to match exactly.

If you are having a difficult time getting a guide to move only a fraction (it moves too far when you drag it), try zooming in on the image with your Zoom Tool. When you zoom in, your mouse movements are based on the current view, so you can drag the guide over pixel by pixel. You can zoom back out by pressing the Alt key while clicking, double-clicking on the Zoom Tool in the Tools Panel (brings you to 100 percent), or by using the Set Magnification drop-down menu located in the bottom-right corner of the main window.

If your guides and slice are not showing up when you reenter the Button Editor Active Area tab, click the Show slices and hotspots button, found on the bottom-right of the Web section in the Tools Panel.

When you preview your document in the browser, the fox button should slide out like a drawer when the mouse passes over it, as shown in panel 6.

7. Now that you have completed the fox, practice by repeating the same process with all of the images on the page. After you have completed the images, add hotspots to all of the rectangles.

You may have issues getting into the hawk silhouette image because of the size of the fox image. The easiest way to overcome this issue is to select the fox button and open the Layers Panel. In the Layers Panel, hide the Fox layer by clicking the eye icon to the left in the layer. After you have completed your hawk button, click the eye icon again to show the Fox layer. If you don't unhide the Fox layer, it is displayed when you preview the document in a browser from Fireworks.

When you have finished all of these steps, you should congratulate yourself: you have created all of the basic components for an interactive page. You are now getting command over some of the best features in Fireworks MX 2004.

SUMMARY

In this chapter we explored how Fireworks MX 2004 can be used to create page layouts. Along the way, we discovered buttons and some behaviors that help make your output dynamic. We also looked at masks and how they can really add a nice effect when applied.

Now we are going to move on and look at a few more features. We will also be exploring publishing and output from Fireworks MX 2004 with "Exporting, Optimizing, and More Effects in Fireworks MX 2004."

12

Exporting, Optimizing, and More Effects in Fireworks MX 2004

W hen working with Web design in Fireworks MX 2004 (or any other application), one of your greatest concerns is output. Many of the rules used by graphic designers and the print world are thrown out the window because of the medium on which the material will ultimately be published—the World Wide Web.

On the Web, content is usually accessed by some form of a browser. Many different types are available, but this book focuses on the primary style—the browser that came with your computer or that you downloaded.

When speaking of browsers on a personal computer, one of the first limitations that comes to mind is monitor resolution. As was discussed previously, a monitor is capable of displaying images only at 72 dpi, whereas in print 300 dpi or higher is preferred.

Another issue is bandwidth. Users' access to the Internet is limited by their connections. If they are on dial-up, it can take some time for their browsers to load and display pages, especially if the page contains many images. When using Fireworks MX 2004 to create and modify images (even vector images are output as bitmaps upon export for the Web), this limitation should immediately be a concern.

We want our users to see content that is visually exciting and loads quickly. Otherwise, we may lose the user. Fortunately, Fireworks MX 2004 provides excellent tools, discussed in this chapter, for optimizing your images to be as small as possible but still look great.

Another concern is interactivity. Although we have created buttons, how can we be sure they will appear correctly when your page is published? This topic is also explored here.

And what about some more effects? You will see more about creating animations in this chapter. Well, there is a lot to cover, so let's get busy.

ALL ABOUT SLICES

Slices are how Fireworks adds HTML and formats content to be published to Web pages. In simple words, the program actually slices your document and publishes the results.

If we did not have the capacity to create slices, we not only couldn't add HTML and behaviors, but your output would be nothing more that one giant graphic, a graphic that would take an exorbitant amount of time to load. You also could not add any other content on the portion of the page covered by the graphic. On the other hand, having your images split up in smaller areas not only loads the page quicker but also affords you the ability to have more complex graphics than would normally be available.

When using slices, you assist Fireworks in cutting up your document into different areas. Some area are only images, others are images with JavaScript and HTML added, and still others are either blank or set for HTML.

All of these chunks are then published as tables, nested tables, or layers. All of these options work hand in hand with Dreamweaver to add more content in the future.

To start looking at slices, open up your completed *categories.png* file. Your current document should resemble that shown in Figure 12.1.

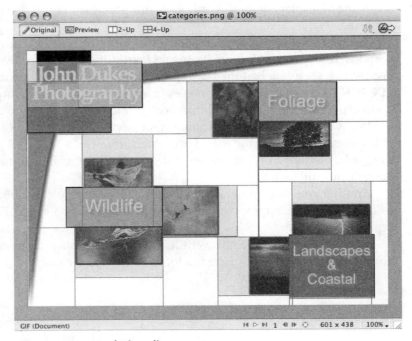

FIGURE 12.1 Exploring slices.

Within the figure notice the areas covered with semitransparent green and aqua blocks. The green areas are slices. Fireworks created both of these blocks automatically when we made our buttons and hotspots.

The green slices are created for buttons and the aqua blocks for hot spots. Right now the rest of the page is not sliced. If we don't slice the rest of the page, we will be stuck with the way Fireworks decides to treat content on export. Worse still, if we pick the wrong setting on export, these areas will not be published at all.

Hotspots are not slices, although they resemble them. They are representative of the HTML that will be generated to create a link or clickable region on a portion of an image. This distinction becomes important later when we are optimizing.

We are going to manually place the rest of your slices on the page, creating two types: image slices and HTML. The image slices are for any area that will have an image or portion of an image, and the HTML is for blank areas. Use HTML for these blank areas to keep the file size down.

Let's start adding slices, as shown in Figure 12.2.

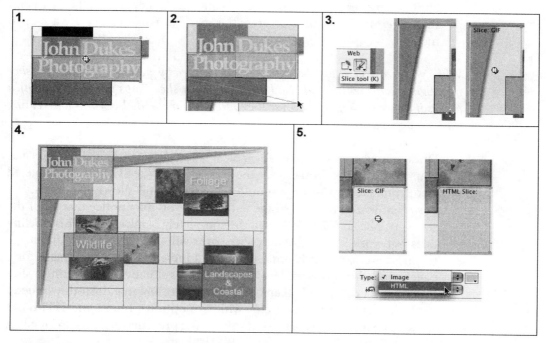

FIGURE 12.2 Adding slices to *categories.png*.

1. For your first slice, look at the top-left corner of the document by the logo. Notice that the logo is not completely covered by the hotspot. This situation is the same for the other rectangles on the page.
2. Instead of creating new slices to cover the corner graphics, simply modify the hotspot currently there to make a larger clickable area, which is not a bad thing. Because nothing else clickable can cause an overlap in this area, it won't hurt. Often, it is good to have a larger clickable region to make it easier for users to navigate. With this in mind, by expanding the hotspot, we are improving the design. Use your Pointer Tool to drag each corner out to cover all three rectangles, as shown in panel 2 of Figure 12.2.
3. Now break out the Slice Tool to start filling in the rest of the page. The Slice Tool is located in the upper-right area of the Web section of the Tools Panel (or by pressing the K key). Underneath the Slice Tool is the Polygon Slice Tool. This tool is for creating irregularly shaped slices. Be careful when using this tool; try not to create too many Polygon slices. Doing so can be tough on the browser when it loads pages because it adds complexity to the page. We will be drawing basic rectangle slices. To create a slice, follow the same procedure you used for creating rectangles. Pressing the Shift key creates a perfect square. Pressing the Alt key creates the slice from the center out. You can also press the spacebar while you create a slice to move it.

When you create slices to fill areas currently marked by guides, if you start the slice just slightly outside the guide (only slightly), your slice snaps to the guide, which makes it easier to completely cover the space. This method also works for creating slices on page edges.

TIP

4. Draw enough slices to cover all blank areas on the page. For small areas, use your Zoom Tool so you can see the areas easier. When you have completed all of your slices, your page should resemble what is shown in panel 4.
5. Now that you have covered the entire page you may notice that all of the slices are labeled Slice: GIF, even the completely blank spaces. This labeling does not work for you because Fireworks will create a blank white image for these areas, which is not efficient and increases the time it takes for a page to load in a browser. We can correct this situation by selecting a slice that covers a completely blank area. After selecting it, a drop-down menu opens in the Property Inspector with two options: Image and HTML, as shown in panel 5. Select HTML. This setting prevents an image from being created. Repeat this process for all blank areas.

It is important that you use the HTML slice type for only completely blank areas. If even a portion of a graphic is in the slice area, you must leave it as an image. Otherwise, the portion of the image that appeared in the slice is not exported, which will not look good in your design.

Now that we have sliced up *categories.png*, let's take a more in-depth look at HTML using *background.png* and referring to Figure 12.3.

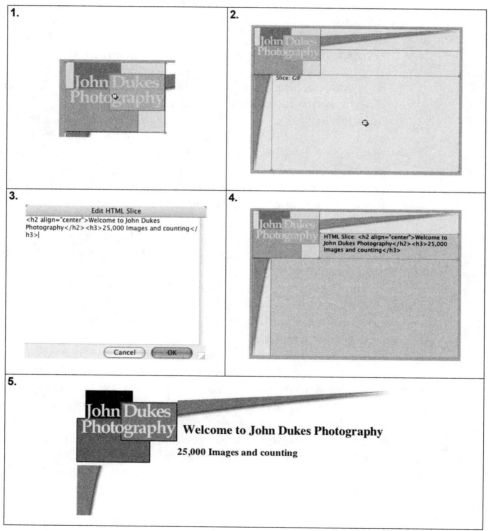

FIGURE 12.3 Exploring HTML slices.

1. The first thing we are going to do is resize the hotspot in the top-left corner so that it covers all three rectangles.

2. Next draw a total of four slices: one across the top to cover the right side of the background graphic; another directly underneath the graphic to cover the entire area from the bottom of this slice to the bottom of the hotspot; a third that covers the bottom portion of your background graphic; and a fourth for the rest of the space.

3. After you have placed all of your slices, you see that two of them are covering completely blank areas. Convert them to HTML slices in the Property Inspector. After you convert them, an Edit button appears. When you click it, the Edit HTML Slice window opens. In this window you can type any HTML text you want to display in the slice. Remember, you must type the HTML, tags and all.

4. After you have added text in the Edit HTML Slice window, it appears in the slice on the stage, as shown in pane 4.

5. Press the F12 key or click File > Preview in Browser to see the results displayed in a browser. Notice that the text is on the page. Also take note that the design is broken up. Look at how the bottom part of the background graphic is separated from the rectangle above. This separation is because you added text, and, upon publication, the table cell had to expand to fit the text, which knocks everything out of alignment.

As you have just seen, Fireworks allows direct HTML input, but you may have unforeseen results. The addition of HTML is useful if Fireworks is the only product of the suite you own.

The first problem of using HTML text in Fireworks is that you must hand-code all of the HTML used. This is not necessarily a bad thing if you are comfortable with hand-coding, but you don't have the control that is available with Dreamweaver. Also, you are limited with what you can add to the page. If you plan to use Cascading Style Sheets, you still need to edit the HTML in another text editor.

The other issue is that you can have unforeseen results with the output. Fireworks tries to put all of the data into a table or layers. When using layers, the control is more precise, but layers are not compatible with a wide range of browsers. Tables are the best choice for maximum browser compatibility. The issue arises when you look at the result. Fireworks provides you few options to modify the tables when they are published. To have the greatest degree of control, create your basic graphics layout in Fireworks, then use Dreamweaver to add all of your text and other content.

Creating a Swap Image

You can use slices for more than standard demarcation of images versus HTML upon export. They can be used to add a link to an image or even add more behaviors. Let's look at another behavior available with slices—the swap image.

A swap image at its core is similar to a rollover button. A rollover button, in fact, is a form of swap image. JavaScript dictates that when the mouse passes over the Up image, the image is swapped for an alternate image. When the mouse moves off the image, the swap image is replaced again (usually with the original).

Three images can actually be involved in a rollover. When the page loads, the first image appears. When a user's mouse passes over this image, a new image takes its place. After the user moves his mouse off the image, it is replaced again, usually with the original image, which is what gives the impression that only two images are involved, but it does not have to be this way. You could dictate that a third, different image be used. For this exercise, however, stick with the traditional, two-image convention.

The magic of a swap image is that the image that is swapped does not have to be the original image the user passed over; it can be any image on the page. This practice is commonly known as a *disjointed rollover*. Fireworks enables this functionality by using slices. We create a disjointed rollover, as shown in Figure 12.4.

1. Create a layout on the canvas with four black rectangles sized at 113x36. Place the following text on the buttons: Lighthouse, Gator, Flower, and Tree. The text should be white, 20-point, boldface Arial. The text that reads *Move your mouse over the buttons to see the Images* should be black, 22-point, boldface Arial.

2. When you have completed all of your rectangles, slice all the relevant information on the page. Also add a slice above the instructions sized at 145x95. Those dimensions make it large enough to accommodate all of the images that will be used.

3. You have two methods to add a swap image behavior. The first is to select a slice and click the target that appears. In the pop-up menu, choose Add Swap Image Behavior. The second method is to click the target of a selected slice, then drag your mouse, while holding down the button, to the target slice. This action opens a minimized Swap Image dialog box that allows you to choose a frame. You will learn about frames later in this chapter. For now, click the More Options button.

4. The Expanded Swap Image window opens. In this window are options that allow you to define which slice you want to swap and where you should get

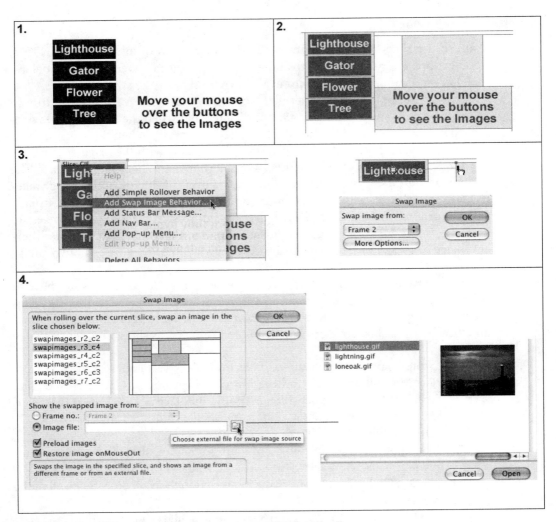

FIGURE 12.4 Using a swap image to create a disjointed rollover.

the image. You can also select Preload images and Restore the image on-MouseOut. Let's explore these options:

a. In the first section, choose which slice you want to swap. You have two methods available here. You can either choose from the list of slices on the left or choose from a visual representation of the page on the right. If you have not named each of your slices in the Property Inspector when you made them, you may find it easier to use the visual representation on the right. The Fireworks default naming scheme is efficient but not quick to read.

When you drag a behavior to the target slice, notice that the slice has been preselected for you when you open the expanded Swap Image dialog box. This preselection cuts steps and eliminates any confusion with your target slice.

b. The next area determines what image you want to substitute for the image being swapped. You have two options here. You can choose a Frame number or an Image file. Select Image file and navigate to your first image. We will be using the same images you used for the buttons in the *categories.png* file. These images are located in the *Fireworks/Chapter 11/button images* folder on the CD-ROM.

Be sure you select the Image file option before you browse for an image.

c. Make sure Preload images is selected. This setting is important upon publication. If images are not preloaded in the background, the user must wait for the image to download, degrading the user's experience.
d. Leave the Restore image onMouseOut option selected. This option causes the image to disappear when the user moves his mouse off the triggering slice.

Now that you have set up your first swap image, preview it in the browser. If all is well, you should see the lighthouse picture appear when you mouse over the lighthouse rectangle and disappear when you move away.

Repeat all of these steps to create the rest of your swap images. Use the following files for each rectangle: Gator—*gatorclose.gif*, Flower—*flower.jpg*, and Tree—*loneoak.gif*. After you have added all of your slices, preview them again in the browser. Save your file as *swapimages.png*.

Removing Behaviors

If you make a mistake or just no longer need a behavior, you can use one of two methods to remove it. The first method is the easiest. Click the blue line that shows your behavior, then click the OK button when Fireworks prompts you to confirm your action.

The second method is to select the slice with the behavior you want to delete. After selection, click the target in the middle and choose Delete All Behaviors. Keep in mind this command deletes all behaviors used on a slice. If you have more than one behavior used on a slice, you may want to use the first method.

Adding a Status Bar Message

Another behavior you can add to a page is a status bar message. A status bar message is text that is displayed on the status bar at the bottom of a browser window. Let's add status bar messages to *swapimages.png*, as shown in Figure 12.5.

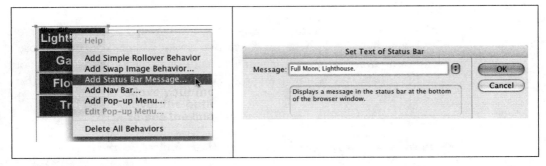

FIGURE 12.5   Adding a status bar message.

Adding a status bar message is a simple procedure. Select the slice to which you want to add the behavior and click the target in the center. When the pop-up menu appears, choose Add Status Bar Message, as shown in panel 1 of Figure 12.5. The Set Text of Status Bar dialog box opens. Add the following text for each of your rectangles:

- Lighthouse—*Full Moon, Lighthouse*
- Gator—*Baby Alligator close-up, Florida Everglades*
- Flower—*American Vetch*
- Tree—*Lone Oak Silhouette*

When you preview the page in a browser, the messages should appear in the status bar. This procedure works on most but not all browsers.

Using status bar messages is often considered bad form in Web sites design, so use them sparingly. Often users cannot even see them or may experience browser support issues.

The Behaviors Panel

Within Fireworks MX 2004, all behaviors can be modified or removed through the Behaviors Panel. This panel, accessed by clicking Windows > Behaviors, is a one-stop place to work with behaviors. Let's explore this panel using *swapimages.png*, as shown in Figure 12.6.

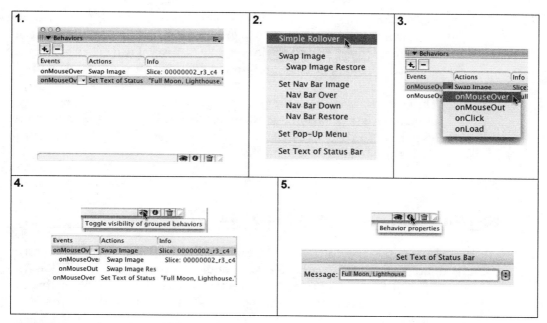

FIGURE 12.6   The Behaviors Panel.

1. Whenever you have a slice selected on the stage, you can see what behaviors have been applied to it in the Behaviors Panel. Panel 1 shows the Lighthouse slice selected with two behaviors listed: onMouseOver and onMouseOut.

2. If you click the Add behavior button (plus sign), a pop-up menu appears. This menu, which is similar to the pop-up menu that appears when you click the target icon on a slice, gives you yet another way to add a behavior to a slice you have selected on the canvas. You can also remove a behavior by selecting it in the list and clicking the Remove Behavior button (minus sign). The trashcan icon in the bottom-right corner of the panel also removes a behavior.

3. One of the most important reasons to use the Behaviors Panel is to change an existing event. Events are actions users take with the mouse or something that occurs with the browser. You can choose from four events. The first three are the user events onMouseOver (the mouse is moved over a slice), onMouseOut (the mouse is moved over an object and is moved off), and onClick (the user has clicked the slice). The last event is the system event of onLoad, which occurs when the page is loaded. You can see the available events by clicking the drop-down arrow that appears when an event is selected.

4. In the bottom-right corner are three buttons. The first of these is an eye icon, which displays all items in a grouped behavior. For example, we are using Swap Image. This behavior actually consists of two behaviors that are grouped: onMouseOver and onMouseOut. Click the eye icon again to edit your events.

5. The next icon available is the *i* on a disc. This icon opens the dialog box you used to define a behavior. For example, if we select the onMouseOver event with the action of Set Text of Status Bar, the original dialog box appears, allowing you to adjust the status bar.

ANIMATIONS IN FIREWORKS MX 2004

Fireworks MX 2004 enables you to create animations. Not all animations found on the Web are created with Flash. Another popular form of animation is the Animated GIF, and Fireworks has built-in functionality to assist you in creating this format. You start this section by looking at the Frames Panel and then frame-by-frame animations.

The Frames Panel

Any time you work with animations in Fireworks, you must have the Frames Panel in focus. The Frames Panel works similarly to the Frames Panel in Flash, but it is not as clearly laid out.

When you are using Fireworks for creating animations, your frames and layers are in separate panels. With them both being vertically aligned, you don't have as clear a representation as you find with the Flash Timeline. The Frames Panel coexists with the History Panel, as shown in Figure 12.7.

As you can see in Figure 12.7, the Frames Panel consists of several components. First is the main window where you can see the frames themselves. This area is where you can navigate throughout time in the animation.

Below the main window are several buttons. The first of these is Onion Skinning. As you have found previously with Flash, this feature is an invaluable aid to see where you are coming from and where you are going to with adjacent frames. When you press this button a pop-up menu appears, allowing you to modify your preferences.

The next button, GIF Animation Looping, allows you to adjust your looping. By default, when a GIF animation is created, it continuously loops. Here you can define a specific number of times for it to loop. This setting is important. Some-

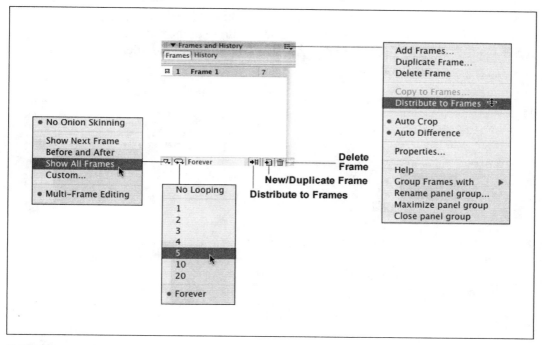

FIGURE 12.7 The Frames Panel.

times animations on a page can be distracting, so by limiting the number of cycles they play, you can tone down the effect.

After GIF Animation Looping is the Distribute to Frames button. This feature works in a similar manner to the command found in FreeHand MX.

The New/Duplicate Frame button appears next. This icon provides a handy way to add another frame to your animation while you are building it.

In the far-right-bottom corner is the ever-familiar trashcan icon, which when pressed deletes the selected frames.

In the top-right corner is the Options menu, as in most other panels. This menu provides more options.

Frame-by-Frame Animations

The first style of animation we will explore is the traditional frame-by-frame animation. Let's create a simple example using the reliable old bouncing ball, as shown in Figure 12.8.

1. Create a new document. A size of 300x300 should suffice.
2. On the new document, create an ellipse in the bottom-right corner. If you want, give it a Radial gradient and nudge the gradient to make it appear more realistic.

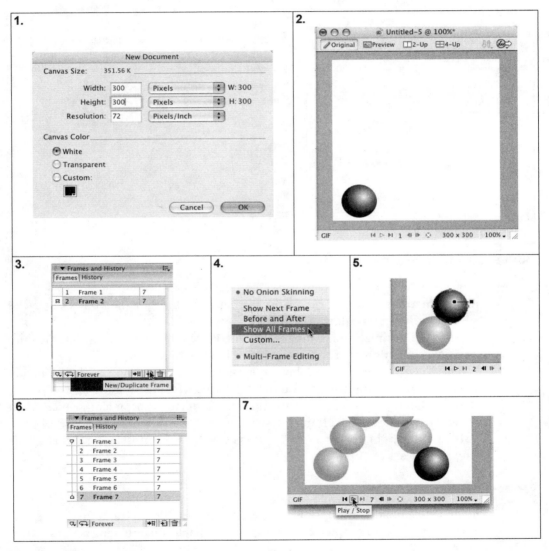

FIGURE 12.8 Creating a frame-by-frame animation.

3. After you have completed your ball, copy it by clicking Edit > Copy (or right-click [Control + click on a Macintosh] > Edit Copy). Add a new frame in the Frame Panel by clicking the New/Duplicate Frame button.
4. Press the Onion Skinning button and select Show All Frames to place your ball easier.
5. In the new frame, paste your ball, then move it up and to the right.
6. Continue the process of adding new frames, pasting the ball, and moving the ball until you have enough frames for the whole cycle of movement. The ball should bounce up to the upper-center of the screen and back down to the bottom-right corner.
7. After you have completed the animation, test it by clicking the Play/Stop (the open white triangle that points to the right) button in the bottom of the main window. To stop the animation, click the button again while it is playing. (The button becomes a square while the animation plays.)

You have now created your first frame-by-frame animation. Yes, it is just as tedious to make an animation as it was in Flash. Let's explore other options.

Using Distribute to Frames

One way of automating the creation of an animation is to work in conjunction with FreeHand. Remember that although Fireworks has many of the vector features available in FreeHand, it does not have all of them.

One of the features not available in Fireworks is the Blend Tool. To explore working with multiple programs, create a blend in FreeHand and then bring the result into Fireworks.

To get started, create a new document with a canvas size of 400x400, 72 dpi, and a canvas color of white. It's time to create our animation, as shown in Figure 12.9.

1. To start, perform the following steps using FreeHand:
   a. Create an ellipse that has a red fill, black 1-point stroke, and dimensions of 31x31.
   b. Create a six-pointed star shape with a purple fill, a 1-point stroke, and dimensions of 58x58. After you complete it, adjust the vertices in the Object Panel so they are both set to 29. This setting turns the stars into a polygon.
   c. Press Alt/Option and drag a copy of your polygon to create a clone. Change the vertices to 61 and 24 in the Object Panel. While in the Object Panel, change the fill color to blue. Rotate your star approximately 20 to 25 degrees.

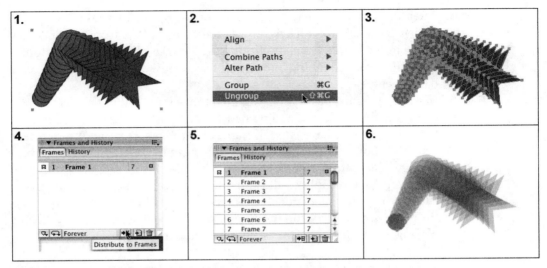

FIGURE 12.9   Using Distribute to Frames.

d. Now that your shapes are created, select the Blend Tool. Click the circle and drag your mouse to blend it into the polygon shape. After blending, change the number of steps in the Object Panel to read 10.

e. Blend the Polygon into the star shape.

f. Select all of your objects and click Edit > Copy (or Ctrl/Command + C). Paste these objects into your new Fireworks document.

2. After you have pasted and positioned your FreeHand MX shapes, you may notice that they are grouped. We can't have items grouped when working with the Distribute to Frames feature. Click Modify > Ungroup (or Ctrl/Command + Shift + G, or right-click [Control + click on a Macintosh] > Ungroup) to break them apart.

3. Now you see that all of your objects are separated.

4. In the Frames Panel click the Distribute to Frames button.

5. Notice only one object is now shown on the canvas. Each object is on its own frame, and only one frame is visible at a time. The Frames Panel has been populated as shown in panel 5.

6. If you activate Onion Skinning and click Show All Frames, you can see the path of your animation. Press the Play button to watch it.

You have now seen how the Distribute to Frames feature works. You have also seen that you can use FreeHand in conjunction with Fireworks to leverage the strengths of both programs. You are not limited to using only copy and paste between the programs, either. You can open or import a FreeHand document directly into Fireworks.

When you import a document from FreeHand, you are given extra options. You can choose to have either all layers in the FreeHand document converted to frames or all pages converted to frames. This option is invaluable, because you may wish to create advanced vector graphics in FreeHand and then use Fireworks to either place them on a Web page or animate them.

You can also distribute multiple objects to frames. These objects can be created within Fireworks or imported. The possibilities are endless. Some crafty individuals have even created video transitions using Fireworks.

Using Tweens and Graphic Symbols

Another way to work with animations in Fireworks is to use tweens with graphic symbols. This practice is similar in principle to what you find in Flash. Let's create another ball and look at this principle, as shown in Figure 12.10.

1. Create another ball shape like you did in the previous example. Then click Modify > Symbol > Convert to Symbol (or press the F8 key). Give the symbol the name *ball* and Type of Graphic in the Symbol Properties dialog box.
2. After you complete your symbol, press Alt/Option and drag out two copies of the symbol. Lay them out in the manner shown in pane 2 of Figure 12.10.

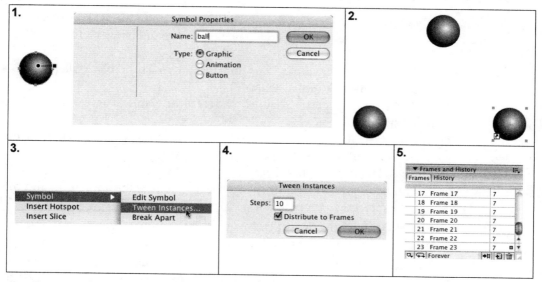

FIGURE 12.10   Using tweens and graphic symbols.

3. Select all instances of the ball on the stage, then right-click [Control + click on a Macintosh] and click Symbol > Tween Instances (or Modify > Symbol > Tween Instances).

4. The Tween Instances dialog box appears. In this dialog box you can define how many steps the animation should take between each position. You can also select Distribute to Frames. This action completes the tweening and frame distribution in one shot. If you don't use this option, all the instances appear on the canvas at once. This practice can be handy if you want to tweak the movement further and then distribute the result to frames. Select Distribute to Frames and click OK.

5. You should now see that your Frames Panel has been populated. Play your animation to see how it turned out.

Although using tweens in Fireworks can make creating an animation simpler, they are different in terms of file size than those in Flash. In Flash, tweens are not only convenient but also reduce the final movie file size because they are repeated. This is not the case in Fireworks. Any kind of animation you make is larger than just a static image of a single frame because each frame adds size to the final document. Therefore, animations can lead to large file sizes very quickly. Special care should always be taken when creating Animated GIFs with Fireworks.

Creating Animation Symbols

The last method this chapter addresses for creating animations in Fireworks is using animation symbols. We will create one, as shown in Figure 12.11.

1. Let's create another ellipse. This time just give it a solid black fill. After you create it, convert it into a symbol.

2. In the Symbol Properties dialog box, give it the Name of *grow* and the Type of Animation.

3. The Animate dialog box opens, in which you can type an explicit value for what you want to happen. The categories include:

   Frames: Defines how many frames you use to complete the animation. Be careful here—the more frames you use, the cleaner the animation, but the file size increases exponentially.

   Move: Defines how many pixels you want the animation to travel. The animation is currently set to 150 pixels.

   Direction: Defines the direction of the animation. When you click the drop-down arrow to the right, a dial appears. You can twist the dial to

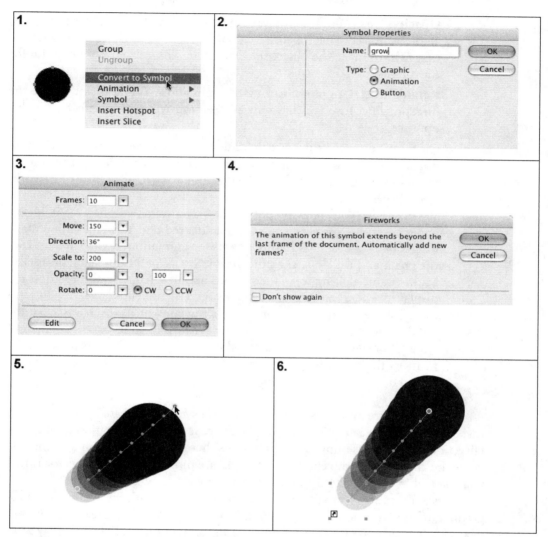

FIGURE 12.11   Creating an animation symbol.

manually choose the direction. You can also type a number to represent degrees. The value of 36 degrees is used in Figure 12.10.

Scale to: Scales the object to a specific size. If you want the object to grow as the animation progresses, type in what the final size will be. The Scale to value in the figure is 200 here, which will make the symbol increase to twice its initial size.

Opacity: Determines the object's transparency. We can determine if we want the object to have transparency at the start or finish. Choose 0 for the first field to make the object slowly appear. This setting can be useful for transitions.

Rotate: Rotates an object during the animation. You also can choose the direction. Because you have an ellipse, you will see no effect with this option.

4. Click OK. Fireworks prompts you to add new frames. Because you have not added any frames prior to creating this symbol, we don't have enough frames in the document to handle the animation. Click OK for Fireworks to create the needed frames.

5. We now have your new symbol on the stage. When you first see it, it may appear as just a line with a green dot and a red dot. Turn on Onion Skinning for all frames. This feature reveals the animation. If you still don't see the green and red dots, click the Onion Skinning button again and select Multi-Frame Editing from the pop-up menu. The green and red dots are displayed where the animation begins (green) and ends (red). If you want to adjust the distance the animation is traveling or its direction, click the red dot and drag it to a new location, as shown in panel 5.

6. After you have moved the red dot, the animation modifies its path to conform to the new dot placement. You can also move the starting point (green dot) in the same manner.

Another feature available after an animation symbol is created is the Property Inspector. Here you can adjust Frames, Opacity, Scaling, and Rotation (along with Direction). The only settings you can't adjust here are the direction and the distance the animation is traveling. Another feature of the Property Inspector is that you can add Live Effects to the animation symbol after creation.

These procedures wrap up the section on animation with Fireworks. As a program, it offers several animation features. It is more robust than FreeHand but not nearly the powerhouse that Flash is for creating animations. Ideally, you may want to consider making many of your animations in Flash.

This lack of power in animation doesn't leave Fireworks, or even FreeHand, out of the loop. You often use these programs in conjunction with one another. You can use Fireworks to manipulate images and vector graphics before bringing them into Flash, and do the same in FreeHand with vector graphics.

Both Fireworks and FreeHand have image-editing capacity that goes far beyond what Flash has to offer. Because you are working with Macromedia Studio MX 2004 as a package, leverage everything it has to offer.

IMPORTING GRAPHICS

Before output is covered, let's explore how to input graphics into Fireworks. Just as you have a broad range of image-editing capacities, you also have a broad range of formats you can input. You can import and open the following image types:

GIF (Graphics Interchange Format): One of the two most popular Web image formats. It supports up to 256 colors and can be both transparent and animated. It is the ideal format for displaying line art and large flat-color planes. Much of your vector art will be exported in this format.

JPEG (Joint Photographers Experts Group): As a format, JPEG is commonly used for photographic images. It is the other most popular compression method on the Web and can support millions of colors.

PNG (Portable Network Graphics): Some degree of confusion surrounds this format. Fireworks stores its working files in a PNG format, but it is not the same thing as what you find on the Internet. Application-specific settings are contained in Fireworks PNG files. The open-standard PNG found on the Web was developed as an alternative to GIF. It can support up to 32-bit color, allows transparency, and can be progressive. It is like a blend of GIF and JPEG. Although it was developed to be a superior compression mechanism, it has never really caught on and doesn't have the nearly ubiquitous support that GIF and JPEG do.

WBMP (Wireless Bitmap): This black-and-white format was created for use with the Wireless Application Protocol (WAP). WAP, a 1-bit (black and white) format, is commonly used with cell phones and PDAs.

TIFF (Tagged Image File Format): If you want to have high-resolution images suitable for printing, TIFF is a great format to choose. It is supported by most applications but is a poor format for the Web because of its large file sizes.

BMP: Microsoft uses this bitmap format within Windows for many of the operating system graphics. It is widely available to many applications, but like TIFF, it creates files too large for the Web.

PICT: Apple uses this as a primary format, much the same as Microsoft uses BMP. It also is a poor choice for Web graphics due to file size.

In addition to the previously mentioned graphic file types, Fireworks allows the import of files created from specific graphic applications, including not only SWFs and FreeHand documents but also those created using Adobe® Photoshop®, Adobe Illustrator®, and CorelDRAW®.

When opening files created in these other applications, one of the issues you may run into is when a font used in the image is not installed on your computer. Fortunately, Fireworks gives you the option to Maintain Appearance. This option causes the text to be held as a graphic unless you try to modify it. If you try to change the text, you then must define a substitute font.

You may also encounter an issue with Encapsulated Post Script (EPS) files. Fireworks tries to import them as raster images. To combat this situation, you may want to open these files in FreeHand, save them, and then open the saved FreeHand file with Fireworks.

You can also pull pictures in directly from a scanner or digital camera by clicking File > Scan. You must first set up the TWAIN settings for each device. This procedure may be an extra step, but it is better than converting files from applications that came with your device. The fewer steps you take en route to Fireworks, the better your result usually is.

The last method of import discussed is the old-fashioned copy and paste. Often, this method is the easiest way to get graphics into Fireworks. You can copy and paste from many image applications, text editors, and even Dreamweaver (although it is usually best to stay in Dreamweaver and call Fireworks from within).

One new feature of Fireworks MX 2004 is the ability to work on many image files in their native format. If you open a JPEG, for example, and make changes, you can just click File > Save to save the image with the changes. This feature is an improvement over previous versions of Fireworks in which you had the added process of exporting files back out to the original format.

OPTIMIZING

Before any graphics are exported for the Web, they should be optimized. Optimization is the process of choosing the best file type for clarity of the image and size. One note of importance with Fireworks is that even though graphics drawn with the tools inside the application may be created as vectors, they are converted to a raster format for the Web. Fireworks can create vector output in the form of .swf files, FreeHand 10, or Adobe Illustrator 7, but this is not its specialty. Use FreeHand for vector output. The .swf export is useful mainly if you want to create content in Fireworks and then bring it into a Flash movie.

You have two primary formats you can comfortably choose for the Web: GIF and JPEG. Fireworks has wonderful capabilities for optimizing these formats.

Let's discuss these two formats and when they should be used, starting with GIF.

GIF, or Graphics Interchange Format, in general, is your format of choice when exporting line art and basic vector graphics with flat colors. It also works well with text. This format uses a compression scheme known as Lempel-Zif-Welch (LZW). The way the format operates is based on the number of colors used in an image. Although you have 256 colors available, it is likely you are not using all of them.

The compression scheme is based on a table. Let's say you have an image that is 75 pixels wide and is made up of red, white, and blue bars. (Each color consists of 25 pixels.) This information could be expressed by repeating each of the colors 25 times each, as in red, red, red, and so on. Using the GIF LZW scheme, you could say 25 red, 25 white, and 25 blue. You are shrinking the file size significantly without losing the integrity of the image. This compression method is why GIF is known as a *lossless* format. You achieve a smaller file size by using fewer colors. After all, if they aren't in the image, you don't need information about them anyway.

The JPEG, or Joint Photographers Experts Group, format, on the other hand, is considered a *lossy* format. As a format, it is dependent on the fact that the human eye doesn't have the perception to see minor color changes in transitions, so it throws some of those bits away, which gives it its name as a lossy format. You are actually losing information in the image. If you compress the image too much, it keeps throwing out data, and your eye will begin to perceive it. This color loss is especially apparent with flat colors and images with sharp, contrasting edges. This is an ideal format for photographs because they tend to contain more subtle color changes.

So does this mean we should always use GIF for vector art and JPEG for photographs? Not necessarily. If you created vector graphics that made heavy use of gradients, you will run into limitations with GIF because it can handle only 256 colors. The result may show a banding effect, which can be unsightly.

On the other hand, if you are working with a photograph of an object with large planes of flat color and sharp, contrasting edges (like a sign), you will notice degradation immediately when compressing in a JPEG format. In this case, you may benefit by using GIF as your compression format. Be sure to experiment with both formats to find the best compromise of image versus size.

The Preview Buttons and Optimize Panel

When optimizing graphics for publication in Fireworks MX 2004, you work primarily in two areas: the Optimize Panel and the Preview buttons located at the top of the main window. These items are shown in Figure 12.12.

Figure 12.12 contains four panels. Panel 1 shows the Optimization Panel, which is where you choose formats and specific settings. The other three panels display previews of how the output looks. Preview gives a full-window view of the file

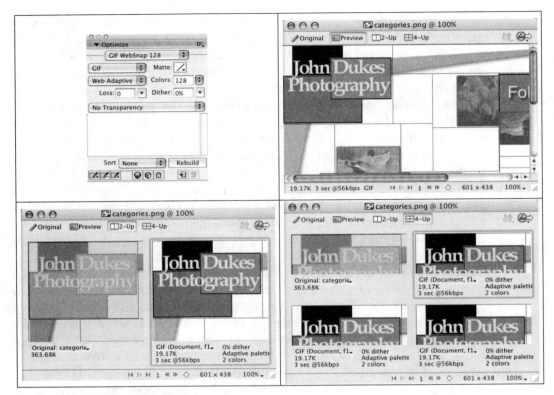

FIGURE 12.12 Optimization tools.

size and final appearance of your current output settings. The 2-Up and 4-Up windows provide a comparison view of the original versus the output format.

You will likely spend most of your time in the 2-Up and 4-Up windows. It is handy to have the option to visually compare the original to your chosen format and settings.

Remember, you are always performing a bit of a dance when optimizing for the Web. You must choose the smallest possible format to accommodate bandwidth, but, at the same time, you want the image to look good. These dual requirements make things difficult, but the more time you spend tweaking the settings, the better a compromise you will have.

The first trick to optimizing, believe it or not, is using slices. Every image slice you create is a separate image, which gives you great flexibility because you can be more specific with your settings. You can choose GIF for one part of a graphic and JPEG for another. You can even adjust levels differently for individual slices.

Optimizing the Logo as a GIF

Let's begin looking at optimization by opening *categories.png*. This image has a nice mix of slices and graphics to help you understand what each setting does. The following procedure is shown in Figure 12.13.

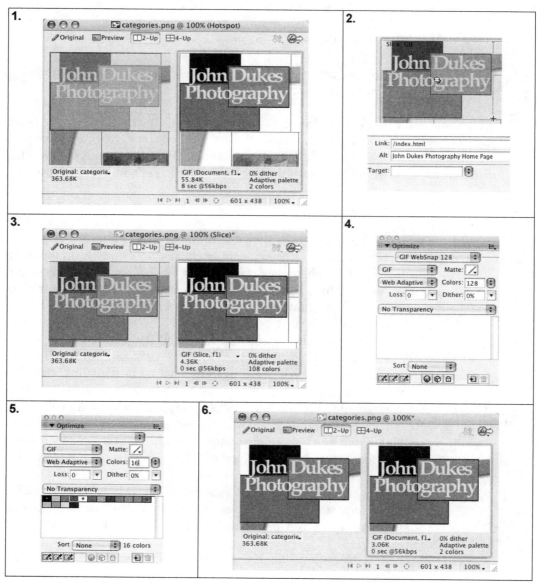

FIGURE 12.13 Optimizing the logo.

1. In this step we are using the 2-Up window to see both the original and preview of the screen. Start by optimizing the logo section of your document. You can choose this slice by clicking directly on the individual slice to be optimized with the Pointer Tool either in the original or preview view. (Your cursor becomes a pointing hand in these windows.) You can also move the document in the window using the Hand Tool, which is activated from the Tools Panel by pressing the H key. (Pressing the spacebar temporarily invokes the Hand Tool.)

Be careful to not click and drag with the mouse when you are selecting areas. This action causes the objects to actually be moved in the document.

Notice the preview window shows that the graphic is currently going to be exported at the size of 55.84 KB. That can't be right. Let's look closer at the preview window on the right. Notice it says GIF (Document, F1). You are not looking at an individual slice; we are looking at the whole document. Let's address this situation.

2. The reason why we are not looking at the logo portion alone is because it has not been sliced. It has a hotspot, but this is not the same thing as a slice. You must actually slice the image itself to use it for output. We have two choices when doing this. We can either create a slice directly on top of the hotspot or just simply replace the hotspot with a slice and add a link to it. The second option is better in this case because we want the entire logo area to be a link and having an image map over this area is redundant.
   a. Delete the hotspot in your original view.
   b. Draw a slice over the area as shown in panel 2 of Figure 12.13.
   c. Within the Property Inspector, add the Link and Alt attributes as shown. You can click the drop-down arrow next to link and click */index.html* again. The drop-down menu contains previous links you have created in the document. The same applies for the Alt field.
3. After we have sliced the logo, notice that when you click the slice, the export file size is a much more reasonable 4.36 KB. This file actually is pretty small already and could be used on the Web with few issues, but we will still tweak it a bit more. After all, graphics do add up.
4. Because this slice contains basic flat colors, the ideal choice is to use GIF as the export format. This format has most likely already been selected for you. Let's see what's available in the Optimize Panel with GIF as the chosen format:
   a. The top drop-down menu contains the following preset compression settings for the Web:

GIF Web 216: Changes all colors to match what is considered the Web-safe palate of 216 colors. The Web-safe palette was created based on 8-bit color or 256 colors. This setting came out of equipment limitations from several years ago. Video cards didn't have the capacity to support more than 256 colors at a time. Unfortunately, not all operating systems could agree on how 40 of these colors would be represented. The extra colors were thrown out, and the 216-color palette was designed for maximum compatibility. Many of these limitations have gone by the wayside now with newer equipment that displays at a 16-bit (65,536 colors) resolution or higher.

GIF WebSnap 256: Converts any color not in the 8-bit color palette available for GIF to the nearest Web-safe counterpart.

GIF WebSnap 128: Works in the same manner as GIF WebSnap 256, but the palette is limited to 128 colors.

GIF Adaptive 256: Contains only the colors used in the actual image. You can have up to 256 colors.

JPEG: Better quality automatically converts your JPEG to a level of 80%, which usually looks close to the original.

JPEG: Smaller files use the JPEG setting of 60%, which results in a smaller file but a loss of quality.

Animated GIF WebSnap 128: Works in the same way as GIF WebSnap 128 but is for use with Animated GIFs.

b. Underneath the presets to the left is the Export file format pop-up menu in which you can choose a specific format. This menu includes all formats available with Fireworks.

c. To the right of the Export file format menu, you can choose what color your matte will be.

d. The Indexed Palette menu appears if you choose a format that has these items available. Indexed Palettes are different preset color groups available with a format.

e. If the Indexed Palette option is available, you can further refine in the Colors area how many colors are actually used.

f. You can use the Loss option to compress the graphics even further. Be gentle with this setting—Macromedia recommends using no more than a 15-percent maximum. This setting is not the same thing as JPEG; it is a preprocessing of the GIF before compression is applied.

g. Use the Dither option when you don't have enough colors to accomplish a transition. It alternates similar colors in a pattern of dots giving the illusion of a more gradual transition. This method can add significantly to the file size and should be used sparingly.

5. Now that we have explored your options for GIF, let's modify the settings for the logo. All we are going to do is look at the colors. Notice inside of the Optimize Panel that the image is set to 128 colors. Well, there can't be that many colors in the logo. Let's go to the extreme and change Colors to 16.

6. Click the Hide slices and hotspots button in the bottom-left corner of the Web section in the Tools Panel so we can get a better visual comparison between the original and the preview. Notice that the file size has been decreased to 3.06 KB, and it still looks pretty close to the original. This file size drop is 25 percent more than just the default. It pays to individually optimize your graphics.

Use the Hide slices and hotspots button to get a better comparison when you are previewing the output with the original. But remember you need to press the Show slices and hotspots button again after you finish previewing. If slices are hidden, you can't select a single slice while optimizing.

Optimize the rest of your rectangles. Remember, you must add image slices to them. For the rest of your rectangles, add the image slice in addition to the preexisting hotspots.

When you are finished with *categories.png*, optimize all of the graphics in *background.png*. Remember, you must resolve the issue with the hotspot on the logo in this file as well.

Optimizing the Buttons as JPEGs

Let's look at JPEG optimization in Fireworks. Because the buttons are actually images, we want to optimize these as JPEGs using the following procedure, shown in Figure 12.14.

1. Start with your yawning fox button. If it is not in view, use your Hand Tool to shift the canvas and move it into place. Now activate the Pointer Tool and select the slice. Notice when you are in the preview view, as your mouse moves over the slice, you see the Over state of the button. This state works well because there is more to see. Fireworks has defaulted this image to GIF and 128 colors. It doesn't look bad and the file size is relatively small at 4.97 K, but we can do better.

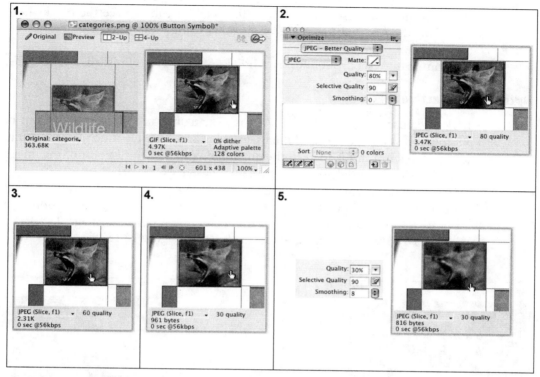

FIGURE 12.14   Optimizing the buttons as JPEGs.

2. In the Optimize Panel, click JPEG—Better Quality from the presets at the top of the Optimize Panel. You can see that the file size has decreased dramatically to 3.47 K, and this decrease is at the higher quality of JPEG. This efficiency is the result of working with a photograph, which what JPEG is specialized to handle.

3. If you change the percentage to 60% under Quality, you notice that the picture has degraded slightly, but it's still not terrible. The file size has decreased dramatically again to 2.31 K. We are now well under half of where we started.

4. By bringing the quality down to 30%, you can see how the JPEG becomes terribly blocky and the image has degraded severely. Obviously, we won't want to compress to this degree.

5. Fireworks also offers the option of Smoothing. This feature combats the blocks created when images are compressed. When we set smoothing to 8

on the image currently with a 30% quality, you can see the blocks have toned down, but the image would still be unusable.

Optimize the rest of your buttons as JPEGs. After you have finished, save your file.

Optimizing Selective JPEGs

A trick often used on JPEGs for the Web is to actually optimize selected regions in a photograph at a high level and then set the background to a much lower setting. The theory behind this is to keep the quality high for the focal point of the image and let the background degrade because many users won't care.

For example, if you have a group of people in a photograph, you are most likely concerned with how clear their faces are. Within Fireworks, you can optimize their faces at a high level and set everything else to a lower percentage. Let's start this process by preparing your graphic, as shown in Figure 12.15.

FIGURE 12.15 Preparing the JPEG graphic.

ON THE CD

1. The first thing you must do is create a new document. Size doesn't matter, but make the resolution 72 dpi and choose a canvas color of white. Click File > Import and open *Fireworks/Chapter 12/tarantula.jpg*. In the stage you see that your cursor now looks like an upside-down *L*. Click anywhere on the canvas to place your image. When the image is placed, click Modify > Canvas > Fit Canvas or click the Fit Canvas button in the Property Inspector. Notice that the image is huge. As it stands now, it is far too large for the Web, both in file size and screen real estate. You can see the exact size of the canvas by looking in the bottom-right corner of your main window, as shown in panel 1 of Figure 12.15.

NOTE

As of Fireworks MX 2004, you can open JPEGs and other image files directly. You can then make changes and save the original by clicking File > Save. The reason why we are not using this method and are creating a new Fireworks PNG file is that you don't destroy the original photograph. We can turn back many settings in a Fireworks PNG.

2. To get the actual size under control, resize the image. Select the image and click Modify > Transform > Numeric Transform. The Numeric Transform dialog box opens. This dialog box allows you to explicitly scale, resize, and rotate your graphics by typing numeric values. Scale your graphic to 50%.
3. After scaling, the tarantula is a much more reasonable size, but the canvas is still much too large. Click a blank area on the canvas, and click the Fit Canvas button in the Property Inspector.
4. Now, let's get rid of some of the background. The star of this show is the tarantula, not the garage door or the ground. Choose the Crop Tool from the Tools Panel and use it to draw a rectangular shape around the tarantula, as shown in panel 4. You can move and resize the crop area with your mouse, if needed.
5. After you have selected the area for cropping, double-click the selection. Fireworks recreates the image, using only your selected area, as shown in panel 5.

We have prepared your base image, and now it's time to optimize. We will create a selective JPEG and optimize the parts of the photo separately, as shown in Figure 12.16.

1. Select the tarantula using any of your selection tools (Marquee, Lasso, Magic Wand). You might find it easiest to use the Magic Wand for this task, as well as pressing Shift + click to keep adding to your selection.

FIGURE 12.16 Creating and optimizing a selective JPEG.

2. After the tarantula is selected, click Modify > Selective JPEG > Save Selection as JPEG Mask. This command changes the tone of the tarantula, telling you it has been selected as a mask.

3. If you look in your 2-Up window you see that at the defaults of 80% quality and a Selective Quality (the tarantula), the file size will be 27.82 K upon export.

4. Modify the Quality to 40%. It's just concrete, so it makes little difference. Also tone back the Selective Quality to 80%. The background starts to ap-

pear blocky, so set Smoothing to 1 to tone it down. Now you have an image with a file size of 12.25 K, less than half of the original size, and the tarantula is still clear enough to scare people. Oddly enough, by toning back the background, the tarantula pops even more. Save your file as *tarantula.png*.

Batch-Processing Images

One of the handiest options available in Fireworks MX 2004 is the ability to batch-process images. It is one thing to optimize a single image, but what if you have a whole folder of them? The Fireworks MX 2004 Batch Process dialog box makes short work of this task. Use it to optimize multiple files and even create thumbnails. Let's look at this utility in Figure 12.17.

ON THE CD

1. Click File > Batch Process to begin. The Batch Process window opens to walk you through the process. Navigate to the folder containing the files you want to process. You can choose a single image, add all images in the folder, or remove an unwanted image. Navigate to the *Fireworks/Chapter 12/batch* folder on the CD-ROM. Select Add All and click Next.

2. Now add your first step of the process by selecting Scale from the left and clicking the Add button in the middle. Your ultimate goal is to scale down all the images in size, optimize them, and rename them. With the Scale Option you have multiple choices. You can choose Scale to Size if you know the specific pixel size you want, Scale to Fit Area (which is handy if you have a set area on the screen in which all images need to fit), and Scale to Percentage. Choose Scale to Percentage and type 15.

3. Next select Export from the left and click the Add button. With the Export setting you can set your optimizations. In the Settings menu at the bottom you can choose from all of the Fireworks presets. You can also click the Edit button to open the Export Preview window in which you can refine your settings.

4. Select Rename and add it to the process. Rename is a great tool when you are running this utility. It is especially useful if you are saving the files into the same folder you are using for the batch process because it prevents you from overwriting the original files. Select Add Prefix and type the word *Web* on the right. You can also add a suffix.

5. When you click Next, the Batch Process window opens, in which you can choose where you want to save your files. Select a folder on your hard drive, because you can't write to the CD-ROM. You can also choose how you want to handle backups. Backups are how files are handled in the output folder. When Backups is left unchecked, files in the folder that have the

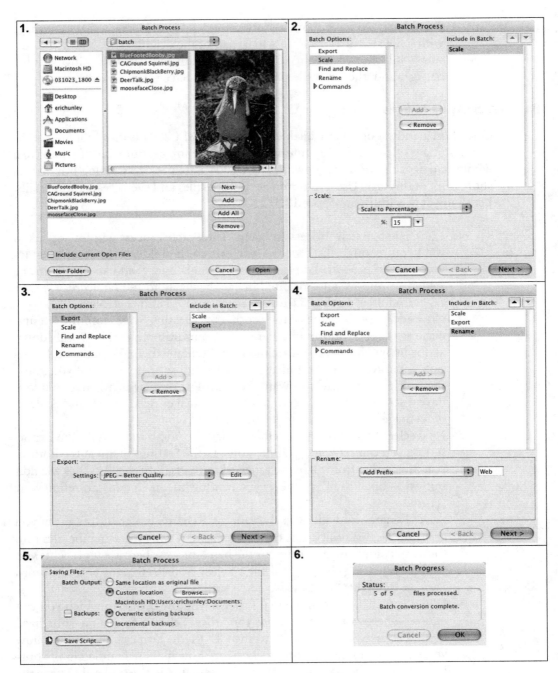

FIGURE 12.17 Batch-processing images.

same name are overwritten. When it is checked, you have two options: Overwrite existing backups, which overwrites previous backups of the files, and Incremental Backups, which stores all copies and resolves conflicts by appending a number to the filename. Leave this option unchecked and click the Batch button.

6. When the process is running, a progress window appears, letting you know which stage is occurring in the process. When the batch process is complete, the program window tells you the process is complete; click OK. Keep in mind that the entire process can take some time if you have many files. It may even seem as if your computer is locked up. Just wait it out; it should eventually be complete.

As you can see, numerous options are available in the Batch Process window. We have completed just one process. Take the time to explore and experiment with this utility. It can be a real assistance to your workflow.

EXPORTING HTML

You will wrap up the coverage of Fireworks by exploring HTML. Because the goal was to create an actual Web layout, it will be a relief to finally do so.

Fireworks allows you to create all of your graphics, add behaviors and HTML, and then export the entire document as HTML. When exporting to HTML, you use layers or tables and save to HTML or other file types.

As of Fireworks MX 2004, you now have the option of exporting your content to another Web page type, such as ColdFusion (.cfm), Server-Side Includes (.shtml), PHP (.php), JSP (.jsp), or ASP (.asp). This capability takes another step out of the process in creating HTML for use in Dreamweaver.

Open your *background.png* file. If you have not optimized this file already, do so before continuing. We will use this file for exporting HTML, as shown in Figure 12.18.

Figure 12.18 contains four panels. Let's look at the content of each and determine what settings to use based on the options given.

1. Panel 1 contains a view of the Quick Export button and the menu it opens. In this menu, you have all of your available export options. You can export to Dreamweaver, Flash, FreeHand, and Director, as well as other applications. Choosing Dreamweaver > Export HTML because you are using this application as part of Macromedia Studio MX 2004. This command opens

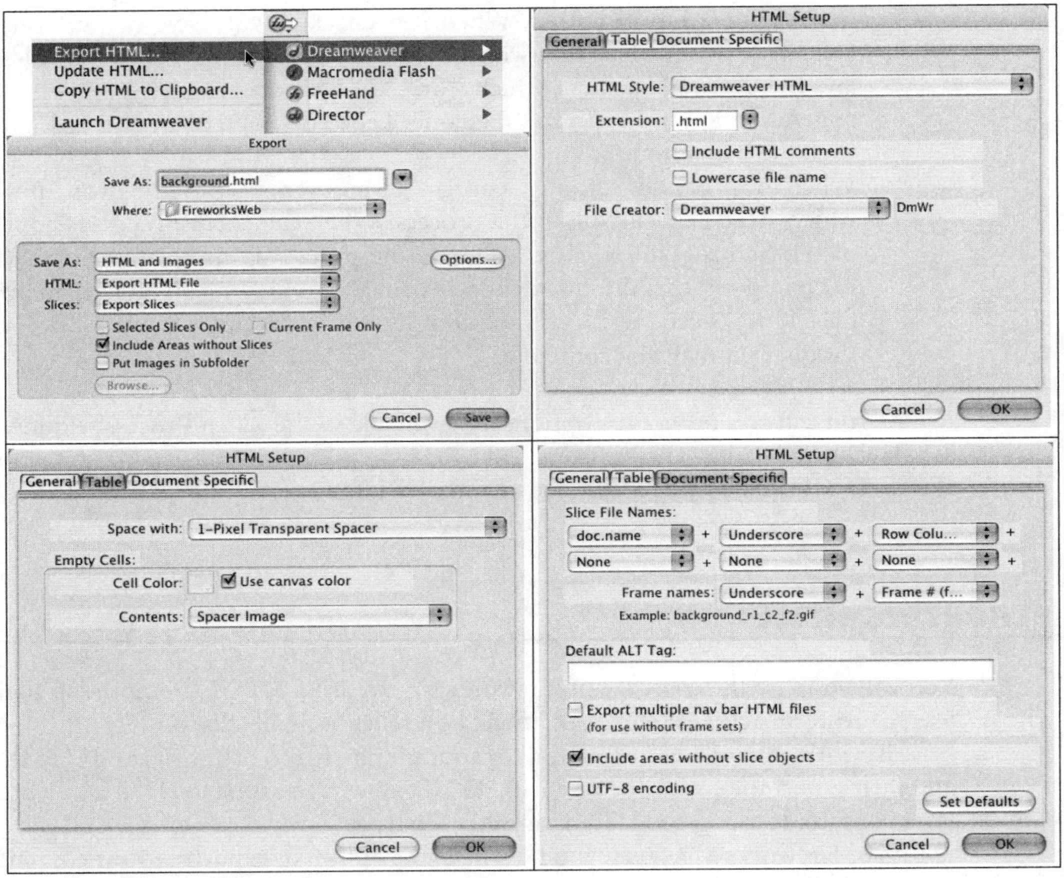

FIGURE 12.18   Exporting HTML.

the Export window. Here, you can choose where you want the file to be saved as well as other options. This menu is the same one that appears when you click File > Export instead of the Quick Export button. Let's look at what the menu offers:

Save As: Automatically displays HTML and images because you have clicked Dreamweaver > Export HTML. When you click File > Export instead of the Quick Export button, if you have added HTML attributes to your page, HTML and Images appears. If you have only an image created, it shows Images only. Other options you can choose under Save As are Dreamweaver Library, CSS Layers (if you want to use layers instead of tables), Director, Layers to Files (creates a separate file for every layer),

Frames to Files (creates a separate file for every frame), Lotus Domino De-signer, Macromedia Flash SWF, Illustrator 7, and Photoshop PSD. We will use HTML and Images.

HTML: Provides the option to Export HTML File. This option is impor-tant in your output. You need Fireworks to create an actual HTML docu-ment, which is what contains all of your JavaScript and links.

Slices: Determines how you want slices to be handled. You can choose to use None, Export Slices, and Slice Along Guides. Slice Along Guides allows you to place guides in the document that Fireworks uses to slice up the document. The problem with this method is that it does not support be-haviors.

Selected Slices: Exports only the slices you have selected. This option is lo-cated underneath the Slices field. Next to this option is the option to use the current frame only. You can use frames in Fireworks to achieve a sim-ilar result to the multipage option in FreeHand.

Include Areas without slices: Ensures that every part of the document is exported.

Put Images in Subfolder: Keeps images in a separate folder away from your HTML files, for organizational purposes. Fireworks creates a folder named *images* by default.

2. To the right of the HTML settings is an Options button, which opens the General tab in the HTML Setup window. In here you can adjust the fol-lowing settings specific to the HTML output:

HTML: Determines which HTML editor is to be used as a target. Options include Dreamweaver HTML, FrontPage® HTML, generic HTML, Go-Live® HTML, Dreamweaver XHTML, generic XHTML, and GoLive XHTML. These programs are the most popular used in HTML editing. If you are planning to export to one of these programs, pick the specific pro-gram from the list for maximum behavior compatibility. Choose Dreamweaver HTML here.

Extension: Defines the file extension to which you will export. As of Fire-works MX 2004 you can choose from multiple formats. Select .html.

Include HTML comments: Describes the content.

Use lowercase filename: Formats the final output files using lowercase file-names. Using lowercase filenames is a good idea if you are using Fireworks. You are going to be importing the files into Dreamweaver, so you don't have to worry about this.

File Creator: Causes the operating system to associate the file with the selected program. Keep the selection on Dreamweaver.

3. The next tab in HTML Setup is Table. Here you choose how you want your cells to be placed. The spacing options are 1-Pixel Transparent Spacer, Nested Tables—No Spacers, and Single Table—No Spacers. A 1-Pixel Transparent Spacer is an image that is 1 pixel high. This setting forces the table cells to be the width of the pixel. Nested Tables creates tables within tables to achieve a desired layout. This setting is preferable if you have a complicated document. Single Table—No Spacer lays out the document as a single table. Be careful when using this setting. Macromedia states that it may not display correctly in some cases. You will use this setting and see how to adjust the table cells using Dreamweaver. Wrapping up this tab is the Empty Cells area with the Cell Color checkbox and the Contents text box. Cell Color determines the background color of any empty cell. Use the default of Use canvas color. The Contents field allows you to choose how an empty cell is held open to insert content in another application. Your choices are None, Spacer Image, and Non-Breaking Space. None stands a risk of being collapsed when you want to do further editing. Spacer Image adds a 1-Pixel transparent GIF, and Non-Breaking Space uses a series of the HTML   entities in row. Empty Cells are only created when you don't have Fireworks set to include areas without slices, so you can ignore it.

4. The Document Specific tab allows you to adjust how Fireworks labels files upon output. It is usually best to leave this tab as it is.

After you have adjusted all of your settings, click OK. You are returned to the Export window. Once here, navigate to your *FireworksWeb* folder that you created in the beginning of the Fireworks section of this book, and click the Save button.

You have now published your first HTML document. Follow the same process for *categories.png*, only this time choose Nested Tables—No Spacers in the HTML Setup Table tab.

SUMMARY

This chapter concludes the coverage of Fireworks MX 2004. As you can see, there is nothing quite like it on the market. You won't find many applications that are created so specifically for creating Web graphics. It's now time to move toward Dreamweaver MX 2004. But before delving into that, let's take a brief interlude and see where it all comes from with "An HTML Primer."

13 An HTML Primer

Ｗe have learned about Flash MX, FreeHand MX, and Fireworks MX, and will look at Dreamweaver MX in upcoming chapters. Now let's pause and explore the past.

HISTORY OF HTML

The Hyper Text Markup Language (HTML) is the primary language used for the Web today. Although many technologies are available, HTML is the glue that ties all these components together. It took many years before HTML was created, with several steps along the way.

GML and SGML—The Origin

It all started with SGML, or Standardized General Markup Language. SGML is what is known as a meta markup language. In other words, its job is not to format data but to describe it.

In the late 1960s, it was common practice among large publishers to format every piece of data as a specific format name. This system worked, but it was dependant on having specific programming and equipment that understood the instructions. Stanley Rice, a New York book designer, suggested that a universal catalog of editorial structure tags be created. Instead of a specific instruction, a term such as *heading* could be used. The specialized equipment, in turn, could translate the universal terms into the formatting available.

Another individual who was influential to the concept of separating information from format was William Tunnicliffe, chairman of the Graphic Communications Association (GCA) Composition Committee. He brought up this topic in a meeting at the Canadian Government Printing Office in 1967. The committee adopted this principle and developed GenCode.

Charles Goldfarb, leading an IBM research project, created the Generalized Markup Language (GML) with the assistance of Edward Mosher and Raymond Lorie.

By 1980, the first working draft of SGML, based on GML, was published, and by 1983, it began to be adopted by the United States Internal Revenue Service and Department of Defense.

On to HTML and the WWW

The development of SGML was running almost parallel with the growth of the Internet. The Internet had unlimited potential because of its capability to connect millions of computers into a giant worldwide network, but it was essentially incomplete. No Web browsers existed at this point, and no way was available for documents to be posted and viewed. If you wanted a document, you had to download it to your hard drive and use the proper application to open it.

The World Wide Web and HTML were created to overcome this major limitation. Tim Berners-Lee, a scientist at CERN (l'Organisation Européenne pour la Recherche Nucléaire [European Organization for Nuclear Research]) invented the World Wide Web in 1990. He also created HTML as a language to work with the Web. A copy of the original HTML draft can be found on the World Wide Web Consortium Web site at *www.w3.org/History/1991-WWW-NeXT/Implementation/HyperText.m.*

The driving principle behind the Web is hypertext and the all-important link. Hypertext is the principle of combining pieces of text and images to complete whole documents with relationships. It is very similar to how people think—starting with one thread of thought and then drifting to a related thought as conclusions are formulated. Using the principle of hypertext turns the Web into an almost living entity.

Hypertext uses standard referencing mechanisms as its model, like dictionaries and footnotes in scientific notation. The truly revolutionary principle within is not only having the capability to have a footnote on the bottom of a page forcing the user to seek out a referenced document, but actually *linking* it to the document with a simple click.

HTML STRUCTURE

As a language, HTML uses a system of programming called *tags*. Tags are contained within angle brackets: <tag>. Two elements are available within the angle brackets: the tag name and attributes, which further define the tag. (Not all tags have attributes, and they are not always required.) Values are used to define attributes as follows:

```
<tagname attributename="value">
```

Two basic types of tag are used: *closing* and *empty*. Tags that close have both an opening and closing tag with a slash before the tag name in the closing tag (`<tag>Content</tag>`) and content in between. Empty tags have only a single opening tag.

Core Tags

The highest level of structure in HTML contains the core tags. These tags are required to have an HTML document. Starting at the top, you have what is often referred to as the *root tag*: `<html>Page Content</html>`. All information within the Web page must be contained within the opening and closing `<html>`.

Usually placed directly after the opening `<html>` is the opening `<head>` tag. The head of the document is for all information not displayed on the page. The most well-known item within is the `<title>` tag, which displays the title of the document in the top of the browser window. The `<title>` tag is not mandatory but should always be used. The title is the most basic information used by search engines to describe your page. Without it, you see your page listed as Untitled Document, which is considered unprofessional, so treat the title as an essential tag.

Other uses for the head section of the document are for `<meta>` tag, which gives further information about the page in addition to instructions for the browser, such as redirection and the language in which the document should be read. `<meta>` tags can be seen as information about the document itself rather than the content within.

Over time, Dynamic HTML (DHTML) was created. It is not a specification itself but rather a term describing the use of multiple technologies to extend Web pages. The most notable components of DHTML are JavaScript and Cascading Style Sheets. JavaScript is a client-side scripting technology (it runs in the user's browser) that helps pages be more interactive with effects such as images that swap when the user's mouse hovers over them. Cascading Style Sheets were developed to give more formatting options to HTML and to separate the formatting from the content. Both of these references are often found in the `<head>` of the document so that they load first and are always available during the life of the page.

Following the closing `<head>` tag is the opening `<body>` tag. The body of the document is where you find all information that is displayed on the Web page. If you want information to be seen by the user, it must be inside the opening and closing `<body>` tags. The basic structure of an HTML document follows:

```
<html>
    <head>
        <title></title>
    </head>
    <body>
    </body>
</html>
```

With the basic tags, you have a Web page. It won't be much to look at because it is totally blank, but you always have these tags on your page as a basic template.

White Space, Comments, and Case

In HTML, white space is generally ignored. What this means is that the code listed previously could just as easily been written as `<html><head><title></title></head><body></body></html>` with no ill effects.

There are two camps on this issue, both of which have sound arguments. The first set of designers and developers feels that putting some degree of space between elements makes the code far easier to read and thus more approachable. If an error occurs on a line and only so much content is on the line, it is easier to track the error, unlike in a file where the entire page is one giant line. Pages can be quite long as more and more elements are added.

The second set feels that although white space is generally ignored, it must be parsed. This theory is correct because the browser must go through the code to determine what to do with it—even white space. This parsing does cause a slight penalty in performance on the page, but it is usually negligible.

We can compromise between the two thoughts by breaking up the code into line breaks, but use no more than one line break between tags. This way, we can read the code more easily but still be able to see more of it at once without scrolling. If you want, you could delete all white space after the page is proven functional, but not before.

HTML comments must also be addressed. Comments are used to add notes to code and can be referenced later. They are available in the source but are invisible to the users.

Comments are an invaluable tool and should be used in any form of programming. By using them, you can note what you are trying to accomplish in a certain area of a document or script. It may seem silly because developers are so possessed with the creation of the page at the time that it seems they will never forget what was intended—but who would remember all of the programming a year or two later?

One comment is available in HTML, and it works for both a single line and multiple lines. An HTML comment starts with a left-angle bracket, an exclamation point (commonly referred to as a "bang" in programmingese), and followed with two dashes. The text of the comment follows and is closed with two dashes and a right-angle bracket:

```
<!-- I'm an HTML comment,
  so you can't
see me on the page -->
```

The last thing to discuss is case. Throughout all HTML standards (1–4.01), using uppercase or lowercase text did not matter. It was common practice for developers to use all uppercase for their HTML tags and lowercase for scripts so they could more easily differentiate between them. Times have changed, and with the use of XHTML coming into practice (XHTML is covered later in this chapter), lowercase should always be used.

Block-Level Tags

Let's jump into the body of the document by looking at block-level tags. Block-level tags are larger-level tags that contain major content like headings, paragraphs, and lists, to name a few. Let's look at a basic HTML document:

```
<html>
    <head>
        <title>A Basic Web Page</title>
    </head>
    <body>
        A Basic Web Page
    </body>
</html>
```

Open your favorite text editor and type the preceding code. If you are using Notepad, you must select All Files in the drop-down menu in the Save As dialog box and type *sample.html* in the File Name text box. If you are using a Macintosh, use TextEdit. The issues in a Macintosh are a bit more complicated. First, make sure that you choose Format > Make Plain Text. When you are prompted to Convert Document to Plain Text?, click OK. When you save the document, click File > Save As. Then, in the drop-down menu that reads Western (Mac OS Roman), select Unicode (UTF-16). Make sure you uncheck Hide extension and save the file as *sample.html*. When the dialog box prompting you to Save Plain Text opens, click Don't Append. This option causes the document to be saved as an HTML page.

Make certain you use an actual text editor. A word processing program like Microsoft Word should never be used because it adds extra information that can cause issues with the HTML file when it is displayed.

The point of all of this trouble is to show how any text editor can be used to write HTML. That flexibility is one of the great benefits of HTML—it was designed to be written with any basic text editor. The code you typed results in the page shown in Figure 13.1.

This page is a great start, but notice that you have nothing more than plain text reading "A Basic Web Page." The Web page is displaying exactly what we have told it. The title of the page is A Basic Web Page, as seen in the top of the window. The text on the page reads the same thing, but it doesn't stand out. This brings you to

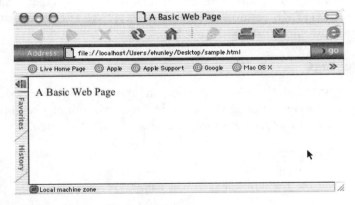

FIGURE 13.1   A basic Web page.

the first block-level tag, the heading. Six levels of headings are displayed with the tags <h1> through <h6>. The results of these tags are shown in Figure 13.2.

You will notice right away that after the <h4> tag, the headings are smaller than the normal text of A Basic Web Page. This decrease in size is by design. Although the headings may be smaller, they still stand out. Also notice how each heading (no matter how small or large) is on its own line. This is because headings are block-level elements, meaning they literally take up a imaginary block running across the page. By default, nothing coexists on the same line. (Exceptions, like images, are covered later.)

The next block-level tag is the paragraph tag, denoted by <p>, which, according to original HTML standards has an optional closing tag. When a paragraph is used, the block of text has an empty space, one line deep, separating it from the previous paragraph or text, similar to double-spaced text in a word processor.

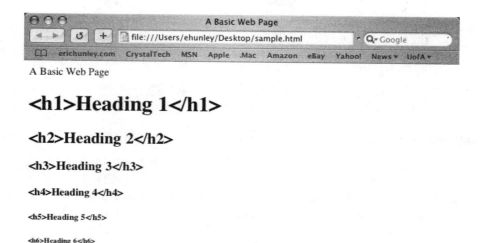

FIGURE 13.2   The six heading levels available.

An alternative to a paragraph is the `<blockquote>` tag. A block quote causes a block of text to be indented on both sides with space above and below. Figure 13.3 shows the results of `<p>` and a `<blockquote>` on a page.

A common block-level element used to visually separate content on a page is the `<hr>` (horizontal rule) tag. This tag simply creates a visible line across the page with space above and below.

FIGURE 13.3   Comparing paragraphs and block quotes.

The last block-level element discussed is the <pre> tag. The <pre> tag stands for preformatted text and is unique in that it is the one tag that uses spaces put in by the designer. Although the typical behavior of HTML is to strip all white space and line returns, save one space, <pre> makes use of these. When you place content within an opening and closing <pre> tag, the browser renders it using a monospace font by default, and all your spaces, tabs, and line returns are preserved.

Introducing Attributes

Within HTML, tags are further defined with attributes. If no attributes are defined, you are leaving the formatting up to the browser, which will act in its default manner. This is why all of the formatting tags we have created so far are left-aligned. Left alignment is the default browser behavior for these block-level tags.

Attributes are declared after the tag name as shown:

```
<tag attribute="value">
```

Let's begin by looking at the tags we have been working with—the block-level tags. When dealing with block-level tags, your main attribute is alignment. You have three choices: left, right, and center. Left is the usual default when dealing with block-level tags and is often considered the easiest to read with long blocks of text.

Figure 13.4 is your sample page with different values applied to the `align` attribute.

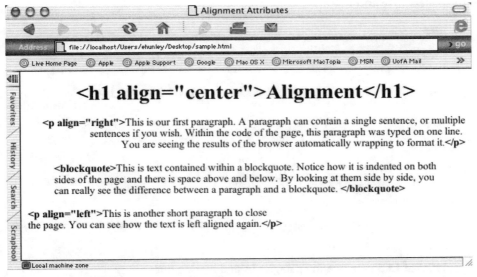

FIGURE 13.4 Using the `align` attribute on block-level tags.

The `<div>` Tag

When you must align multiple elements on a page that share the same value, it can be rather tedious to state the attribute inside each one. This is where the `<div>` tag can be handy. Surrounding all of the block-level elements with one `<div>` tag affects all of them at once. You can override the `<div>` tag on a single element if you want to have it aligned differently. The following code taken from your sample Web page demonstrates the principle:

```
<html>
    <head>
        <title>Alignment Attributes</title>
    </head>
    <body>

        <div align="center">

        <h1>Alignment Principles</h1>
        <h2>Looking at the Div tag</h2>
        <p align="left">This is our first paragraph. A
paragraph can contain a single sentence, or multiple
sentences if you want. Within the code of the page,
this paragraph was typed on one line. You are seeing
the results of the browser automatically wrapping to
format it.</p>

        </div>

    </body>
</html>
```

Notice in the example how the paragraph has an `align="left"` attribute? By explicitly stating that the paragraph is left-aligned, the attribute overrides the `<div>` tag. You can think of this as a rule of specificity, or that which is closest to the text wins. Because the `align` attribute is within the `<p>` tag surrounding the text, it is closer to the content reflected in the paragraph and wins.

Line-Level Elements

The next level of element examined is the line-level element. Line-level elements are used to manipulate words within a block-level element. Whereas block-level tags affect larger areas, such as an entire element, line-level tags are more finite. They can be used to change a single word or several words.

The key thing to remember about line-level elements is that they can never be placed around a block-level element—this breaks the nesting rules within HTML. The browser may display the content correctly (browsers are made to be forgiving), but the pages are invalid. If you want an entire block-level element to be modified with a line-level tag, place the opening line-level tag just after the opening block-level tag, then close it immediately before the closing block-level element.

Two of the most popular line-level elements are bold and italic, which are represented as `<b>content</b>` and `<i>content</i>`, respectively. However, they really are not the proper choice for HTML. The proper tag to use for bolding a section of text is `<strong>`; use `<em>` (emphasize) for italic. These tags are compatible with screen readers. Screen readers often ignore `<b>` and `<i>` tags but will stress the content between `<strong>` and `<em>` appropriately for vision-impaired visitors to your Web site.

Another popular line-level tag is the `<font>` tag. The `<font>` tag is interesting because it has no effect on text. It requires attributes to further define how it affects your content. The two most popular attributes are `size` and `color`. Seven sizes are available within HTML, appropriately named 1 through 7, representing 20-percent increments. They are referred to in either a relative or an absolute manner.

Relative uses +/− the number that it is relative to the current font size. For example, if you want to have a font appear to be one size larger than the default, type `<font size="+1">`. This attribute causes the selected content to be 20-percent larger than the current size. Figure 13.5 displays the results of font sizing.

It is important to avoid using too small of a font because it is difficult for users to read. The user's platform can also cause issues. Fonts appear smaller on Macintosh computers because they use 72 dpi (dots per inch) as the default resolution versus the 96 dpi on Windows machines.

Font color can be determined by using one of two methods: name or RGB value. When declaring a color by name, you must declare one of the 16 known colors that can be displayed in any browser on any platform. These colors are Aqua, Black, Blue, Fuchsia, Gray, Green, Lime, Maroon, Navy, Olive, Purple, Red, Silver, Teal, White, and Yellow. A known color is declared as `<font color="black">`, for example. Other nonstandard names may work in some browsers, but they are not displayed in all browsers on all platforms.

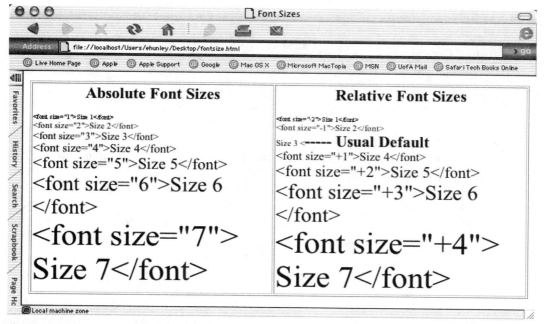

FIGURE 13.5 Absolute and relative font sizing.

The second method of declaring a font color value is by defining its RGB attributes. RGB stands for Red, Green, Blue, and the hexadecimal number represents how much of each is used to display the color. The color is declared with a preceding # (hashmark) followed by the RGB value, as in `<font color="#000000">` (the RGB value for black). The # is a flag denoting that the upcoming information is in a hexadecimal format.

The `<font>` *tag has been officially deprecated by the W3C (World Wide Web Consortium) and will be removed from a future version of XHTML. The preferred method of coloring and sizing text is with Cascading Style Sheets. This chapter discusses the* `<font>` *tag only for familiarity when exploring and revising current Web sites.*

NOTE

The last line-level tag discussed is the line-break tag, `<br>`. This tag is used at line level on any block-level element to cause a line of text to be broken to the next line. It differs from a `<p>` tag in that it is at the line level and breaks only to the next line, whereas a `<p>` tag adds an empty line of space between elements. It is a useful tag when you want to have items displayed without extra space between them, such as for a contact information block.

The <img> Tag

The <img>, or image tag, has enough importance that it is explored separately. Like the <font> tag, without attributes, <img> has no functionality on its own. Common attributes used with the <img> are src (source), align, width, height, and alt (alternate text).

The src attribute is arguably the most important attribute because it is used to give the browser the path to the actual image. Because the image is not text, it cannot be embedded directly on the page. When you give the browser the source information, it retrieves the image separately, then places it on the page where you have declared it with the <img> tag. The source of the image can be local (on the same server as the page) or remote (another Web site or location). When you choose a remote image, you must include the protocol (usually *http://*) in the path, or the image will not load correctly. For example, you would use the syntax <img src="http://www.domainname.com/imagefilename.ext" >. The *http://* flags the browser, letting it know that the image is not stored in the Web server filesystem and that it must go back out to the Internet and retrieve it.

The align attribute, when used with an image, is different from what we saw with block-level tags like <h1>–<h6> and <p>. First, only two values are available—left and right—because where the other block-level elements align to the actual page, images align to the text that follows them.

The default behavior of an image is to be placed on the page as a block-level element with no text around it. The first window in Figure 13.6 demonstrates this. If you want the image to have the text after it wrap to it, use the align attribute. The second window in Figure 13.6 shows the result of <img src="images/mtgoat.jpg" align="left">. Notice how the image is placed to the left of the text.

Now let's look at the width and height attributes of the <img> tag. It is sometimes thought that width and height can be used to resize images on the page to make them larger or smaller. This is untrue. Although width and height can cause an image to appear as a different size on the page, they do not change the physical file size of the image.

When width and height are used in an attempt to make an image appear larger, pixelation occurs, which does not look good. On the opposite note, if width and height are used to shrink an image, the image will appear clear, but the physical size still does not change. Therefore, a large image displayed at a small size makes the page load just as slowly as if it were displayed at its full size. If you want to resize an image, use a graphics application to modify it, not the browser.

Image width and height attributes should be considered as placeholders for the browser. This practice gives the user a better experience. If width and height are not used, the browser loads all of the text in a tight block, then retrieves the image and

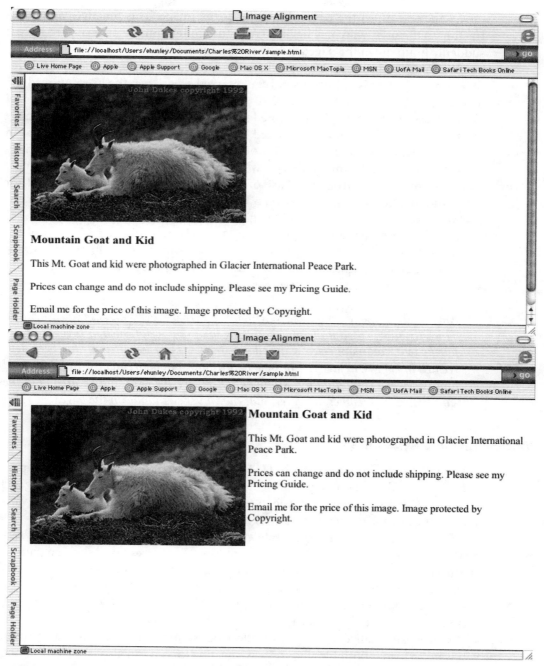

FIGURE 13.6 Using the `align` attributes with images.

moves the text down the page while it loads the image. This practice can be distracting to the user, who may begin to read the content on the page only to have it suddenly jump down the page when the image appears.

When `width` and `height` are used for the image, the space for the image is reserved, and the text is placed around the reserved area. Then the user can read the text without having it suddenly moved.

The last `<img>` tag attribute covered is `alt`. Often called an *alt tag* (it's actually an attribute), it is frequently overlooked. You use the `alt` attribute to display text in place of a picture, in case the user is not displaying images. This text is especially important for visually impaired users who cannot see the image but should know what the content is (through the use of a screen reader). It is also important for users who may be viewing the page on other devices or have a poor bandwidth connection. These users often turn off images to load the pages more quickly.

In either case, the text you put in the `alt` attribute is displayed instead of the image. This text is also displayed when a user mouses over the image in most browsers. The syntax of the tag including `alt` is something like `<img src="images/filename.ext" width="100" height="100" alt="Another description of the picture.">`.

Another attribute commonly used with images is `name`, *or its modern equivalent* `id`. *This attribute is used if the image is going to have a script, such as JavaScript, referring to it, commonly seen with rollover images. The* `name` *attribute has been deprecated in HTML in favor of the new* `id` *attribute, but both can be used for forward and backward compatibility. Many designers give the* `name` *and* `id` *attributes the same value. Remember, however, that they must be unique on the page.*

Anchor Tags and Hyperlinks

Possibly the most important tag in HTML is the anchor tag, `<a>`. It is how hyperlinks are created. Without hyperlinks, the Web would be nothing more than a giant hard disk with no real connectivity between files. Three primary attributes are available for the anchor tag: `href`, `name`, and `id`.

The `href` attribute is used to create a link. The syntax used for hyperlinks is formatted as `<a href="filepath.html">Linked text or image</a>`. As with a path to an image, you can refer to a local or remote file. Three types of reference are available: remote or absolute path, local-document relative, and local-root relative.

A remote link must have the entire path, including the *http://*. As with images, these characters flag the browser to go out to the Internet.

A local path relative to the document can be as simple as the filename of the page you want to load if both files live in the same directory. It can also involve climbing up and down directories to find the file. The format is to use `../` for every parent directory (directory above the current) and then the path back down if there is any.

For example, if the current file lives in `siteroot/products/product1/support/page.html`, but the image is located at `siteroot/images/imagename.ext`, you could call it from the document using the path `../../../images/imagename.ext`. This code tells the browser to go up three directories, then into *images*, and select the file. The process using this type of relative path is commonly known as *bottom-up*.

The alternative is to path off of the root with a method known as *top-down*. This method involves using a preceding / (slash) in the path. A preceding slash tells the browser to go all the way to the root of the site. Using the previous example, the path would be `/images/imagename.ext`. This method is useful if you use the same image or link in multiple locations throughout the site because the path is location independent.

When you are pointing to a page outside of your current Web site, it is often popular to use the `target` attribute. The `target` attribute comes from frames and has four values: `_self`, `_blank`, `_parent`, and `_top`. The first attribute, `_self`, is the default. It simply tells the browser to load the new page into the current browser window. Next is `_blank`, which tells the browser to load the new page into a new browser window. Your current page is still open in the current window.

Then is `_parent`, which is used with frames. In frames, your window may be split into multiple panes, with one controlling the others. This pane is known as the *parent frame*. When you select the value of `_parent`, the new page loads into the parent frame.

The last value is `_top`. This target breaks the frameset and loads the new page in the current window, with all panes disappearing.

With standard Web pages, you would only consider using `_blank`, which loads the content into a new window. This target is popular if you want to link to an external Web site. This way, if the users close the window with the external site, your site is still there.

The syntax for adding the target attribute is `<a href="http://www.externalsite.com/" target="_blank">Linked text or Image</a>`.

When you decide to use an image instead of text to place your link, simply drop in an image tag where you would place your clickable text like this: `<a href="newpage.html"><img src="imagename.ext"></a>`. An issue you may encounter is that a blue border surrounds an image by default when using a link (much the same as text is underlined). You can stop this by adding a `border` attribute to the `<img>` tag as follows:

```
<a href="newpage.html"><img src="imagename.ext" border="0"></a>.
```

The other main attribute used with an anchor tag is the `name` or `id`. Whereas `href` can be thought of as a pointer to another location, `name` or `id` can be thought of as a target. This method is especially popular for navigating long Web pages, such as FAQs (Frequently Asked Questions). It is used in combination with an `<a href="">` to be fully functional.

The process works when you surround content lower on the page with `<a name=`
`"chosenname" id="chosenname">Content</a>`. The `name` or `id` you give the tag must be
a single word or multiple words with a dash or underscore tying them together.

On the upper part of the page, create a pointer to your target in the following
manner: `<a href="#chosenname">Linked Text or Image</a>`. Notice the #. This is a
flag to the browser stating that the link is internal to the page. It can also be pointed
to an internal link on another page by using the syntax of `<a href="otherpage`
`.html#chosenname">Linked Text or Image</a>`. Figure 13.7 displays the use of hyperlink types.

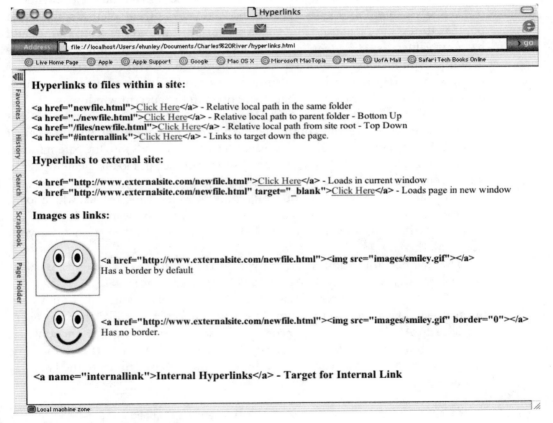

FIGURE 13.7 A look at hyperlinks.

Some confusion exists over the use of name *or* id *as an attribute. The* name *attribute
has been deprecated and will be removed in the future. The main issue, however,
is that* id *is a new attribute and is not supported by many older browsers. The rec-
ommendation is to use both in the same tag for maximum compatibility.*

A Look at Lists

In the modern world, pithiness has become a standard. Rather than writing long passages in these days of sound bites, short concise comments are popular. Bullet statements have entered nearly every environment, and HTML allows their creation in the format of lists. Three list types are available in HTML: unordered (bulleted), ordered (numbers and letters), and definition lists (term and definitions).

Let's first look at unordered lists. Unordered lists come in three character types: bullets (now called *discs*), open circles, and squares. The default is the bullet character. Unlike the tags we looked at previously, lists involve more than one tag. You first use the overall list tag. In the case of an unordered list, it is `<ul>`. Then you need to tag the items in the list. For both unordered and ordered lists, that is `<li>`. The overall code required to make an unordered list is:

```
<ul>
     <li>Item 1</li>
     <li>Item 2</li>
     <li>Item 3</li>
</ul>
```

This code makes a three-item bulleted list. To make an ordered list with the default values of numbers 1, 2, 3, use the `<ol>` tag as shown:

```
<ol>
     <li>Item 1</li>
     <li>Item 2</li>
     <li>Item 3</li>
</ol>
```

If you want to change your list type, use the `type` attribute. The different `type` attributes follow:

`<ul type="disc">` (previously was `bullet`, but the term has been deprecated): Available for unordered lists. It creates a solid circle. This is the default unordered list type.

`<ul type="circle">`: Available for unordered lists. Creates a hollow circle.

`<ul type="square">`: Available for unordered lists. Creates a solid square.

`<ol type="1">`: Available for ordered lists. Creates numbers next to each item. This is the default ordered list type.

`<ol type="A">`: Available for ordered lists. Creates an uppercase letter sequence.

`<ol type="a">`: Available for ordered lists. Creates a lowercase letter sequence.

`<ol type="I">`: Available for ordered lists. Creates an uppercase roman numeral sequence.

`<ol type="i">`: Available for ordered lists. Creates a lowercase roman numeral sequence.

As you can see, multiple options are available with ordered and unordered lists. Let's look at another important attribute, start. When you have a large ordered list and must interrupt it with other content, how do you get the list to resume where you left off? That is where the start attribute comes in.

To use this attribute, populate your list with items until you come to the point where new content is added to the page. Close your list. Add your content, then create a new ordered list with the start attribute reflecting the number with which to resume counting. This attribute works with all types of lists. For example, if you leave off on the letter *D*, set your start attribute to equal 5, and the new list will begin on the letter *E*. An example follows:

```
<ol type="A">
    <li>Item A</li>
    <li>Item B</li>
    <li>Item C</li>
    <li>Item D</li>
</ol>
<p> New content needed on the page.</p>
<ol type="A" start="5">
    <li>Item E</li>
    <li>Item F</li>
    <li>Item G</li>
</ol>
```

The unordered/ordered list item discussed next is the nested list. A nested list is a list within a list. Be careful when using these types of lists because it can be confusing to make sure you follow the nesting rules properly. A nested list must be declared within the open and close of a list item. An example of a nested list follows:

```
<ol type="I">
    <li>Item I
        <ol type="A">
            <li>Item A</li>
            <li>Item B</li>
            <li>Item C</li>
        </ol>
    </li>
    <li>Item II</li>
```

```
<li>Item III
    <ol type="A">
        <li>Item A</li>
        <li>Item B</li>
        <li>Item C</li>
    </ol>
</li>
</ol>
```

Notice in the example that Item I and Item III each have a list within them, whereas Item II does not. Item I and Item III do not have the `</li>` until after the `</ol>` of the sublist within. This is how you can create an outline format. Figure 13.8 shows the results of multiple ordered and unordered lists.

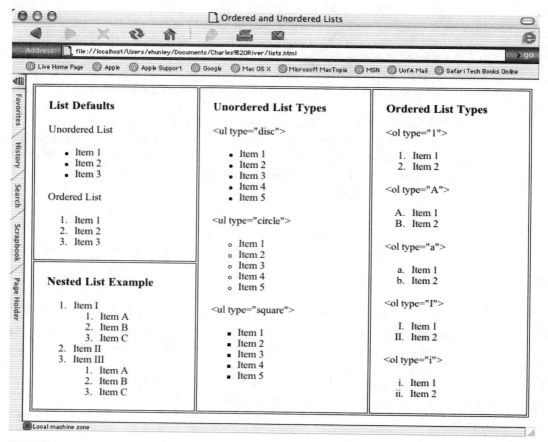

FIGURE 13.8 Looking at ordered and unordered lists.

The last list type covered is the definition list, creatively tagged <dl>. The definition list differs from the other lists in that it uses three tags. The first tag is the <dl>, which starts off the list. Next we have the <dt> (definition term) tag, which is aligned to the left of the page. Last is the <dd> (definition description), which is indented from the <dt>. This list type is commonly used with the <b>, or preferably the <strong> tag around the content in the <dt> to bold the definition term.

A Look at Tables

Tables could be considered the designer's best friend. Using everything we have learned up to this point, you may have discovered that you don't have much control over layout on a page. This is where tables come in. Prior to the use of tables, the only layout mechanism available was the <pre> tag and align attributes in images and block-level elements. Although these attributes may work to a degree, they have nowhere near the power available with tables.

Every table opens with an appropriately named <table> tag. Within this tag, you have <tr> (table rows) tags, which hold rows of <td> (table data cells) tags, which hold the actual content. You can also use <th> (table header cells) tags instead of <td> tags on the first row in the table if you want the text to be centered and bolded by default.

Other technologies, like layers with CSS (Cascading Style Sheets), have been written as a replacement for tables, but for forward and backward compatibility, you can't beat tables for formatting. Tables contain both rows (<tr>) and cells (<td>) for laying out all of your content, with the basic structure being:

```
<table>
    <tr>
        <td>Actual Content</td>
        <td>More Content</td>
    </tr>
</table>
```

Tables contain rows, which in turn contain cells or headers. Cells contain all of the content. They can contain not only any element on a page we have seen so far but even other tables, using a method called *nested tables*. Figure 13.9 shows basic and nested tables.

As you can see from Figure 13.9, a nested table is nothing more than a table within a cell of another table. Let's now look at some table attributes.

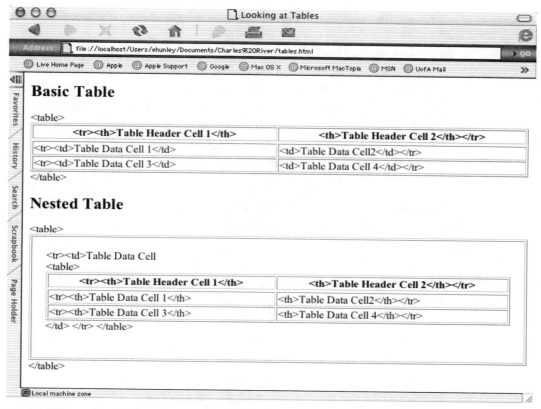

FIGURE 13.9 A look at basic and nested tables.

Attributes of `<table>`

align: Determines how the table is aligned on the page. Values are left, right, and center. This attribute has been deprecated in preference to CSS.

bgcolor: Specifies the background color of the table.

cellpadding: Specifies how much space surrounds the content within a cell.

cellspacing: Specifies the amount of space between cells.

border: Specifies if a border appears around all the cells in a table and how thick it is.

Attributes of `<tr>`

align: Aligns data within all cells in a row unless overwritten by `<td align="">`. Values are left, right, and center.

bgcolor: Adds a background color to all cells within a row.

valign: Affects the vertical alignment of data in cells within a row. Possible values include top, bottom, middle, and baseline. The default is middle. This attribute is one of the most valuable available in table rows and cells. With the default being middle, sometimes when you place content on a Web page with an image in one cell and text in an adjoining cell, you may encounter some problems. You may want the top of the image to align with the top of the text in the next cell, but when you add text that is longer than the height of the image, the image floats down the page. By setting the `valign` attribute to `top` in either the `<tr>` or `<td>` tag, all of the data stays aligned at the top of the cells, effectively stopping the drift.

Attributes of `<td>`

align: Aligns data within cells. Values are left, right, and center.

bgcolor: Adds a background color to cells.

colspan: Allows a cell to extend beyond its normal width to encompass however many cells are declared.

height: Provides the browser with a recommended height. This attribute has been deprecated.

rowspan: Acts in the same manner as `colspan`, only for rows.

valign: Affects the vertical alignment of data in cells. Possible values include top, bottom, middle, and baseline. The default is middle.

width: Provides the browser with a recommended width. This attribute has been deprecated.

With the availability of multiple attributes within the three primary tags making up tables, you have a great deal of control over content. Tables with attributes are shown in Figure 13.10.

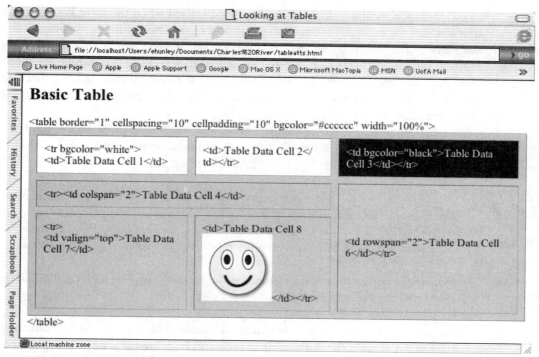

FIGURE 13.10   Adding table attributes.

Exploring Forms

The last HTML element covered is the form. Forms are the only way to collect input from a user in standard HTML and are extremely important for any type of e-commerce site.

Like many other tags, forms open with the self-explanatory `<form>` tag. The form is a major element that can contain multiple elements, including tables, but they cannot contain other forms. Tables often are used to format the form fields with the text in a neat manner. The form has several attributes. Among the most important are the `name`/`id`, `action`, and `method` attributes. The `name` attribute is important because the form is not an independent entity; it works in conjunction with another script or program, which is often expecting data from a form of a particular `name` or `id`. The `name` attribute has been left in for backward compatibility.

The `action` attribute identifies the path to the script that will handle the contents of the form. It is initiated when the Submit button is pressed.

The method attribute dictates what method is used when the form is submitted to a script. Two methods are available: get and post. The get method appends the contents of the form to the end of the URL when the form is submitted. This method is not secure. URLs requested are added to server log files, which are often available over the Internet. The get method must never be used when collecting personal or financial information from users. This is the default method, so if you don't explicitly state post, get is used.

The alternative is the post method. The post method is more secure than get because it sends the information in the body of the document and not the URL. It can also send more information than the get method can.

Although the get *method is less secure, it is not always a bad method to use. Most search engines use the* get *method for searches. This method allows them to parse the server log files to find out what search terms are more popular so they can optimize their service. The key thing to remember is to never use* get *if security is involved.*

Within the form, your main element is the `<input>` tag. The input is defined by the type attribute. Several type attributes follow:

`<input type="text" name="fieldname">`: Creates a basic text field for collecting user input. This is the default input type and is created if type is not specified. Other attributes available with this type are width, which is the visible character width of the field, and maxlength, that sets a limit on the amount of characters the user can input.

`<input type="password" name="fieldname">`: Acts in the same manner as a text field, but the input is displayed as asterisks to prevent someone from reading over the user's shoulder.

`<input type="checkbox" name="fieldname" value="assignedvalue">`: Collects multiple predefined options. The name attribute is critical for this input type because related checkboxes share the same name. The value is determined by the developer to represent what each checkbox will return. If you want to have one of the checkboxes preselected, you can use the checked="checked" attribute on the desired checkbox.

`<input type="radio name="fieldname" value="assignedvalue">`: Similar to the checkbox, but restricts the user's choice to only one. To have one option button preselected, use the checked="checked" attribute.

`<input type="submit value="label">`: Creates the specialized Submit button. This type works in conjunction with the form action and method. When it is pressed, all data in the form is collected into a list and sent to the script URL listed in the action. The `name` attribute is not as critical on this element because its primary function is just to submit rather than pass any data on its own. You can use the `value` attribute to change what the label on the button reads. Otherwise, it reads whatever the browser default is, usually Submit or Submit Form.

`<input type="image name="fieldname" src="imagename.ext" alt="Alternate Text">`: Makes an image act as a Submit button. It can take normal image attributes; and the `alt` attribute should be used.

`<input type="reset value="label">`: Clears all user input on the form when clicked. Again, you can use the `value` attribute to relabel the button.

`<input type="button value="label"`: Creates a basic push button. The `value` attribute is used to give it a label. Another script is usually tied to it.

`<input type="hidden name="fieldname">`: Passes information that you don't want to be seen on the form. This can prove valuable for controlling form input.

Let's now look at another tag available within forms, `<textarea>`. The `<textarea>` tag is handy for when you want to have a greater amount of user input in a field. It can also be used to display text in a smaller area on a page because it creates scroll bars when the text extends beyond the height of the box. The format for the text area is a bit different in that it requires a separate closing tag, even if you do not have text in it. Its basic format is `<textarea></textarea>`.

The text area has the following attributes to define how it is displayed and what can be entered:

name: Assigns a name to the element for association with the data.

rows: Specifies how many visible lines are in the box.

cols: Specifies the width of the box in characters.

readonly: Makes the text area read-only. This attribute is useful if you don't want the user to be able to enter data, such as when you want the text area to only display content.

The last tag discussed in forms is `<select>`. It is used in different tasks. The first task is to create a menu in which the user can select either one or multiple items, depending on whether you choose the `multiple="multiple"` attribute. This field is useful for when you have a long list of selections from which to choose, such as a list of U.S. state postal abbreviations. You can have all 50 entries in a field that takes up only one line. A portion of the code to accomplish this follows:

```
<select name="state">
  <option>AL</option>
```

```
    <option>AK</option>
    <option>AZ</option>
    <option>AR</option>
</select>
```

Notice the overall tag is `<select>`, and each item to select is an `<option>`. This format is similar to a list. If you want the form to display more than one item at once, you specify how many rows you want displayed by using the `size="number"` attribute. If you want to have an option to be preselected, use the `selected="selected"` attribute within the `option` tag.

You also can give the user the ability to choose more than one option by using the `multiple="multiple"` attribute as follows:

```
<select name="items" size="4" multiple="multiple">
   <option selected="selected">Item 1</option>
   <option>Item 2</option>
   <option>Item 3</option>
   <option>Item 4</option>
 </select>
```

Another option available with the `select` tag is the ability to have submenus by using the `<optgroup>` tag. Note that support for this tag is a bit spotty with browsers. Older browsers do not display the content. The basic syntax for using `<optgroup>` to create submenus follows:

```
<form name="myform" action="somescript.cgi" method="post">
    <select name="menu">
<option selected="selected">Choose One</option>
        <optgroup label="Menu 1">
            <option>Item 1</option>
            <option>Item 2</option>
            <option>Item 3</option>
        <optgroup label="Menu 2">
        <option>Item 1</option>
            <option>Item 2</option>
            <option>Item 3</option>
        <optgroup label="Menu 2">
</select>
<input type="submit" value="Send">
</form>
```

Figure 13.11 shows various options available on forms.

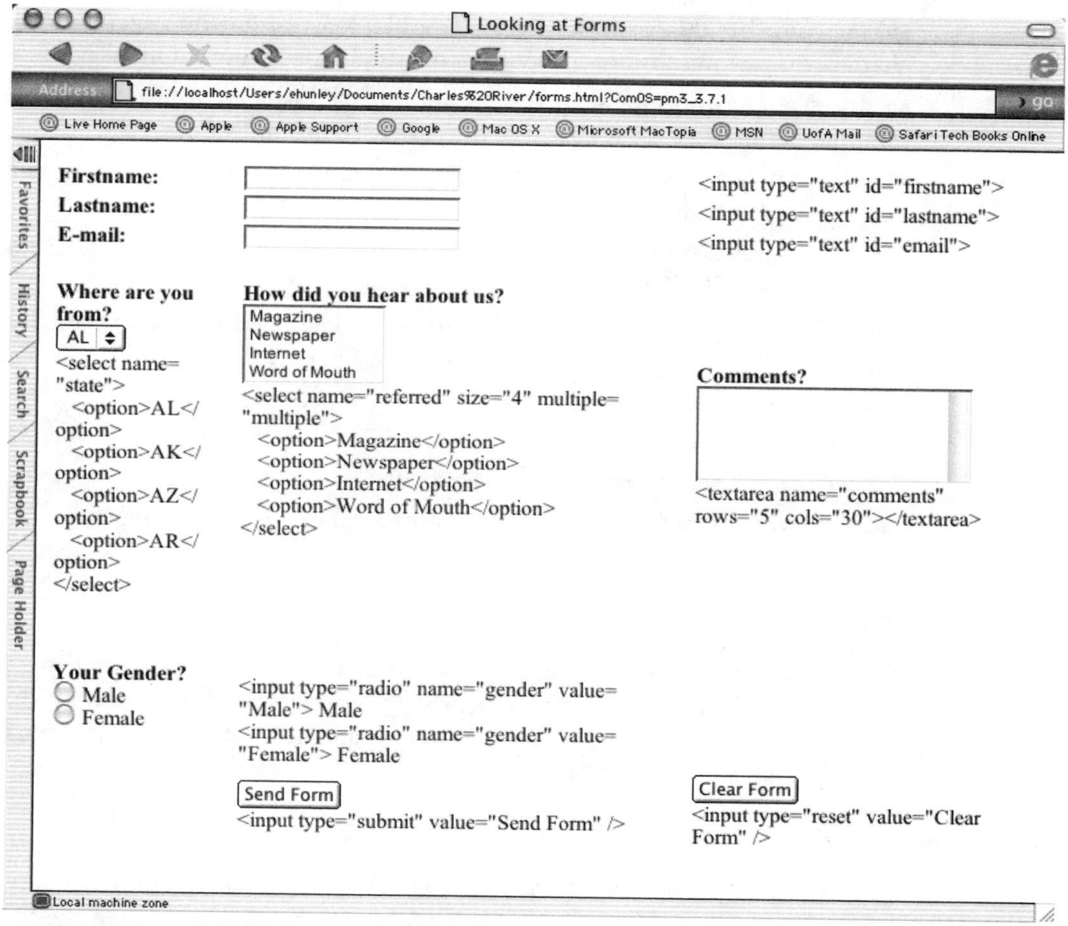

FIGURE 13.11   Looking at form elements.

HTML Special Characters

Within HTML, you sometimes need to use a character that is either not available or is already a part of the language but would cause conflicts. This is where special characters come in.

All special characters in HTML start with the ampersand (&) character, then the name or code for the character, and then end with a semicolon. An example is &, which is the special character for the &, which requires a special character because it is part of the language. A short list of some common special characters follows:

** ** (**non-breaking space**): Provides a blank space on the page. Use this character if you want more spaces than the single space allowed in HTML.

" (**straight quote**): Creates a quotation mark inside of your text. Quotation marks can cause issues because they are used around values.

< (**left-angle bracket**): Creates a less-than sign. Because this character is part of a tag, it can cause issues on the page.

> (**right-angle bracket**): Creates a greater-than sign. Like the less-than sign, it is part of an HTML tag.

& (**ampersand**): Creates an ampersand. This character is used to start special characters in HTML, so using it in text causes a conflict.

©: Creates a copyright symbol.

™: Creates a trademark symbol.

®: Creates a registered trademark symbol.

° (**degree symbol**): Creates a degree (for temperatures) symbol.

¢: Creates a cent symbol.

£: Creates a pound sterling symbol.

This list is by no means complete. A good place to look at character entity references is on the W3C Web site at *www.w3.org/MarkUp/html3/latin1.html*. This page has a listing of special characters that were available as of HTML 3 for maximum compatibility with older browsers.

Within the `<head>` Tag

As was mentioned previously, the head of the HTML document is for hidden information. The content within is usually more about the page itself than the formatting of the document. This is where you find information for search engines to help the page be listed.

Outside of the `<title>`, the most prominent tag seen in the head is `<meta>`. It is defined by its attributes and has many functions. Two main defining `<meta>` attributes are `http-equiv` and `name`.

The first attribute we will look at is `http-equiv`. This is used to act as an HTML header, or instructions to the browser on how to handle the page. Some of its popular values are:

Content-type `<meta http-equiv="Content-Type" content="text/html; charset=iso-8859-1">`: Gives information on the page type.

Refresh `<meta http-equiv="refresh" content="http://www.sitename.com/">`: Used to redirect the browser to another page.

Expires `<meta http-equiv="expires" content="Mon, 25 Aug 2003 12:00:00 GMT">`: Informs the browser when the contents of the page expire.

Pragma `<meta http-equiv="pragma" content=""no-cache">`: Prevents browsers from caching (storing a copy of) the page.

Window-target `<meta http-equiv="Window-target" content="_top">`: Prevents a browser from displaying the page within a frame.

The second attribute is the `name` attribute. It is supposed to be for content that is not related to HTTP headers. However, more and more blurring occurs in the distinction over time and with different browsers. At any rate, some of the most popular meta `name` tags follow:

Author `<meta name="author" content="Eric Hunley">`: Identifies the author of the Web page. Many HTML editors fill in this tag or use the alternative `<meta name="generator" content="toolname">`.

Description `<meta name="description" content="A sentence or two">`: Provides a description of either the company or content on the page for search engines.

Keywords `<meta name="keywords" content="word1, word2, etc.">`: Creates a comma-separated list of keywords related to the content on the page. Be careful to not use too many because some search engines interpret that as search spamming. Twenty or fewer is a fairly safe bet.

Robots `<meta name="robots" content="all">`: Instructs robots or spiders (programs used by search engines to build their databases) how the site should be handled. Several values are available:

all: Page is indexed and all links followed with subsequent pages indexed.

none: Page is not indexed and no links are to be followed.

index: Page is indexed.

noindex: Page is not indexed, but links are followed.

follow: Links are followed.

nofollow: Page is indexed, but links are not followed.

noimageindex: Images on the page are not indexed, but text may be.

noimageclick: Images are not linked directly.

Combinations: Robot values can also be combined to achieve a more granular effect, for example: `<meta name="robots" content="index, nofollow">`. This code states that the page should be indexed, but links should not be followed.

Rating `<meta name="rating" content="general">`: Adds a rating to the content on your page. Some values include `"general"`, `"14 years"`, `"mature"`, and `"restricted"`.

One of the unfortunate issues with `<meta>` tags and their attributes is that they are not consistently followed by browsers and search engines. You must be certain that you understand your audience's capability and should research up-to-date information on search engines that you want to interact (or not) with your site.

Other tags you frequently see in the head of an HTML document are script tags and links to stylesheets. The head is an ideal location for these tags because often the content of the programming must be available when the content on the page loads. The head ensures that the scripts and styles are loaded and available throughout the life of the document.

The DOCTYPE Declaration

At the top of an HTML document, you often see what is known as the DOCTYPE declaration. This item states what standard was used to write the page. It is used to validate the pages using an HTML validator and as an assistant for browsers to render the elements properly. By following the exact standards and declaring the doctype, your odds are greatly increased at having your content displayed correctly.

The DOCTYPE declaration is the first thing listed on the page before the opening `<html>` tag. An example DOCTYPE declaration follows:

```
<!DOCTYPE HTML PUBLIC "-//W3C//DTD HTML 4.01 Transitional//EN"
"http://www.w3.org/TR/html4/loose.dtd">
```

Note that the DOCTYPE declaration is case sensitive.

THE FUTURE WITH XML AND XHTML

HTML and SGML have served well over time, but they are becoming dated. New languages have been created to help overcome this effect.

XML

SGML is a powerful but complex language that has grown over the years. Due to its age, much of it seemed a bit cryptic, so the W3C put together a committee to create a subset of SGML that would have the power of SGML but more of the simplicity of HTML. This was the birth of XML.

The basic principle of XML is to separate content from formatting, or to create self-describing data. You can create your own tags to label the data in a meaningful manner. For instance, if you are making a page with contact information, you may have the following code in HTML:

```
<html>
    <head><title>Contacts</title></head>
<body>
<p><strong>Sally Smith</strong><br >
<em>Customer Service Rep</em><br>
<em><strong>Acme International</strong></em><br>
123 Main Street<br>
Anywhere, Arizona, 85733<br>
(602) 555-5252<br>
sally@acme.com</p>
</body>
</html>
```

Although this code would display adequately in a browser, we really have no picture of what the data means. The same information written in XML follows:

```
<?xml version="1.0"?>
<contacts>
    <contact>
        <lastname>Smith</lastname>
        <firstname>Sally</firstname>
        <position>Customer Service Rep</position>
        <company>Acme International</company>
        <address>123 Main Street</address>
        <city>Anywhere</city>
        <state>AZ</state>
        <phone>(602) 555-5252</phone>
        <email>sally@acme.com</email>
    </contact>
</contacts>
```

Notice how the code now has some meaning. We don't know how it will display or what will display it, but we can look at the raw data and derive meaning. This is the power of XML. Whereas HTML is all about formatting of data for display, XML is about describing the data.

By pulling out the formatting elements, the data can now be moved around to any number of applications. The data is used not only on the Web but in desktop software. This opens up sharing of data with many applications and developers. Now developers can create the data with any application they want and send it out as XML. It doesn't matter if you don't have the same program; your program just needs to know how to read the XML.

XHTML

One of the first challenges with XML was how to bridge the gap to HTML. The answer was to write an XML application based on HTML 4.01. This led to the creation of XHTML.

XHTML is based on HTML 4.01, but it follows XML syntax rules. To make the language clearer and ultimately easier to work with, XML contains very strict syntax rules.

The primary rules are that it doesn't allow tags that don't close, it is case-sensitive, and all attributes must have values within quotes. The way it affects tags from HTML follows:

Case-sensitive: All tags must be written in lowercase text.

All tags must close: This requirement is handled in two ways:

- If a tag is surrounding content, such as a `<p>`, `<li>`, or `<tr>` tag, you must put a closing tag on the end, such as `</p>`, `</li>`, or `</tr>`.
- If the tag is an empty tag, or a tag with no content on the page, you must make it self-closing. For example, a `<br>` (break) tag must now be written as `<br />`. (There must be a space between the tag name and closing slash.) Some other tags affected are `<hr />`, `<img src="imagename.ext" alt="My Image" />`, and `<input type="text" name="firstname" />`.

All attributes must have values in quotes: This requirement is handled in two ways:

- For some Boolean selections, HTML 4 allowed for short tags, as in `<input type="checkbox" name="item1" checked>`. This shortcut method is not allowed in XHTML because `checked` has no value. To properly write this tag to be XHTML compliant, you must type `<input type="checkbox" name="item1" checked="checked" />`. While the `checked="checked"` may feel redundant, it is correct because it is the only possible value available for the attribute. This attribute was already defined in HTML 4, but the language allowed the shortcut.
- In HTML 4.01, not all values required quotation marks. For example, `<td align=right width=100>` would be interpreted by a browser. In XHTML, however, all values must be within quotation marks. The preceding tag must read `<td align="right" width=100>`.

Although these rules may seem picky and tedious to follow, they actually make the language easier to work with and offer greater consistency in the pages created. For example, you could get away with not having quotation marks in some but not all values. Who wants to try to remember when it is allowed? XHTML forces consistent and clear rules that cause less headaches in the long run. A good reference point for XHTML rules is located on the W3C Web site at *www.w3.org/TR/xhtml1/*.

Another important rule with XHTML is that, in an effort to enforce accessibility standards, all images must have the `alt` *attribute.*

SUMMARY

Your quick tour through HTML and related technologies is now complete. Why did we need to look at it? After all, doesn't Dreamweaver take care of all of this coding for you? Well, yes and no.

Even though we are about to embark on your Dreamweaver MX 2004 tour, we still must know what is going on behind the scenes. Although Dreamweaver MX 2004 does a fantastic job of creating clean, seemingly hand-coded pages, you will sometimes need to hand-code because a page still doesn't validate after creating it with the program.

Also, sometimes it is easier to open the Code view in Dreamweaver and just start typing. Plus, you may want to use CSS with Dreamweaver. One of the best features in Dreamweaver MX 2004 is that it allows you to create CSSs quickly and easily. However, with much of CSS, you must know the tag name you want to affect. This is a primary purpose of this chapter.

HTML is not going away any time soon. Millions of Web sites prove this point. You need to feel comfortable with some of the basic tags so you can see what results you are achieving. We are now ready to move on and look at "Exploring Dreamweaver MX 2004."

14   Exploring Dreamweaver MX 2004

In the previous chapters we used Flash MX 2004, FreeHand MX, and Fireworks MX 2004 to create all of your graphical content for the Web site. Now you are going to start creating your actual Web site using Dreamweaver MX 2004.

Dreamweaver was initially created in the late 1990s by Macromedia after they purchased FutureWave SmartSketch and changed it to Macromedia Flash.

At this time, Macromedia was changing directions as a company. They decided to start to really focus on creating content for the Internet. They felt that the Internet was going to be the way of the future.

They then took a hard look at their product line and dropped several applications to streamline their focus. They also began work on Dreamweaver.

When they were developing Dreamweaver, they sought the opinions of Web designers and developers around the world to see what was needed for a development environment. This research established a reputation for Macromedia as a company that really listened to and interacted with its customer base.

When Macromedia released Dreamweaver to the public, it was snapped up. It exceeded all expectations within the company and became one of the best-selling products in the history of the company. Dreamweaver MX 2004 is the sixth full release of this powerful program

Dreamweaver MX 2004 is an incredible tool. It not only is excellent for creating clean-coded pages that appear as if they were written by hand, but also serves as a powerful site builder and control point. Anytime you move pages or even images on a Web site, you are asking for trouble. Even with just a couple of files moved, you may find a flurry of broken links and your navigation stops dead. That's where Dreamweaver MX 2004 comes in. While everything you create is within your Dreamweaver MX 2004-defined site, Dreamweaver keeps track of all your links and updates them for you when you move a file.

When you open Dreamweaver MX 2004, you are greeted with a Start page, as you have seen in Flash MX 2004 and Fireworks MX 2004. This page is shown in Figure 14.1.

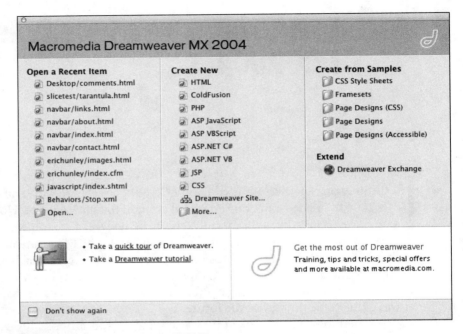

FIGURE 14.1 The Dreamweaver MX Start page.

The Start page is similar in functionality to that of the other core Studio MX 2004 products. You can open recent pages from a list, click the Open Folder icon to browse for a file, and create new files. As you can see, you can create a myriad of file types using Dreamweaver MX 2004. You can not only create straight HTML, but you can also create a page used with a server-based technology like PHP and Cold-Fusion. You also can create a new site or use the Create from Samples feature. As with the other Studio MX 2004 products, you also have options to access Macromedia Exchange for extensions and, of course, take a tour or read a tutorial.

EXPLORING THE WORKSPACE

Dreamweaver MX 2004 runs equally well on both Windows and Macintosh computers. And, like the other new Web applications in Macromedia Studio MX 2004 (Fireworks MX 2004 and Macromedia Flash MX 2004), it's compatible with Macintosh OS 10.2.6 and above, the latest Apple operating system based on a Unix core. The interface looks very similar in both operating systems, making the transition from one machine to another easy for Web designers.

Figures 14.2 and 14.3 show the interface on both Windows and Macintosh. Both versions of the application have the same overall layout. The main difference in Windows is that the panels (on the right side of the screen) are locked in place, as opposed to free-floating, as in the Macintosh.

Other differences are evident in the Tabbed Navigation and Collapsible Panels. These features are offered in the Windows version only.

As with the other products in the Studio MX 2004 family, you can press the F4 key to collapse all panels and give yourself more room. However, pressing the Tab key does not collapse panels in Dreamweaver MX 2004.

After you create a new page (HTML will do fine in this instance), you see the same basic layout shown in Figures 14.2 and 14.3. Touring it clockwise, you see the main menu bar at the top of the window, which is where you can access nearly every program setting and advanced features.

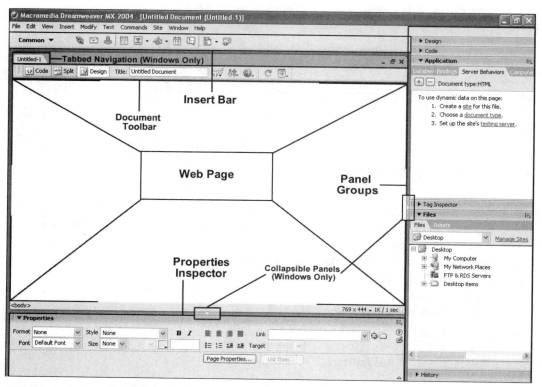

FIGURE 14.2 The Dreamweaver MX 2004 interface on Windows.

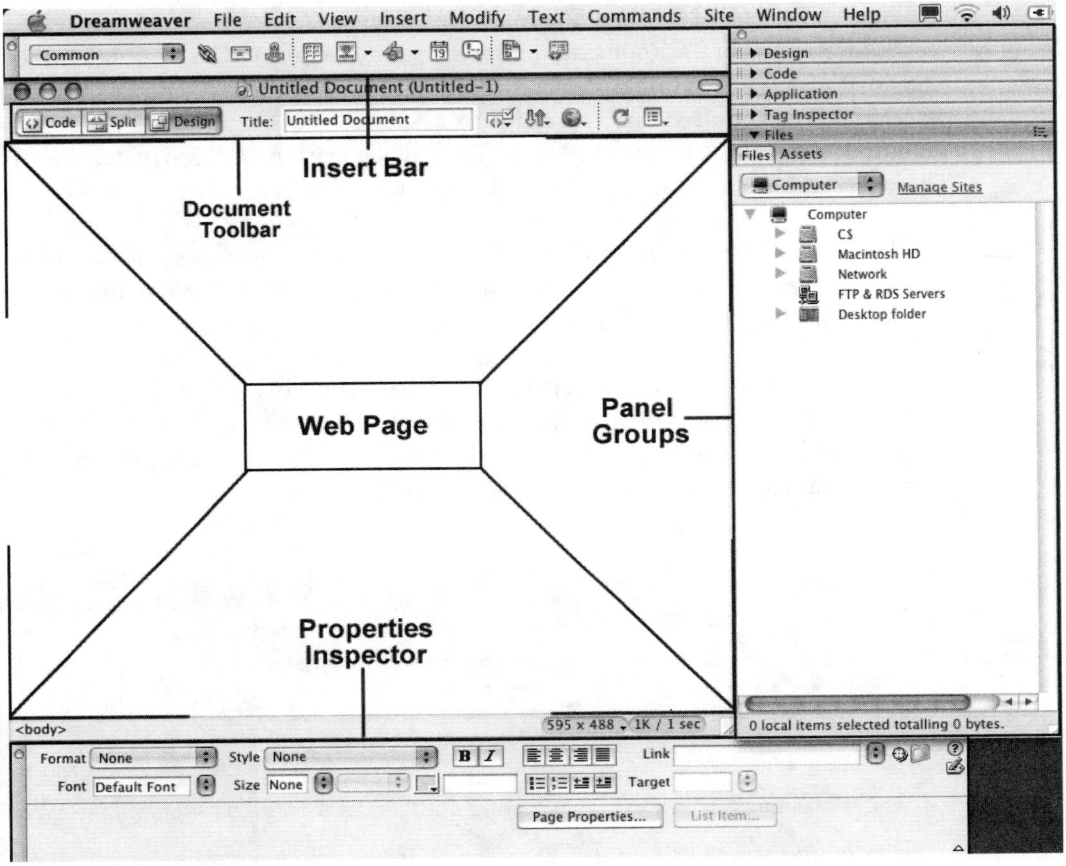

FIGURE 14.3   The Dreamweaver MX 2004 interface on Macintosh OS 10.3.

Directly underneath the menu bar is the Insert bar. If you don't see this, click View > Toolbars > Insert. This bar is where you can insert commonly used items onto your page.

Underneath the Insert bar is your document. By default, the first time Dreamweaver MX 2004 runs, it opens to Design view and appears to be a blank page. If you have chosen another view before you closed the program previously, Dreamweaver opens in the last-used view.

At the top of your document is the Document Toolbar. Again, if you don't see this, click View Toolbars > Document. In this toolbar, you can adjust document-specific views and settings.

On the right side of the interface is the Panel sets. These elements offer added functionality to the program, much as you have found in the other Studio MX 2004 products.

On the bottom of your screen is the Property Inspector. The Property Inspector was initially offered in Dreamweaver 4 and has been carried across Flash and Fireworks since version MX. It offers the one-stop shopping ability to adjust whatever you currently have selected in the document.

The Insert Toolbar

As you know, the Insert Toolbar enables you to insert commonly used items into documents within Dreamweaver. But what are some of these commonly used items?

With HTML documents, items inserted can vary because so much is available that can appear in a Web page. When you add the capacity to work on server-side programming documents, the list grows rapidly.

One of the best qualities of the Insert Toolbar is its capability to adapt to whatever type of document you are working on. If you are working on an HTML document, you have a set number of options to choose from. However, if you find yourself working on a ColdFusion document, you find the options change and new categories appear. Let's look at this in Figure 14.4.

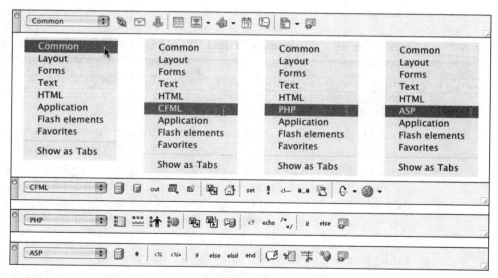

FIGURE 14.4 Using the Insert Toolbar with different document types.

As you can see from the figure, whenever a new file type is created, new categories appear. The figure also displays the new categories. The file types of HTML, ColdFusion, PHP, and ASP VBScript were used for the figure.

Let's start exploring what is available with general HTML. You have eight categories, with the option to Show as Tabs. The Show as Tabs option was added for users of previous versions of Dreamweaver products, which have the Insert Toolbar layout with tabs going across the window instead of the pop-up menu. The Insert Toolbar has been redesigned to consolidate categories to keep closely related items with one another.

TIP

Sometimes it is easier to have a constant view of all available categories by reverting to the Tabbed view. You can change back by choosing Show as Menu from the Options menu in the top-right corner of the Insert Toolbar (if you are currently in Tabbed view).

Within HTML, your categories start with Common, which contains some of the most frequently inserted components in pages. Some of these elements can also be found in other categories but are duplicated here for convenience. Let's look at what is available in this category:

Hyperlink: Inserts a hyperlink in the document. When used, you can type the text that should act as the link; the destination URL; the Target for how it will load (in the same window, new window, and so on); the Title of the link; the Access Key for a single-letter keyboard shortcut; and Tab index. You have other ways to create a hyperlink within Dreamweaver MX 2004 that you will more commonly use. The main purpose of choosing this item on the Insert Toolbar is for the addition of the Access Key and Tab index without having to dig into the HTML code.

Email Link: Inserts an e-mail link in the document. Your options here include Text and Email. You do not have an Access Key or Tab index option.

Named Anchor: Inserts a named anchor, which is used to place a target within a Web page. They are commonly used when a page has a great deal of content, such as a FAQs (Frequently Asked Questions) page. Instead of requiring the user to scroll to find a list item, you can set up a link from the top of the page. Your only option is to name the tag.

Table: Inserts a table. When inserting a table, you can choose the relevant parameters, including how many rows and columns the table contains, Cell Spacing and Cell Padding, and Table Width. Tables are explored more later.

Images: Contains a submenu of commonly inserted image types. After an item is chosen, it remains visible on the Insert Toolbar.

Image: Inserts a basic image.

Image Placeholder: Inserts an image placeholder for an image to be placed later. It can be a helpful tool if you are waiting for an image to be complete and want to continue designing the rest of your page.

Fireworks HTML: Inserts pages created in Fireworks MX 2004.

Navigation Bar: Creates navigation bars, similar to the option in Fireworks MX 2004.

Draw Rectangle Hotspot: Creates a rectangular hotspot. Hotspots are used for creating image maps or portions of an image as a link. You used this option in Fireworks MX 2004.

Draw Oval Hotspot: Creates an oval hotspot.

Draw Polygon Hotspot: Creates a polygon-shaped hotspot.

Media: Contains a submenu of inserted image types. After an item is chosen, it remains visible on the Insert Toolbar.

Flash: Inserts .swf files.

Flash Button: Provides a selection of premade SWF buttons.

Flash Text: Creates a line of text that is added to the page as an SWF element. This option is useful if you want to use a customized font or include a rollover behavior on text.

Shockwave: Inserts files created in Macromedia Director.

Applet: Inserts Java applets.

Param: Adds controlling behaviors to an imported object, such as an SWF.

ActiveX: Inserts custom ActiveX components.

Plugin: Specifies if a plug-in should be used on the page and where to find it on the hard drive. Choose this option if you have a target audience with Netscape Navigator.

Date: Adds the current date on your page. This option is useful if you want to show when your page was last updated. You can also select the option to Update automatically on save, so you don't have to remember to change the date every time you make changes.

Comment: Allows you to add HTML comments. Comments are statements about a document that appear in the source code but are not visible when the document is displayed in a browser.

Templates: Contains a submenu of the options to create templates. You will explore templates later. Options in the submenu include:

Make Template
Make Nested Template
Editable Region
Optional Region
Repeating Region
Editable Optional Region
Repeating Table

Tag Chooser: Adds any tag to the code. It opens up a window with a huge assortment of tags from which you can choose.

The other categories outside of Common are Layout, which offers advanced page-layout tools including layers, tables, and frames. Following this is Forms, used for adding form tags and fields to your page.

The Text category offers some of the most commonly inserted text-formatting tags used in HTML, including headings, bold, italic, and more. Next, you can choose from HTML where you have additional tags such as meta tags, frames, and scripts. Application offers options for connecting external data sources such as databases. Flash Elements provides one menu item, Flash Element. A Flash Element is a component created in Flash MX 2004 to add functionality to your page. The Favorites category allows you to create your own customized set of menu items.

The Document Toolbar

The Document Toolbar allows you to adjust the view of your document. Like the Insert Toolbar, it is dynamic; it is displayed differently according to what view you are currently using.

Three views, chosen from the left of this toolbar, are available: Code, Split, and Design. Code hides all visual elements and allows you to work exclusively on the source code of a document. Split allows you to see both Code and Design views at the same time. Design previews what the page will look like in the browser. It allows you to visually create elements in a What You See Is What You Get (WYSIWYG, pronounced wiz-ee-wig) manner.

In the center of the Document Toolbar is the Title field. It is important to title your documents, or else they appear on a search engine as Untitled Document, which is likely to turn away many users. Dreamweaver performs a courtesy by placing this front and center of the document as a reminder.

On the right are five buttons, four of which have submenus. The first button is No Browser/Check Errors. This button helps you if you want to check if your page is compatible with a browser you don't have installed on your computer. The menu offers options such as Autocheck on open, which alerts you of compatibility errors when you open the document. It also allows you to navigate through errors. You can adjust what browsers you want to check against by clicking Settings.

Next to No Browser/Check Errors is File Management. This option allows you to perform uploads and downloads in addition to checking files in and out. Having it placed here in the document is convenient. You can perform all of these options in the Sites Panel or from Sites on the main menu bar. By using it here, however, the option is specific to the open document. If you choose Put from here, Dreamweaver puts the current page up, whereas if you use the Sites Panel, you must navigate to the current document first.

Preview/Debug in Browser comes next. It is a quick shortcut to check your page in a browser. You can edit your browser preferences here, too.

Refresh Design View redraws your document. Use this option if you have changed content and the changes aren't reflected on screen.

The Visual Aids button offers different options that reflect what type of view you are currently using. If you are in Design view, the option allows you to toggle different Visual Aids like Table borders on and off, which are shown even if you don't have one in the final document. By having Visual Aids on, you can more easily see where items are in the document.

When you are in Code view, you have options related to text editing, like Line Numbers and Word Wrap. The Split view contains all options from both categories.

Panel Groups

Panel groups are used to give you further options when developing your page. Let's look at some of these in Figure 14.5.

Design Panel: Contains two tabs—CSS Styles and Layers. CSS Styles allows you to add CSS to your page and edit them within this same panel. Layers gives you a centralized location to manage your layers.

Code: Offers two tabs—Snippets, in which you can insert individual chunks of code into your document; and the incredibly useful Reference Panel. The Reference Panel offers you the ability to look up tags and attributes, and how they should be used for HTML, as well as similar help for other languages like Cold-Fusion, PHP, JSP, JavaScript, SQL, and ASP.

Application: Offers several tabs to assist you with connecting to external data.

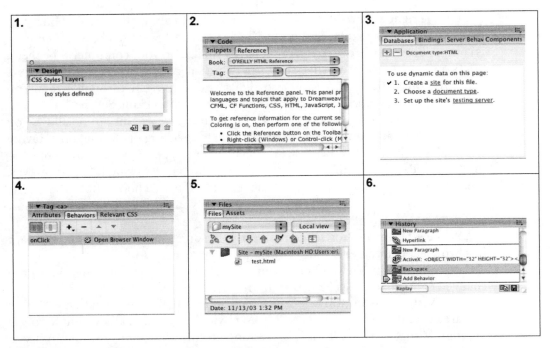

FIGURE 14.5 Panel groups in Dreamweaver MX 2004.

Tag Inspector: Contains three panels. Attributes lists current attributes on any selected object and allows you to further define it. Behaviors adds JavaScript to your selected object. It works in a similar manner to the Behaviors tab in Fireworks MX 2004, but you have many more options to pick from in Dreamweaver. Relevant CSS gives you another listing of CSS that has been applied to the selected object.

Files Panel: This group contains two tabs—Files and Assets. Files can be thought of as your Sites Panel. Here you control files and define if they are local or remote. Assets is a laundry list of images, links, colors, scripts, templates, and other media you have used on your site.

History: Acts in the same manner as the History Panel in Flash MX 2004 and Fireworks MX 2004. It is a visual representation of your Undo record and can be used to replay steps or save them as a command sequence.

The Property Inspector

The Property Inspector works in the exact same manner as those in the other Studio MX products. It reflects what is chosen in the page. Let's look at it in Figure 14.6.

Notice we have four versions of the Property Inspector showing. The first is when text is selected. Notice we have all of the standard text options of Style, Bold/Italic, Paragraph Alignment, and Size. You also have the added options of Link, Target, and Format.

Next is the Property Inspector with an image selected. Here we have a preview of the image, its Source, Width, Height, and other editing options.

With the Flash button selected you have yet another set of attributes from which to choose. These options are related to its File Location, Quality, Alignment, and other parameters.

CSSStyle, which completes the group, contains one option visible—Edit Style Sheet.

You will use the Property Inspector constantly, as we have in the previous applications. It is one tool that really makes Macromedia products stand out.

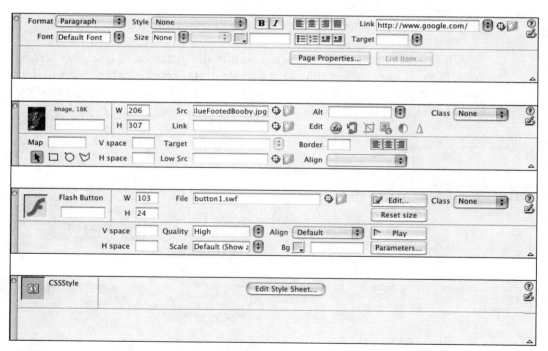

FIGURE 14.6   Different views of the Property Inspector.

CREATING YOUR SITE

It's time to create your first site. Files edited in Dreamweaver are usually related to a site, so it is a good idea for you to create one before we start moving content around.

You are going to now use the Files Panel. The Files Panel has two tabs: Files and Assets. At this point we are concerned about Files.

Previously, a menu bar was located in this panel, but it has been removed as of Dreamweaver MX 2004. Now the following options are found under the Options menu in the top-right corner of the pane:

File: Offers options for general file activity, such as creating a new file or folder, opening files, renaming files, and deleting files. It also offers some extra options, like the ability to check links and preview the page in a browser.

Edit: Offers options for general editing—Cut, Copy, Paste, Duplicate, Find, and Select. It sets itself apart by dealing with two locations, local and remote.

View: Provides viewing options. Do you want to refresh the view? How do you want to view the files—as files or maybe a map? You will explore more View options when we have some files to view.

Site: Provides options for site maintenance and creation.

The Files Panel alone is enough to justify the purchase of Dreamweaver MX 2004, but it is just the beginning. Let's create a site. You have three ways of doing this (Dreamweaver MX 2004 is full of options that tailor to each user's workflow), shown in Figure 14.7.

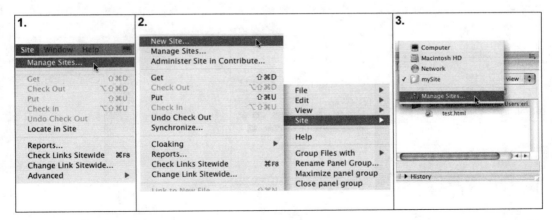

FIGURE 14.7 Creating a new site.

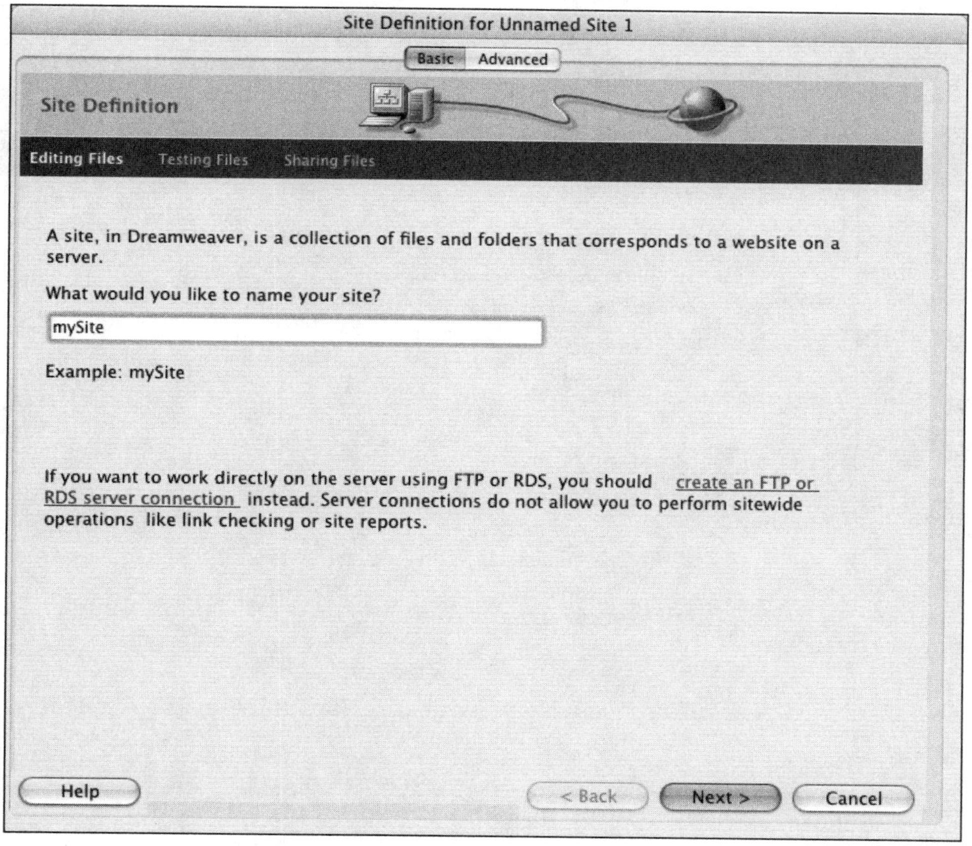

FIGURE 14.8   Site Definition window.

1. Click Site on the main menu bar and choose Manage Sites. From there, click the New button.
2. In the Files Options menu, click Site > New Site.
3. In the drop-down menu in the Site pop-up menu in the Files Panel, shown in panel 1 in Figure 14.7, select Manage Sites and select the New button.

Whichever way you go about it, the result is initially the Site Definition window with the Basic tab in focus, as shown in Figure 14.8. If the Basic tab isn't in focus at this time, click it now. Now let's set up your first site.

1. Within the field "What would you like to name this site," type an easy name to remember (your business or domain name would be a great choice) and click Next. This action opens Editing Files, Part 2, shown in Figure 14.9.

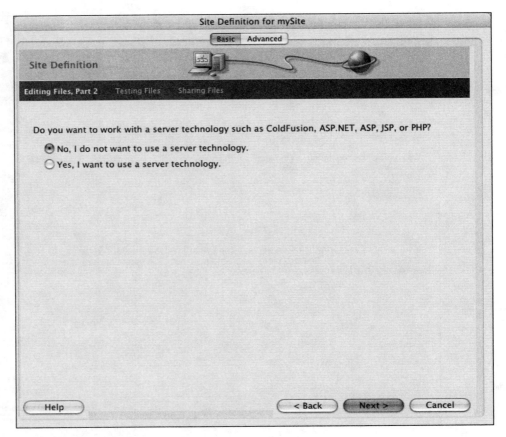

FIGURE 14.9 Editing Files, Part 2.

2. One of the greatest features of Dreamweaver MX 2004 is that it offers Web professionals the ability to make server-side pages, like ASP, PHP, and, of course, ColdFusion. In previous versions of Dreamweaver, you had the ability only to create basic Web pages. Then Macromedia came out with Dreamweaver UltraDev™, which had a focus on server connectivity. With Dreamweaver MX 2004, Macromedia has married the two into a single application with a competitive price. Select No, I don't want to use a server technology. You can change this later, if necessary. Click Next. The Editing Files, Part 3 window opens, as shown in Figure 14.10.

3. Now we come to the Editing Files window in which we have two options: **Edit local copies on my machine, then upload to server when ready (recommended):** Essentially creates all files locally and uploads all at once. Choose this option.

■ **Edit directly on server using local network:** Choose this option if you are in-house on the same network as the Web server, doing development on a site. This option keeps all the files in a central location.

4. Below the options in the Editing Files window, we see Where on your computer do you want to store your files? By default, Dreamweaver wants to put your site files in My Documents (Documents on a Macintosh). This placement is an improvement over previous versions of Dreamweaver, which wanted to put your site files by default in C:\Program Files\Macromedia\Dreamweaver\Sites\. My Documents (or Documents on a Mac) is a far better storage location for files on your computer. Most programs default to this location, and it is easier to back up. Often, network administrators automatically back up the folder to the network. You are going to take this one step further and add the word *sites* in the path so it reads . . .

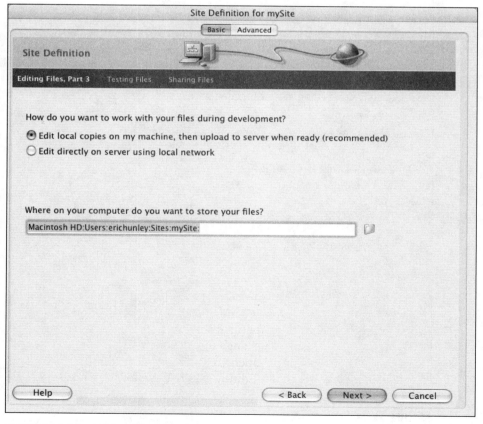

FIGURE 14.10 Editing Files, Part 3.

My Documents\sites\sitename (or Documents/Sites/sitename on a Mac), with the assumption that this is not the only site we will be working on. You are a Web professional, after all. Dreamweaver automatically creates your new folder when you click Next and move to the Sharing Files window, shown in Figure 14.11.

5. You are now at the Sharing Files window. Remember, a Web server is, in general, nothing more than an amped-up file server. Every Web page is, in fact, a document. This step is where we determine where to put your files. By default, Dreamweaver displays the Local/Network option when you first enter this window, but FTP is by far the most popular method of moving files. Let's look at all of the options:

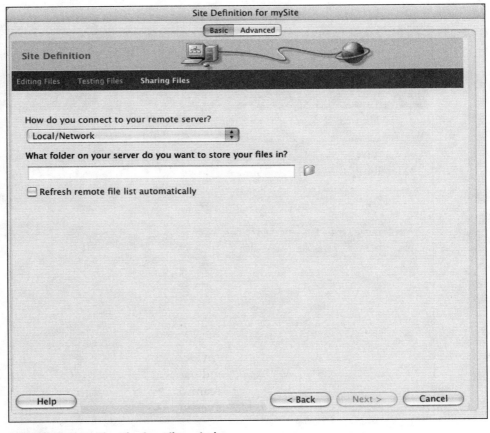

FIGURE 14.11   The Sharing Files window.

None: Enables you to build your entire site while waiting for a location to upload. This option would be your choice if we didn't have a Web host to provide space for your files.

FTP: Moves files using the File Transfer Protocol (FTP). This option is the most common type of file access to a Web host. This option would be your choice if we use a standard hosting service.

Local/Network: Connects to your server directly over a LAN, where both your computer and the Web server reside.

RDS (Remote Development Services): Allows users to remotely connect to ColdFusion servers and databases. You must be running a ColdFusion server to use this option.

WebDAV (Web-based Distributed Authoring and Versioning): Allows susers to work on documents and collaborate directly on the server. You must be running Internet Information Services 5 or higher, by Microsoft, or another compatible server.

6. You also must choose What folder on your server do you want to store your files in? Often, hosting services have you store content in either www or pub-lic_html as a folder. You have access at a higher level, but any Web pages must be stored in the appropriate folder. You can set the root folder here. This option means less synchronizing is required for checking your content.
7. If you have Local/Network selected, the last item is if you want to Refresh remote file folder automatically. It is not recommended that you check this. If you do, make certain you have a high-bandwidth connection or little network traffic, because every time you upload content, Dreamweaver combs through your remote site to refresh all file lists. As your site grows, this process can be very time consuming.
8. If you have a Web host available, set up FTP now.
   a. After you select FTP on the drop-down menu, you are greeted with the window shown in Figure 14.12.
   b. Enter your hostname (mycompany.com) or IP address of the Web server.
   c. Choose the remote folder, if it applies. The figure shows a folder with a / (slash), which means "root" because that is what the sample hosting service requires.
   d. Enter your login name, provided by your hosting service, and password.
   e. Underneath your login and password, you can select Use Secure FTP. This option is new to Dreamweaver MX 2004 and is one of the most important features in this version of the program. Macromedia rewrote the entire FTP engine to support this option with Dreamweaver MX 2004 and Macromedia Contribute. FTP as a protocol sends your infor-

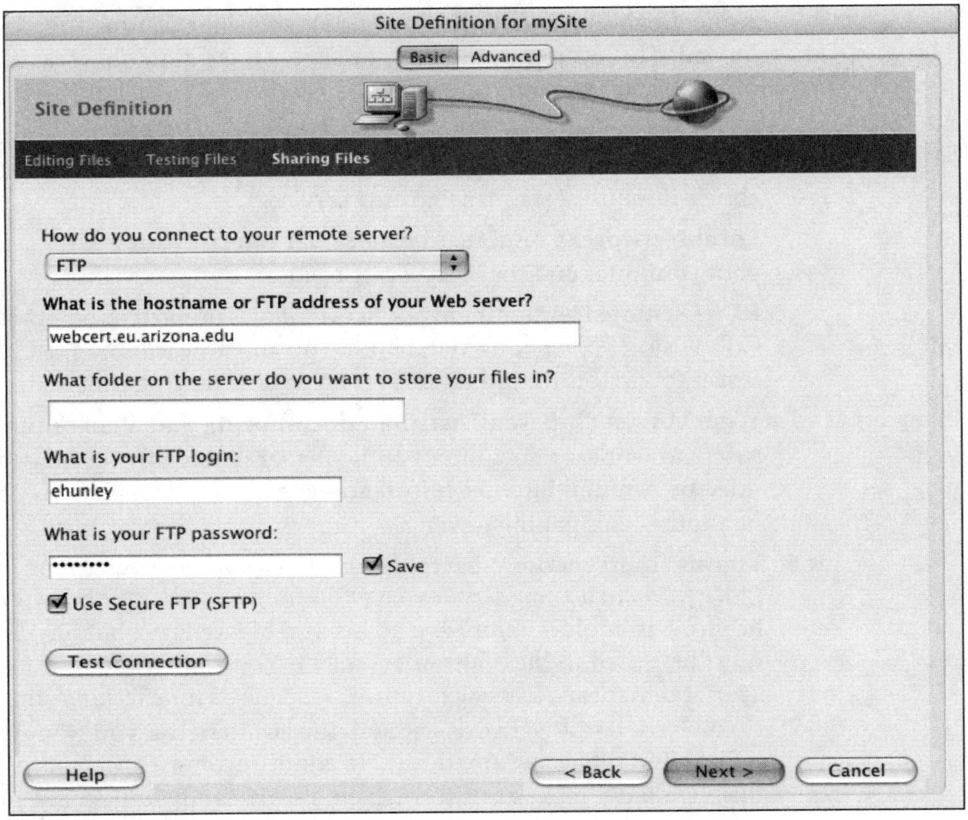

FIGURE 14.12 FTP Setup.

mation in what is known as clear text. What this means is if someone has what is known as packet sniffer tied into the network, he can capture your login and password. With this information, he has the master keys to your Web site. Due to this serious issue, many companies and even universities are using Secure FTP, which encrypts information before it is sent. Previous versions of Dreamweaver had little to no support for Secure FTP, rendering them useless for site maintenance with the server in this environment. Site maintenance is one of the reasons to own Dreamweaver as a product, so having Secure FTP capabilities is a necessity. It may be an under-the-hood upgrade, but this doesn't lessen its importance.

f. Click Test Connection to see if the settings worked. If you see the message shown in Figure 14.13, all is well.

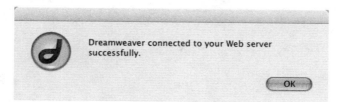

FIGURE 14.13   Successful FTP connection message.

9. The Summary screen now appears, and you can finally click Done. You now are able to see, in your Files window, your newly defined site. You can also see the site by choosing Manage Sites from the Sites pop-up menu, by clicking Site > Manage Sites on the main menu, or by clicking Site > Manage Sites in the Files Panel Options menu. Both the Files Panel and Manage Sites window with the new site listed are shown in Figure 14.14.

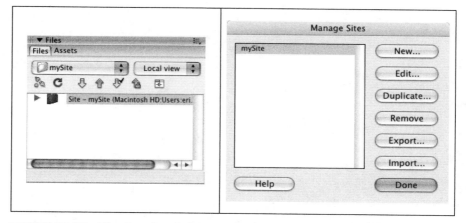

FIGURE 14.14   Files Panel and Manage Sites window with the new site listed.

SUMMARY

In this chapter we had an opportunity to tour the Dreamweaver MX 2004 interface. You also created your first site in the program so your files can be managed efficiently. Dreamweaver MX 2004 should be the central point for all content we create using Macromedia Studio MX 2004. Let's move on now and start "Creating Pages with Dreamweaver MX 2004."

15 Creating Pages with Dreamweaver MX 2004

In the previous chapter, we created our first site, mySite. This site will be the basis of all content created in Dreamweaver MX 2004 from here out. Now, this book is all about integration between the products in the Macromedia Suite MX 2004, so we are going to start things a bit differently. Roundtrip HTML is usually discussed late in documentation about Dreamweaver and Fireworks, but we are going to discuss it now.

ROUNDTRIP HTML

Roundtrip HTML is one of the primary reasons to buy Studio MX 2004 as a complete package. You can buy each of the products independently and they are powerful in their own right, but using them together is what sends the package over the top.

Roundtrip HTML is the process of creating content in one of the Studio MX 2004 applications (namely Flash MX 2004 and Fireworks MX 2004) and bringing that content into Dreamweaver MX 2004. It also works for content created in Free-Hand MX and brought into Flash MX 2004 or Fireworks MX 2004. After the content is brought into Dreamweaver, its association to the original application is not forgotten.

If you want to make any changes or refine the content, just open the application with which you authored the content from within Dreamweaver and make modifications in the original program. After you make the changes, the original application re-saves the source file and re-exports the result, and the updated material is reflected in Dreamweaver. This action is the round trip.

Roundtripping with Fireworks MX 2004

In Fireworks MX 2004, we created two page designs for use on a Web site: *background.png* and *categories.png*. We will learn about Roundtrip HTML using these files.

First we must import content from Fireworks, as shown in Figure 15.1.

Initially we create a new HTML page. You may be asking yourself why we are creating a whole new page when Fireworks created not only the images but also the HTML page that went with them? The simple reason is because we created those pages as a *base* for later use in Dreamweaver.

Those files do work if you have Fireworks MX 2004 as a standalone product, but we are using it as part of an entire package. We want Dreamweaver MX 2004 to

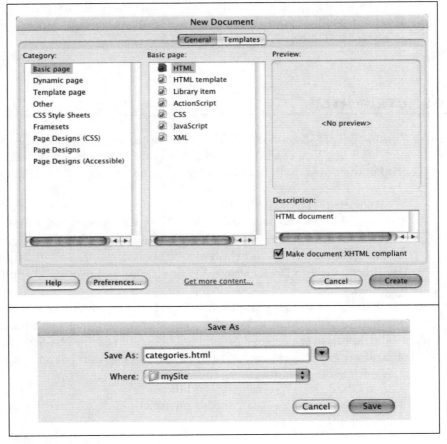

FIGURE 15.1 Creating a new Web page.

control all of the files in our site and be our management program; therefore, we pull those files into Dreamweaver.

To create a new page we can use the Start Page, but instead let's click File > New. In the New window, you can create numerous types of pages, as shown in panel 1 of Figure 15.1. Select Basic and choose HTML from the list.

Do you see the option in the bottom-right corner of Make document XHMTL compliant? XHTML is the modern HTML standard for Web content. Select this option so Dreamweaver will add all the necessary code for the page to be compliant.

If many of your users will be using older browsers, it is advised to leave this option unchecked.

Next, we need to save the file. You must save a file before you add any outside content to it. If you haven't saved the file, Dreamweaver has no way to associate any external files with your page.

Remember, the program keeps track of not only all the contents in your site but also how files relate to one another. It cannot have this knowledge without knowing the location of the original file. Save the file by clicking File > Save (Ctrl/Command + S). Notice that the target director defaults to mySite? This location is exactly where we want the file saved, so click the Save button.

Now that we have saved our Web page, we can actually bring content into it, as shown in Figure 15.2.

To import Fireworks content, click the Images button and select Fireworks HTML. This field is called Fireworks HTML because we are importing not only the images but also the Web page that Fireworks MX 2004 generated for you. This option opens the Insert Fireworks HTML dialog box, in which you have two options: Browse, and Delete file after insertion. Use the option Delete the file after insertion when you have created the Fireworks content specifically for Dreamweaver and don't want the original file cluttering up your hard disk.

We are going to leave this option unchecked for now (just in case any issues arise) and browse for our Fireworks content. Remember, you should have stored it in your FireworksWeb folder located in My Pictures if you are on Windows, or Pictures if you are using a Macintosh.

When you select the *categories.html* file, you are prompted with a confirm dialog box asking you if you want to copy your files into your site. This dialog box opens because Dreamweaver associates your Web site exclusively with the folder you created along with your site, and these files are located outside of that folder. This prompt is a good thing; space on your Web server is often limited, so you should keep working files off of it. You want to put files only for the public on the Web server. Leave your working files on your hard disk.

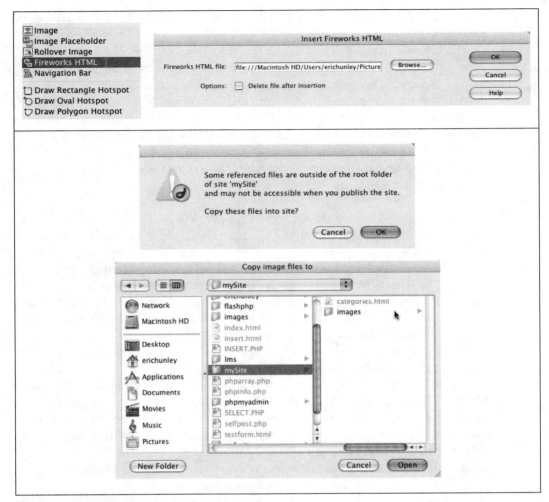

FIGURE 15.2 Inserting Fireworks MX 2004 content.

Click OK. The Copy image files to window opens, prompting you to select a location for your images. Create a new folder called *images*, then select the newly created images folder and click the Open button. Once inside the images folder, click the Open button again.

When you return to the main screen, you see that all of your Fireworks content is now in place, as shown in Figure 15.3.

We now have our base page. The first thing you must do is give the page a title. You can do this in the Document Toolbar in the Title field. Give it the title of *John*

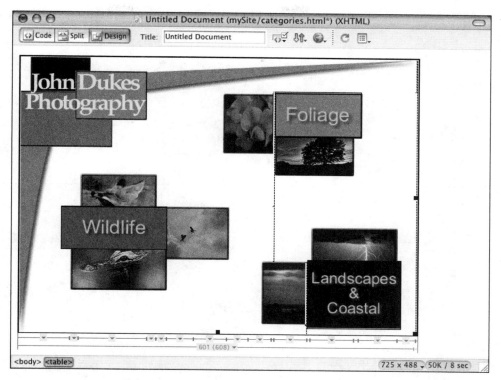

FIGURE 15.3   Our page with Fireworks content.

Dukes Photography—Categories. This title helps the page to be displayed better in search engines.

Now we need to explore what round tripping is about. Let's imagine that our client really likes the logo but feels that the purple rectangle is too tall. He also wants the blocks to have a slight drop shadow effect. No problem—we will use Roundtrip HTML, as shown in Figure 15.4.

1. First we need to select the object in question. In this case, click the logo portion of the page. When it is selected, the Property Inspector displays it. In the Property Inspector, click the FW button next to Edit.
2. A new window titled "Find Source for Editing opens." In this window, we have two options: Use a PNG and Use This File. This choice is another neat feature of Macromedia Studio MX 2004. You don't even have to have a file created in Fireworks for it to do the editing. It is just as happy editing an

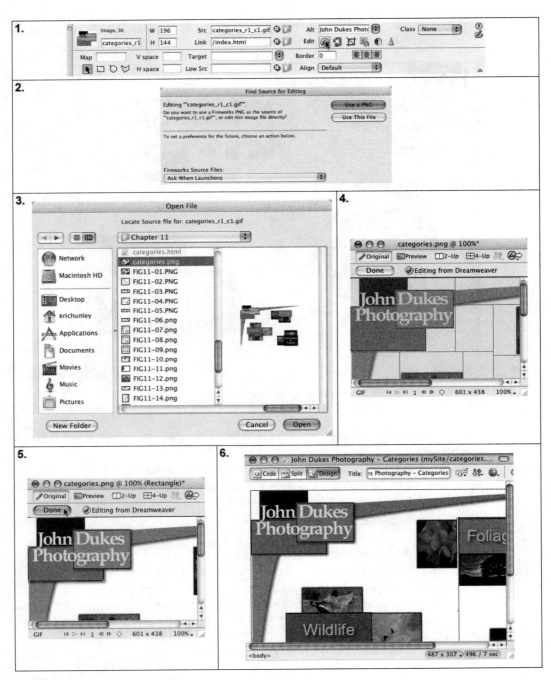

FIGURE 15.4 Roundtrip HTML with Fireworks MX 2004.

image file created in another application. For now, though, choose Use a PNG because the file was created in Fireworks.

ON THE CD

3. Now the Open File window opens. Here you can navigate to your original file. If you have not saved *categories.png* onto your hard disk, you need to do so now. You can copy it from the CD-ROM in *Dreamweaver/Chapter 15*. Navigate to the file and click the Open button.

4. Now you see something different. You are in Fireworks MX 2004, but at the top of the window is the title "Editing from Dreamweaver" with a Done button next to it. Fireworks knows this file is coming from Dreamweaver.

5. The first thing you must do is to turn off slices by clicking the Hide Slices and Hotspots button on the bottom-left corner of the Web section of the Tools Panel. When you have completed this, you ungroup your logo and the text on it by selecting the area and clicking Modify > Ungroup (or right-click [Control + click on a Macintosh] + Ungroup or Ctrl/Command + Shift + G twice). When you have ungrouped this section of the document, select the purple rectangle and give it a height of 66. You see a white area between the rectangle and the swoosh in the document. This space is because of the white rectangle you placed behind the logo. Select the white rectangle and give it a height of 121. After you have adjusted the heights of these two elements, select the aqua rectangle and go into the Property Inspector. In the Property Inspector, add the Live Effect of Drop Shadow with an offset of 3. Do the same with the purple rectangle. When you have finished adjusting the image, click the Done button.

6. You are now returned to Dreamweaver, which reflects the changes you have just made in Fireworks.

Let's revisit this process so you can get the scope of what just happened. You clicked one button in Dreamweaver, which then prompted you to find the original file. After you found the file, you were taken to Fireworks—you didn't even have to open the program. Then you made your changes and pressed one button.

When you pressed that button, the original file was saved and the content was re-exported to Dreamweaver. Then Fireworks closed the document (and itself if you didn't already have it open), and the focus was returned to Dreamweaver. The Dreamweaver view was also refreshed—all with the click of a single button. Now, *that* is efficiency. Welcome to Roundtrip HTML.

Roundtripping with Macromedia Flash MX 2004

Now that we have used Roundtrip HTML with Fireworks, let's try the same with Flash. We will use our dice game created earlier, as shown in Figure 15.5.

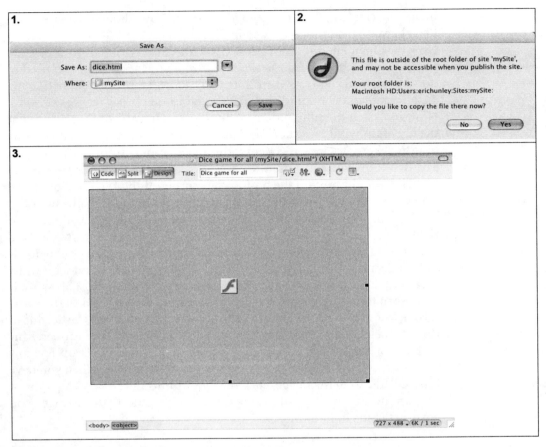

FIGURE 15.5   Bringing Flash MX 2004 content into your page.

1. Create a new file in Dreamweaver. You won't have to choose Make document XHMTL compliant because this option was retained in the program from the last file you created. Once completed, save this file as *dice.html* in your mySite folder.

ON THE CD

2. After saving your file, type *Dice game for all* in the Title field of the Document Toolbar. After you create a title for your document, click the arrow to the right of the Media button in the Insert Toolbar. From the menu, select Flash. This option opens a Select File window. Navigate to your completed *dice.swf*. (Not the .fla file, the .swf file—the .swf file is used for publication.) If you don't have this file, copy *dicerevised.fla* and *dicerevised.swf* from the *Flash/Chapter 15* folder on the CD-ROM to your hard

drive. When you have selected *dice.swf* (or *dicerevised.swf*), click the Choose button. You will again see the confirm dialog box, shown in panel 2 of Figure 15.5, asking if you want to copy the file to your site. Choose Yes and select the images folder you created previously.

3. You now see a big gray box with the Flash icon in the middle of it on your page, as shown in panel 3. This is normal. If you want to play the Flash Movie, you can click the Play button in the Property Inspector. When you are ready to edit again, press the Stop button, which toggles with Play.

Now that we have brought our Flash movie into Dreamweaver, let's get the backgrounds to match. Right now, the dice game is on an island of green.

Click the Play button in the Property Inspector so you can see the contents of the Flash movie, then click an empty area of the page. You see a new button in the Property Inspector called Page Properties, provided the Property Inspector is expanded. If it is not expanded, click the downward-pointing triangle in the bottom-right corner. Click the Page Properties button and select the swatch in Background color from the Page Properties window that appears.

After you have clicked Background color, move the Eyedropper Tool over the background of the Flash movie in your page. This tool tells you what the RGB value of the background color is (#00FF00). Take note of this value, and pick the color in your Color Selection window.

If you can't find the color, select any color. When the focus returns to the Page Properties window, type the proper color value in the field next to Background Color, and press Enter/Return. Click the OK button. When you return to your page, the background color matches that in your Flash movie.

Now that we have the Flash movie all set on the page, we realize that we should have a small copyright statement on the page. We resolve this issue, as shown in Figure 15.6.

1. Select your Flash movie and press Edit in the Property Inspector, as shown in panel 1 of Figure 15.6.
2. This action opens the Locate Macromedia Flash Document File window. From here you must navigate to the original *dice.fla* file or the *dicerevised.fla* file copied from the CD-ROM.
3. You are now inside Flash. Notice it has Editing From Dreamweaver as the title on the top of the window, along with the Done button. You may notice that the Timeline has been collapsed. If you need to do work within the Timeline, just click the word *Timeline* to expand it. In the top-center area of the stage, type *Copyright 2004* and your name. When finished, click the Done button.

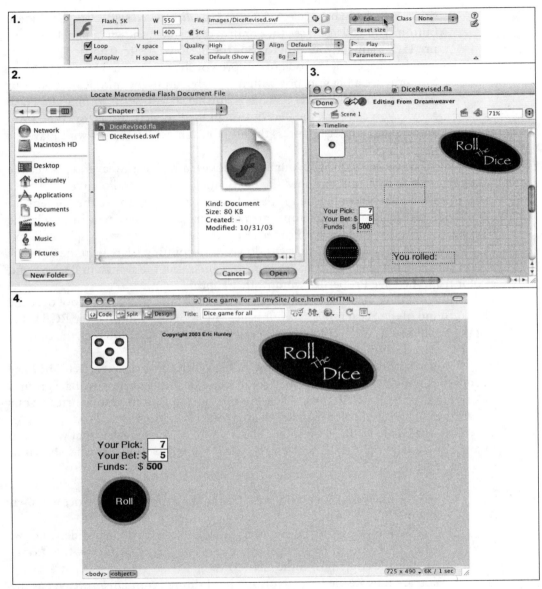

FIGURE 15.6 Roundtrip HTML with Flash MX 2004.

4. You are returned to Dreamweaver. Notice that the copyright statement now appears in your Flash movie after you click the Play button in the Property Inspector.

When you associate an original PNG or SWF file with content in a page, you are not prompted to navigate for the original file after that point.

You have now completed Roundtrip HTML with two applications: Flash MX 2004 and Fireworks MX 2004. As you can see, this integration can significantly help with your workflow. Now let's learn how to add content to Dreamweaver.

SETTING UP PAGE PROPERTIES

At the outset of the creation of any Web page you should set up properties. You can do this by clicking any blank area of the page and selecting the Page Properties button in the Property Inspector. You also can click Modify > Page Properties.

The Page Properties window has dramatically changed from previous versions of Dreamweaver. Let's explore what is available, as shown in Figure 15.7.

1. To open Page Properties, you can either click a blank area of the document and choose the Page Properties button in the Property Inspector or click Modify > Page Properties (or press Ctrl/Command + J).
2. The Appearance Category window opens. In this window, you can set up general parameters for the page, including font style used on the page as a default, font size, Text color, Background color, and Background image. It is often a good idea to explicitly choose the Text color and Background color because your users may have set their browser preferences to something different from what you intended. Imagine if you had only black text specified and a user sets a default background color of black. As far as having a background image on the page, you should think carefully before you choose this option. Some very real issues arise when using background images. They can make the page difficult to read and can also add to the file size. These issues are why, when you look on the Web at most large, professionally created sites, you notice a distinct lack of them. Your last options in this area are to specify each margin.
3. The next window you can work with is the Links window. In this window, you can change how your links appear on the page. Be careful when you change the appearance of links. Users are familiar with the standard color and style and may not recognize your links if you modify them, particularly if you choose Never Underline.
4. Headings is a convenient location to set the look for each heading style you use on your page.

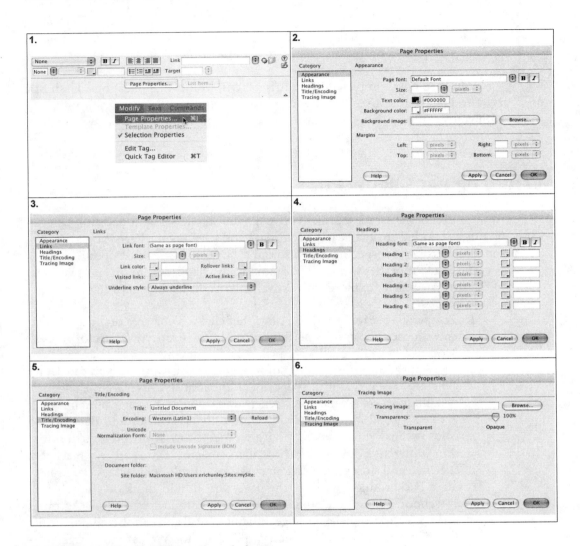

FIGURE 15.7 The Page Properties window.

5. Title/Encoding allows you to add a title and set the language for your page.
6. Tracing Image allows you to set a background image for the authoring view of your page. The image is not published with the page, and your users never see it. Tracing images are especially helpful when you create layouts based on images provided to you. We will work with a tracing image later.

ADDING HEAD CONTENT

Whenever you want your site to be listed properly (or at all) by a search engine, use meta tags in the head of the document. The head of an HTML page is where information that describes the page itself is listed. This behavior is the specialty of the meta tag. As you discovered in Chapter 13, "An HTML Primer," several meta tags are available to you. We focus here on two: keywords and description, as shown in Figure 15.8.

1. To begin, we will change the Insert Toolbar to reflect the HTML category by clicking the pop-up menu (it should currently reflect Common) and selecting HTML from the list.
2. Now let's add some keywords, which are found under the Meta button (two tags) on the menu. Keywords help search engines match your site according to search terms. They can be very useful, but don't use too many. In earlier days on the Internet, some unscrupulous designers loaded the dictionary as keywords to increase traffic to their sites. Often these sites contained porn or distributed pirated software, so something had to be done. As a result, if a search engine sees too many keywords, instead of increasing a site's rank, it reduces it. For this example, we use Nature, Pho-

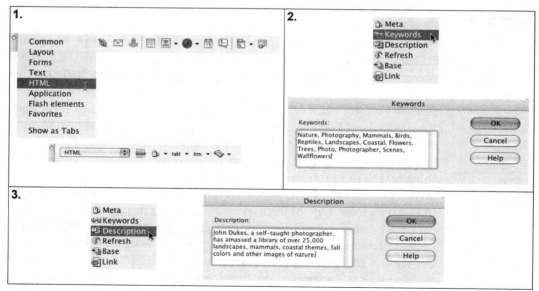

FIGURE 15.8 Adding head content.

tography, Mammals, Birds, Reptiles, Landscapes, Coastal, Flowers, Trees, Photo, Photographer, Scenes, and Wallflowers. Notice how these terms are all relevant to a nature photographer.

3. Now we add a descriptive phrase to the site using the Description option. This option is also found under the Meta button. When the dialog box opens, type *John Dukes, a self-taught photographer, has amassed a library of over 25,000 landscapes, mammals, coastal themes, fall colors, and other images of nature.* This sentence controls what search engines use as the description when they display the site.

Head content is not seen by users, but it is very important to your page. It would be neglectful to not mention the most important tag that lives in the head section: Title. Remember to give every page a title. This element is the most important qualifier used by search engines.

ADDING TEXT AND IMAGES TO YOUR PAGE

Now we can look at visible content on the page. When you add content to a page, you can use the Insert Toolbar, drag in items, or simply type. Let's start by looking at text.

Adding Text

Text is one of the most common components you will add to a Web page. Essentially, most HTML documents on the Web comprise text and images. Using the Property Inspector, creating text is a breeze. We start exploring text, as shown in Figure 15.9.

1. Adding text in Dreamweaver is as easy as clicking and typing on the page. Your text should be defaulted to the Paragraph format, as shown in panel 1 of Figure 15.9. If the Property Inspector shows the Format as None, adjust it to read Paragraph. Underneath Format is Font. It reads Default Font initially. Default Font means Dreamweaver uses whatever font the user's browser is using as its default. To the right is Style. This option is important in Dreamweaver. One of the major changes with this version of the application is extensive Cascading Style Sheet (CSS) support. The HTML styles used in previous versions have been dropped in the default setup. (You can change this in the General setting in the Preferences window, accessed by clicking Edit > Preferences on Windows, or Dreamweaver > Preferences on Macintosh.) You also have other standard formatting options like bold,

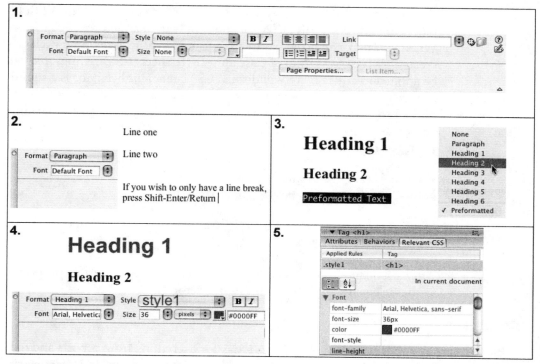

FIGURE 15.9 Adding text to a page.

italic, and alignment, as well as the opportunity to add a URL in the Link field.

2. When you type text and press the Enter/Return key, a new paragraph is created. Paragraphs automatically insert a blank line between themselves. If you want to drop to the next line without the double-space effect, press Shift + Enter/Return. This key combination creates a line break, which drops your cursor to the next line. Keep in mind that the text is still part of the paragraph or heading.

3. You have nine choices available to you under Format: None, Paragraph, six Heading levels, and Preformatted. Headings are used for sectional demarcation within a document. Six are available, aptly named Heading 1 through 6. Heading 1 is the largest; they get progressively smaller as the numbers increase. Preformatted is a unique type of text. The normal behavior of HTML is to display only one white space, no matter how many spaces and carriage returns are in the code. The Preformatted option causes

the white space to be counted and defaults to a monospace font. With tables being available, this tag is not commonly used anymore.

4. When you make any changes to a tag using Dreamweaver, a new .class is created. A .class is a group of Cascading Style Sheet (CSS) settings that can be applied to any tag. We will discuss CSS later. This behavior is a significant change from previous versions of Dreamweaver. In all earlier versions of the program, HTML styles were used. For example, to make a heading change as we have shown, a font tag would be added to the code after the H1 tag as follows:

```
<h1><font face="Arial,Helvetica,sans-serif"
color="blue" size="4">Heading 1</font></h1>
```

Font tags have been deprecated from HTML since version 4.01 and will likely be removed from the language in favor of CSS.

5. After a style has been created, you can quickly see and adjust its properties in the Relevant CSS Tab of the Tag Inspector.

Using Lists

Lists are commonly used in Web pages today for everything from reports and outlines to FAQs. With this kind of popularity, they must be included in Dreamweaver MX 2004.

HTML offers three list types: Ordered, Unordered, and Definition. The first two (Unordered and Ordered) are shown in Figure 15.10.

1. The first list type we will explore is formally known as an unordered list. It also has the common nickname of bulleted list. This list type can have three types of bullet: a solid circle, a hollow circle, and a filled square. You can also add image icons when you hand-code the HTML. Start by typing the statement *My List:*. Press the Enter/Return key and follow it with *Item 1*, *Item 2*, and *Item 3*. (Press the Enter/Return key between each.) When you have created the components of your list, highlight Items 1, 2, and 3 with your mouse and click the Unordered List button in the Property Inspector. This option turns your selection into an unordered list, as shown in panel 1 of Figure 15.10.

2. If you want to add a subitem to Item 1, place your cursor on the end of the list item and press the Enter/Return Key. This action creates another first-level list item. To demote this item, press the Text Indent button, located to the right of your list buttons. You can also press the Tab key as a quick

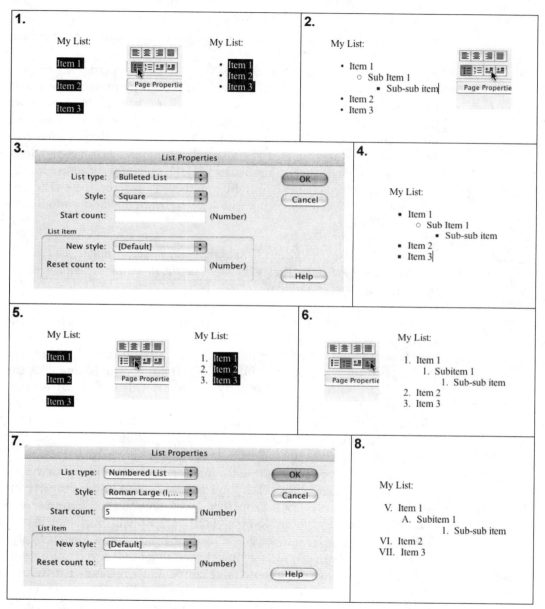

FIGURE 15.10 Using unordered and ordered lists.

shortcut. This action creates what is known as a *nested list*, or a list within a list. Dreamweaver displays the new nested list with a hollow circle as its bullet icon. If you press the Enter/Return key, another subitem is created. When you press the Tab key or click the Text Indent button, this subitem is delineated by a solid square.

3. If you want to change a value in a list, use the List Properties dialog box. The List Item button becomes available in the Property Inspector if you have placed your cursor within a list item. If you have highlighted more than one list item, the button is unavailable. The List Properties window is divided into two parts: List type and List item. List type dictates what type of list you are using: Bulleted (Unordered), Numbered (Ordered), Directory, or Menu. Style determines what type of icon you want to use for the list. Start count is available only for numbered (ordered) lists. The List item options allow you to change the selected list item without modifying the rest of the list.

If you are inside a table cell, the List Item button may not be available. You can select List Properties by clicking Text > List > Properties no matter where your list is located or how much of it is selected.

4. If you have selected Square in the Style pop-up menu under List type, your list items in the primary list begin with squares.

5. Create another set of text beginning with *My List*. Add Items 1, 2, and 3, as you did before. When completed, highlight Items 1, 2, and 3 and click the Ordered List button in the Property Inspector. This option, by default, numbers your items as 1, 2, and 3.

6. This time, if you add a list item and press the Tab key or click the Text Indent button, you find that another ordered list starting at 1 is created. This will happen each time you indent.

7. To change the type of counter used in an ordered list, place your cursor within a list item and either click the List Item button in the Property Inspector or click Text > List > Properties. Here, you can choose from several styles of counters, including Number (1, 2, 3 . . .), Roman Small (i, ii, iii . . .), Roman Large (I, II, III . . .), Alphabet Small (a, b, c . . .), and Alphabet Large (A, B, C . . .). As you can see, you have everything needed to create an outline. After Style, you can choose Start count. Enter a number to resume counting if you want to continue from a previous list. This option uses a number no matter what type of list you are using. For example, if you enter 5 and are using an Alphabet Large list, the count resumes at E.

8. This list was created by selecting Roman Large with a Start count of 5 with the cursor placed in the first list item. Alphabet Large was selected for the first nested list, and the second nested list was left with the default (Number).

The last type of list, the Definition list, is not available in the Property Inspector. You must select it by clicking Text > List > Definition List in the main menu. A Definition list splits each list item into two parts: the term (DT) and the definition (DD). The definition is displayed underneath the term and is indented.

Adding Images

We have learned how to add text to pages in Dreamweaver MX 2004. Now it's time to add the second-most popular type of content on Web pages: images.

First, you must create a new HTML page. Next, save this page as *saw-whetowl.html*. We will insert an image, as shown in Figure 15.11.

1. Images are easy to add to a Web page in Dreamweaver. If you don't currently have Common selected in your Insert Toolbar, change to it now.

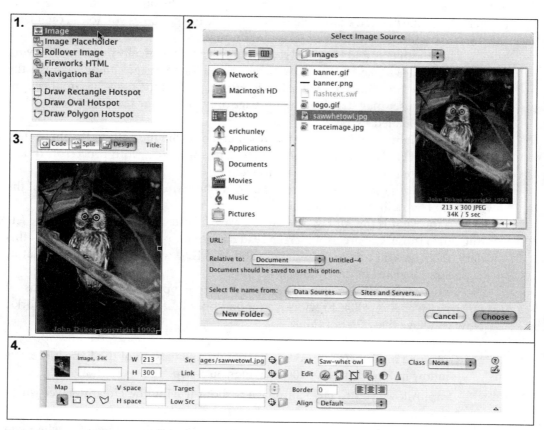

FIGURE 15.11 Adding images.

Within the Common category, just click the downward-pointing arrow next to the Images button to open the pop-up menu and select Image. If you don't see the Image icon, you may have selected another item before this point, such as the Flash option. If you don't recognize the icons, it is the fifth button from the left.

2. When you have pressed this button, navigate to the *Dreamweaver/Chapter 15/Images* folder on the CD-ROM, select *sawwhetowl.jpg*, and click the Choose button. You are prompted with a confirm dialog box asking if you want to copy the file to your site folder. Choose Yes and copy the file to the images folder in MySite.

3. Now you see the owl picture on the stage.

4. When you click the new picture, a new set of options appears in the Property Inspector.

The Property Inspector now allows you to name the image on the top-left corner next to the preview of the image. Naming the image allows you to call on it later if you are adding a behavior or script in the page.

The Width (W) and Height (H) attributes are automatically populated for you. It is a good idea to have a width and height noted for an image. Doing so causes the browser to reserve the space while it is loading a page. If the space has not been reserved, your user may start reading the page only to have the text jump down when the image is loaded.

To the right of W and H is Src, which contains the file path to the image file. Remember, HTML cannot actually embed an image like a word processor. It uses a pointer to tell your browser where to fetch it.

Underneath the Src field is Link, which is where you add a URL if you want the image to have a link attached to it.

To the right is the Alt tag. We must always fill out the Alt tag or we will be letting down those who are using screen readers. Not only that, if we don't fill out this field, the page will not be considered valid HTML if we check it with a validator. Type *Saw-whet owl* in the Alt text box.

Underneath Alt are the Edit options. These options have changed as of Dreamweaver MX 2004. Previously you had only Edit, which opened Fireworks. Now you have five other options:

Optimize in Fireworks: Takes you straight to a version of the Export Preview window in Fireworks MX 2004, saving you a step.

Crop: Allows you to crop an image without leaving the Dreamweaver workspace.

Resample: Allows you to change the size of the original image file when you have changed the display size of the image.

Brightness/Contrast: Allows you to modified these settings in the image without leaving Dreamweaver.

Sharpen: Allows you to modify the sharpness of an image without leaving Dreamweaver.

On the far right is the option to add a CSS class to the image. This closes out our options on the upper half of the Property Inspector.

On the lower half of the Property Inspector you can add hotspots in the same manner as you did in Fireworks. You can also change the alignment and spacing around the image.

Within this area is the option to choose Low src, which specifies that a lower-resolution copy of the image should be loaded first. This setting can be used if an image may take a while to download and you want to give the users a preview of what is coming.

Let's start exploring alignment with images, as shown in Figure 15.12.

Figure 15.12 is split into two areas. The upper area covers aligning the image on the page, and the lower covers aligning the image with text.

An HTML <img> tag doesn't have an attribute to align it on a page in terms of left, center, and right. You must nest the <img>tag inside of another tag that does the alignment for you. Dreamweaver, by default, wraps the image in a <p> (paragraph) tag, which has a CSS class with an align rule applied. Let's look at this.

In the upper-left panel of Figure 15.12, you see that the image is aligned to the left on the page, which is the default alignment for an image. An image is considered a block-level element, so, by default, it takes up a certain area on the page with other content falling below.

In the Property Inspector, click the Align Center button, as shown in the top half of Figure 15.12. This option adds a <p> tag around the image, and the image is aligned to the center of the page, as shown in the upper-right panel.

You can see the new tag that was added on the bottom-left corner of the page. The tags read <body>, <p>, and then <img>. The paragraph is the element that is actually aligned.

Now let's look at aligning an image with text. Click the Align Center button again to return the image to its original alignment.

ON THE CD   When the image has been placed back on the left, we need to get our text. Navigate to the *Dreamweaver/Chapter 15/* folder on the CD-ROM and open *owlstory.txt*. Notice that Dreamweaver can open a text file with no problem.

When the text file is open, click Edit > Select All (or press Ctrl/Command + A) and click Edit > Copy (or press Ctrl/Command + C). Change to your *sawwhetowl.html* page by choosing Window and selecting the page or by clicking its tab, if you are using Windows.

When you are in your Web page, click to the right of your image and click Edit > Paste (or press Ctrl/Command + V). Your page should resemble the bottom-left panel in Figure 15.12.

Notice that the text is all aligned underneath the image, which is the default behavior. Remember that an image is a block-level element, so it takes up an entire segment of the page, just as a heading or a paragraph would.

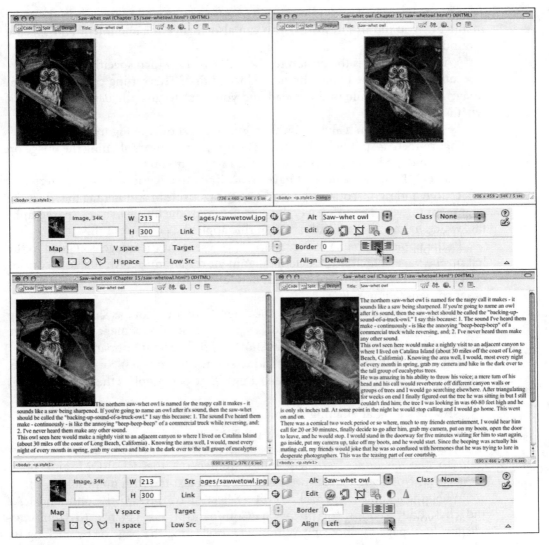

FIGURE 15.12 Aligning images.

We can modify this behavior by using the Align pop-up menu found in the Property Inspector. Several options are available, but we are concerned with two: Left and Right. When you choose the Left or Right value, the image aligns itself with all text following on the side specified. Take note, the image aligns itself to the text following it, not to the page.

Select Left from the menu. You see that the text has wrapped itself around the image, as shown in the bottom-right panel of Figure 15.12.

It is important to understand that the image aligns itself with any text following the image. If you create the text first and then insert your image, you notice no change.

Notice how the text is aligned tightly against the image. This arrangement makes it difficult for users to read the text. To correct this, add a value of 5 in the H space field to give the image a 5-pixel buffer, adding some white space between the image and text. Now the text is much easier for users to read.

Flash Text and Buttons

Flash Text and Buttons, features in Dreamweaver MX 2004, don't fit neatly in any category. They can be considered a form of an image, but they are, in fact, small Flash movies that can be modified for a page.

These components can be placed on a Web page to offer more interactivity. Create a blank HTML page for creating these components. We will explore using Flash Text and Buttons, as shown in Figure 15.13.

To create Flash Text, make sure you have Common selected in your Insert Toolbar. When this category is selected, click the drop-down arrow to the right of the Media button (sixth from the left) and choose Flash Text from the options.

The Insert Flash Text window opens, allowing you to choose your font, size, bold, italic, and alignment. Choose Century Gothic with a size of 30 and bold. You can also choose colors for its Up and Rollover states. Choose blue for Color and red for Rollover color.

In the next menu, type what you want the text to read. We will type *This is Flash Text*. If you leave the Show font option checked underneath this text area, Dreamweaver previews how the font will appear.

The Link field and Target pop-up menu allow you to make the Flash Text a link to another page and determine how it will load. We'll leave these options alone.

Our last option is to change the Bg color (background color) of the text. This option is important if your Web page has any background color other than white because your Flash Text appears inside of a white box, which can be unsightly against a colored background. The easiest method of changing this field is to click

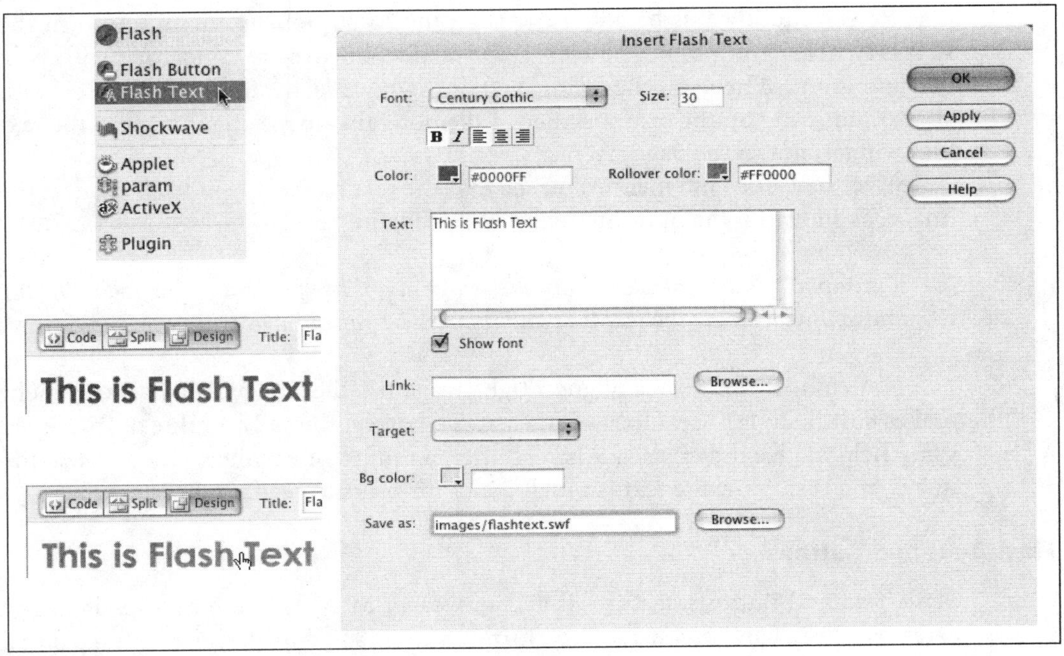

FIGURE 15.13   Adding Flash Text.

the swatch and then move the Eyedropper Tool that appears over your page background and click. The swatch then reflects the color you have sampled. Take note of this color so you can enter it in the BG color box.

The last field available is the path to which you want to save the Flash Text. An important consideration here is that if you are linking the Flash Text to a file within your site, using a relative link (as in *index.html*), you must save the file in the same directory as the current document. Otherwise, the Flash Text will be confused as to where it points because the link attributes are carried within the .swf file created and not the actual Web page.

The primary uses for Flash Text are for Rollover states and for using a custom font. The second reason is probably the best argument for using Flash Text. If you want to use a customized font on your Web page and don't want to turn it into an image, this features offers you another option.

Now let's look at creating a Flash Button, as shown in Figure 15.14.

1. To insert a Flash Button, click the drop-down arrow next to the Media button, as you did before. This time, select Flash Button.

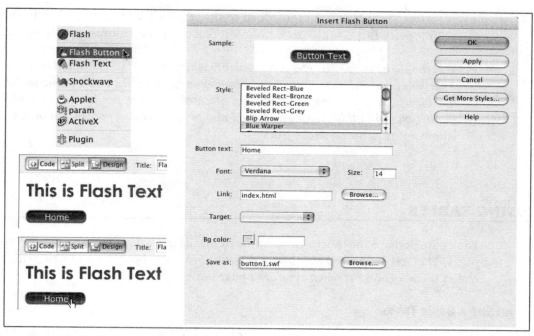

FIGURE 15.14   Creating a Flash Button.

2. The Insert Flash Button window appears. Here you can select from numerous premade styles and see a preview of the style in Sample. Choose Blue Warper.
3. Underneath Sample, type what should appear on the button in the Button text field. We will type *home*.
4. After entering the text for the button, you can choose the text font, size, link, and target. We will use Verdana with a font size of 14. Add a link to *index.html*. Let's leave target alone.
5. As with Flash Text, you can choose a Bg color (background color). You should change this setting if your page does not have a white background.
6. The Save as command determines where the file should be saved in the site. The same issue with links and Flash Text applies here. Because we are using a relative link, leave this field alone so that the file is saved in the same directory as our page.
7. When the button is complete, click Apply to see it on the page, or OK to return to the page. You can also press the Get More Styles button, which opens your browser to the Dreamweaver Exchange on the Macromedia Web site where you can download more button styles.

8. After the button has been added to the stage, click the Play button in the Property Inspector to preview how it reacts when the mouse passes over it.

You should be concerned about accessibility when using Flash Text and Buttons. After you have inserted either of these components, you must add a name within the Title field in the Property Inspector (located in the upper-left corner under Flash Text or Flash Button). You should also provide an alternate means of navigation for users with a screen reader.

USING TABLES

Tables are perhaps the most well-established means of formatting content on Web pages. They are supported by a broad range of browsers, both old and new, which makes them a good bet when creating a page layout.

Inserting a Basic Table

We start exploring tables in Dreamweaver by inserting a basic table. You can do this by clicking the Table button (fourth from the left) in the Common category of the Insert Toolbar. We will create a new blank HTML page and explore inserting a basic table, as shown in Figure 15.15.

After clicking the Table button, you are greeted with the Insert Table dialog box. Here you can choose from multiple options.

Initially, you choose how many rows and columns you want to use. Rows are from left to right and columns are up and down (much like a spreadsheet or database table). If you multiply these numbers together, you arrive at the total number of cells you have available for data.

Next, you can select the table width. Here you have the option to use an absolute or relative width. An absolute width causes the table to display at a width of the number of pixels selected, no matter how large the browser window is. This setting can result in a horizontal scroll bar if the user's browser is displaying an area narrower than the table width.

It is often a good idea to use relative width, which causes the table to take up a specified percentage of the browser window. When you use this setting, the table adjusts to the current browser display.

You choose absolute width when you type a number and select Pixels from the menu to the right. Relative is chosen when you select Percent. Set the table to 80 percent.

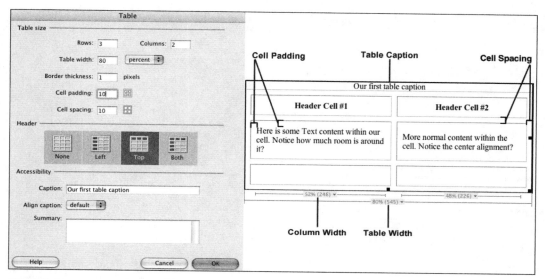

FIGURE 15.15 Inserting a table.

After defining the width, you can set Border thickness if you want a visible border between cells and around the table, Cell padding, and Cell spacing. Cell padding and Cell spacing are often confused. If you look at the right panel of Figure 15.15, you can see the difference between these options.

Cell spacing determines how much space is between each cell. This setting can be seen clearly when you have a border turned on, as shown in Figure 15.15.

On the other hand, cell padding is the amount of space between the content of a cell and its edges. This setting is also shown in Figure 15.16.

If you don't have a border turned on, it is difficult to see the difference between cell spacing and cell padding.

Next you can define if you have header cells. Header Cells display their content centered with bold text. You can choose from multiple layouts.

Next is Accessibility, where you can determine if you have a caption for the table. By default, a caption is shown above the table and centered, but you can modify this placement in the Align Caption menu.

The Summary field provides a description of the table that can read by a screen reader but is not seen on the page.

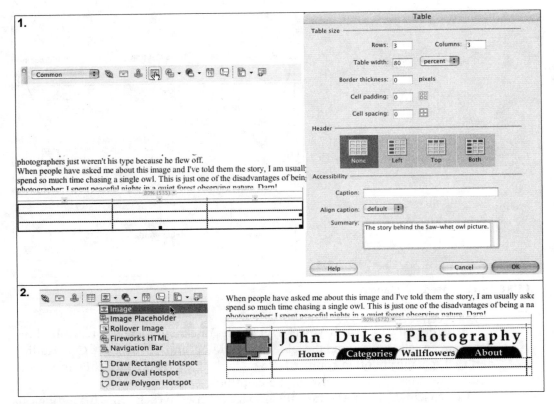

FIGURE 15.16   Inserting a table for layout.

Using a Basic Table for Layout

Now that we have learned how to create a basic table, let's create one and use it for a page layout. We will use your *saw-whetowl.html* file, as shown in Figure 15.16.

1. Place your cursor at the end of the text within your page and click the Table button on the Insert Toolbar. This action opens the Insert Table dialog box. Give the table the following properties: Rows 3, Columns 3, Table Width 80 Percent, Border Thickness 0, Cell padding 0, Cell spacing 0, Header None, and a summary statement of *The story behind the Saw-whet owl picture*. When finished, click the OK button.

ON THE CD

2. Now, we must insert some images created in Fireworks. Place your cursor inside the left cell on the top row, and select image from the Images menu on the Insert Toolbar. When your Browse menu appears, navigate to the

Dreamweaver/Chapter 15/images folder on the CD-ROM and select the *logo.gif* file. You are prompted to copy your files into the site. Do so, and save the image in the images folder. The new image should appear inside the cell. Repeat this process to insert another image. The second image is called *banner.gif* and is also located on the CD-ROM in the *Dreamweaver/Chapter 15/images* folder. The result should resemble what is shown in panel 2 of Figure 15.16.

We continue with the panels shown in Figure 15.17.

3. Select all of the text and the owl image above the table on your page, as shown in panel 1 of Figure 15.17. An easy way to select this content is to place your cursor after the end of the text, click and drag all the way up the page and to the left of the owl picture.

4. When you have selected all of the text and the owl image, click the selection and drag it into the very center cell within your table. If this proves difficult, click Edit > Cut (or press Ctrl/Command + X), click inside the center cell, and click Edit > Paste (or press Ctrl/Command + V). You should now see the content inside of your table.

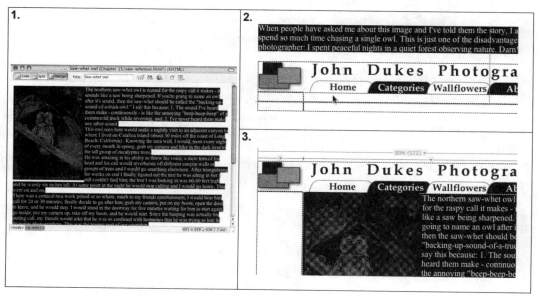

FIGURE 15.17   Continuing our layout with a table.

Preview your results in the browser by clicking File > Preview in Browser, pressing the F12 key, or selecting your browser from the Preview/Debug in Brower button menu found in the Document Toolbar. Your result should resemble that shown in Figure 15.18.

FIGURE 15.18   The saw-whet owl story, previewed in Internet Explorer.

Adjusting Table Properties

Now that we have all the content in our table, let's explore manipulating the table to display our content on the page.

Currently, our page looks pretty good, but we can refine it more and resolve some minor issues.

First, the logo image in the top-left corner is floating all by itself. It might look better if our content were underneath it. Second, the page might look nicer if we centered the table. Third, maybe we should consider putting a thin black border around the content so it appears to be a tabbed document.

Let's tackle these changes, as shown in Figure 15.19.

1. Select your entire table. A quick shortcut for doing this is to click anywhere within a cell, and click the `<table>` tag shown in the Tag Selector on the bottom of your document window, as shown in panel 1 of Figure 15.19. After selecting the table, select Center from the Align menu in the Property Inspector. This option centers your table on the page. Other options available include Default (Left), Left, and Right.

The Tag Selector, located at the bottom of the document window, is an incredibly handy tool. If you have a rudimentary knowledge of HTML tags, it can assist you in navigating within your page. For example, selecting within a table cell is difficult if the cell contains only an image. The Tag Selector makes this task easy. When you click the image, you see in the Tag Selector that `<td>` is located to the left of the `<img>` tag. Just click the `<td>` tag to select the cell.

2. Now that we have the table centered, we want the text to take up the entire row. To accomplish this, click inside of the left cell in the middle row and drag the mouse until all cells in the row are highlighted.

3. When the cells are selected, click the Merge Cells button in the Property Inspector. This option conveniently creates a `colspan` attribute of 3 for the first cell and moves your content into it. `colspan` and `rowspan` are attributes used with cells in a table. `colspan` allows a cell to take up more than one column of space; `rowspan` works in the same manner, only with rows.

4. Now, we will add a border to our modified cell. To do this, we must add a CSS style. Although we are adding CSS to this page, we will not be discussing it until later. Expand your Design Panel group and select the CSS Styles Tab, as shown. When the tab is in focus, click the New CSS Style button in the lower-right corner (second button) in the panel to open the New CSS Style dialog box. Here we type the Name *field .border.* (Make sure you include the dot.) Underneath this, select Class (can apply to any tag). Also, select This Document Only under Define In and click the OK button.

5. This procedure opens the CSS Style definition for .border window. In this window, select Border from the left under Categories. You should now be in the Border window, shown in panel 6. For the first option of Style, making sure that Same for all is checked, click the arrows to the right of Top, and

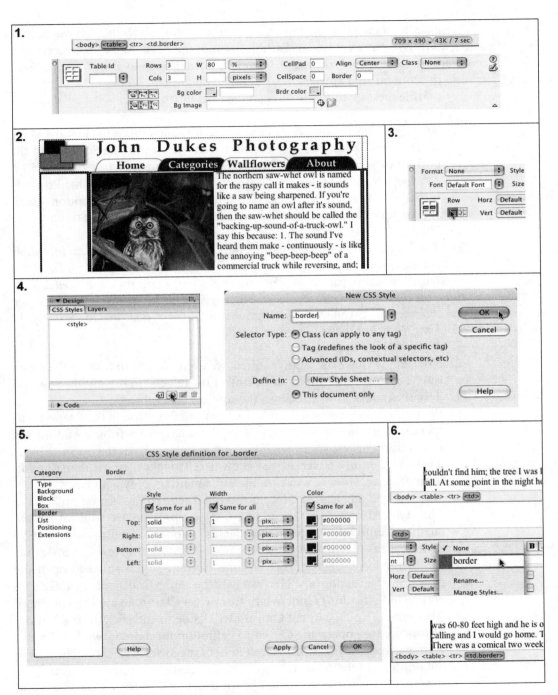

FIGURE 15.19 Adjusting our table properties.

select Solid from the menu. Under Width, type *1* next to Top, and again make certain that Same for all is checked. Under color, select black under Top and leave Same for all selected. When you are finished, click the OK button.

6. Now let's apply your new style. Click anywhere inside of the cell that contains the owl picture and click <td> in the Tag Selector underneath the document window. When you are sure that the cell is selected, choose .border from the Style menu in the Property Inspector. If you look at the Tag Selector, you can see that the <td> now says <td.border> and a border appears around the cell.

With these steps, we have accomplished everything we set out to do with our document. However, as is often the case in Web design, as soon as you resolve some issues, others appear as a result of your changes or oversight.

Currently, we don't have a heading to describe the document; this is an oversight. Another issue is that our text is butted up against the border we added, which makes reading the text more difficult. We need to resolve these issues, so before the document is ready for publication, you need to take a couple last steps.

1. Go into your Design Panel again and select the CSS tab. Press the New CSS Style button to create a new style.
2. Within the New CSS Style dialog box, type the name of *.margin* (making sure to include the dot), and choose Class (can apply to any tag). Under Define in, select This document only, and press the OK button.
3. The CSS Style definition for .margin window opens. Select Box from the left, and under Margin type *5* for Right, Bottom, and Left. Now we apply these setting to our text to separate it from the cell border.
4. Press the OK button to return to the HTML document. In the HTML document, select all of the text within the table and change Format to Paragraph in the Property Inspector.

   After changing the text format to Paragraph, select .margin from the Style menu in the Property Inspector. You see the text move away from the cell border.
5. Now we need to add a heading. Deselect all of your text by clicking a blank area of the page, and then click the space before the first word in the document. Type *Saw-whet Owl*.
6. Select the new text you have typed and change Format to Heading 2 in the Property Inspector. The new text should be placed above your other text in a larger font. While the new text is still selected, press the Align Center button in the Property Inspector to place the heading in the center, between the image and cell border.

7. Now, you must complete the images. Select the logo in the top-left corner of the page (the three rectangles) and type *Logo* in the Alt field in the Property Inspector.

8. Select the owl picture and type *Saw-whet owl* in the Alt field.

9. Select the John Dukes Photography banner on the top of the page and type *John Dukes Photography* in the Alt field.

10. With the banner image selected, create rectangular hotspots around each of the tabs. For each tab, add Alt text and a link, as shown in Table 15.1.

TABLE 15.1   Alternate Text and Links

Tabs	Alt Text	Link
Home	John Dukes Photography Home Page	/index.html
Categories	Categories	/categories.html
Wallflowers	The Wallflowers collection	/wallflowers.html
About	About John Dukes	/about.html

These last steps have completed your page. As you can see, you have a great deal of control when configuring tables in Dreamweaver. Preview the page in your browser; it should resemble that shown in Figure 15.20.

Using the Layout Mode for Tables

You have seen that tables are an important tool for creating page layouts. However, they can be a bit difficult when designing more complex layouts. Tables were initially created for tabular data (like a spreadsheet), so they can be a bit unwieldy and nonintuitive for creating a large design.

Dreamweaver enables you to tackle more complex tables with ease by offering the Layout Mode. The Layout Mode sets up your page like a pasteboard where you can freely draw in cells and add content anywhere you want.

Let's say that our client wants to have the content on a particular page laid out in a specific manner. He has provided you with a JPEG that shows the layout and wants you to duplicate it on the page.

This project is a perfect opportunity to use Layout Mode. Create a new HTML document named *wallflowers.html*. We will explore using Layout Mode in conjunction with a tracing image, as shown in Figure 15.21.

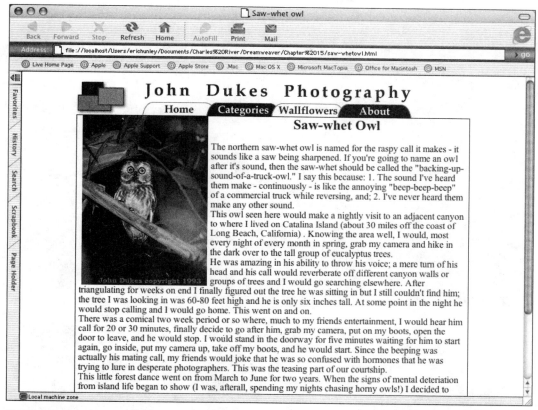

FIGURE 15.20   Our completed table layout.

Don't forget to give the page a title. We will name it Wallflowers.

Our client has provided us with an image he wants to be represented exactly on a Web page. He has displayed his photos previously in a gallery with this layout, and it has proven successful. Click Modify > Page Properties and select Tracing Image from the Categories list. Now browse to the *Dreamweaver/Chapter 15/images/* on the CD-ROM and select *traceimage.jpg*. When you press the Choose button after navigating to the image, you are prompted to copy the image to your site. This time, press the No button. The reason for pressing No is that the tracing image is something we are using to visually lay out the page. We don't want this file to be published to the Web site. Original files used for tracing can be quite large, and space is at a premium. When you have loaded this image, change the Transparency

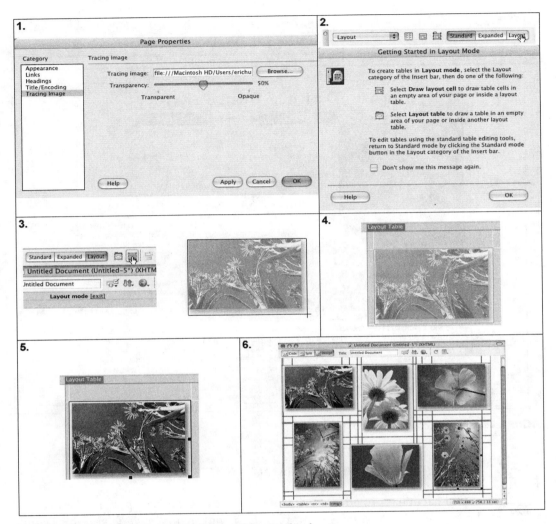

FIGURE 15.21 Using the Layout Mode with a tracing image.

to approximately 50% so you can tell the difference between the tracing image and the images you place on the page. Press the OK button to return to your page.

If you want to turn off the visibility of your tracing image while you are working on the document, click View > Tracing Image > Show. You can also adjust its placement on the page by clicking View > Tracing Image > Adjust Position or View > Tracing Image > Adjust Position. Click View > Tracing Image > Reset Position to remove adjustments.

The next step is to change into the Layout Mode. Select the Layout category from your Insert Toolbar and click the Layout button. When you have done so, you should see the dialog box shown in panel 2 of Figure 15.21. Press the OK button to return to the document.

When you return to your Web page, you notice that the appearance has changed and an exit link appears on the top of the page. This link provides a way to leave Layout Mode. While we are here, we have two options to begin laying out our content. We can press the Layout Table button and draw our table on the Web page, or we can click the Draw Layout Cell button and draw our cell on the page. Dreamweaver creates the table for us. Let's choose the second option and draw a cell around the image on the top-left area.

While you are drawing the cell, don't worry about covering the entire image area (including the drop shadow). Often, it can be helpful to cover slightly less than the content area when you are inserting an image because the image winds up expanding the cell for you. This practice creates a tighter fit, which looks better in your final result.

Once we have drawn the cell, you can see that a layout table has been created, and we now have a rectangle representing the cell. If your cell is not placed correctly, click the outline of the cell. When it appears as a blue rectangle with small squares surrounding it, you can move the cell to adjust its position. You can move it into place by using either your mouse or, to be more precise, your arrow keys. (Pressing Shift + the arrow keys moves the cell more pixels at a time.) When moving the cell into place, focus on the top-left corner of the cell. This is the point from which it expands when you insert an image.

Click inside of your newly created cell and insert an image. It is easier to click Insert > Image from the main menu because you would need to switch back to the Layout category in the Insert Toolbar otherwise. (Anything option available on the Insert Toolbar is also available in the main menu.) When the Insert Image dialog box opens, navigate to the *Dreamweaver/Chapter 15/Wallflowers/* folder on the CD-ROM, select *Sneeze.jpg* and click the Choose button. When you are prompted to copy the image to your site, do so. Place it in your images folder.

Continue the layout process to place the rest of your cells on the page. Either while you are placing the cells or after you have completed them, insert the rest of the images from the *Wallflowers* folder on the CD-ROM. To complete the first row, choose *Tethered.jpg* and *Sunbathe.jpg*. The second row consists of *Perseph.jpg*, *Gaia.jpg*, and *AlmostThere.jpg*. Click the exit link to return to Standard Mode. Your final result should resemble what is shown in pane 6 of Figure 15.21. Notice how many rows and cells there are? Imagine how difficult it would be to create this table using just the Standard Mode, as we did previously.

When you attempt to adjust the size or position of cells that contain an image, it is easy to inadvertently resize the image instead of the cell. Pay close attention to what you have selected. If you see a blue rectangle with small squares, you are adjusting the cell, which is correct. If instead you see a black box with small squares, you have selected the image accidentally.

After you preview the page in your browser, you should see that the page is not complete. As an added challenge, accomplish the following tasks:

- Center your table on the page.
- Merge the center cells in the top row and insert *banner.gif* inside the new spanned cell.
- Insert *logo.gif* in the top-left corner of the page.
- Put Alt tags and links on all of the images, as shown in Table 15.2.
  When you have finished all of the Alt tags and links on the images, you must create an image map for the banner by adding hotspots as before. Use the same attributes as you did previously.

After you have completed all of the previous steps, you no longer need the tracing image. Because the table is now centered, in fact, the tracing image is distracting. Click Modify > Page Properties and select Tracing Image from Categories list. Clear the path shown in the Tracing Image field by selecting it and pressing your Delete key. When it is clear, press the OK button to return to your page.

Now you are ready to preview the page in your browser. Your results should resemble that shown in Figure 15.22.

TABLE 15.2 Alternate Text and Links

Image	Alt Text	Link
logo.gif	Logo	blank
banner.gif	John Dukes Photography	blank
Sneeze.jpg	The Sneezeweed Family Reunion	sneeze.html
Tethered.jpg	Tethered Wings, Link	tethered.html
Sunbathe.jpg	Sunbathing, Link	sunbathe.html
Perseph.jpg	Persephone's Return, Link	perseph.html
Gaia.jpg	Gaia's Lantern, Link	gaia.html
AlmostThere.jpg	Almost There, Link	almostthere.html

FIGURE 15.22   Your final result, after modifications.

ASSETS IN DREAMWEAVER MX 2004

We close this chapter by taking a look at a helpful panel: Assets. This panel acts as a centralized repository of assets you have used within your site. It can be convenient when you want to reuse components on more than one page.

The Assets Panel is located in the Files Panel group, along with the Files Panel. You can access it by clicking the Assets Tab. In this panel, you can choose from several categories. The Assets Panel is shown in Figure 15.23.

Panel 1 in Figure 15.23 shows what images are currently used in our site. Notice, because we have *banner.gif* selected, a preview of the image appears in the upper half of the panel. This preview is helpful if you have many images with similar names. Nine buttons are available to the left to choose which type of asset you are seeking. We have currently pressed the first button, Images. The other buttons

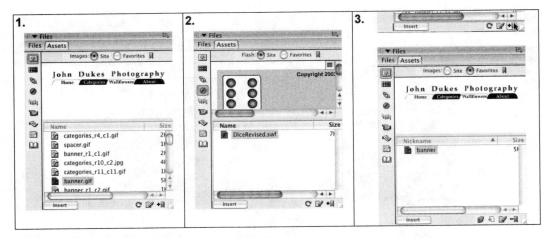

FIGURE 15.23   The Assets Panel.

are Colors, URLs, Flash, Shockwave, Movies, Scripts, Templates, and Library. Content can be added to the page simply by dragging it into the document window or by clicking the Insert button, located in the bottom-left corner of the panel.

If you have recently brought content into Dreamweaver and don't see it listed in the Assets Panel, click the Refresh button on the bottom-right (first button) of the panel in the Site View. If you still can't see the content, choose Recreate Site List from the Options menu in the top-right corner of the Assets Panel.

In the second pane we have selected Flash. Notice that our dice game has appeared in the preview window. You can preview the Flash asset selected by pressing the Play button in the top of the preview window, as we have done here to see the content.

If you are planning to reuse content frequently and don't want to navigate through all assets in your site, you can select the asset in question and press the Add to Favorites Button in the bottom-right corner of the panel. When you click the Favorites button, you see only the content you have previously added.

SUMMARY

In this chapter, you have learned how to place content in your page and create layouts using tables. These tasks take up the majority of your time when using Dreamweaver. It's now time to move on and explore "Site Management and More Dreamweaver Features."

16 Site Management and More Dreamweaver Features

It's now time to wrap it all up, and Dreamweaver MX 2004 is the program to do it. We have come a long way to get here and are almost through our design wheel.

We have discovered FreeHand MX and created a site diagram with it. We then explored the incredible power of Flash MX 2004. As an application, it's deceiving—it appears to be a simple little program to create small animations for the Web. Only when you explore it further do you see the power that can be unleashed.

Next, we started to create content with Fireworks MX 2004. It, too, offers more than meets the eye. Much of the public perceives it as simply a photo-editing tool, but it is a Web graphics machine. The ability to work with both vector and raster graphics, as well as adding HTML, is liberating to the Web designer.

We took a brief look at HTML. This chapter may seem out of place, but it is important to understand the language behind Web design. Macromedia products were not built for you to avoid HTML; they were created to enhance your usage of it.

Finally, we began to look at Dreamweaver MX 2004. This application is the centerpiece of your Web development. All content should eventually travel through Dreamweaver MX 2004 when you are using the whole suite.

Now it is time to put it all together. We will discuss more features available to you in Dreamweaver MX 2004, and then we will discuss site management. Site management is part of both the Build and Maintain stages in our design wheel.

Let's start exploring other Dreamweaver MX 2004 features with a look at templates and how they can assist you with repeating content in your site.

USING TEMPLATES

Templates are useful tools if you have repeating content on multiple pages. For example, consider our use of *banner.gif*. We used it in two documents, and each time we did, we were stuck with creating hotspots, along with their links and Alt text.

Not only is this labor redundant, but it is also prone to errors. It is easy to omit an Alt attribute or link when you are in a hurry. Wouldn't it be easier if we had to create all this information only once and not worry about it any more? Wouldn't it be even better if we could both address the repeating content and avoid having to go to every page when something, like the company logo, changes? Templates take care of this for you. Let's begin exploring the creation of templates, as shown in Figure 16.1.

1. Click File > New (or press Ctrl/Command + N) and select HTML Template from the list, as shown in panel 1 of Figure 16.1. Also select Make document XHTML compliant. After you press the OK button, you are brought to the document window, where it appears as if you are making a straightforward Web page. The only difference you see is that <<<Template>> is displayed within the title bar of the document window.

2. Insert a standard table using the following properties: Rows 3, Columns 3, Table width 80 Percent, Border thickness 0, Cell padding 0, Cell spacing 0, and Header None. In the Summary field, type *Content for John Dukes Photography*, and click the OK button.

3. After the table has been placed in the document window, add *banner.gif* and complete all links and Alt text. Also insert *logo.gif* in the upper-left corner of the page. When you have completed this, center the table, merge the middle three cells into one, and add a solid black 1-pixel border to your merged cell. While you are adjusting the table, use your mouse to make the table taller and the middle merged cells higher. Your result should resemble what is shown in panel 3.

When you are inserting banner.gif *and* logo.gif, *you can pull them from the Assets Panel.*

4. When your content is complete, click File > Save (or press Ctrl/Command + S). You see the warning displayed, as shown in pane 4. Take note of what it is telling you and press the OK button.

5. You now see the Save As Template dialog box. This dialog box is a bit different from what you have seen before. Dreamweaver automatically creates a special folder that contains all templates for the site. Type the name *general* in the Save As field and press the Save button.

Leave your template open and click File > New (or press Ctrl/Command + S). While in the New Document window, look at the top-center area. You see two buttons: General and Templates. Press the Templates button.

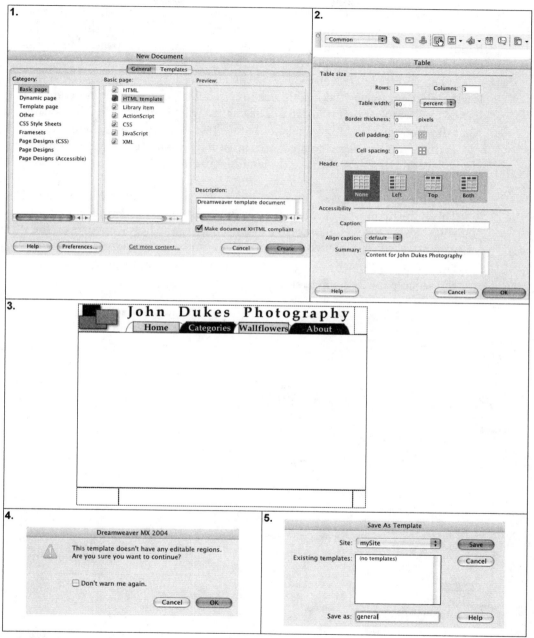

FIGURE 16.1 Creating a template.

You are now in the New from Template window. On the left you see mySite, with general selected in the center. On the right is a preview of the template—a handy feature if you have many templates. Make sure Update page when template changes is checked, and press the OK button.

When you try to click anywhere on the new page, you are greeted with the following alert message: Making this change would require changing code that is locked by a template or a translator. The change will be discarded." This warning is what the message shown in panel 4 of Figure 16.1 was alerting you about.

To have modify pages created, you must have what are known as editable regions. Several types of region are shown in Figure 16.2.

Editable Region: Allows the addition of any type of content within the region. This is the main type of region you will be inserting into a template. In this pane, you see what the region looks like in the template and how it appears on the Web page attached to it. Notice that the content can be changed on the Web page.

Optional Region: Contains specific content that cannot be changed. As you can see in pane 2, the field shown on the Web page has the same content from

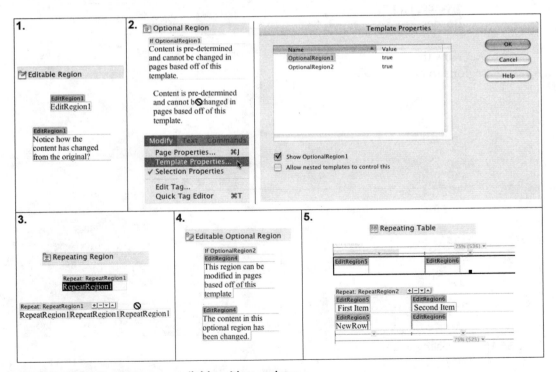

FIGURE 16.2   Region types available with templates.

the template shown above it. Notice the cursor is showing the No icon. What makes these regions optional is that you have the choice of whether or not the field appears in a page created from the template. You can choose this by clicking Modify > Template Properties. In this window, highlight the Optional field in question and uncheck Show OptionRegion to hide the region.

Repeating Region: Contains predetermined content that cannot be modified. Only the designer can add or subtract from the total number of regions. You can see in pane 3 the repeating region created in the template. Just underneath it is how it appears on the Web page. Notice the plus sign (+), minus sign (–), and two arrows. The + was clicked twice, creating two repeats of the original (the minus takes them away), but as the pointer icon shows, the content cannot be changed. You must create an editable field within the region to change content.

Editable Optional Region: Allows contents to be edited later. This is similar to an optional region. Notice that the content has changed in the Web page.

Repeating Table: Creates a table with fields that can have content inserted. New rows can also be added by pressing the plus sign (+). The table shown was created much like a standard table with a Row value of 1, Columns of 3, and Border thickness of 1.

Now that we have learned what region types are available to use, let's add some regions to our general template, as shown in Figure 16.3.

1. Switch back to your template, and in your merged cells in the middle row, add an editable region. Rename it to *content*.
2. When you have placed the content editable region, you see that it is in the center of the Web page. Correct this placement by clicking within the cell and choosing Top under Vert in the Property Inspector. This option adds the `valign="top"` attribute to your cell, which overrides the default behavior of `"middle"`. You may now want to delete the content inside the editable region and press your Enter/Return key a few times so you can more easily see the Web pages attached to this template.
3. Your revised template, complete with the expanded editable region, is shown in pane 3. Save your file and return to your Web page.

ON THE CD

We now must add content to your Web page created from the template. First, you notice that you have the editable region showing in the merged cell. Click inside, navigate to *Dreamweaver/Chapter 16/images*, and choose *Mesaguaro.jpg*. When prompted, copy it into your images folder in mySite.

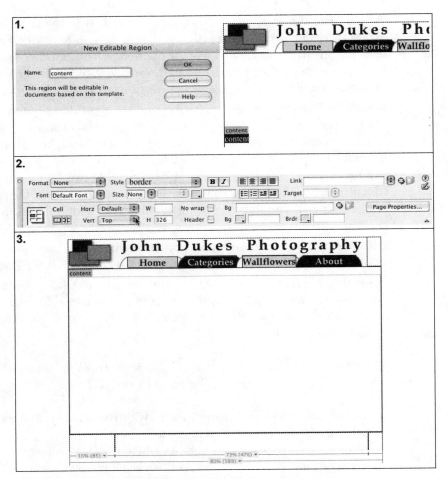

FIGURE 16.3 Adding an editable region to our template.

After you have added your image, click File > Open (or press Ctrl/Command + O), and choose *aboutjohn.txt* located in the *Dreamweaver/Chapter 16/* folder. When the file opens, click Edit > Select All (or press Ctrl/Command + A) and then click Edit > Copy (or press Ctrl/Command + C). Return to your new document using either your tabs (Windows) or by clicking Window in the main menu (both operating systems). Paste the text onto the page, after the image, by clicking Edit > Paste (or press Ctrl/Command + C).

When you have added the text to your page, you see that the image is resting on top of the text. Click your image to select it and choose Right from the Align menu in the Property Inspector.

Now you have your graphic and text aligned on the page with one another. You see that the text is running up against the border of your merged cells. We must create a new style to stop this from occurring. However, we cannot add a style in this page. Because the page is based on a template, we have no access to add CSS content. We can apply the content, but we cannot create it. We must create the style in the general template.

Change the active document to *general.dwt* and expand your Design Panel, if it is currently not open. In the panel, select the CSS Styles Tab, and click the New CSS Style button in the bottom-right corner of the panel.

In the New CSS Style dialog box, type *.margin* (including the dot) in Name, choose Class for Selector Type, This document only under Define In, and press the OK button. The CSS Style Definition for .margin window opens. Select Box from the Category list and enter *5* pixels for Right, Bottom, and Left (making certain you have Same for All unchecked), and press the OK button.

You cannot apply this style within the template, so you must go back to your Web page. In the Web page, select all of the text, and pick .margin from the Style menu in the Property Inspector. You now have a margin around all of the text on the page and your workspace should resemble that shown in Figure 16.4.

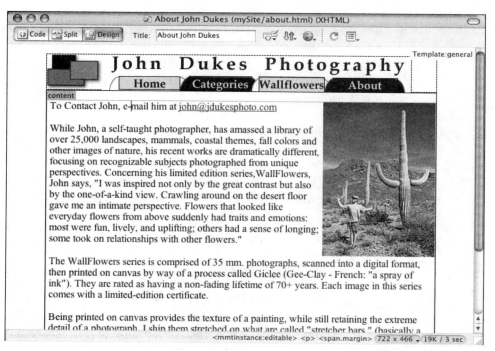

FIGURE 16.4 The completed *about.html* Web page based on the general template.

Another method to create a template is to save a pre-existing Web page. For this example, we will import our *background.html* content that we created in Fireworks MX 2004.

1. Create a new HTML page. If you are in the Template window, press the General button in the top-center area of the screen to get to normal pages. Select Basic Page: HTML and click the Create button. Save the page as *back.html*.

ON THE CD

2. Click the Images button in the Insert Toolbar and choose Fireworks HTML. Navigate to your FireworksWeb folder. If you do not have this folder, navigate to the *Dreamweaver/Chapter 16* folder on the CD-ROM. Select *background.html* and click Open. When prompted, copy the images into your images folder in mySite.

3. Your imported Fireworks content is on the stage. Select your table and choose Center under the Align menu in the Property Inspector.

4. Now, click File > Save As Template, enter the name *background* in the Save As field, and click Save. When you are asked to update links, click the OK button.

5. All that needs to be done at this point is to create an editable region and tweak a cell. Place your cursor inside the largest cell in the table and insert an editable region.

6. In the cell on the left side of the page, click the image. With the image selected, click <td> in the tag selector in the bottom of the document window, and choose Top in the Vert menu of the Property Inspector. This option sets the valign attribute to top in the HTML code. Save your template; it is now complete.

NOTE

*The Vert menu in the Property Inspector allows you to set what may be one of the most important attributes you can create with tables—*valign. *By setting this attribute to* top, *you don't have to worry about having content in the adjacent cell running past the bottom of the page. If you leave it unselected, it defaults to* center, *which causes the image to seemingly float away from the logo above it.*

CASCADING STYLE SHEETS (CSS)

Cascading Style Sheets (CSS) as a technology was initially developed by the World Wide Web Consortium (W3C) as a means to address shortfalls in HTML formatting. The W3C created them as a method of separating the content of a page from its formatting.

When HTML was initially created, it was meant to be a quick and efficient means of putting data on the Web. Most original documents posted were scientific and not prone to colorful themes. This all changed, however, as the Web grew.

Businesses began to take an interest in the Web as another means for marketing, and later selling products, and the public awareness of the Internet grew.

Initially, the primary products marketed on the Web were technology based, often computers themselves. The limitations of the Web and HTML were not of a grave concern because most of the audience was involved with technology and understood its limitations.

As the public awareness of the Internet grew, these limitations were no longer acceptable. Web design suddenly became a viable field of employment, and a new breed of designers were pulling every trick possible to create engaging content.

They faced issues with limitations in technology. Also, perhaps more important, there were limitations with browsers that displayed HTML.

In the early days of the Web, a graphical browser named Mosaic took the world by storm. It later became Netscape Navigator. After a time, Microsoft became interested in the Internet as a way to expand their influence and came out with Internet Explorer (IE).

This is where the problems started. To be competitive with one another, Microsoft and Netscape began to introduce proprietary features within their browsers to maintain and increase market share. This led to a designers' nightmare.

Worse still, HTML was treated in a loose and supposedly friendly manner by the browsers. Because not many good tools were on the market and educational opportunities were limited, most designers taught themselves HTML, along with bad habits.

Both Microsoft and Netscape designed their browsers to be forgiving to bad coding habits. This flexibility is still in place today. After all, if the browsers suddenly enforced strict rules for HTML code, millions of Web sites already on the Web would not function, and the sad truth is many people would assume it was the browsers' fault.

When compounded with the proprietary nature of browsers, Web designers had an outlandish situation, often having to design two versions of every page.

This is where the W3C stepped in. It was created as a standards-creating committee to oversee Web design and development. Designers and browser manufacturers could finally look to a central location for guidelines.

One of the issues addressed was the extremely limited capacity in formatting that HTML provided. With the massive growth of the Internet and more professional graphic designers working on material, the limitations of HTML were quickly brought to light.

Professional graphic designers were used to working in print with well-established, robust technologies. Their talents were seriously compromised when working on the Web. To address this need, the W3C came up with the idea of CSS, which would enable much greater control of formatting but still keep the actual HTML content separate. The advantage of keeping format separate from the content allows pages to grow more beautiful without the HTML language growing out of control.

CSS offers the ability to have a single stylesheet control the formatting of every page on a site connected to that stylesheet. Imagine if you had a site with 900 pages (not an uncommon occurrence). Then your manager informs you that the company is no longer using navy blue as its theme color; it has chosen to go with a royal blue. He also informs you that all of the text on all of the pages must be modified to reflect this by Monday (it is now Friday) when the company is having a big marketing rollout.

With original HTML, this situation would be highly stressful. You would have to open every Web page individually and modify all font attributes on each. However, with CSS, if you have designed your site well, you can modify attributes on one page. Every page in the site then reflects those changes. Instead of taking all weekend to change your theme, you could finish it in minutes.

If that is not enough of a reason to use CSS, here is another. The W3C is beginning to enforce the use of the language. As of HTML 4.01, HTML style attributes were deprecated and are slated for removal. The W3C is possibly attempting to help designers help themselves.

Let's explore CSS and the CSS Definition dialog box, as shown in Figure 16.5.

To create a new style, click the New CSS Style button in the CSS Styles Panel to opens the New CSS Style dialog box. In this dialog box, you have several choices:

Selector Type (Class, Tag, and Advanced): Use a Class if you are creating a style that will be used in special instances. We created two classes previously: .border and .margin. Tag allows you to redefine the characteristics of an HTML tag. When you click the arrows to the right of Name field, you are presented with a menu of available HTML tags. Using Tag is a great choice when you are building a theme for a site. For example, if you want to set all of your Heading 1 tags to be a font size of 24, Arial, and navy blue, choose the H1 tag option. Every H1 in every page attached to the stylesheet shares these attributes, unless specifically changed. The last option, Advanced, applies to links. You can use these settings to change the way hyperlinks are displayed. Be careful when using this setting, because unexpected link formats can often be confusing to users.

Define in: Determines whether a style applies to the current documents or to a New CSS file. The advantage of using New CSS file is that you can create an ex-

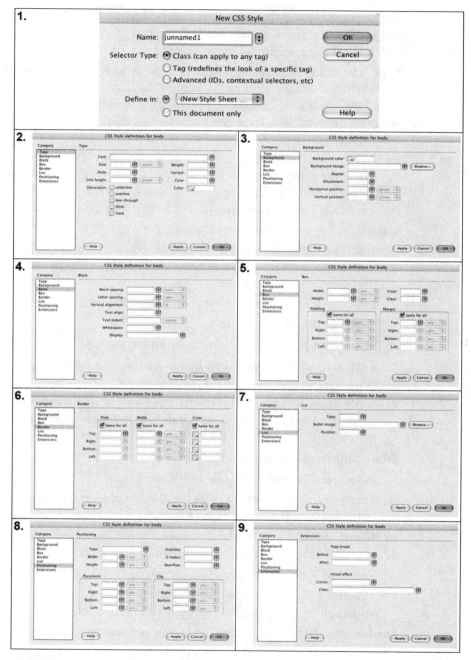

FIGURE 16.5   The CSS Definition dialog box.

ternal stylesheet and then attach as many documents as you want to it. When this option is chosen, a new dialog box prompts you for both a location in which to save the document and a name.

Type: Defines font attributes, such as Font (typeface), Size, Weight (level of boldness), Style (italic, oblique), Variant (Small-caps), Line height (leading, or space between lines), Case (all uppercase or lowercase), Decoration, and Color. Many of these options have Normal as an option. This option overrides another stylesheet, if one is attached to the page.

Background: Applies background images and color. Background images are considered by many to be a bad idea for pages. They tend to make reading content difficult and can add unnecessary size to a Web page. Most high-level, professionally created Web sites do not have background images.

Block: Contains the following advanced text settings:

> **Word Spacing:** Defines the space used between words. This setting is not displayed in the Dreamweaver workspace. You must preview the page in the browser to see it applied.
>
> **Letter Spacing:** Defines the space between letters.
>
> **Vertical Alignment:** Aligns text within the line.
>
> **Text Align:** Aligns text horizontally on the page.
>
> **Text Indent:** Indents the first line in a paragraph or text block.
>
> **Whitespace:** Handles white space in a document. The Pre option makes all white space count and be displayed. Normal disregards all extra white space, allowing only one space total. No wrap only wraps text (feed to the next line) if a break tag (`<br>`) is used.

Box: Controls placement of objects in a Web page.

> **Width and Height:** Controls width and height.
>
> **Float:** Determines how the object has other objects float around it. Similar in principle to the `image align` attribute.
>
> **Clear:** Specifies which sides do not work with layers. When a layer is on the specified side, the object moves below.
>
> **Padding:** Acts like cell padding, but works with borders or margins.
>
> **Margin:** Defines the amount of space between the border of an element and another element. This option is similar in principle to cell spacing.

Border: Sets the type, thickness, and color of borders around content.

List: Customizes lists. You can specify the bullet character, type, and position.

Positioning: Controls the placement of layers on your Web page.

Extensions: Contains three options—Pagebreak, Cursor, and Filter. Pagebreak forces a page break between areas when a user prints the document. Support for this option among browsers is spotty. Cursor changes the user's cursor to reflect the selected icon when it passes over an object with the style applied. Filter is used to apply special effects, like drop shadow or invert to objects on a page. Be selective with this option because it is supported only by cutting-edge and very modern browsers.

CSS is a powerful tool to use for formatting elements on your pages. It is the wave of the future. The only concern you should have when using CSS is browser support. Browsers have been slow to adopt some of the features, and it is a good idea to stick with older formatting options like text font, color, weight, and style. Your odds are best when using these rules because they offer the most universal support. You should test your Web site in as many browsers as possible when implementing styles.

CSS is easy to apply when using Dreamweaver. The following steps demonstrate how quickly you can make sweeping changes with CSS:

1. Create an HTML document and save it as page1.html. On the document, create a Heading 1 that says Heading 1, a Heading 2 that says Heading 2, and a paragraph that says This is my paragraph. Save the file and then click File > Save As. Name it page2.html.

2. Expand your CSS Styles Panel and click the Add CSS Style button. Select Tag under Selector Type and choose H1 from the list. You also want to use the option Define in (New Style Sheet File) and click the OK button. Name the file *styles* and save it to mySite.

3. In the CSS Style Definition dialog box, select Arial, Helvetica, sans-serif for Font, 36 px for Size, Weight of 800, Style of Oblique, Case of Uppercase, and color of Red. Click the Apply button and look on the Web page. You should see a change immediately for Heading 1.

4. Change Category to Background in the CSS Style Definition dialog box and choose a background color of Blue. Click the Apply button. You see that the area behind the text is now a blue block.

5. Now change Category to Block and add a Letter spacing of 1 ems and Text-align of Center. The measurement of ems is used for horizontal spacing and is relative. It literally means the width of the letter *m* according to the current font size and style. Another measurement is ex, which is the height of a lowercase *x* in vertical spacing. When you have made your entries, click Apply to see the changes. The letters are now spread out in your heading and the text is centered on the page. You can also use negative values to bring letters closer together.

6. Choose Border in the Category list. Add a border Style of Solid, a Width of 3 px, and a Color of black. Make certain that Same for all is selected. Press the OK button. You are returned to the document window.

7. Click anywhere in Heading 2, and press the Add CSS Style button in the CSS Styles Panel. Notice H2 and tag are already picked for you, and styles.css is shown in the New CSS Style dialog box. Click the OK button, and create a unique style for Heading 2. Repeat this procedure for your paragraph.

8. Now we can see the magic of CSS. Click File > Open and open *page1.html*.

9. You see that Heading 1, Heading 2, and your paragraph are in their default states. Let's do something about this. In your CSS Styles Panel, click the Attach Style Sheet button in the bottom-right (first button) of the panel to open the Attach External Style Sheet window. Browse to styles.css, which you created. Make sure that you have Add as Link selected. You have two methods of attaching an external stylesheet: Link and Attach. More browsers support the Link method, so you will use this method most often. There is no real functional difference between Link and Attach, so you won't be sacrificing anything. Click the OK button to attach the stylesheet to your document, using Link.

10. Now look at your page. Notice that all of your elements share the same styles as *page2.html*—and you haven't had to do anything on this page. If you make changes to any of the styles in your stylesheet, both pages will reflect them.

Dreamweaver also provides sample CSS stylesheets for your use. They can be a great starting point, and you can build from there. These stylesheets can be found as a link when you are in the Attach External Style Sheet window at the bottom of the dialog box. You also can create a stylesheet separately from a Web page by clicking File > New and choosing CSS in the Basic Page category. You can also choose a predefined CSS stylesheet from either the CSS Stylesheets or Page Design (CSS) categories.

USING LAYERS

Layers work hand in hand with CSS. For this reason, they are often called *CSS layers*.

Layers offer you a great deal of control when formatting Web pages. Not only can you place them wherever you want on the page, they can overlap one another, be moved dynamically, or hidden by adding scripting.

The only issue with using layers is the lack of widespread browser compatibility. Also, the way they are sometimes displayed can be unpredictable. For this reason, you may find yourself using tables if you are designing for a large audience.

A great feature of using layers in Dreamweaver is that you can convert them to tables after you have created them. This capability enables you to create two versions of the same page with ease, or even use layers as an alternative to the Layout Mode. Let's explore layers, beginning with Figure 16.6.

1. Drawing a layer is as simple as drawing a rectangle. Let's look at this principle using our Wallflowers page again to get a comparison of layers versus Layout Mode. Create a new HTML page and save it as *layers.html*. Click View > Tracing Image > Load (another method of adding a tracing image to a page), navigate to *traceimage.jpg* located in the *Dreamweaver/Chapter 15/images* folder on the CD-ROM, and click the Choose button. You are prompted to copy your image into your site. Click the No button because we are not publishing the image. This action opens the Tracing Image Category in your Page Properties window with Tracing Image path already populated. Change your Transparency slider to approximately 50% and click the OK button. You are back on your page, complete with a tracing image in the background.

2. Select Layout from the Categories menu in the Insert Toolbar. In Layout, choose the Draw Layer button (third button from the left). Draw a rectangle around the top-left image (*sneeze.jpg*) on the page, as shown in panel 2 of Figure 16.6. Notice that when you click the layer outline, you see a new rectangle complete with sizing handles on all sides and a handle on the top. Use this handle to move the layer around on the page. If you want to move multiple layers at the same time, you can select them by pressing Shift + click.

3. After you draw the rectangle, name the layer *sneeze* in the Layer ID field in the Property Inspector. Draw rectangles around all other images in the tracing image and name each layer. For the rest of the first row, the names are *tethered* and *sunbathe*. For the second row, use the names *perseph*, *gaia*, and *almostthere*. If you open the Layers Panel (found under Design with CSS Styles) you see all of your named layers.

4. Insert the following images into the layers: *sneeze.jpg*, *tethered.jpg*, *sunbathe.jpg*, *perseph.jpg*, *gaia.jpg*, and *almostThere.jpg*. Remember to add Alt text for each (*Sneezeweed Family Reunion, Tethered Wings, Sunbathing, Persephone's Return, Gaia's Lantern,* and *Almost There.*) You also must add links for each image (*sneeze.html, tethered.html, sunbathe.html, perseph.html, gaia.html,* and *almostthere.html*). Your final result should resemble what is shown in panel 4 of Figure 16.6. Remember to clear out the tracing image in the Page Properties Tracing image field because you no longer need it.

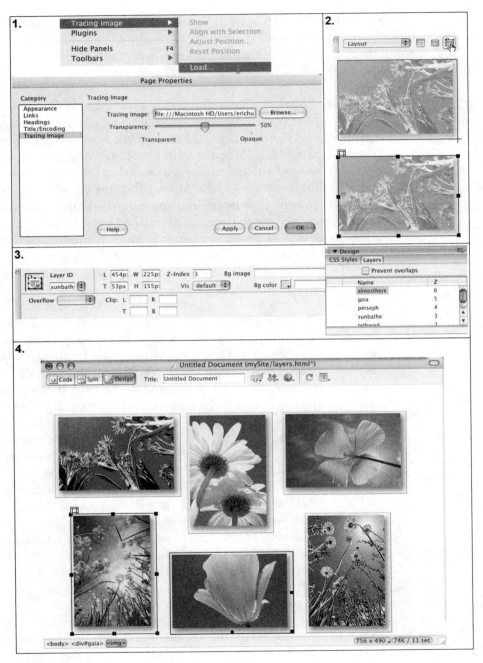

FIGURE 16.6 Drawing layers.

The important elements you see in the workspace are the Layers Panel and the Property Inspector. The Layers Panel enables you to see all of the layers on the page in a centralized location. It also displays their Z-Index, which is the level at which they reside, also known as the stacking order. The higher the Z-Index, the higher the layer rests in the stacking order. This order provides the ability of the layers to overlap one another.

You can adjust layer visibility by clicking the eye in the panel. Each time you click it, you go to another setting. These settings include Default (layer is visible, no icon in the panel), Visible (open eye icon in the panel), and Hidden (closed eye icon). You also can click the header eye icon in the top of the column to toggle all the layers at once between Visible and Hidden. (Default is not an option.)

In the top of the panel, you have the option to Prevent overlaps. This option prevents the layers from overlapping when you are positioning them, in case you plan to later convert them to tables.

The Property Inspector provides numerous options for a selected layer. You can change the Z-Index and visibility, like in the Layers Panel, with the additional option of Inherit for visibility. Inherit is used when you have nested layers (layers within layers). If you set Inherit on the inner layer, it inherits the status of its parent. You can also adjust a layer's positioning by explicitly typing values in the L (Left) and T (Top) fields. These values determine how far the layer is placed from the edges of a Web page. Clip determines how much of the layer is visible at any given point. This option is commonly used with JavaScript to create a wipe effect (not supported in all browsers).

Overflow determines how the browser handles content that takes up more space than a layer's current size. Settings include Visible, which stretches the layer to fit the content; Hidden, which does not show the extra content; Scroll, which causes the browser to add scroll bars to the layer, whether needed or not; and Auto, which allows the browser to display scrollbars only when needed.

One of the best features of using Dreamweaver MX 2004 to work with layers is its ability to convert layers to tables and vice versa. In fact, many designers use layers and the Convert to table option instead using of Layout Mode. You may also find this method easier.

Let's convert our page to a table.

1. Click File > Save As and name the page *layertotable.html*.
2. Click Modify > Convert > Layers to Table.
3. The Convert Layers to Table dialog box opens. Here, you have options for your Table layout and Layout Tools. Table layout gives you the option of Most accurate, which creates as many cells as necessary to preserve your positioning. Smallest: collapse empty cells causes cells that are smaller than

the size you specify to collapse, creating a less-complex table. You can also choose Use transparent GIFs for keeping the width of empty cells constant by filling the last row with 1-pixel transparent GIFs, and Center on page to center the final table. Within Layout Tools, you have the options of Prevent layer overlaps (overlaps are not allowed in tables), Show layers panel, Show grid, and Snap to grid. Prevent layer overlaps prevents issues with tables. Show layers panel opens the Layers Panel and keeps it in focus. Show grid and Snap to grid work together to assist you in accurate layout.

4. Choose Most Accurate, Use transparent GIFs, Center on page, and click the OK button. You have now converted your layers to a table. Wasn't that simple? You may find this method even easier than using the Layout Mode.

ADDING BEHAVIORS

Just as you have behaviors available to you in Fireworks MX 2004, you can find behaviors in Dreamweaver MX 2004. In fact, Dreamweaver supports even more behaviors than Fireworks.

For a start, we must discuss which behaviors we are seeing. Dreamweaver offers two types: behaviors and server behaviors.

Behaviors user client-side scripting, namely JavaScript. Client-side means that the user's browser runs the scripts.

On the other hand, server behaviors are written in a server-side scripting language, of which you have several from which to choose. Server-side scripts are run on the server, and they tend to be more powerful.

Server behaviors are used for security. For example, you would never want to use a client-side script to connect to your database directly because doing so would cause the code making the connection visible to the world in the Web page source code. On the flipside, you wouldn't want to have a server rolling images over for the users when their pointer passes over them because this would be a terrible waste of resources.

Each type of script has its place. In this section, we discuss client-side scripting called behaviors. We will add some simple behaviors to our Web site, as shown in Figure 16.7.

1. For these behaviors, open the *layers.html* Web page you created earlier. The first behavior we will add is a status bar message. Expand your Tag Inspector and click the Behaviors Tab. Now, click a blank area of the Web page, then click the Add behavior button in the Behaviors Panel. This ac-

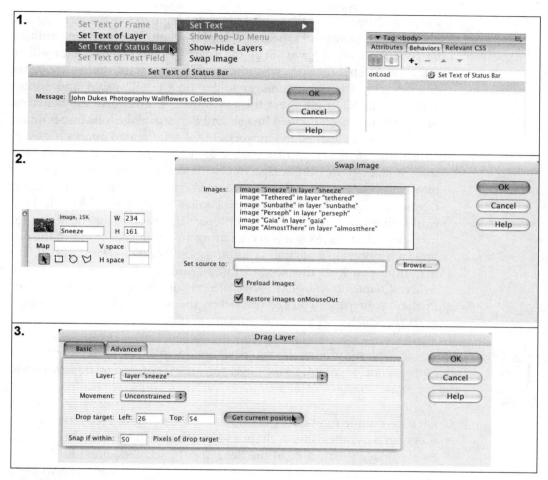

FIGURE 16.7 Adding behaviors.

tion opens a long list of choices. Click Set Text > Set Text of Status Bar. Within the resulting dialog box, type *John Dukes Photography Wallflowers Collection*. Preview the document in your browser. You should see the new message in the status bar. This behavior is also found in Fireworks MX 2004.

ON THE CD

2. Now we will create some basic swap images. You must name all of your images so that the JavaScript generated by Dreamweaver has a way to communicate with them. Name the images *Sneeze, Tethered, Sunbathe, Perseph, Gaia*, and *AlmostThere* in the Title field in the top-left side of the

Property Inspector, next to the preview window. Click *sneeze.jpg* and choose Swap Image from the Add Behavior menu. The Swap Image dialog box opens, displaying a list of all the images on your page. *Sneeze* will already be selected for you. This image is what we want, so browse to the *Dreamweaver/Chapter 16/images* folder on the CD-ROM and choose *WallflowerLndOver.gif*. Press the OK button to complete the behavior. Make sure that both Preload Images and Restore images onMouseOut are checked. As you learned in Fireworks MX 2004, Preload images is used to ensure that images are available when the user mouses over an object. Restore images causes the image to revert to the original when the user moves his mouse away. You have now created your first swap image in Dreamweaver. If the process seems similar to what you found in Fireworks, that is because, in fact, it is. Repeat this process for the rest of the images on the page. When you are setting a swap image for any of the pictures positioned in a portrait fashion, choose *WallflowerPortOver.gif*. The first time you load this second image, you must navigate to *Dreamweaver/Chapter 16/images* to select it and copy it to your images folder. Preview your page. You see that when the mouse rolls over an image, users see which sizes and quantities are available.

When you display text on an image, as we do in step 3, you must be certain the same information is repeated on the target page. If it is not, you are neglecting those who are unable to read text on images, such as users with screen readers.

3. Let's have some fun with layers now. We are going to set up the page so users can move the pictures about and line them up as they see fit. Click the *Sneeze* image to select it. In the Behaviors Panel, click the Add Behavior button and choose Drag Layer. The Drag Layer window opens, giving you options to choose the layer. Leave it with layer *sneeze*, as it is. Under this option, you have movement options. You can use the default of Unconstrained, which allows the user to drag the layer anywhere on the page, or Constrained where you can set limitations in all directions. We will use Unconstrained. If you want your image to snap into place when it is moved near a location, you can adjust Drop target. Click the Get current position button so the layer target is at its original location. When Get current position is selected, Snap within is automatically populated for you with 50 pixels. If the user is within that distance and releases his mouse button, the image snaps into place. Leave this value at 50. Repeat the same procedure for all of your layers, and test the page in your browser. Your layers should allow themselves to be dragged.

If you are a Macintosh user, you must test Drag Layer with Internet Explorer. Safari does not support this behavior as of Version 1.1.

As you can see, you can have some fun using behaviors. Behaviors also have some practical purposes.

Three of the most practical behaviors are Check Browser, Check Plugin, and Goto URL.

Check Browser: Allows you to see what browser the user has and redirect it to another page, if necessary. This option can be important if you are using features that may not be supported by some of your target audience's browsers. You can create different versions of your pages and move users to those pages when they arrive.

Check Plugin: Operates on the same principle as Check Browser. If a user does not have the Flash Player or another type of plug-in, for example, you can send him to an HTML-only portion of your site without forcing him to download software.

Goto URL: Redirects users to a URL. You can used this option if you have moved your site to another location. You can also use it for customized 404 Page not Found pages.

SERVER BEHAVIORS

Dreamweaver has incredible capabilities to connect to databases with built-in server-side support written in several languages. Although it is beyond the scope of this book to cover connecting to databases using the Dreamweaver interface, some great resources are out there.

PHP and ColdFusion are two of the most popular means to connect to databases using Dreamweaver MX 2004. You don't even need to see the code—Dreamweaver does the background programming for you.

If you want to explore these two languages further, *ColdFusion MX Web Application Construction Kit* is a great resource for learning about programming ColdFusion. If you want to explore communication between PHP and Dreamweaver, consider *Dreamweaver MX: PHP Web Development* by Gareth Downes Powell, Tim Green, and Bruno Mairlot.

Also, tutorials covering connectivity with Dreamweaver MX 2004, ColdFusion MX, and PHP are available at *www.erichunley.com*. On the site, there are also tutorials exploring how to install and configure ColdFusion on a Macintosh for use as a development machine.

CREATING FORMS

Forms are a common element found on Web pages. They are the only method of gathering user information with HTML.

Dreamweaver MX 2004 offers the ability to create forms in an easy and efficient manner. You can access forms under the Insert Toolbar in the Forms category.

When using forms, keep in mind that forms are utterly worthless by themselves; you must use them in conjunction with scripts (primarily server-side). Although the form collects data, you must have some sort of programming to receive and act upon the data.

Let's look at our different form fields. Create a new HTML file and save it as *forms.html*. The next procedure is shown in Figure 16.8.

1. Select the Forms category in the Insert Toolbar. The first tag you use when creating a form is the `<form>` tag itself. This is also the first tag available in the category. Click the page, then press the Form button. A new form is inserted on the stage where you clicked. In the Property Inspector the following fields are available:

   Form name: Allows you to name your form. It is important to name forms if you want JavaScript to be used with them. We will call this form *myForm*.

   Action: Defines the action a script should take. Remember, a form cannot work on its own. It must have an action. This action is usually set as a path to a script on the server. For testing purposes, enter mailto:*youremailaddress@yourdomain.com*. This action causes the form fields to be added to an e-mail message, as long as you are using a standard e-mail client like Outlook Express. You will have issues if you are using America Online (AOL) or a Web-based e-mail service. These issues are why you shouldn't use this method in a production environment.

   Target: Works in the same manner as target for links.

   Method: Determines how the data is sent. You have three choices.

   > **GET:** Send the information in the URL of the browser request. This method is not secure and has limitations of how much text can be sent.

   > **POST:** Sends the information in the body of the request and allows more information to be passed. Although it is more secure than GET, it is not truly secure. Your information can still be seen if a packet sniffer is used. To truly make the data passed from a form secure, you must use some form of encryption, like Secure Hypertext Transfer Protocol (HTTPS). The default method is GET, so be careful when you choose this option.

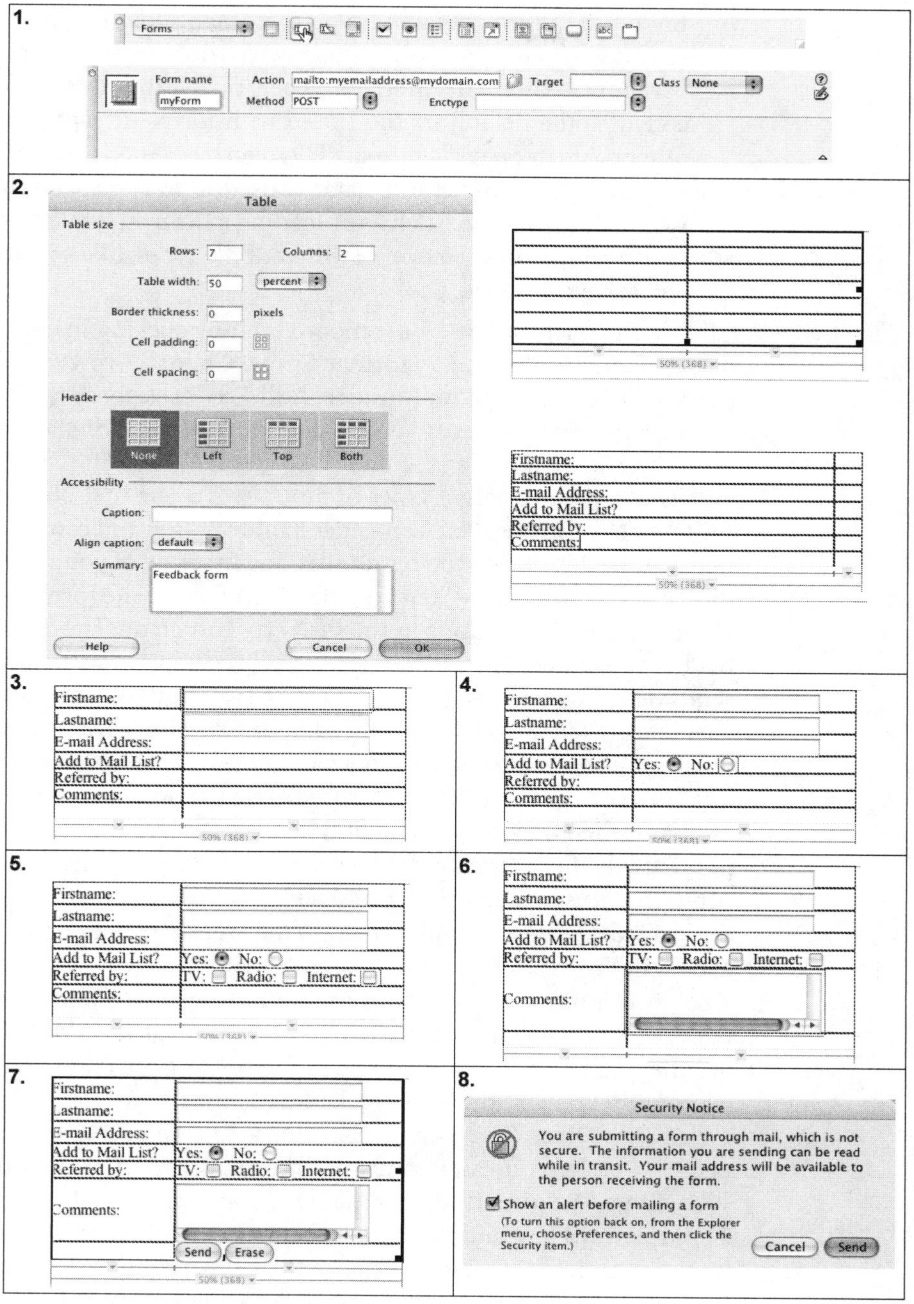

FIGURE 16.8   Using forms.

Enctype: Determines what type of content you are submitting. You have two options—application/x-www-form-urlencoded and multi-part/form-data. The first, Enctype application/x-www-form-urlen-coded, is the default method used with forms. It replaces spaces and other characters so a legitimate URL can be created. The second type of encoding, multipart/form-data, is used if you are sending more advanced information, such as uploading a file from the user's hard disk. It also allows presentation of different file types, like spreadsheets. We will leave this blank.

2. Click in the form and insert a standard table by clicking Insert > Table. Tables are commonly used to format forms. Choose 7 rows, 2 columns, no border, 50% width, and no header. Add Feedback form in the Summary Field. In the left column of your table, enter the following text: *Firstname:*, *Lastname:*, *E-mail Address:*, *Add to Mail List?*, *Referred by:*, and *Comments*.

3. Forms comprise different types of input fields. The first one we explore is the text field. This field collects general information and can accept any textual input. Click inside the right cell in the first row of your table, and click the Text Field button. When you place this field in the form, you find that you have multiple options in the Property Inspector. The TextField name field is where we type *Firstname.* (It is important to name any field that sends data so the script can refer to it.) Char width determines how many characters wide the field is displayed. Max Chars sets how many characters are actually allowed. Type changes the type of field you are using. (Multi line converts the Text Field into a TextArea; Password turns user input into asterisks when they type it; and Single line is the default.) Init val is used to populate the field with data. Wrap is used if you have changed the type to Multi line. Insert two more Text Fields in the following two rows. Name these fields *Lastname* and *E-mail.* Your result should resemble that is shown in Figure 16.8.

4. The next options we explore are radio buttons and radio groups. Essentially, they are the same thing. Radio buttons are grouped together by having the same name, which tells the browser to treat them as a group and allow only one option to be picked at a time. When you insert a radio group with Dreamweaver, you can choose to format them by using <br /> tags or a table. You can also choose how many to insert and their values. We will use radio buttons and name them appropriately to group them. Type the word *Yes:* and press Radio button on the Insert Toolbar. This action inserts the first radio button. In the Property Inspector, name it *mail-list,* and set at Checked value of Yes. The Checked value is what is sent to

the script if this button is chosen. Also change the Initial state to Checked. This setting causes Yes to be the default value. Click the cell and place your cursor to the right of the radio button, add a space, and type *No:*. Insert another radio button with the name of *maillist* and value of No. These two buttons are now tied to one another; the user can choose only one.

5. Checkboxes are the same as radio buttons in structure, but they allow the user to pick more than one option at a time. We are going to create checkboxes for our Referred field. In the cell to the right of Referred, type *TV:*, insert a checkbox (fifth button), type *Radio:*, insert a checkbox, type *Internet:*, and insert your last checkbox. Now, select each checkbox, give them each the name of *Referred*, and values of Radio, TV, and Internet.

6. The last input field we create is the TextArea. You have two ways to go about creating this element. You can create a Text Field and then set it to Multi line. The second method is to use Textarea (fourth button) in the Insert Toolbar. We will use the second method. Click in the cell to the right of Comments and insert a TextArea. Notice that it is displayed as Text Field in the Property Inspector. Name this *comments* and leave the rest of the setting at their defaults.

7. Last, we must insert two buttons. One is to submit the form and the other resets or clears the form. Click in the right cell of the last row. Choose Button (third from the right) in the Insert Toolbar, add a space, and add another button. Click the first button to select it. You now can change settings in the Property Inspector. Buttons are simplistic. You can give them a name, but it is not really necessary unless you are referring to them from a script. You also can change the Label (what the user sees on the face of the button). We will call this button Send. Buttons provide users a way to initiate an action. The default Action is Submit, which sends the form data to the location specified in the Action field in the <form> tag. You can also choose None, which makes the field dependent on another script tied to it. Reset form erases all data in the form and sets it back to its initial state. We will leave this button with the Action Submit form. We will also leave the name alone because we are doing nothing but having this form submit information. Select the second button, set its Action to Reset form, and change its label to Erase.

8. Add the Title Feedback form and preview your form in your browser. When you fill out the form, you may be presented with the warning shown in panel 8. This warning alerts you that your form data is being transferred via e-mail client, which is not secure. Your users will see this warning, which, in addition to e-mail client compatibility, is a reason why you should not use this method for production.

Creating a Jump Menu

The Jump Menu item is listed underneath Form. It is made up of both form fields and JavaScript. This element can be a handy extra navigation feature on your page. Let's add one to *forms.html*, as shown in Figure 16.9.

1. Click your table to select it. If needed, use the Tag Selector to help you pick the correct tag. When the table is selected, choose Center in the Align Menu. The table should be in the center of the page.
2. Place your cursor directly underneath the table. Now click the Align Center button in the Property Inspector.

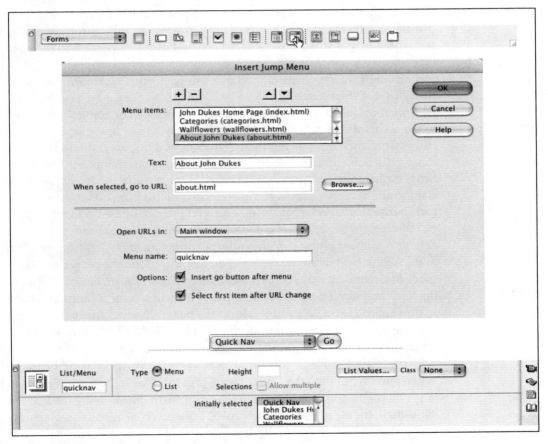

FIGURE 16.9 Adding a Jump Menu.

3. In the Forms category of the Insert Toolbar, press the Jump Menu button (sixth from the right). The Insert Jump Menu dialog box opens. In this dialog box, you can choose what you want to name each of your selections and add links for navigation.

4. For the first field, type *Quick Nav* with no link. This field acts as a label. Press the plus sign (+)button to add a new selection. Label this *John Dukes Home Page* (link *index.html*). Continue pressing the plus sign and add the following entries: Categories (*categories.html*), Wallflowers (*wallflowers.html*), and About John (*about.html*).

5. If you make an error, you can select a menu item and press the minus sign (–)to delete it, or press the up or down arrows to shift its position.

6. On the bottom of the button, you have two Options: Insert go button after menu and Select first item after URL change. Select both of these. Insert go button after menu allows the user to press the Go button should the URL not automatically change. Select first item after URL change causes the selection to be reverted to Quick Nav when your user returns to the page.

7. Name the menu *quicknav* and press the OK button. When you return to the page, you see the menu reflected in the Property Inspector. You can adjust your menu choices at any point by clicking the List Values button.

CLEANING UP HTML

Two areas are available to assist you with cleaning up your HTML code. You may have either inherited a site that has some sloppy code or used an application that created pages with extraneous code that must be stripped.

If you are planning to update your site to be XHTML compliant, you may find clicking File > Convert > XHTML to be of great assistance. It doesn't catch everything for you in the conversion, but it does do the lion's share of the labor for you.

Clicking Commands > Clean Up HTML/Clean Up XHTML can fix poorly coded HTML/XHTML. Which option appears depends on what type of page you have created. The option appearing matches the current page in the document window.

The other option you find in the Commands menu is Clean Up Word HTML. Microsoft Word has been converting documents to HTML for the past several versions, but it sometimes leaves extra code that you might not find desirable. This option can help clean up the pages.

SITE MANAGEMENT

The primary tool used in site management within Dreamweaver MX 2004 is the Files Panel. In this panel, you can upload, download, and synchronize your local folder with the folder on the server.

The Files Panel

The Files Panel is your one-stop resource for keeping your site up to date. This panel is shown in Figure 16.10.

1. If you click the last button to the right within the Files Panel, you can expand the view in your workspace to enable you to see both your local and remote (on the server) files at the same time. Within this view, you can simply drag files back and forth between the local site and remote server. The drop-down menu on the left allows you to determine what site you want to view and contains the Manage Sites option. Let's look at our buttons:

   a. To connect to the remote server, press the first button on the top of your panel.

   b. You can refresh all of your files by clicking the second button.

   c. View Site FTP Log opens the FTP log so you can view your FTP activity.

   d. Within the next set of buttons are your views (shown with the Panel expanded). You can choose to view Site Files, a Testing Server (used when you have a server installed locally), or a Site Map. (A home page must be set up for this option to be available.)

   e. After the view buttons are Get and Put. These options download and upload selected files and folders between the local and remote sites.

   f. Next are the options of Check In and Check Out. These options cause the files to be marked as in use on the server if you have Check In/Check Out enabled on your site (accessed under Remote Info in the Advanced View). This option prevents multiple individuals on a design team from working on the same files at the same time.

2. If you want to have a site map view of your site, click the Site Map button. This button offers the choice of Map and files or Map only. When you first click it, you may see the message shown in panel 2 of Figure 16.10, warning you that you are unable to create a site map because of the lack of a home page. Click the Manage Sites button, which takes you to the Manage Sites dialog box. Click the Edit button.

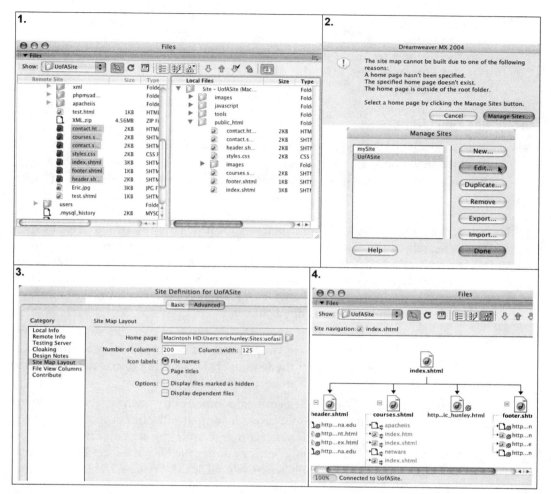

FIGURE 16.10 The Files Panel.

3. The Advanced View of the Site Definition dialog box opens. Choose Site Map Layout from Categories. In this screen, you can navigate to your home page and have options to set up your map view.

4. When you return to the expanded Files Panel, you see a visual representation of your site.

Other options available to work with your site include Synchronization settings. If you click Site > Synchronize from the Files Panel Options menu, the Synchronize

Files dialog box opens. Here you can synchronize all of your files in both directions. You can choose to use selected remote or local files only, or the entire site. You can also choose the direction (Put newer files to remote, Get newer files from remote, or Get and Put newer files). Use this dialog box if you want to perform a large-scale synchronization.

The Results Panel Group

The Results Panel group is one of the most valuable resources in Dreamweaver MX 2004. In this group you find an array of tools to assist you with site maintenance. We will explore some of the panels found within this group, as shown in Figure 16.11.

Search: Opens the Find and Replace dialog box. This powerful tool enables you to search in the files or in the source code itself, or construct very specific searches. You can search an individual page, a folder, or the whole site. Be very careful when you use Find and Replace on either a folder or the whole site, with files that are not open. When the operation is performed on files that were closed, the Undo option is not available.

Validation: Validates your pages to a W3C standard. You can adjust what document type you want to base your validation on by selecting Settings under Validate (the top button on the left edge). This setting opens the Preferences window with the Validator category selected.

Target Browser Check: Determines compatibility with selected browsers. When you are concerned about browser compatibility but don't have copies of all your target browsers, this panel comes to your rescue. You can change your targeted browsers by choosing Settings under the Check Target Browsers button. This window also opens when you click the Preview/Debug in Browser menu in the Document Toolbar.

Link Checker: Allows you to check links for the page or even the entire site. You can check for Broken Links, External Links, and Orphaned Files.

Site Reports: Provides multiple types of reports. You can determine what files are checked out by users, if untitled documents exist, if missing Alt text exists, and more. It can be useful for getting workable information about the status of your site.

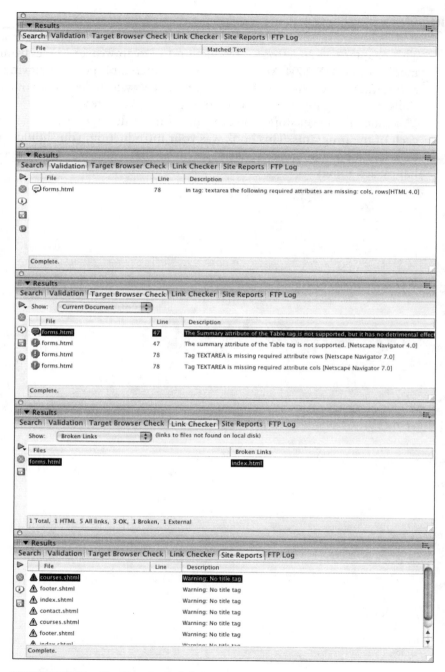

FIGURE 16.11   The Results Panel group.

SUMMARY

This chapter concludes our introduction to Dreamweaver MX 2004 and Macromedia Studio MX 2004. You can now see the incredible power of having all of these applications integrated, and you are on your way to unleashing your new-found skills in creating highly interactive and creative Web sites.

Education never stops, however, and you should explore advanced material on each of the programs. This book was your introduction; you should feel empowered to understand or quickly learn anything that is thrown at you. Good luck and happy designing!

A | Other Resources

This listing of resources on the Web, listed by category, can assist you with Web site development.

MACROMEDIA PRODUCTS

Macromedia Web site—*www.macromedia.com*: The main source for all that is Macromedia. Areas that you should check out are the Macromedia Exchange and the Developer Center (Devnet).

Macromedia FreeHand

Macromedia FreeHand Support Center—*www.macromedia.com/support/freehand*—Provides support from Macromedia.

www.freehandsource.com: Offers tips and resources for the program.

FreeHand for Cartographers—*www.applemaps.co.uk/f4c*: Provides information about using FreeHand for Cartography (mapmaking).

Mike's Sketch Pad—*www.sketchpad.net/freehand.htm*: Offers tutorials on FreeHand.

Professional FreeHand Tips and Tricks—*www.tema.ru/f/r/e/e/h/a/n/d*: Offers additional FreeHand tutorials.

About.com FreeHand Tutorials—*http://graphicssoft.about.com/cs/freehandtutorials*: Contains more tutorials and links to FreeHand resources.

Macromedia Flash

Macromedia Flash Support Center—*www.macromedia.com/support/flash*: Provides support from Macromedia.

Flashkit—*www.flashkit.com*: Represents possibly the largest Macromedia Flash support site on the Web. This site offers thousands of Flash movies that have been generously uploaded from developers worldwide. These uploaded movies include the source FLAs so you can open them and see how developers achieved results. Keep in mind that many of the files were made using earlier versions of Flash, so the programming techniques may be outdated.

***www.moock.org*:** The Web site of the highly regarded author and developer Colin Moock.

***www.actionscript.org*:** Provides a great resource for learning ActionScript.

***www.flashmagazine.com*:** Dedicated to programs that create Flash movies (.swf).

Ultrashock—*www.ultrashock.com*: Offers more tutorials and source FLAs.

Literally hundreds of Web sites about Flash are on the Internet. Use your search engine to keep looking. New ones pop up every day.

Macromedia Fireworks

Macromedia Fireworks Support Center—*www.macromedia.com/support/fireworks*: Provides support from Macromedia.

Fireworks MX Zone—*www.fwzone.net*: Offers tutorials and resources for Fireworks users.

About.com Fireworks Basics—*http://graphicssoft.about.com/cs/fireworksbasics*: Provides tutorials and links to Fireworks resources.

***www.ultraweaver.com*—**Offers written and video tutorials on Fireworks.

Playing with Fire—*www.playingwithfire.com*: Offers tutorials, tips, and tricks with Fireworks.

Macromedia Dreamweaver

Macromedia Dreamweaver Support Center—*www.macromedia.com/support/dreamweaver:* Provides support from Macromedia.

DMX Zone—*www.dmxzone.com*: Offers tutorials and extensions for Dreamweaver.

Dreamweaver MX Support—*www.dreamweavermxsupport.com*: Provides tutorials and extensions for Dreamweaver.

Dreamweaver Fever—*www.dreamweaverfever.com*: Provides tutorials and extensions for Dreamweaver.

Dreamweaver FAQ.com—*www.dwfaq.com*: Offers tutorials and extensions for Dreamweaver.

GENERAL WEB DEVELOPMENT

The following all-purpose links can assist you with Web development. Accessibility and usability links are in this section.

Bobby—*http://bobby.watchfire.com/bobby/html/en/index.jsp*: Offers information about checking Web sites for accessibility.

Vischeck—*www.vischeck.com*: Allows you to check how color blind users will see your site.

W3C—*www.w3.org*: The World Wide Web Consortium determines the standards for HTML.

HTML Validator—*http://validator.w3.org*: Validates your Web pages in addition to the built-in validator found in Dreamweaver MX 2004.

Web Pages That Suck—*www.websitesthatsuck.com*: Showcases helpful and not-so-helpful Web sites to explain usability.

User Interface Engineering—*www.uie.com*: Offers information about usability.

Usable Web—*www.useit.com*: Contains links to resources on usability.

PROGRAMMING RESOURCES

Some resources that can be of assistance when you are ready to take your Web sites to the next level follow.

ColdFusion—*www.macromedia.com/software/coldfusion*: Provide support for the Macromedia application server.

PHP—*www.php.net*: Provides information about this open-source server-side programming language.

Perl—*www.perl.com*: Provides information about this open-source server-side programming language.

Comprehensive Perl Archive Network (CPAN)—*www.cpan.org*: Contains the central depot of Perl resources.

MySQL—*www.mysql.com*: Provides an open-source relational database management system.

JS-Examples—*www.js-examples.com*: Provides a great resource for learning JavaScript.

B   About the CD-ROM

This CD-ROM contains support files for exercises in the book, trial versions of all the software included in Macromedia Studio MX 2004 for both PC and Macintosh, a copy of all figures used in the book, and an Open Source Web server bundle for Windows, including Apache, MySQL, PHP, and Perl. A description of the directory structure and what is contained within follows:

CRWeb Install: Contains the setup file for an open-source Web server package, including Apache, MySQL, PHP, and Perl.

Dreamweaver: Contains support files for the Dreamweaver MX 2004 portion of the book.

Figures: Contains full-color copies of all images used in the book.

Fireworks: Contains support files for the Fireworks MX 2004 portion of the book.

Flash: Contains support files for the Flash MX 2004 portion of the book.

FreeHand: Contains support files for the FreeHand MX portion of the book.

Trials: Contains trial versions of all programs covered in this book for both Windows and Macintosh.

Many of the files used in this book can only be opened with Macromedia Studio MX 2004 products. If you do not own a copy of the software, install the trial versions found on this CD-ROM

SYSTEM REQUIREMENTS

CRWeb

The CRWeb package is for Windows versions 98/2000/XP. It is not Macintosh compatible. Most of the applications contained in the package are already built into

OS 10, with the exception of MySQL, which can be downloaded from Apple for free at *www.apple.com/downloads/macosx/unix_open_source/completemysql.html*.

Macromedia Dreamweaver MX 2004

The system requirements from Macromedia for this software follow:

Windows:

- 600 MHz Intel Pentium III processor or equivalent
- Windows 98 SE (4.10.2222 A), Windows 2000, Windows XP, or Windows Server 2003
- 128 MB RAM (256 MB recommended)
- 275 MB available disk space
- To Install, double-click dwmx2004_trial_en_win.exe and follow the on-screen prompts.

Macintosh:

- 500 MHz Power PC G3 processor
- Mac OS X 10.2.6 and later, 10.3
- 128 MB computer RAM (256 MB recommended)
- 275 MB available disk space
- To Install, double-click Dreamweaver MX 2004 Installer and follow the on-screen prompts.

Macromedia Fireworks MX 2004

The system requirements from Macromedia for this software follow:

Windows:

- 600 MHz Intel Pentium III processor or equivalent
- Windows 98 SE (4.10.2222 A), Windows 2000, Windows XP, or Windows Server 2003
- 128 MB RAM (256 MB recommended)
- 150 MB available disk space
- To Install, double-click fwmx_2004_en.exe and follow the on-screen prompts.

Macintosh:

- 500 MHz Power PC G3 processor
- Mac OS X 10.2.6 and later, 10.3
- 128 MB computer RAM (256 MB recommended)
- 100 MB available disk space

- To Install, double-click FW_Client_Installer and follow the on-screen prompts.

Macromedia Flash MX 2004

The system requirements from Macromedia for this software follow:

Windows:

- 600 MHz Intel Pentium III processor or equivalent
- Windows 98 SE (4.10.2222 A), Windows 2000, Windows XP, or Windows Server 2003
- 128 MB RAM (256 MB recommended)
- 275 MB available disk space
- To Install, unzip FlashMX2004-en.zip, double-click Install_Flash_MX _2004.exe and follow the on-screen prompts. The other documents included in the ZIP file are instructional PDFs. You will need to have Adobe Acrobat to read them.

Macintosh:

- 500 MHz Power PC G3 processor
- Mac OS X 10.2.6 and later, 10.3
- 128 MB computer RAM (256 MB recommended)
- 215 MB available disk space
- To Install, UnStuff FlashMX2004-en.sit by double-clicking. When the files have been extracted, open the new FlashMX2004-en folder and mount Install_Flash_MX_2004.dmg by double-clicking on it. This will make the Flash MX 2004 File Available. Install the program by double-clicking and following all prompts. The other documents included in are instructional PDFs. You can use Preview or download Adobe Acrobat to read them.

Macromedia FreeHand MX 11.0.1

The system requirements from Macromedia for this software follow:

Windows:

- 600 MHz Intel Pentium III processor or equivalent
- Windows 98 SE (4.10.2222 A), Windows 2000, or Windows XP
- 64 MB of free available system RAM (128 MB recommended)
- 100 MB available disk space
- To Install, double-click freehand1101_en_trial.exe and follow the on-screen prompts.

Macintosh:

- 500 MHz Power PC G3 processor
- Mac OS X 10.2.6 and later, 10.3
- 64 MB RAM (128 MB recommended)
- 70 MB available disk space
- To Install, double-click FreeHand MX Installer and follow the on-screen prompts.

INSTALLATION

To Install the CRWeb Package, simply double-click the *setup.exe* file in the *CRWeb Install* folder. However, some items must be checked:

- If you are installing the package on a computer that has Internet Information Services (IIS) installed, you must shut down the service. Do this by clicking Start > Settings > Control Panel > Administrative Tools > Services and finding Internet Services Manager on the list. (If it is not listed, you are okay.)
- You must allow the server to be installed to c:\crweb. Do not change the folder name or the program locations after installation. The configurations and the CRWeb Control Panel are hard-coded to run from that location.
- Use the CRWeb Control Panel, accessed by clicking Start > Programs > CRWeb Control Panel (also located on the Desktop or Quick Launch Toolbar), to start and stop (Window 98 and ME) or install and remove the services (Windows NT/2000/XP).
- To uninstall the package, remove the Apache and MySQL services and use the Uninstall utility accessed by clicking Start > Programs > CRWeb Control Panel.
- Any updates or revisions to the text can be found at *www.erichunley.com*.

C Open Source Licenses

APACHE SOFTWARE LICENSE (APACHE AND MOD_PERL)

```
===================================================================
* The Apache Software License, Version 1.1
*
* Copyright (c) 2000-2004 The Apache Software Foundation.  All
* rights
* reserved.
*
* Redistribution and use in source and binary forms, with or
* without
* modification, are permitted provided that the following
* conditions
* are met:
*
* 1. Redistributions of source code must retain the above copyright
*    notice, this list of conditions and the following disclaimer.
*
* 2. Redistributions in binary form must reproduce the above
*    copyright
*    notice, this list of conditions and the following disclaimer
*    in the documentation and/or other materials provided with the
*    distribution.
*
* 3. The end-user documentation included with the redistribution,
*    if any, must include the following acknowledgment:
*        "This product includes software developed by the
*         Apache Software Foundation (http://www.apache.org/)."
*    Alternately, this acknowledgment may appear in the software
*    itself if and wherever such third-party acknowledgments
*    normally appear.
*
```

```
* 4. The names "Apache" and "Apache Software Foundation" must
*     not be used to endorse or promote products derived from this
*     software without prior written permission. For written
*     permission, please contact apache@apache.org.
*
* 5. Products derived from this software may not be called
*     "Apache", nor may "Apache" appear in their name, without prior
*     written permission of the Apache Software Foundation.
*
* THIS SOFTWARE IS PROVIDED "AS IS" AND ANY EXPRESSED OR IMPLIED
* WARRANTIES, INCLUDING, BUT NOT LIMITED TO, THE IMPLIED WARRANTIES
* OF MERCHANTABILITY AND FITNESS FOR A PARTICULAR PURPOSE ARE
* DISCLAIMED.  IN NO EVENT SHALL THE APACHE SOFTWARE FOUNDATION OR
* ITS CONTRIBUTORS BE LIABLE FOR ANY DIRECT, INDIRECT, INCIDENTAL,
* SPECIAL, EXEMPLARY, OR CONSEQUENTIAL DAMAGES (INCLUDING, BUT NOT
* LIMITED TO, PROCUREMENT OF SUBSTITUTE GOODS OR SERVICES; LOSS OF
* USE, DATA, OR PROFITS; OR BUSINESS INTERRUPTION) HOWEVER CAUSED
* AND ON ANY THEORY OF LIABILITY, WHETHER IN CONTRACT, STRICT
* LIABILITY, OR TORT (INCLUDING NEGLIGENCE OR OTHERWISE) ARISING IN
* ANY WAY OUT OF THE USE OF THIS SOFTWARE, EVEN IF ADVISED OF THE
* POSSIBILITY OF SUCH DAMAGE.
*
============================================================================
*
* This software consists of voluntary contributions made by many
* individuals on behalf of the Apache Software Foundation.  For
* more information on the Apache Software Foundation, please see
* <http://www.apache.org/>.
*
* Portions of this software are based upon public domain software
* originally written at the National Center for Supercomputing
* Applications, University of Illinois, Urbana-Champaign.
*/
```

PHP SOFTWARE LICENSE

```
--------------------------------------------------------------------
                    The PHP License, version 3.0
     Copyright (c) 1999 - 2004 The PHP Group. All rights reserved.
--------------------------------------------------------------------
```

Redistribution and use in source and binary forms, with or without modification, is permitted provided that the following conditions are met:

1. Redistributions of source code must retain the above copyright notice, this list of conditions and the following disclaimer.

2. Redistributions in binary form must reproduce the above copyright notice, this list of conditions and the following disclaimer in the documentation and/or other materials provided with the distribution.

3. The name "PHP" must not be used to endorse or promote products derived from this software without prior written permission. For written permission, please contact group@php.net.

4. Products derived from this software may not be called "PHP", nor may "PHP" appear in their name, without prior written permission from group@php.net. You may indicate that your software works in conjunction with PHP by saying "Foo for PHP" instead of calling it "PHP Foo" or "phpfoo"

5. The PHP Group may publish revised and/or new versions of the license from time to time. Each version will be given a distinguishing version number.
Once covered code has been published under a particular version of the license, you may always continue to use it under the terms of that version. You may also choose to use such covered code under the terms of any subsequent version of the license published by the PHP Group. No one other than the PHP Group has the right to modify the terms applicable to covered code created under this License.

6. Redistributions of any form whatsoever must retain the following acknowledgment:
"This product includes PHP, freely available from <http://www.php.net/>".

THIS SOFTWARE IS PROVIDED BY THE PHP DEVELOPMENT TEAM ''AS IS'' AND ANY EXPRESSED OR IMPLIED WARRANTIES, INCLUDING, BUT NOT LIMITED TO, THE IMPLIED WARRANTIES OF MERCHANTABILITY AND FITNESS FOR A PARTICULAR PURPOSE ARE DISCLAIMED. IN NO EVENT SHALL THE PHP DEVELOPMENT TEAM OR ITS CONTRIBUTORS BE LIABLE FOR ANY DIRECT,

```
INDIRECT, INCIDENTAL, SPECIAL, EXEMPLARY, OR CONSEQUENTIAL DAMAGES
(INCLUDING, BUT NOT LIMITED TO, PROCUREMENT OF SUBSTITUTE GOODS OR
SERVICES; LOSS OF USE, DATA, OR PROFITS; OR BUSINESS INTERRUPTION)
HOWEVER CAUSED AND ON ANY THEORY OF LIABILITY, WHETHER IN CONTRACT,
STRICT LIABILITY, OR TORT (INCLUDING NEGLIGENCE OR OTHERWISE)
ARISING IN ANY WAY OUT OF THE USE OF THIS SOFTWARE, EVEN IF ADVISED
OF THE POSSIBILITY OF SUCH DAMAGE.

-----------------------------------------------------------------------

This software consists of voluntary contributions made by many
individuals on behalf of the PHP Group.

The PHP Group can be contacted via Email at group@php.net.

For more information on the PHP Group and the PHP project,
please see <http://www.php.net>.

This product includes the Zend Engine, freely available at
<http://www.zend.com>.
```

MYSQL LICENSE

G GNU General Public License

Version 2, June 1991

```
Copyright © 1989, 1991 Free Software Foundation, Inc.
59 Temple Place - Suite 330, Boston, MA   02111-1307, USA

Everyone is permitted to copy and distribute verbatim copies
of this license document, but changing it is not allowed.
```

21.4 Preamble

The licenses for most software are designed to take away your freedom to share and change it. By contrast, the GNU General Public License is intended to guarantee your freedom to share and change free software—to make sure the software is free for all its users. This General Public License applies to most of the Free Software Foundation's software and to any other program whose authors commit to using it.

(Some other Free Software Foundation software is covered by the GNU Library General Public License instead.) You can apply it to your programs, too.

When we speak of free software, we are referring to freedom, not price. Our General Public Licenses are designed to make sure that you have the freedom to distribute copies of free software (and charge for this service if you wish), that you receive source code or can get it if you want it, that you can change the software or use pieces of it in new free programs; and that you know you can do these things.

To protect your rights, we need to make restrictions that forbid anyone to deny you these rights or to ask you to surrender the rights. These restrictions translate to certain responsibilities for you if you distribute copies of the software, or if you modify it.

For example, if you distribute copies of such a program, whether gratis or for a fee, you must give the recipients all the rights that you have. You must make sure that they, too, receive or can get the source code. And you must show them these terms so they know their rights.

We protect your rights with two steps: (1) copyright the software, and (2) offer you this license which gives you legal permission to copy, distribute and/or modify the software.

Also, for each author's protection and ours, we want to make certain that everyone understands that there is no warranty for this free software. If the software is modified by someone else and passed on, we want its recipients to know that what they have is not the original, so that any problems introduced by others will not reflect on the original authors' reputations.

Finally, any free program is threatened constantly by software patents. We wish to avoid the danger that redistributors of a free program will individually obtain patent licenses, in effect making the program proprietary. To prevent this, we have made it clear that any patent must be licensed for everyone's free use or not licensed at all.

The precise terms and conditions for copying, distribution and modification follow.

21.5 TERMS AND CONDITIONS FOR COPYING, DISTRIBUTION AND MODIFICATION

1. This License applies to any program or other work which contains a notice placed by the copyright holder saying it may be distributed under the terms of this General Public License. The "Program", below, refers to any such program or work, and a "work based on the Program" means either the Program or any derivative work under copyright law: that is to say, a work containing the Program or a portion of it, either verbatim or with modifications and/or translated into another language. (Hereinafter, translation

is included without limitation in the term "modification".) Each licensee is addressed as "you". Activities other than copying, distribution and modification are not covered by this License; they are outside its scope. The act of running the Program is not restricted, and the output from the Program is covered only if its contents constitute a work based on the Program (independent of having been made by running the Program). Whether that is true depends on what the Program does.

2. You may copy and distribute verbatim copies of the Program's source code as you receive it, in any medium, provided that you conspicuously and appropriately publish on each copy an appropriate copyright notice and disclaimer of warranty; keep intact all the notices that refer to this License and to the absence of any warranty; and give any other recipients of the Program a copy of this License along with the Program. You may charge a fee for the physical act of transferring a copy, and you may at your option offer warranty protection in exchange for a fee.

3. You may modify your copy or copies of the Program or any portion of it, thus forming a work based on the Program, and copy and distribute such modifications or work under the terms of Section 1 above, provided that you also meet all of these conditions:

    a. You must cause the modified files to carry prominent notices stating that you changed the files and the date of any change.

    b. You must cause any work that you distribute or publish, that in whole or in part contains or is derived from the Program or any part thereof, to be licensed as a whole at no charge to all third parties under the terms of this License.

    c. If the modified program normally reads commands interactively when run, you must cause it, when started running for such interactive use in the most ordinary way, to print or display an announcement including an appropriate copyright notice and a notice that there is no warranty (or else, saying that you provide a warranty) and that users may redistribute the program under these conditions, and telling the user how to view a copy of this License. (Exception: if the Program itself is interactive but does not normally print such an announcement, your work based on the Program is not required to print an announcement.)

These requirements apply to the modified work as a whole. If identifiable sections of that work are not derived from the Program, and can be reasonably considered independent and separate works in themselves, then this License, and its terms, do not apply to those sections when you distribute them as separate works. But when you distribute the same sections as part of a whole which is a work based on the Program, the distribution of the whole must be on the terms of this License, whose permissions for other licensees extend to the entire whole, and thus to each and every part regardless of who wrote it. Thus, it is not the intent of this section to claim rights or contest your rights to work written entirely by you; rather, the intent is to exercise the right to control the distribution of derivative or collective works based on the Program. In addition, mere aggregation of another work not based on the Program with the Program (or with a work based on the Program) on a volume of a storage or distribution medium does not bring the other work under the scope of this License.

4. You may copy and distribute the Program (or a work based on it, under Section 2) in object code or executable form under the terms of Sections 1 and 2 above provided that you also do one of the following:
    a. Accompany it with the complete corresponding machine-readable source code, which must be distributed under the terms of Sections 1 and 2 above on a medium customarily used for software interchange; or,
    b. Accompany it with a written offer, valid for at least three years, to give any third-party, for a charge no more than your cost of physically performing source distribution, a complete machine-readable copy of the corresponding source code, to be distributed under the terms of Sections 1 and 2 above on a medium customarily used for software interchange; or,
    c. Accompany it with the information you received as to the offer to distribute corresponding source code. (This alternative is allowed only for noncommercial distribution and only if you received the program in object code or executable form with such an offer, in accord with Subsection b above.)

The source code for a work means the preferred form of the work for making modifications to it. For an executable work, complete source code means all the source code for all modules it contains, plus any associated interface definition files, plus the scripts used to control compilation and installation of the executable. However, as a special exception, the source code distributed need not include anything that is normally distributed (in either source or binary form) with the major components (compiler, kernel, and so on) of the operating system on which the executable runs, unless that component itself accompanies the executable. If distribution of executable or object code is made by offering access to copy from a designated place, then offering equivalent access to copy the source code from the same place counts as distribution of the source code, even though third parties are not compelled to copy the source along with the object code.

5. You may not copy, modify, sublicense, or distribute the Program except as expressly provided under this License. Any attempt otherwise to copy, modify, sublicense or distribute the Program is void, and will automatically terminate your rights under this License. However, parties who have received copies, or rights, from you under this License will not have their licenses terminated so long as such parties remain in full compliance.

6. You are not required to accept this License, since you have not signed it. However, nothing else grants you permission to modify or distribute the Program or its derivative works. These actions are prohibited by law if you do not accept this License. Therefore, by modifying or distributing the Program (or any work based on the Program), you indicate your acceptance of this License to do so, and all its terms and conditions for copying, distributing or modifying the Program or works based on it.

7. Each time you redistribute the Program (or any work based on the Program), the recipient automatically receives a license from the original licensor to copy, distribute or modify the Program subject to these terms and conditions. You may not impose any further restrictions on the recipients' exercise of the rights granted herein. You are not responsible for enforcing compliance by third parties to this License.

8. If, as a consequence of a court judgment or allegation of patent infringement or for any other reason (not limited to patent issues), conditions are imposed on you (whether by court order, agreement or otherwise) that contradict the conditions of this License, they do not excuse you from the conditions of this License. If you cannot distribute so as to satisfy simultaneously your obligations under this License and any other pertinent obligations, then as a consequence you may not distribute the Program at all. For example, if a patent license would not permit royalty-free redistribution of the Program by all those who receive copies directly or indirectly through you, then the only way you could satisfy both it and this License would be to refrain entirely from distribution of the Program. If any portion of this section is held invalid or unenforceable under any particular circumstance, the balance of the section is intended to apply and the section as a whole is intended to apply in other circumstances. It is not the purpose of this section to induce you to infringe any patents or other property right claims or to contest validity of any such claims; this section has the sole purpose of protecting the integrity of the free software distribution system, which is implemented by public license practices. Many people

have made generous contributions to the wide range of software distributed through that system in reliance on consistent application of that system; it is up to the author/donor to decide if he or she is willing to distribute software through any other system and a licensee cannot impose that choice. This section is intended to make thoroughly clear what is believed to be a consequence of the rest of this License.

9. If the distribution and/or use of the Program is restricted in certain countries either by patents or by copyrighted interfaces, the original copyright holder who places the Program under this License may add an explicit geographical distribution limitation excluding those countries, so that distribution is permitted only in or among countries not thus excluded. In such case, this License incorporates the limitation as if written in the body of this License.

10. The Free Software Foundation may publish revised and/or new versions of the General Public License from time to time. Such new versions will be similar in spirit to the present version, but may differ in detail to address new problems or concerns. Each version is given a distinguishing version number. If the Program specifies a version number of this License which applies to it and "any later version", you have the option of following the terms and conditions either of that version or of any later version published by the Free Software Foundation. If the Program does not specify a version number of this License, you may choose any version ever published by the Free Software Foundation.

11. If you wish to incorporate parts of the Program into other free programs whose distribution conditions are different, write to the author to ask for permission. For software which is copyrighted by the Free Software Foundation, write to the Free Software Foundation; we sometimes make exceptions for this. Our decision will be guided by the two goals of preserving the free status of all derivatives of our free software and of promoting the sharing and reuse of software generally.

21.6 NO WARRANTY

12. BECAUSE THE PROGRAM IS LICENSED FREE OF CHARGE, THERE IS NO WARRANTY FOR THE PROGRAM, TO THE EXTENT PERMITTED BY APPLICABLE LAW. EXCEPT WHEN OTHERWISE STATED IN WRITING THE COPYRIGHT HOLDERS AND/OR OTHER PARTIES PROVIDE THE PROGRAM "AS IS" WITHOUT WARRANTY OF ANY KIND, EITHER EXPRESSED OR IMPLIED, INCLUDING, BUT NOT LIMITED TO, THE IMPLIED WARRANTIES OF MERCHANTABILITY

AND FITNESS FOR A PARTICULAR PURPOSE. THE ENTIRE RISK AS TO THE QUALITY AND PERFORMANCE OF THE PROGRAM IS WITH YOU. SHOULD THE PROGRAM PROVE DEFECTIVE, YOU ASSUME THE COST OF ALL NECESSARY SERVICING, REPAIR OR CORRECTION.

13. IN NO EVENT UNLESS REQUIRED BY APPLICABLE LAW OR AGREED TO IN WRITING WILL ANY COPYRIGHT HOLDER, OR ANY OTHER PARTY WHO MAY MODIFY AND/OR REDISTRIBUTE THE PROGRAM AS PERMITTED ABOVE, BE LIABLE TO YOU FOR DAMAGES, INCLUDING ANY GENERAL, SPECIAL, INCIDENTAL OR CONSEQUENTIAL DAMAGES ARISING OUT OF THE USE OR INABILITY TO USE THE PROGRAM (INCLUDING BUT NOT LIMITED TO LOSS OF DATA OR DATA BEING RENDERED INACCURATE OR LOSSES SUSTAINED BY YOU OR THIRD PARTIES OR A FAILURE OF THE PROGRAM TO OPERATE WITH ANY OTHER PROGRAMS), EVEN IF SUCH HOLDER OR OTHER PARTY HAS BEEN ADVISED OF THE POSSIBILITY OF SUCH DAMAGES.

21.7 END OF TERMS AND CONDITIONS

21.8 How to Apply These Terms to Your New Programs

If you develop a new program, and you want it to be of the greatest possible use to the public, the best way to achieve this is to make it free software which everyone can redistribute and change under these terms.

To do so, attach the following notices to the program. It is safest to attach them to the start of each source file to most effectively convey the exclusion of warranty; and each file should have at least the "copyright" line and a pointer to where the full notice is found.

one line to give the program's name and a brief idea of what it does.

```
Copyright (C) yyyy    name of author

This program is free software; you can redistribute it and/or modify
it under the terms of the GNU General Public License as published by
the Free Software Foundation; either version 2 of the License, or
(at your option) any later version.

This program is distributed in the hope that it will be useful,
but WITHOUT ANY WARRANTY; without even the implied warranty of
MERCHANTABILITY or FITNESS FOR A PARTICULAR PURPOSE.  See the
GNU General Public License for more details.
```

```
You should have received a copy of the GNU General Public License
along with this program; if not, write to the Free Software
Foundation, Inc., 59 Temple Place - Suite 330, Boston, MA  02111-
1307, USA.
```

Also add information on how to contact you by electronic and paper mail.

If the program is interactive, make it output a short notice like this when it starts in an interactive mode:

```
Gnomovision version 69, Copyright (C) 19 yy  name of author

@dis:Gnomovision comes with ABSOLUTELY NO WARRANTY; for details type
'show w'.
This is free software, and you are welcome to redistribute it
under certain conditions; type 'show c' for details.
```

The hypothetical commands `'show w'` and `'show c'` should show the appropriate parts of the General Public License. Of course, the commands you use may be called something other than `'show w'` and `'show c'`; they could even be mouse-clicks or menu items—whatever suits your program.

You should also get your employer (if you work as a programmer) or your school, if any, to sign a "copyright disclaimer" for the program, if necessary. Here is a sample; alter the names:

```
Yoyodyne, Inc., hereby disclaims all copyright interest in the
program
'Gnomovision' (which makes passes at compilers) written by James
Hacker.

 signature of Ty Coon , 1 April 1989
Ty Coon, President of Vice
```

This General Public License does not permit incorporating your program into proprietary programs. If your program is a subroutine library, you may consider it more useful to permit linking proprietary applications with the library. If this is what you want to do, use the GNU Library General Public License instead of this License.

Index

A

Accessibility panels, Flash, 133
Actions, adding, 225
ActionScript
  adding, 220
  applying, 265–277
  code comments in, 225–226
  events, 254
  literals, 226–229
  loops, 244–247
  objects, creating, 250–252
  overview, 223
  variables (*See* Variables, ActionScript)
ActionScript Dictionary panel, Flash, 132
Actions Panel, ActionScript, 223–225
Action tool, Freehand, 84
Add Effect Button popup menu, Freehand, 66
Add Motion Guide option defined, 189
Add Points tool, Freehand, 86
Addresses, 4
Align panel, 96–97, 336
Alpha Channel masks, 355
Alt attribute defined, 339, 416
Anchors
  named, 125, 285
  tags, 416–418
Animations
  Fireworks, 376, 382–384
  Flash
    actions, adding, 110
    enhancing, 122
    overview, 86–87, 107–112
    testing, 110
  frame by frame, 159–162, 377–379
  movement in, 161
  and movie clips, 197
  symbols, 382–384
Apache software license, 537–538

Appearance tab described, Fireworks, 358
Arc tool, Freehand, 35–36
Array.concat() method defined, 235
Array.join() method defined, 235
Arrays, Flash
  associative, 234–235
  methods, 235
  multidimensional, 234–235
  overview, 233–234
Array.sort() method defined, 235
Array.toString() method defined, 235
Arrow tool described, Flash, 127, 135–137
Assets panel, Dreamweaver, 495–496, 498
Assets Panel Shapes tab, Fireworks, 317–319
Attributes, HTML, 410
Auto Shapes tool, Fireworks described, 315–317
Axis, adding Flash, 170, 171

B

Ball example
  creating, 159–166
  finishing, 173–175
Bandwidth profiler, Flash, 294–295
Behaviors
  Dreamweaver
    adding, 514–517
  Fireworks
    adding, 375
    removing, 373, 375
  Flash
    choices, 213–215
    custom, 215–221
    defined, 210
  server, 517
Behaviors Panel, Fireworks, 374–376
Bend popup menu, Freehand, 66
Bend Tool, Freehand, 48, 76
Betting, code for, 273–275

Bevel and Emboss menu, Freehand, 68
Beveled rectangle shape, creating, 316
Bézier handles, Freehand, 19–20
Bezigon Tool, Freehand, 30–32
Bitmaps
    BMP format defined, 385
    graphics
        fills, using, 153
        and masks, 352–355
        overview, 13–14
    tools, Fireworks, 321–330
    WBMP format defined, 385
Blend tool, 79, 84–85, 326, 379
Blockquote tag defined, HTML, 409
Blur effect defined, 209
Blur menu, Freehand, 69
Body tag defined, HTML, 405–406
Boolean() function defined, 233
Box symbols, Freehand
    scaling and placing, 98–99
Break/ continue command and loops, 246–247
Brushes, creating Freehand, 64–65
Brush strokes, Freehand, 62–65
Brush tool described
    Fireworks, 326
    Flash, 128, 148–149
Burn tool, Fireworks, 326–327
Butt defined, 61
Buttons
    creating
        Dreamweaver, 479–482
        Fireworks, 341–343, 361
        Flash, 205–208, 281–283
    frames available, 205
    instances, editing, 347–350
    optimizing, 387–388, 392–394
    properties, 262–263
    states of, 343–347, 362
    text, adding, 349
    Web sites, adding to, 350–352

C

Cactus, creating, 24–27, 144
Calligraphic Pen tool, Freehand, 34–35
Calligraphic strokes, Freehand, 65
Canister icon, creating Freehand, 103
Cascading Styke Sheets (CSS)
    .class defined, 472
    content, adding, 503
    and Dreamweaver, 509–510
    overview, 504–510
Case in HTML, 406–407
Cel animation, history of, 162

Chamfer rectangle shape, creating, 316
Charts, making, 83–84
Chart tool, Freehand, 83–84
Checkboxes, creating, 521
Circles, creating, 36–38, 313–314
Client-server relations, 2–3
Clock image, creating, 317
Clones
    duplicate, location of, 347
    output, controlling, 328
Code comments, ActionScript, 225–226
Code hinting
    and cursor issues, 283
    defined, 224
    generating, 265
    with object names, 264–265
Cog image, creating, 317
Color Mixer Panel, Freehand, 87, 152
Colors
    custom and swatches, 87
    Fireworks, 300–301
    Flash, 156
    Freehand, 21, 56
    text and, 413
    and transitions, 392
Color Swatches panel, Flash, 151–153
Comments in HTML, 406–407
Comparison operators applied, 240–241
Concantenation operator defined, ActionScript, 228
Conditionals, Flash, 240–244
Cone gradient described, Freehand, 56
Connector tool, Freehand, 84, 104–106
Content
    accessing, Web sites, 365
    adding, 340–341, 469–470, 503
    displaying, 126
    external, editing, 52–53
    placing, 114
    sharing, 107
Contour gradient described, Freehand, 56
Copyright statements, removing, 350
Copy to Grid effect defined, 209
Counting loop defined, 245–246
Coyote, creating, 139, 142
Crop tool, Freehand, 86
Crop tool described, Fireworks, 312
CRWeb package, 533, 535–536
CSS. See Cascading Styke Sheets (CSS)
CSS Definition dialog box, 506–509
Cube image, creating, 317
Current Direction tool, Freehand, 85
Curves, creating, 19, 24

Custom fills, Freehand, 54
Cylinder image, creating, 317

D

Data, converting, 232–233
Datatypes, variable viewing, 229, 232
Date object defined, ActionScript, 250–251
Delete Layer option defined, 189
Design cycle diagram, 7
Design panels, Flash, 132–133
Development panels, Flash, 133
Dialog boxes, coding in XML, 217, 219
Dice game example, 198, 200–202, 204, 265–277
Distort tool described, Fireworks, 311, 312
Distributed Duplicate effect defined, 209
Distribute to Frames, Freehand, 379–381
Divide tool, Freehand, 86
div tag defined, HTML, 411
DOCTYPE declaration, HTML, 432
Document Panel, Freehand, 113
Documents
    creating new, 112–113, 297–306
    objects, organizing, 114
    root-relative, 339
    saving, 304–308
    symbols, placing, 95–96
Document Toolbar, Dreamweaver, 444–445
Dodge tool, Fireworks, 326–327
Domain names, 4, 5
Domain Name System (DNS) overview, 4–5
Do statement defined, ActionScript, 247
Doughnut shape, creating, 316
Down state defined, 205
Drawings, adjusting Fireworks, 337
Dreamweaver. *See* Macromedia Dreamweaver MX 2004
Drop Shadow effect defined, 209
3D Rotation tool, Freehand, 73
Duet popup menu, Freehand, 66, 68
Dynamic Text defined, 140

E

Editable regions, 500–503
Effects tools, Freehand, 71–84
Elements, HTML, 411–413
Ellipse tool
    Fireworks overview, 313–314
    Freehand overview, 36–38
Embedded devices defined, Flash, 120–121
Embedded Video option defined, Flash, 213
Emboss tool, Freehand, 86
Envelope, creating Freehand, 103

Environmental variables and client-server relations, 3
EPS files and Fireworks, 386
Eraser tool
    Fireworks, 326
    Flash, 128, 154–155
    Freehand, 48–49
Event handlers, ActionScript, 259–262
Events, 254, 375
Expand effect defined, 209
Expand Path menu, Freehand, 68
Expand Stroke tool, Freehand, 86
Explode effect defined, 209
Export Area tool described, Fireworks, 312
Extensible Markup Language (XML)
    dialog boxes, coding, 217, 219
    and Flash behaviors, 215–221
    principles of, 432–434
External variables, ActionScript, 252–254
Extrude tool, Freehand, 74–76
Eyedropper tool, 128, 154, 329

F

Feathering defined, 323
Files Panel, Dreamweaver, 448, 524–526
Fills
    bitmaps and, 153
    Fireworks, 309–311
    Flash, 137, 148
    Freehand, 14, 54–60, 69–71
    types of, 54–60
Fill Transform tool described, Flash, 128, 151–153
Find and Replace tool described, Flash, 157
Fireworks. *See* Macromedia Fireworks MX 2004
Fisheye Lens tool, Freehand, 73–74
Flash. *See* Macromedia Flash MX 2004
Flash Element defined, 444
Flash Text, Dreamweaver, 479–482
Flow diagrams, creating Freehand, 104–107
Folder symbol, Freehand
    arranging, 99–100
    creating, 94–95
Font color, determining, 412
Fonts, sizing, 413
For...in loop defined, 246
For loop defined, 245–246
Forms, 425–429, 518–521
Fractalize tool, Freehand, 86
Frame by frame animation, 159–162, 377–379
Frames
    adding, 283
    buttons and, 205

Frames (*cont.*)
  defined, 159
  and guides, 169
  in HTML, 417
  identifying, 125
  image, creating, 317
  keyframes, 124, 162, 163
  navigating, Flash, 214
  types of, 124
  wireframes, creating, 12–13, 91–106
Frames Panel, Fireworks, 376–377
Frameworks, Freehand, 12–13
Freeform Tool, 47, 320
Freehand. *See* Macromedia Freehand MX 2004
Freehand 10 Stroke Inspector, 21
Free Transform tool described, Flash, 128, 149–151
FTP setup, Dreamweaver, 453–455
Functions, ActionScript, 248–249

G

Gertie the Dinosaur, 161
getDate() method defined, ActionScript, 250
getDay() method defined, ActionScript, 251
getFullYear() method defined, ActionScript, 251
getHours() method defined, ActionScript, 251
getMinutes() method defined, ActionScript, 251
getMonth() method defined, ActionScript, 251
getYear() method defined, ActionScript, 251
GIF images
  defined, 385
  exporting files in, 387
  files, optimizing, 389–392
  publish settings, 286, 293
gotoAndPlay() action defined, 254
gotoAndStop() action defined, 254
Gradients
  fills, 54–57
  modifying, 152, 153
  types of described, 56
  and vector graphics, 14
Gradient Tool, Fireworks, 330
Graphic Hose tool, Freehand, 81–83
Graphics, 15, 62, 390. *See also* Images; Raster Graphics; Vector Graphics
Grayscale and masks, 355
Groups, placing, 336
Guide layers, 169, 172, 187–188

H

Hand tool described, Flash, 156

Head tag defined, HTML, 405, 408, 409, 430–432
Help panel, Flash, 132
History panel, 133–134, 336
Hit state defined, 205, 206–207
Horizontal rule tag defined, HTML, 409
Hotspots
  adding, 338–339, 477
  defined, 338
  resizing, 370
  vs. slices, 367
Hotspot Tool, Fireworks, 339
House icon, creating Freehand, 102
HTML. *See* Hypertext Markup Language (HTML)
HTML Output Assistant, Freehand, 116–117
Hyperlinks, creating, 416–418
Hypertext defined, 404
Hypertext Markup Language (HTML)
  editing, 523
  elements, 411–413
  exporting, 399–402
  frames, 417
  history of, 403–404
  image behavior, default, 414
  lists, 419–422, 472–475
  nesting rules in, 412
  publish settings, 286, 290–293
  roundtrip, 457–467
  slices, exporting to, 369
  special characters in, 429–430
  structure of
    block-level tags, 407–410
    core tags, 405–406
    overview, 404–405
  style attributes, 506
  white space in, 406–407

I

Icons, creating Freehand, 101–103
if/else conditional statement applied, 242, 274
if/else if/else conditional statement applied, 242–243
Images
  adding to Web page, 470–472, 475–479, 493
  batch-processing, 397–399
  behavior, default in HTML, 414
  edges, feathering, 323
  and graphic symbols, 197
  maps defined, 338
  optimizing, 386–399
  and pixelation, 414
  resizing, 395, 494

scaling, 350, 351, 478
symbols and, 197
and text, 339, 516
tracing, 491–492
Web sites, adding, 470–472, 475–479, 493
img tag defined, HTML, 414–416, 477
Ink Bottle tool described, Flash, 128, 153
Inner Bevel menu, Freehand, 68–69
Input Text defined, 140
Insert Layer Folder option defined, 189
Insert Layer option defined, 189
Insert Toolbar, Dreamweaver, 441–444
Instances
    buttons and, 347–350
    defined, 347
    modifying, 94
    and movie clips, 197, 199, 200
    timelines and, 199
Interactivity, adding Flash, 210–221
Internet Protocol (IP) defined, 4
Intersect tool, Freehand, 86
int() function defined, 233

J

Join options, Freehand, 61
JPEG images
    buttons, optimizing, 392–394
    defined, 385
    exporting files in, 387
    publish settings, 286, 293
    regions, optimizing, 394–397
Jump menus, creating, 522–523

K

Kerning defined, 320
Keyframes, 124, 162, 163
Knife tool
    Fireworks, 321
    Freehand, 48–49

L

Labels, Flash, 283, 286
Languages
    loose typed *vs.* strong typed, 229–230
    setting, 134
Lasso tools
    Fireworks, 323–325
    Flash, 127
Lathe tool, Freehand, 76
Layer Context Menu options, Flash, 189–190
Layers
    CSS, 510–514

Flash, 126, 159, 172, 188–190
Freehand, 114–115
guide, 19, 172, 187–188
masks, 184–187
movement in, 161
objects and, 112
tables, converting to, 513–514
Layers Panel, Freehand, 114–115
Leading defined, 320
Lens fill, Freehand described, 57–58
Library, Freehand, 88, 93
Library panel, Flash, 132, 152
Licenses, open source, 537–547
Line tool
    Fireworks, 312
    Flash, 135–137
    Freehand, 35–36
Line tool described, Flash, 127
Links, creating, 416–418
Lists, HTML, 419–422, 472–475
Literals, ActionScript, 226–229
Live Effects
    Fireworks, 331
    Freehand, 51, 66–69, 87
Lock/Unlock All Layers option defined, 188–189
Logarithmic gradient described, Freehand, 56
Loops, ActionScript, 244–247
L-shape, creating, 316

M

Macintosh
    platform and documents, saving, 304–306
    Projector images, publish settings, 286, 294
Macromedia Dreamweaver MX 2004
    assets in, 495–496
    behaviors, adding, 514–517
    buttons, creating, 479–482
    and CSS, 509–510
    overview, 437–438
    Property Inspector, 447, 470–472
    resources, 530–531
    system requirements, 534
    user interface, 438–441
Macromedia Fireworks MX 2004
    animations, 376, 382–384
    behaviors, 373, 375
    buttons, creating, 341–343, 361
    colors, options for, 300–301
    content, adding, 340–341
    documents, creating, 297–306
    EPS files and, 386
    events, changing, 375

Macromedia Fireworks MX 2004 (*cont.*)
  fills, 309–311
  HTML input, 370
  HTML roundtripping, 458–463
  masks, 352–356
  navigation bars, creating, 345
  output issues, 365
  overview, 297
  panels, 303
  Property Inspector, 302–303, 349, 384
  and raster graphics, 297
  resources, 530
  slices (*See* Slices, Fireworks)
  strokes, 308–309
  swap images, creating, 371–373
  symbols, 341, 381–384
  system requirements, 534
  tweens, 381–382
  user interface, 301–304
  and vector graphics, 11, 297
  vector tools, 312–321
  vs. Freehand, 11, 332
Macromedia Flash MX 2004
  animations, 86–87, 107–112, 122
  arrays, 234–235
  bandwidth profiler, 294–295
  behaviors, 210, 213–221
  buttons, creating, 205–208, 281–283
  colors tools, 156
  conditionals, 240–244
  content, displaying, 126
  contextual menus, 134
  fills, 137, 148
  frames, navigating, 214
  and HTML roundtripping, 463–467
  labels, 283, 286
  layers, 126, 159, 172, 188–190
  mask layers, 184–187
  named anchors, 125, 285
  objects in, 149–151, 156–157
  operators in, 236–239, 241
  overview, 119–121
  paths, controlling, 168
  Property Inspector, 128–129, 131, 140
  publishing, 279, 286–294
  resources, 530
  strokes, 137
  symbols, 191–196
  system requirements, 534–535
  timeline, 123–126
  tweening, 162–167, 175–180, 382
  user interface, 121–123

View tools, 155–156
Macromedia Freehand MX 2004
  assets, 87–88
  colors, 21, 56
  content, sharing with Flash, 107
  exporting HTML, 87, 115–117
  images, exporting, 115
  layers in, 114–115
  Live Effects, 51, 66–69, 87
  navigation controls, 110, 111
  objects (*See* Objects, Freehand)
  overview, 11–12
  pages in, 112–114
  points, 27–30
  preferences, adjusting, 30
  publishing in, 107–112
  resources, 529
  strokes, 60–66, 69–71
  symbols (*See* Symbols, Freehand)
  system requirements, 535
  text, creating, 42–45
  user interface, 17–19
  vs. Fireworks, 11, 332
  wireframes, creating, 12–13, 91–106
Macromedia Studio 2004 and the design cycle, 7–9
Magic Wand tool, Fireworks, 325
Marquee tool described, Fireworks, 321–323
Masks
  Alpha Channel, 355
  bitmap graphics, 352–355
  Fireworks, 352–356
  Flash, 184–187
Math object defined, ActionScript, 250
Media option defined, Flash, 214
Menu bar, Fireworks, 301–302
Meta tag defined, HTML, 405
Mirror tool, Freehand, 79–81
Modulus operator defined, 239
Monitor resolution settings, 299–300, 365
Motion, adding, 162
Motion tweening, Flash
  ball example, 163–166
  modes in, 166–167
  overview, 162, 175–180
Mouseovers. *See* Buttons
Movie Clip option defined, Flash, 214
Movie Explorer panel, Flash, 134
Movies
  clips
    creating, 198, 200–202
    instances, 197, 199, 200

overview, 197
  properties, 262–263
demonstrating, 199
frames per second values, 123–134
navigation, adding, 280–286
viewing, 134, 284–285
Multiple with Rotate option, Freehand, 81
MySQL software license, 540–547

N

Named anchors, Flash, 125, 285
Navigation, 110, 111, 345
nextFrame( ) action defined, 254
Number( ) method defined, 233, 237
Numeric Transform dialog box, 395

O

Object Panel, Freehand, 51–53
Objects
  aligning, 203
  creating, ActionScript, 250–252
  Flash, 149–151, 156–157
  Freehand
    depth, adding, 76
    manipulating, 27, 28, 75
    moving, 28, 112
    parts, selecting, 29
    placement values, 99
    points, adding, 86
    shaping, 30
    transforming, 97
  and functions, 248
  graphics symbols and, 191
  and layers, 112
  names and code hinting, 264–265
  overlap considerations, Flash, 156–157
  rotating, 180
  scaling, Flash, 150
  and the Shadow Tool, 77
  symbols and, 191
  tweened, rotating, 205
  visibility, order of, 162
OnClipEvent handler defined, ActionScript,
    257–259
On Handler code defined, Flash, 212,
    255–257
On Release code, events of, 212–213
Operators
  comparison applied, 240–241
  concantenation, 228
  Flash
    arithmetic, 236–239
      assignment, 239
      logical, 241
      precedence, 236
Optimize Panel with GIF, compression settings
    for, 390–391
Output, previewing, 392
Ovals, creating Freehand, 36–38
Oval tool described, Flash, 127, 145
Over state defined, 205, 207–208

P

Paint Bucket tool
  Fireworks, 329–330
  Flash, 128, 153–154
Panel Groups, Dreamweaver, 445–446
Panels. *See also individual panels or applications
    by name*
  collapsing/ expanding, 131, 439
  overview, 18, 303
Panel sets, Flash, 130–134
Paragraph tag defined, HTML, 408
parseFloat( ) function defined, 233, 237
parseInt( ) function defined, 232, 237, 238
Paths
  bottom-up *vs.* top-down, 417
  controlling, 168
  creating Freehand, 19–36
  freeform, 32–34
  manipulation tools, 45–49
  operations, 84–86
  several in sequence, 24
  with sharp corners, 21–22
  with smooth curves, 22–24
Path Scrubber tools described, Fireworks, 321
Paths defined, Freehand, 14
Path Transform tools, Freehand, 47–48
Pattern fills described, Freehand, 58
Pencil Tool
  Fireworks, 326
  Flash, 128, 148
  Freehand, 32–34
Pen Tool
  Fireworks, 312
  Flash overview, 127, 137–139
  Freehand overview, 19–20
Perspective grid, creating, 317
Perspective tool, Freehand, 71–73
PHP software license, 538–540
PICT format defined, 385
Pie shape, creating, 316
play( ) action defined, 254
Playhead function described, Flash, 125

PNG images
  defined, 385
  publish settings, 286, 293
Pointer tools
  Fireworks, 311, 323
  Freehand, 27, 29
Points
  deleting, 33
  Freehand, 27–30, 86
  vectors, manipulating, 311, 336
Polygons, creating
  Fireworks, 314
  Flash, 148
  Freehand, 40–42
Polygon tool
  Fireworks overview, 314
  Freehand overview, 40–42
Polystar tool described, Flash, 128, 146–148
Pop-Up Borders tab described, Fireworks, 359
Pop-Up Menu Editor, Fireworks, 356
Pop-Up menus, creating Fireworks, 356–359
Position tab described, Fireworks, 359
Postscript fills described, Freehand, 58
Preformatted text tag defined, HTML, 410
prevFrame() action defined, 254
Preview buttons and image optimization,
  387–388
Programming resources, 531–532
Projector option defined, Flash, 214
Property Inspector
  and CSS layers, 513
  Dreamweaver, 447, 470–472
  Fireworks
    and animation symbols, 384
    overview, 302–303
    text, modifying, 349
  Flash
    overview, 128–129, 131
    and the Text Tool, 140
Punch tool, Freehand, 86

Q

Quicktime (.mov) images, publish settings, 286,
  294

R

Radial gradient described, Freehand, 56
Ragged menu, Freehand, 68
Raster graphics
  editing, 321–330
  Fireworks and, 297
  overview, 13–14, 66
  transforming into vector art, 77–78
  vs. vector graphics, 15–16

Rectangle gradient described, Freehand, 56
Rectangles, creating, 38–40, 146
Rectangle tool
  Fireworks, 313
  Flash, 127, 145–146
  Freehand, 38–40
Red Eye Removal tool, 329
Redraw Path tool, Fireworks described, 312–313
Release to Layers dialog box, Freehand, 108–109
Replace Color tool, 328
Requests, processing, 6–7
Reshape Area Freeform Tool
  Fireworks, 321
  Freehand, 47–48
Results Panel Group, Dreamweaver, 526–527
Reverse Direction tool, Freehand, 85
Rollover effect, creating, 265–270
Rollovers, disjointed creating, 371–373
Roughen Tool, Freehand, 48
Rounded rectangle shape, creating, 316
Rubber Stamp tool, Fireworks, 327–328

S

Scale tools
  Fireworks, 311, 312
  Freehand, 45–46
Script navigator defined, Flash, 224
Scripts, creating, 223
Scrubbing defined, 125
Select Behind tool, Fireworks defined, 311
Servers, 1–2, 6
Shadow tool, Freehand, 76–77
Shape hints, applying Flash, 181–184
Shapes
  creating, 24–27, 31, 36–45, 316
  simplifying, 33
  and tweening, 166, 181–184
Sharing Files window options, Dreamweaver,
  452–453
Sharpen tool, 69, 326
Show All Layers as Outlines option defined, 188
Show/Hide All Layers option defined, 189
Simplify tool, Freehand, 34–35
Sketch menu, Freehand, 68
Skew tool described, Fireworks, 311, 312
Sky, creating, 180
Sled example
  behaviors and, 210–212
  and motion tweening, 176–180
Slices
  Fireworks
    adding, 367–368
    and behaviors, 375
    defined, 343

and guides, 368
HTML, exporting to, 369
and optimization, 388, 390
overview, 366–367
preselecting, 373
vs. hotspots, 367
Slice Tool, Fireworks, 368
Smart polygon shape, creating, 316
Smudge tool, 76–77, 327
Sound option defined, Flash, 214
Spell checking, Flash, 145
Spiral shape, creating, 316
Spiral tool, Freehand, 35–36
Squares, creating Freehand, 86
Stars, creating
    Fireworks, 314, 316
    Flash, 148
    Freehand, 40–42
Static Text defined, 140, 141
Status bar message, adding, 374
Status Toolbar, Freehand overview, 18–19
stop() action defined, 254
stopAllSounds() action defined, 254
Storyboards, Freehand, 12–13
Streaming defined, 119
Strings panel, Flash, 134
Strokes
    Fireworks, 308–309
    Flash, 137
    Freehand, 60–66, 69–71
Styles, Freehand, 87
Subselection tool
    Fireworks, 311
    Flash, 127, 135–137
Subselect tool, Freehand overview, 28
Surface Button options, Freehand, 75–76
Swap images, creating Fireworks, 371–373
Swatches and custom colors, 87
.swf files, 119, 286, 287–290
switch conditional statement applied, 243
Symbol Editing mode defined, Flash, 192, 193
Symbols
    animations, 382–384
    documents, placing in, 95–96
    Fireworks, 341, 381–384
    Flash
        animating, 196
        creating, 192, 194
        editing, 194, 195
        overview, 191–193
        types of, 191
    Freehand
        box, scaling and placing, 98–99
        creating, 91–96

Folder symbol, 94–95, 99–100
    overview, 88
    and timeline effects, 209
images, 197
objects and, 191
timelines and, 196, 197

T
Tabbed navigation, creating, 317
Tabbed navigation panel, Fireworks, 303–304
Tables
    and browser compatibility, 370
    creating, 402, 482–484
    editable regions, 500–503
    to layers, converting, 513–514
    and layout, 484–486, 490–495
    overview, 422–425, 474
    properties, adjusting, 486–490
Talking bubble, creating, 317
Templates, applying, 497–504
Text
    adding, 100–101, 349, 470–472
    colors in, 413
    creating Freehand, 42–45
    dynamic defined, 140
    fields, properties of, 262–264
    formatting, 140, 349, 478
    images and, 339, 516
    and motion tweening, 175
    properties, controlling, 319
    sizing, 413
    vector graphics and, 44
Text Tool
    Fireworks, 319–320
    Flash, 127, 140–144
Textured fills described, Freehand, 58
TIFF format defined, 385
Tiled fills described, Freehand, 58–60
Timeline Effects, Flash, 208–210
Timelines
    ActionScript, 230–231, 254
    Flash, 123–126
    graphic symbols and, 196, 197, 209
    and instances, 199
    movie clips and, 197
Title tag defined, HTML, 405
Tools panel
    Fireworks, 302
    Flash, 127–128, 134–157
    Freehand, 18, 19, 21
toString() method defined, ActionScript, 233, 251
trace command defined, ActionScript, 227
Trace tool, Freehand, 77–78

Transform effect defined, 209
Transform Handles, Freehand, 47
Transform menu, Freehand, 68, 93
Transform panel, Freehand, 97–98
Transition effect defined, 209
Transparency menu, Freehand, 69
Trigger Data Source defined, Flash, 213
Truth tables applied, 241–243
Tube image, creating, 317
Tweening
    Fireworks, 381–382
    keyframes and, 162
    motion, 162–167, 175–180, 382
    objects, rotating, 205
    shapes, 166, 181–184
Tween Instances dialog box, Fireworks, 382

U

Union tool, Freehand, 86
Up state defined, 205

V

Values, returning and functions, 249
Variables
    ActionScript
        conversion, 232–233
        external, 252–254
        global, 232
        local, 231–232
        and operator precedence, 236
        overview, 226–229
        scope of, 230–232
        timeline, creating, 230–231
        types, 229–230
        undefined, 249
        values, available, 230
    datatypes, viewing, 229, 232
    environmental and client-server relations, 3
Variable Stroke tool, Freehand, 34–35
Vector graphics
    editing, 321–330
    Fireworks and, 11, 297
    and illustrations, 119
    overview, 14–15
    parts of, 308
    raster effects, applying, 66, 77–78
    and streaming, 120
    text and, 44

vs. raster graphics, 15–16
Vector Path tool, Fireworks described, 312–313
Vectors
    advantages of, 15
    capability, maintaining, 51
    output, creating, 386
    points, manipulating, 311, 336
    tools, Fireworks, 312–321
Vert menu, 504

W

WBMP format defined, 385
Web option defined, Flash, 215
Web protocols overview, 4–5
Web sites
    accessibility issues in, 359, 365
    buttons, adding, 350–352
    creating, 280–286, 448–455
    design of, 8, 332, 333
    head content, adding, 469–470
    images, adding, 470–472, 475–479, 493
    layout, creating, 334–338, 360–363
    management of, 524–527
    pages
        background, creating, 334–338
        loading, 111
        properties, setting, 467–468
        server-side, creating, 450
    resources, 531
    status bar message, adding, 374
Wheelchair icon, creating Freehand, 102–103
While loop, coding, 245
While loop defined, 244–245
Windows
    platform and documents, saving, 306–308
    Projector images, publish settings, 286, 293–294
Wireframes, Freehand
    creating, 12–13, 91–106

X

XHTML, principle of, 434–435
XML. *See* Extensible Markup Language (XML)

Z

Zoom tool described
    Fireworks, 363
    Flash, 155